The Shattered Church

How did the Reformation happen? How did the Christian Church with its vision of unity and love among men become split into rival groups?

These are the questions answered in John P. Dolan's brilliant and provocative *History of the Reformation*—termed one of the ten best books of the year by *Herder Correspondence*. In our age of ecumenism, when Christians everywhere are searching once more for mutual respect and unity, those answers are all-important: if we know the past, we will not be condemned to repeat it.

Written by a Roman Catholic, *History of the Reformation* contains an Introduction by the great Lutheran scholar Jaroslav Pelikan, who says that this lively work "will serve both the cause of historical honesty and the cause of ecumenism, for ultimately those two are one."

Other MENTOR-OMEGA Books of Special Catholic Interest

THE PAPAL ENCYCLICALS in Their Historical Context *edited by Anne Fremantle*

For the first time in one volume, the teachings of the Catholic Church as expressed by the Popes in their official letters. (#MQ533—95¢)

THE SOCIAL TEACHINGS OF THE CHURCH *edited by Anne Fremantle*

A companion volume to *The Papal Encyclicals in Their Historical Context*, this book contains papal encyclicals on social problems from Pope Leo XIII to Pope John XXIII. (#MT549—75¢)

TWO CENTURIES OF ECUMENISM: The Search for Unity *by George H. Tavard*

A study of successive efforts at Christian reunion from the Oxford Movement of the last century to the Council of the Church called by Pope John XXIII. (#MT465—75¢)

THE DYNAMICS OF WORLD HISTORY *by Christopher Dawson*

A renowned British historian examines the relation between religion and civilization, and shows Christianity as the central, dynamic force in man's historical progression. (#MQ378—95¢)

HISTORY OF THE
Reformation

*A Conciliatory Assessment of
Opposite Views*

JOHN P. DOLAN

Introduction by Jaroslav Pelikan

A MENTOR-OMEGA BOOK

Published by

The New American Library, *New York and Toronto*
The New English Library Limited, *London*

Nihil obstat:
Louis J. Putz, C.S.C.

Imprimatur:
Leo A. Pursley, D.D.
Bishop of Fort Wayne, South Bend
May 7, 1964

FIRST PRINTING, March, 1967

MENTOR-OMEGA BOOKS are published *in the United States* by
The New American Library, Inc.,
1301 Avenue of the Americas, New York, New York 10019,
in Canada by The New American Library of Canada Limited,
295 King Street East, Toronto 2, Ontario,
in the United Kingdom by The New English Library Limited,
Barnard's Inn, Holborn, London, E.C. 1, England

PRINTED IN THE UNITED STATES OF AMERICA

Acknowledgment

Since there are no notes to the text, acknowledgment must be made to those historians whose recent works have been relied upon in this account of the Reformation: Hubert Jedin, Walter Ullman, Gerhardt Ladner, François Wendell, and the late Maurice Powicke.

Contents

Introduction

The great Protestant theologian and historian, Ernst Troeltsch (see p. 52), once coined the epigram: "We must overcome history by history." By this he meant not only that history, as a bearer of the will and purpose of God, can transcend and break the forms of the past by producing something new, but also that historical research can be a means of renewal and reform if it subjects those forms to honest examination. A prime illustration of Troeltsch's axiom is the history of the Reformation. Scholarship in Reformation history has been shaped as much by the religious and theological presuppositions of the scholar as by the historical materials. A careful study of a volume on the history of the Reformation can give the reader a pretty good idea of the theology of the author—perhaps even a better idea of this than of the theology of the Reformation. Conversely, the more honestly "historical" one's research is, the more carefully will he examine his presuppositions. And as historical research participates in the give-and-take of the scholarly community, everyone's presuppositions come in for review and criticism.

Such review and criticism have dominated recent scholarship in Reformation research. The succinct history of this research in Chapter I of this book can introduce the reader to the currents of scholarly debate and give him a sense of how deep the currents of that debate are. A clearer sense of this can come only from an exposure to the actual data of Reformation research, as these are summarized in the main body of this book. To an extent that the modesty of its scholarly apparatus may belie, Professor Dolan's *History* is based upon extensive study both of the source materials and of the scholarly research produced by Protestant, Roman Catholic, and secular students of the Reformation era. In many ways, his account could be called a *Forschungsbericht*, a report on the present state of scholarly investigation and on its tentative results. Only a working scholar, one who is himself engaged in the investigation of texts and sources, is in a position to summarize and evaluate the work of his colleagues, for his own command of these texts and sources puts him into a position to pass expert judgment on the quarrels among the learned. Yet he cannot claim to have formed his opinions of such a vast subject strictly on the basis of his own research, but must rely on the mining and minting of many other scholars. That is why Professor Dolan alludes to earlier studies, and why someone who has himself been working with these materials will catch many other echoes of these studies in the pages of this book.

Certainly no period in the history of Christianity, except for the age of the New Testament itself, has been the object of as much research and publication as the era of the Reformation. As an editor of *Luther's Works* has opportunity to know, the scholarly presses of Germany, Switzerland, and Scandinavia pour out dozens of volumes every year; there are several journals devoted largely or exclusively to Reformation research; the writings of Reformation figures from all sides continue to be published both in the original languages and in translation; and institutions like the American Society for Reformation Research and the Foundation for Reformation Research are promoting the cause of historical study among scholars in the United States as well as on the Continent. Although it is certainly too much to speak of the emergence of a consensus, all this scholarly work has drastically changed the pictures of the Reformation that had been drawn by the *ex parte* accounts written during the period of Protestant-Roman Catholic polemics. Neither Protestants nor Roman Catholics today would be willing to stand by the charges and the claims of that period, even though authors of tracts distributed by both sides and of articles published in their less responsible popular press may still feel able to get away with slander or with hero-worship.

This does not mean, however, that the presence of theological presuppositions disqualifies the historian for participation in scholarly research, or that the best history of the Reformation would be written by someone who did not care either way about the religious questions being debated in the sixteenth century. As we have discovered in the histories composed by such neutral observers, nontheological or even antitheological presuppositions can be no less damaging to historical understanding and objectivity than explicitly theological ones. One does not have to introduce the red herring of Marxist historiography to make the point that Roman Catholic and Protestant historians have no corner on bias in their evaluation of the past. Is the history of a religious movement or idea better off in the hands of a scholar who cannot understand existentially why people of intelligence should ever have become so agitated about it, or in the hands of someone who has been chastened by modern critical history but who still has a sense of the life-and-death character of the issues at stake? Now that both ways of writing Reformation history have had an opportunity to prove themselves, the notion of a historiography free of theological presuppositions has lost much of its allure.

At the same time, the acknowledgment of theological presuppositions is not tantamount to the acceptance of a partisan position. It seems difficult to imagine how any historian could interpret the Reformation without at least some antenna for the doctrinal questions being debated by the Reformers and their opponents, but it is no less difficult to suppose that the Reformation can receive fair treatment from a writer who divides history between "good guys" and "bad guys." Precisely because the Reformation aroused so many passions and still does, the theological presuppositions of the Reformation historian must include a readiness to hear opinions radically divergent from one's own. Fortunately, such readiness is not really precluded by any confessional differences between Roman Catholics and Protestants, both of whom acknowledge, at least in principle, that neither side in the Reformation had a monopoly on vice or virtue. This was, in fact, acknowledged even in the midst of the heat of controversy by the controversialists on both sides of the sixteenth century, all of whom had frequent occasion to repeat the ancient lament: "My enemies I can manage, but deliver me from my friends!" How much more reason have we, after the passing of so much history, to recognize the validity (if only the partial validity) of the points being made also by those Reformation figures whom the irony of history has placed on the opposite side of the "great gulf fixed" between Roman Catholicism and Protestantism.

It is probably in the honesty with which we see and admit that irony that our age is distinct from earlier times. At least in part, modern developments have brought the irony of the Reformation more vividly to our attention. This is true of both Roman Catholics and Protestants, who must see the sixteenth century differently because of the twentieth. As Professor Dolan's book makes clear in many striking ways, Roman Catholics today have reason to ponder the difference between Martin Luther and the latter-day "enemies of the Church." He battled against the papacy in the name of Catholic Christianity and with a profound sense of the central issues of sin and judgment, grace and salvation. The cruciality of Jesus Christ and of the Cross was fundamental to Luther's entire piety and theology. To put him on the same level with Voltaire and Marx, or even with Descartes and Rousseau, is completely to misunderstand what was at stake for him. It is also to ignore what Roman Catholicism lost when it lost Martin Luther, whom one recent Roman Catholic scholar has called "Augustine's noblest pupil." To put the matter somewhat rhetorically, can Roman Catholicism in the modern world spare the intellectual power, the authentic faith, the biblical understanding, and the Christocentric commitment which were the gift of the Holy Spirit to the Church in the person of Luther the Reformer?

But, to continue in the same rhetorical vein, can Protestantism afford to forget that it was through the Church that the Holy Spirit gave these gifts to Martin Luther? The irony of the Reformation becomes clear also to the Protestant when he views it in the light of subsequent history. For example, one of the principal accusations of the Reformers against the Roman Catholic Church of their day was that it had replaced the divine initiative with human initiative in the establishment of the right relation between God and man, that it was, in the labels of polemical theology, "semi-Pelagian." Roman Catholics have come to admit that this accusation has considerable validity as a criticism of late medieval theology. But in the centuries since the Reformation, Protestantism has repeatedly capitulated to a moralism and a semi-Pelagianism more virulent than anything in the fifteenth century. In the same way, the Reformers' critique of late medieval devotion to the Virgin Mary was not only justified by the state of popular piety and learned theology, but validated by the loyalty of the Reformers to the dogma of Christ bequeathed to them by the ecumenical councils of the first five centuries. That same critique has a hollow sound when it comes from Protestants who no longer understand or accept the Nicene Creed.

Without some such awareness of the irony of the Reformation, we cannot place it properly into the context of the history of renewal and reform in the Church. One of the chief strengths of Professor Dolan's book is its delineation of this context. Ironically, the "Reformers who failed," as Chapter IV describes them, failed both to reform the Church and to split it. Even more ironic was the situation at the Council of Constance in 1415, when John Gerson had to side with the cynical and the corrupt in the condemnation of John Huss. Any modern Roman Catholic who does not recognize the poignancy of that situation cannot understand the bitter irony of Luther's situation a century later. For while both Gerson and Huss were primarily concerned with a reform of the life and practice of the Church, Luther cared most about a reform of its doctrine and a renewal of its structures. In this Luther stood in continuity with the great tradition of reform and renewal throughout Christian history. What he himself called "the succession of the faithful" was the tradition of insisting that, for the Church to be reformed in head and members, its teaching and preaching had to be renewed at their biblical and evangelical roots. Without this, moral reform of clergy and laity was merely a new patch on an old and threadbare garment. Any modern Protestant who imagines that Luther was some novelty that sprang from the brow of history, "the first to burst upon the silent sea," must also come to terms with the continuity of Catholic reform—and that means Catholic reform both before and since the sixteenth century. Whether or not the Council of Trent (1545-63) successfully met the doctrinal challenges of the Reformation is still a matter of theological debate, but no honest Protestant today can ignore the dedication to reform, both moral and doctrinal, that has continued to appear within Roman Catholicism, particularly as that dedication has made its presence known in our own time through the work of the late Pope John XXIII.

By heightening that sense of irony on both sides, a history like that of Professor Dolan can make its contribution to what a nineteenth-century Protestant theologian called "the peace of history," the honesty and balance that can come in the present only from an attempt to be fair and objective about the past. Four centuries of separation have produced a distinct language in each of the traditions, with a consequent inability to understand the other's language. They have produced also a development of thought and teaching that makes some of the earlier controversy meaningless. Repeating Reformation slogans and Counter-Reformation slogans means marching seven times around a Jericho that has long since fallen. The peace of history has graciously descended on many of the debates of the sixteenth century. Most important of all perhaps is the change in the political and social position of Christianity. As Professor Dolan shows, the Reformation was accompanied by—and, in various complicated ways, connected with—the end of the Constantinian era of Christian-Catholic hegemony over Western culture. Now that political history has relieved us of the burden of dominance, it may become possible for both parties to turn once more to the real problems at issue between them. The perspective of the intervening centuries should make those problems more visible, if not more soluble.

But neither the sense of irony about the Reformation nor "the peace of history" will come of itself. Both depend on the continuance of historical research. For all its grasp of the materials and command of the literature, Professor Dolan's book leaves many gaps and must leave them because so much work remains to be done. Perhaps it will suffice to specify two areas of research that await the next generation of scholars. The first is the late Middle Ages in relation to the Reformation. A small group of very able scholars, both Protestant and Roman Catholic, can be given credit for making the relation between the sixteenth century and the two centuries preceding it the most exciting frontier of investigation in Reformation study. For the first time, the vocabulary of Luther and Calvin is being clarified by a study of the very books by which they were nurtured. Many of these books have never been edited in modern times, some of them have never been published. No one can predict at this stage where this research will lead, but this much seems clear: Neither the stereotypes of Roman Catholic defensiveness nor the polemics of Protestant aggressiveness will ever be quite the same after these careful scholars have done their work.

Another field of study to which some historians are turning is the investigation of the relatively minor figures, the "spear-carriers" of the Reformation. So much has been written about Luther, Calvin, and Zwingli that other participants in the Reformation are often ignored. On some of them not so much as one full-length biography has ever been written, and many others have been treated quite summarily in Reformation annals. The collection of vast amounts of primary source material at various American centers, notably at the Foundation for Reformation Research in Saint Louis, will facilitate the study of literally dozens of men who are sometimes thought of as pygmies simply because they were not giants. From such study a revised picture of the Reformation may emerge. We may begin to understand what it meant not only to its leaders but to its participants, perhaps even to the "silent in the land" who did not and often could not write. Both the vigor of popular opposition to the abuses in the old order and the continued devotion of the folk to the ways of the old order may come into view. It should also become more obvious that none of the Reformation parties was the monolith it appeared to be to both friend and foe, and that in some ways there was greater variety within any of these parties than there was between them. This does not make a giant any less gigantic, but it does prevent us from interpreting him as a prima donna.

For readers who know very little about the Reformation, Professor Dolan has provided a lively introduction to what we know about the movement. For students who know something but need to know much more, he has written a history that will deepen their insight and arouse their interest. And for scholars who have worked in both primary and secondary sources, this summary will put many of the facts and issues into a new and different light. Thus it will serve both the cause of historical honesty and the cause of ecumenism, for ultimately these two causes are one.

Jaroslav Pelikan
Titus Street Professor of
Ecclesiastical History
Yale University

"*Was it better to renounce the papacy out of horror for its acts, or to condone the acts out of reverence for the papacy?*"

LORD ACTON

HISTORY OF THE
Reformation

1

The Reformation
in retrospect

*"The historian must beware of confusing a man's cause or
party or religion with his character."*

                                        DAVID KNOWLES

The history of the Reformation has not as yet been written.
It will not be written until the atmosphere is cleared of the
confessional bias that has for over four centuries clouded
so many of the issues that were involved. Unlike the history
of other important epochs of the past, the Crusades for
example or the French Revolution, the Reformation is not
merely an historical event that has taken place and may now
be studied and evaluated on a basis of documentary evidence.
It is a phenomenon that still forms the background of much
of the Western mind. Upon its interpretation often depends
a man's political and ethical outlook. It is an event that is
still taking place.

It must also be borne in mind that the Reformation is an
extraordinarily complicated fact both of itself and in its
centuries-old structure. A study of the vast literature on the
Reformation, and certainly no other period in the past has
so occupied the interest of historians, amazes and confuses
the serious student. Born of self-interest and controversy,
it continues to defy that quality of dispassionate consideration and objective inquiry that must characterize a true understanding of the past. The necessity of going beyond a merely
dogmatic evaluation of the event must be stressed if we
are to approach an adequate interpretation of what was unquestionably the most important event in the history of
Western religious thought since the advent of Christianity.
In this chapter we will attempt to assess some of the various
interpretations that popular historians and writers have given
to the Reformation. They will show that the historian not only
studies history but in a sense contributes to its substance.
For the study of history itself, as we understand it today,
was to a certain extent the product of the Reformation.

21

The earliest views on the Reformation as a movement were those of the reformers who wrote ecclesiastical histories and biographies of Luther and Calvin. The funeral oration delivered by Philip Melanchthon (1497-1560) at the University of Wittenberg on the death of Luther was a biographical sketch of the leader of the reform movement. Melanchthon developed his eulogy in the biography of Luther which he prepared for the second volume of the Wittenberg edition of his complete works in 1546.

Philip Melanchthon, a grandnephew of the scholar Reuchlin, came to the University of Wittenberg in 1518 as a professor of Greek and there he became Luther's loyal companion and collaborator. They were close friends, but their relationship was not free from strain. Often Luther took occasion to upbraid him, yet Melanchthon patiently refrained from making rebuttals. After Luther died, however, he freely and publicly disapproved of some points in the Reformer's doctrine and some of his personal traits and ways. These discordant elements did not appear in the biographical writings where Melanchthon's unqualified praise for Luther testified that he was devoted to him without bound. Luther's distinction as a man was that he lived what he preached. But Luther was not merely a man, for human power was inadequate to explain either such virtue or such theological depth as his. Like the glorious prophets of the old Covenant, Martin Luther was the chosen one of God, given the renewal of the Church, the New Israel, as his mission. Melanchthon found his counterpart in Nehemiah, who had championed the Israelites after their deliverance out of Babylon. The Wittenberg Nehemiah warded off his foes with a sword in one hand, and rebuilt the temple with the other by guarding the Bible and proclaiming its message to the people. Melanchthon considered the Reformation to be a part of a divinely ordained plan which was universally effective both in the Church and in the world. God continually revealed Himself to His chosen race, formerly Israel and now Christianity. He transmitted His word to them through those favored individuals whom He anointed with charismatic gifts. He appointed a chain of messengers which began with Adam and culminated in the God-man, Jesus. The apostles and the Fathers of the Church continued the line of holy men down through the centuries, their task being to let the purity of the Gospel keep the Church ever new. Luther, in Melanchthon's eulogy, was the bearer of God's word in the early decades of the sixteenth century.

Luther's Reformation freed the Roman Church from the slavery of ritualism and Aristotelian philosophy. Ceremonies cluttered man's communion with God; Aristotle's pagan wisdom contaminated the message of Scripture. These two corruptions the Catholic Church had introduced and nursed along. Inflexible and unwilling to reform, Rome was responsible for the breach in Christianity, not the Lutherans.

Melanchthon had ascribed a supernatural dignity to Martin Luther. Johannes Mathesius (1504-65) was the first notable contemporary who lost him in the divine. Mathesius studied under Luther and was on occasion received at his table. In 1566 he published a set of seventeen sermons at Nuremberg which constituted the first significant biography of Luther.

Mathesius' love for his master set the tone of the sermons. Instead of a dry catalogue of moralia, the Bohemian pastor created an ikon of Luther through a series of warm anecdotes. He too, like Melanchthon, was fond of illustrating the consonance between Luther's life and his gospel. Mathesius, the pastor caring for his flock at Joachimsthal, was concerned more with Luther's ethics than his theology. Luther would have done enough, he believed, had he merely published the two catechisms and restored the habit of regular prayer to the masses. Mathesius further regards him as a teacher of civic righteousness: it was God's will that man obey the public authority in every civic duty. This misstatement led later historians to build the legend that Luther was a servile citizen, regardless of the cost.

Like Melanchthon, he saw in history a succession of God's ambassadors to His chosen people. He filled in the picture by including Lucifer whose plottings throughout history prevented the unhindered flow of God's word. Satan had fathered Arius and Mohammed in the East and the anti-Christ Popes in the West, all of whom had demolished the "holy aqueducts of God." The whole Church had been parched—deprived of living water—until God had mercy on His children. He established the University and Church at Wittenberg (where Mathesius had been a student) so that His word again might flow throughout His temporal kingdom.

Mathesius, like many of his contemporaries, felt the imminence of the millennium. In his view Luther was an apocalyptic figure, a superhuman warrior engaged in battle with anti-Christ. The end of the world was at hand, and Martin Luther had been sent with a last warning. He was the messenger dispatched by God in the fourth and final kingdom about which Daniel had written—the Holy Roman Empire of the German nation. The divinization of Luther was now complete. His message and God's word were the same.

At the same time as Protestant historians were tending to the deification of Luther, Catholics were talking about his kinship with the devil. Wildly conceived myths about the circumstances of Luther's death in 1546 were circulating among priests and laymen. Abandoning his faith, so the story was told, Luther committed suicide and a whole troop of devils swooped down on the funeral cortege claiming his body for their own. Johannes Cochlaeus (1479-1552), one of the earliest Catholic biographers of Luther, rose above this kind of caricature, but not far. In the *Historia de Actis et Scriptis Martini Lutheri, 1517-1546,* he would have nothing to do with the tale that Luther was an offspring of the devil, but he dutifully records that Luther was in conversation with an evil spirit during his novitiate. He touched on Luther's vices—pride, avarice, blasphemy—the vices of heretics all, but they were not his major concern.

Cochlaeus made the indulgence controversy his point of departure. He located its root in the depravity of Luther and Staupitz, both Augustinians, who clashed with the Dominican Tetzel. Luther, in Cochlaeus' naive explanation, felt the need of a new cowl, and consequently for a price of forty-two guilders made an attack on indulgences. Cochlaeus was not too upset about Luther's doctrinal aberrations. His capital sins were revolting against the papacy, breaking his solemn vows, and marrying a runaway nun. If Cochlaeus seems too uncritical and naive, Mathesius' unbounded adulation need only call to mind that early Protestant biographers were also innocent of historical moderation.

Cochlaeus was a humanist scholar who had built his reputation by editing and publishing numerous previously unavailable documents important to the student of Church history. Along with the other humanists of the North, Cochlaeus had been a friend of Lutheran renewal at the outset of the Reformation, but he withdrew his allegiance when he realized that Luther would ultimately divide the Church. He put on the mantle of orthodoxy in the *Historia,* carelessly blending genuine scholarship with impassioned exaggeration. It is an interesting aside that later on he indiscreetly advocated a married clergy and Communion under two kinds as a desperate gesture to win back the heretics. He was rewarded with the posthumous listing of some of his works on the Index of Forbidden Books. It is unfortunate that Cochlaeus did not adhere to the sound historical ability which was evidently part of his scholarly equipment, for it has been shown that throughout four centuries no other single book has had so great an influence on Catholic Reformation studies as his biography of Luther.

Equally injudicious was the first biography of Calvin. What Melanchthon and Mathesius had done for Martin Luther, Theodore Beza (1519-1605) did for the Genevan Reformer. The theologian Beza, who was Calvin's close friend and right-hand man, succeeded him after his death in 1564. His *Life of Calvin* was a dutiful panegyric, a memento of devotion to the man he loved as a father. Beza's Calvin, like Mathesius' Luther, had a divine aura. "Never has Calvin had an enemy," he wrote, "who, in assailing him, has not waged war against God." Calvin was God's warrior, who put down Satan's challenge by conquering everyone raised up against him. Calvin's prophetic traits, akin to those of the Old Covenant holy men, apologized for his incontinent fits of temper.

Beza was also indirectly responsible for the earliest full account of events in France during the era of the Reformation. He supervised the writing of the *Histoire Ecclésiastique des Eglises Réformées au Royaume de France* which was published at Antwerp in 1580. Somewhat similar was the Englishman John Foxe's *Acts and Monuments of the Christian Martyrs* (1563). Beza's work was a narrative loosely compiled from documents and contemporary chroniclers and martyrologists like Jean Crespin and Pierre de La Place. In the *Book of Martyrs* Foxe intended to win the sympathy of the people by describing the agonies of those who had died for their faith, an objective Beza shared to some degree. Beza's preface to the first volume of the *Histoire Ecclésiastique* sets forth an interpretation of Church history that ran throughout sixteenth-century Protestant historiography. The Church during the period after the Fathers languished in an age of "barbarism and horrible confusion." The Reformation made "the light of His truth . . . shine beautifully and clear out of the abyss of ignorance and superstition in which it had so long been plunged." It was a brilliant turning point bounded on one side by a millennium of decay and on the other by a new, more hopeful age. Foxe overstated the role of printing in advancing the movement, and as a testimony to the influence he has had on the English Church historians, it has remained a permanent feature in their tradition. The revival of learning providentially prepared the way for the Reformation, for it was the progressive emancipation of the human mind from the superstitions of the Roman Church and the restoration of truth, rational and revealed, in all its splendor. The roles of humanists like Reuchlin and Lefèvre d'Etaples, and of the Reformers Wycliffe and Huss before them, were given proper accreditation.

The real development of the thesis that the Reformation was preceded by a thousand years of decay was left to the writers of the *Magdeburg Centuries*. Matthias Flacius, called Illyricus (1520-75), and six collaborators planned this first Protestant attempt at a complete Church history in 1553 and published it between 1559 and 1574. Indefatigable gatherers of information, they made their massive chronicle a catchall of detail, but they shaped it with uncritical and wholly biased opinions. All things considered, the *Centuries* was little more than a polemical rewriting of ecclesiastical history designed to free Protestantism from its Catholic sources.

Flacius was convinced that the Church after the apostles began an inevitable movement toward anti-Christ and annihilation. The devil contaminated its original purity and its beauty was lost to spot and wrinkle. The compilers of the *Centuries* documented, however speciously, this thesis for the first thirteen centuries of Church history. In their interpretation of the Reformation, projected from Flacius' other works and activities, Luther represented a singular intervention of God in history, a merciful flash of light in the desperate night of the church.

Caesare Cardinal Baronius (1538-1607), a Neapolitan and one of the first members of St. Philip Neri's Oratory, was commissioned to write the official Catholic response to the *Magdeburg Centuries*. Equally massive and equally uncritical, the *Annales Ecclesiastici* began to roll off the Vatican Press in 1588. Baronius used the treasury of data he had collected in the Vatican archives and the Italian libraries to refute the theses of the Protestant writers point by point. He preferred to suffocate their assertions with a blanket of facts, suppressing unwholesome evidence instead of discrediting false conclusions based on it. The *Annales* do not extend to the sixteenth century, but Baronius' interpretation of the Reformation was unquestionably Tridentine.

By Calvinistic standards John Knox's (1505-72) *History of the Reformation in Scotland* was also very orthodox. The five volumes, which had been started by Knox himself and then brought to completion by a number of scribes, were first published in 1584. Knox began to preach the Reformation in Scotland in 1547, but it proved a vain attempt. He spent the next thirteen years in exile, laboring in the French galleys and later more fruitfully in Calvin's Geneva. He returned to Scotland in 1558 and within two years, aided by the English Crown and robber barons in the aristocracy, he had introduced the Reformed Church.

Scotland had suffered under "the same cloud of ignorance that long hath darkened many realms"—the kingdom of the Roman anti-Christ. The evangelist John said that the Babylonian harlot would merchandise in the bodies and souls of men. Did not the Pope traffic in bodies and souls when he sold indulgences and pretended to release men from purgatory? But the God who had summoned light out of darkness had mercifully brought light to some in Scotland and revealed to them how far they had been deceived by the superstitions of Rome.

Knox wrote a record of the activities of the "professors of Jesus Christ" within Scotland, hoping that more would see His light. The work was alternately history and propaganda. In his preface he begged the reader not to take offense if he presented the truth without partiality. His readers need not worry. Knox, always eager to see the hand of God or to defame the Catholic Church, was seldom capable of objectivity.

One of the few Protestant historians of the sixteenth century who enjoyed a reputation for objectivity was John Sleidan (1506-56). In 1544, on Bucer's recommendation, the landgrave Philip of Hesse commissioned Sleidan to write a history of Germany after 1517. Sleidan began in the following year and by 1555 the *Commentarii de statu religionis et rei publicae Carolo V Caesare* was published in twenty-six parts. Evidently Sleidan was so impartial that his book pleased neither Catholic nor Protestant. The Emperor repeatedly denounced him as a liar and Philip Melanchthon could find no fine things to say "of that which is not fine."

Sleidan claimed to give a fair account of the Reformation in Germany by narrating the religious and diplomatic events just as they had occurred. He does not interpret the causes of the movement nor does he sketch the character of Luther or Calvin. Sleidan regarded the Reformation as a religious movement, a triumph for the word of God through the agency of Martin Luther, but he did not separate it from the politics of the German princes. His personal political entanglements, as official historian for the Schmalkald League and an opponent of the Holy Roman Empire raise questions about his impartiality. His book, however, because of its factual completeness, has often been called the best single source for the period.

The sixteenth-century writers who lived in the thick of religious and political turmoil and were passionately involved in it should not be condemned because they did not write emotionless, exact histories of the Reformation. Friends of Luther and Calvin should be expected to produce panegyrics of the men and movement they loved. If a Reformer like Melanchthon could criticize Luther even slightly, he can be praised for it. The Reformers hated the Church of Rome and they were convinced that they were warriors against the anti-Christ. The martyrologists, chroniclers and historians universally condemned the postpatristic Church because it had wandered far from its original purity. The Reformers and their disciples believed that the downfall of that corrupt and decaying institution was preordained in the divine plan. Mathesius regarded Luther as the instrument of God's will, Beza found the finger of God in Calvin, and Knox found it in himself. Cochlaeus and Baronius on the other hand, impassioned defenders of the Catholic Church, should not be condemned for their ardent partiality. They too regarded themselves as warriors for Christ against the heretics, much as the Crusaders were warriors against the Turks. On both sides history had become an instrument of war.

An interesting contribution to the anti-papal histories was made from another quarter by Fra Paolo Sarpi (1552-1623), a brilliant Servite monk who freely censured the corruption of the Renaissance Popes. Fra Paolo was one of the greatest minds of his age, a universal genius like da Vinci. His remarkable memory made him a walking catalogue of the Venetian archives. He joined the Order of Servites at thirteen and later became a protégé of Charles Borromeo, from whom he learned a great deal about the Council of Trent.

Sarpi was a violent partisan of Venice in an age when papal political encroachment still threatened the Republic's mainland territories. It was his advice to the *signoria* that led Venice to resist the Pope's authority by ignoring bulls and denouncing interdicts.

Like many other fervent Christians, Sarpi was sickened by the corruption of the curial and papal autocracy. His outspoken criticism of authoritarianism in the Church made him *persona non grata* to Catholic reformers, especially the Jesuits. He favored the Reformation because it destroyed papal power, but he remained a loyal Catholic. When asked why he adhered to the Roman Church, Fra Paolo answered, "God has not given me the spirit of Luther."

Sarpi's wide knowledge of ecclesiastical history led him to regard the origin of some of the Pope's favored political and financial institutions as corruptions, whereas Rome called them "developments." His *Della Materie Beneficiarie* was a devastating condemnation of the papal system of benefices. More a living polemic than an historical tract, it was a sharp denunciation of the instruments which the Popes used to garner temporal wealth and power.

In 1619, Sarpi, using the pseudonym Pietro Soave, published in London the *Historia del Concilio Tridentino*. His purpose was to expose "the arts employed by the Roman court to prevent the elucidation of true doctrine, and the effectual reformation of the papacy in the Church." His interpretation of the Reformation, based on Sleidan's narrative, was similar to contemporary Protestant accounts. Reform was the fruit of divine intervention and a reaction against abuses.

The Jesuit Cardinal Pallavicini (1607-67) in the official answer to the *Historia del Concilio Tridentino* brought Sarpi's scholarship and honesty into question. The Vatican archives were thrown open to him and through the Jesuit Order he gained access to the libraries of the Roman papal families and Italian religious houses. Pallavicini labored for twenty years on his refutation of Fra Paolo's thesis which was not published until 1659. Unfortunately confined to a direct point-by-point contradiction of Sarpi, he was unable to shape the archival material he had gathered into an interesting narrative. Pallavicini had a distinct advantage over Sarpi and proved him in error on many points. He always gave the name and location of documents he quoted; Sarpi seldom if ever provided the names of individuals whose books he referred to. Pallavicini ended his work with a list of four hundred errors and falsifications he had uncovered to Sarpi's discredit. Pallavicini did not conceal the squabbles that divided the Council Fathers at Trent; his was an honest record of the conciliar events without a suppression of unfavorable evidence. In his *History of the Popes,* the first contribution to the history of the Council of Trent after Sarpi and Pallavicini, Ranke compared the scholarship of the two and preferred the Jesuit. Yet his work was an *apologia mescolata* rather than an impartial history.

Fra Paolo's books were extremely popular in Europe and soon went through numerous editions and translations. He was a propagandist insofar as he used history to popularize his conviction that papal and Jesuit tyranny impeded a true Catholic reformation. A similar position, although in rather different circumstances, was taken by the English poet and pamphleteer John Milton (1608-74). In 1641, Milton, a champion of Puritanism, charged in his first pamphlets that the formalism of the Anglican episcopacy and liturgy obstructed the completion of the Reformation.

After the Long Parliament had impeached Archbishop Laud, the time was ripe for a defense of Puritan religious liberty through a defamation of Anglican ecclesiastical authority. In Milton's view the Reformation had restored the Church to its apostolic spirituality by removing the obstacles which an institutional Church put between God and man. The bishops and their defenders were a "tyrannical crew and corporation of imposters" who, in their ambition for wealth and glory, possessed merely a "temporal, earthly and corporeal spirituality." The liturgy was a Delilah that sapped the spiritual strength of all those who came to depend on her. "The soul . . . finding the ease she had from her visible and sensuous colleague the body in the performance of religious duties . . . shifted off from herself the labour of high soaring any more, forgot her heavenly flight . . ." What value was there to a Reformation that hindered the immediate ascent of the soul to God? Episcopal authority and the liturgy had to be disposed of before the millennium could begin.

By 1644 Presbyterianism had disappointed Milton. He began to realize that the Reformation could not supplant the deeper sources of "this working mystery of ignorance and ecclesiastical thraldom" in one violent upheaval which soon became static. Englishmen had good reason to thank God because doctrinal truth was possessed in their land. But anyone who for this reason would "pitch his tent here," satisfied that the Reformation had been perfectly achieved, did not see the truth.

The virgin Truth had accompanied her divine Master into the world, but after He and His disciples died, "a wicked race of deceivers" hewed her into a thousand pieces and scattered them to the winds. Since then Truth's friends were engaged in a loving search for the parts of her mangled body. The Reformation had not found them all, nor could it until Jesus' second coming. "He shall mould them into an immortal feature of loveliness and perfection."

The light of the Reformation preached by Calvin and Zwingli was a sun that had blinded their disciples. They had been falsely convinced that the Reformation was complete with the unfrocking of a priest and the removal of a bishop's mitre. But even Presbyterianism, in its attempt to prevent schism through tyrannous controls and censorship, prevented the gathering and reunion of Truth's scattered body. England, which had given the Reformation to the world in Wycliffe, the forerunner of Huss, Luther, and Calvin, was rapidly sinking into ignorance and decay through the autocracy of her ministers. Even at that hour God was preparing to use England again as His instrument in reforming the Reformation. "Now once again, by all concurrence of signs . . . God is decreeing to begin some new and great period in His Church, even to the reforming of the Reformation itself . . ."

Milton opposed the Presbyterian clergy's attempt to prevent further dissection of Protestantism by enforcing orthodoxy. This free sectarianism, which Milton accepted as a part of the Christian's continuous search for truth, was to Jacques-Bénigne Bossuet (1627-1704) the internal contradiction and condemnation of the Reformation. Bossuet, Bishop of Meaux and intimate of the Sun King, provided the most significant Catholic interpretation of the Reformation in the "splendid century." Not only was he a theorist of French divine right monarchy, but, remarkably for the seventeenth century, the Eagle of Meaux was a strong advocate for reunion of the Church. *The History of the Variations of the Protestant Churches,* often mistaken for an attack on the Protestant confessions, was a fruit of his irony. Bossuet hoped that once shown the paradoxes and contradictions the Reformers had used to defend their revolution, Protestants would flock back to the Catholic Church. His thesis was that since truth is one, the dissension, division and variation in Protestantism represent its condemnation.

The Reformers produced these differences because they were ignorant of the Church's authority, of its divinely ordained promises and of its very nature. If they had rightly understood what their confessions later expressed—that the Church is "the assembly of saints, wherein the Gospel is rightly taught, and the sacraments rightly administered" (Augsburg Confession)—they would have preserved the unity of the Church. How could the Reformers conceivably accuse the Church of error, Bossuet asked, if the Church *rightly* teaches the good news and *rightly* administers the sacraments? True reformers and sons of the Church were those who worked peacefully for renewal from within, waiting patiently through many delays. On the other hand the radical reformers were proud men who so little understood the Church that they believed it could not survive abuse. In hating the men who befouled the Church with their wickedness, they hated the Church itself.

Instead of confining their attacks to the corruption of the clergymen, bishops and Popes, they attacked the offices of their authority. Once they had eliminated central authority the Reformers learned that their revolution produced not doctrinal renewal but dogmatic relativism and religious anarchy. Out of one revolt burst many others, until the foundations of religious and civil order were undermined. Luther, whose importance in Bossuet's interpretation is out of proportion to the other leaders, was not true to the good news he proclaimed, for the fruit of his evangelization was unchristian sedition and plundering. Bossuet, with Melanchthon, held that the source of the Reformation's success was not theological, but social, economic and political. The people who flocked to the various confessions did not come searching for doctrine; they wanted license and independence. "They seek not doctrine and religion," said Melanchthon, who distressed the imperial towns by restoring the episcopacy, "but power and liberty."

Bossuet's interest in healing the breach between Protestant and Catholic was not merely academic. He participated in a high-level, but unofficial discussion with Protestants on the possibilities for reunion. Bishop Spinola, suffragan of Tina and later ordinary at Neustadt, initiated an exchange of views with Molanus, wise Lutheran Abbot of Lokkum, in the later decades of the seventeenth century. The quality and depth of his irenic attitudes startled his Protestant correspondents, especially his conviction that the content of the Augsburg Confession was not so different from that of the Tridentine decrees. Spinola consulted Bossuet; the Bishop of Meaux gave his hearty approval and also hinted that King Louis XIV was interested. Bossuet was soon drawn into the thick of the exchange. He translated and commented on a *Project for Reunion* that Molanus had drafted. Bossuet, treating Molanus with great charity, said that the Pope would probably grant the concessions the Abbot would demand for the adherence of the Lutheran confessions to Rome. Communion under two kinds, retention of a married clergy, vernacular Scriptures— all these Rome would yield, with the exception of recognizing the validity of Lutheran orders. Bossuet suggested that Luther's translation of the Bible be used, "because of its clearness and elegance."

In July, 1691, Gottfried Wilhelm von Leibniz (1646-1716)

entered the interconfessional exchange with a letter to Mme de Brinon, an intimate friend of the Marquise de Maintenon and a leader at St. Cyr. "All of those," he wrote, "who keep up the schism by throwing obstacles in the way of reconciliation are the real schismatics, and those who are ready to do whatever is possible to bring about visible communion are true Catholics." He succeeded Molanus in the correspondence with Bossuet.

Leibniz scattered comments in his letters for reunion written in the last decade of the seventeenth century which, taken together, form an interpretation of the Reformation. He rose above the emotion and heat of former apocalyptic diatribes to the level of a reasoned historical understanding of the reform movement. He urged Protestants to abandon the unfounded notion that the Bishop of Rome was anti-Christ. He encouraged Catholics to scrap the falsified picture of Luther which hate-literature rather than history had painted. Lutherans should not blame Catholics for the impiety and worldly excesses of the Pope; nor should Catholics, however, condemn the Reformation because of Luther's boorishness.

Leibniz reduced the black period in Church history to two hundred fifty years, 1250-1500, denying that it was the "reign of Satan." Historically, these years were a period of anarchy in German territory and in Europe, caused mainly by the deviousness and plotting of the clergy. The absence of civil order meant a decline in justice, peace and learning. Scholasticism reduced true Christian theology to empty systems. The Pope secularized his priestly office at the expense of genuine piety and worship. In the Tridentine decrees Leibniz saw an admission by the Church that there had been need for reform in scholastic theology and clerical morality.

Leibniz recognized a broad area of agreement between Calvinism and Catholicism in the doctrine of predestination. In his *systema theologicum* he accepted the first Tridentine Canon with the assurance that man is so corrupt as to be unable even to begin "anything good" without divine grace. His theology of justification centered more on love than on faith. Love compelled man to act; good works were then necessary for salvation as signs of an earnest will. Leibniz also conceded to Bossuet in 1692, but with caution, that the Catholic Church had restored the true doctrine of justification at Trent. His attitude toward the sacraments was also Catholic. He admitted in the *systema theologicum* that there was truly a transformation in the bread and wine at the moment of consecration in the Eucharist. Despite his doctrinal Catholicity Leibniz would base reunion on a communal piety rather than a communal faith. He believed that certain theological issues like the damage the fall has done to man were mere quibbling and profited little. Since piety and practice should be the same for everyone, the superior question for Leibniz was whether love of God was requisite for salvation.

Leibniz was full of praise for Catholic teaching but rejected Roman worship with its corruptions. He embraced the Reformation but renounced Lutheran doctrine, while insisting that Martin Luther was not a heretic. His interpretation of the Reformation theology is somewhat of a turning point, for it represents the first time that a secondary principle of the Reformation, freedom of conscience, gained ascendancy over its primary doctrine, justification by faith. The spiritual openness that leads to belief was more important to Leibniz than the content of faith.

In Veit Ludwig Freiherr von Seckendorf (1626-92) we find a Protestant layman who shared Leibniz's preoccupation with Christian reunion. Although a convinced Lutheran, he viewed the division in the Church brought on by the sixteenth-century reform movement as a scandal. "Seckendorf loved the Reformation and grieved over it." He wrote a detailed history of the Reformation as a reply to the account of Bossuet. *Historia Lutheranismi* was first published in 1692, the year of his death, and a second edition followed in 1694. Unlike many of his contemporaries, Seckendorf was very familiar with the writings of Martin Luther. His object in the *Historia* was to present a history of the Reformation from the sources. He was convinced that God had manifested Himself in the achievements of the Reformer and this conviction provided his history with a theological motive. He wanted to study the Reformation as an historical event with the dual intention of understanding the facts objectively and perfecting his own piety.

Seckendorf was fascinated with the early period of the Reformation. In the first seven years of the movement he thought he could see the "real" Luther. He cut away the mystique that had hallowed Luther and wrote about a man rather than an apocalyptic superman. Seckendorf's Luther was still the paramount messenger of God, but he was no longer a mere instrument in His hands. Luther's uncanny drive in the early period, his perseverance and his capacity for work were marvels for Seckendorf. Luther's great achievement was his translation of the Scriptures, an accomplishment that paralleled in importance the introduction of Christianity into Germany. Christianity truly flowered forth in the first years of the Reformation; the princes had not yet stepped in, nor had the confusion, which was soon to reign, yet begun. It was Seckendorf's theological understanding of history that explained for him the later breach between the Lutheran and the Reformed Churches. The Reformation was "the finger of God." It might have proceeded more effectively and rapidly had the Protestants remained one; but He knew what He was about.

Seckendorf's attitudes toward reunion bear a marked similarity to those of Leibniz. Like that philosopher he recognizes the reforms that had been initiated within the Catholic Church since the sixteenth century. Numerous clergy were becoming familiar with the Scriptures; German pastors were imitating the evangelical preaching and vernacular hymnody of the Protestants. Things were improving to such an extent that some of Seckendorf's contemporaries began to wonder if Luther had just cause for breaking with Rome.

Seckendorf set his program for reunion on the same bases as Leibniz. Dogmatic differences may prevail, but there must be unity in holiness and love. He admonished those Lutherans who flirted with immorality because they wanted to demonstrate their disdain for good works. In their conception of a reunion in the Church through the bond of common Christian behavior, both Seckendorf and Leibniz are forerunners of pietism.

Philip Jacob Spener (1635-1705), one of the earliest Lutheran pietists, spent twenty years as a pastor in Frankfurt am Main and in 1691 he became provost of the Nikolaikirche in Berlin. Spener's orthodoxy is unquestionable, but his pietism came into direct conflict with Lutheranism over the essence of Christianity, the shape of the Church and the inner attitudes proper to it. He encouraged Lutherans to manifest a rich spirituality in external works, a doctrine alien to his orthodox hearers. Against those controversialists who took issue with his theology of works, Spener called Martin Luther to witness. He renounced the cult of Luther worship, but insisted that Luther must be imitated as reformer. Luther did not intend the Reformation to be static. The evangelical church must continue it through works without falling back on the principles of the Roman autocracy. He regarded Luther not as *the* interpreter of Scripture, but as a faithful witness to the evangelical idea. Doctrinaire Lutherans, in Spener's opinion, were unfaithful to both Reformer and Reformation. Lutheran consistories that aped Rome in attempting to regulate the particulars of a person's life were acting in opposition to the Christian principle of free conscience.

Spener's teaching on faith, works and conscience were cardinal elements in his interpretation of the Reformation as dynamic, inchoative, always to be advanced. Martin Luther had brought the Church out of Babylon, but the foundation of the Temple was barely started even then in the seventeenth century. The Reformation was not, however, to be pushed ahead by the state. Spener did not approve of the regional Church organization, for nothing appeared to be more oppressive to the Church's spirituality and freedom than secular control. Morality was the area in which the Reformation lacked completion. Luther's followers had misinterpreted his insistence on justification by faith, and as a consequence falsely held good works in contempt. Spener's pietism was a continuing moral reformation through faith and works.

Leibniz, Seckendorf and Spener are representative of the state of religious opinion in Germany at the turn of the eighteenth century. It was a period of transition that ended in the separation of reason and piety from orthodox Christianity. Ethical piety which in Leibniz, Seckendorf and Spener had remained deeply Christian, was alienated from Christian dogma during the Age of Reason. The *philosophes* of the Enlightenment inherited the language of the pietists, but they denatured it and used it in the service of reason. Seckendorf interpreted the events of the Reformation as evidence of divine providence in history; Leibniz and Spener put aside the traditional view that the Reformation was the evangelical restoration of Christian truth and interpreted it as the arrival of Christian freedom of conscience and the dynamic, ever unfinished renewal of piety. To the enlightened men of the eighteenth century, divine providence became reasoned human progress; freedom of conscience became the liberation of reason from faith; and pietism became ethics without Christ, a half-breed Christianity without a Church.

Although the interpretation of the Reformation offered by Johann Salomo Semler (1725-91) showed traces of pietist elements, it was essentially a new, pragmatic treatment. Semler was an "enlightened" theologian who taught at Halle for thirty-nine years. With the pietists, he held that virtue and individuality were superior to dogma. The Reformation was the event that absolved man from servile dependence on dogmatic formulations and an institutional Church. Semler asserted, as had Leibniz with less emphasis, that the fruit of the Reformation was the complete ascendancy of freedom of conscience over dogma in the eighteenth century. Bossuet, in his *History of the Variations of Protestantism,* had charged the evangelical and reformed churches with unfaithfulness to their doctrines, but Semler maintained that this critique was not relevant in the Age of Reason. Luther, he argued, taught that the individual was free to believe what he knew in conscience to be the truth. So, stripping him of his apocalyptic features, he hailed Luther as the bearer of freedom of conscience. Semler had little trouble accommodating his opinion to the fact that Luther insisted on the universality and immutability of dogma. The Reformer had to demand, he explained, universal adherence to his doctrine in order to keep the masses under control. Such an expediency was unnecessary in the eighteenth century when the enlightened man found Christian truth in the order of reason and utility, rather than in the order of faith.

Although reasonableness led Semler to doubt that there was anything miraculous about the radical reformation, he was not so coldly rational as to exclude even the authorship of God. It was an event both explained by the exigencies of history and given as a gift of providence. The divine plan, for Semler and the *philosophes,* was not, however, the preordained salvation of man through time; it was the development of man through enlightened intellectuality and material progress.

Semler applied this idea of providence to the events, advances and abuses which led up to the sixteenth-century era of reform. With pietism he scrapped the old dogmatic idea that the Reformation was a single saving event. Rather it was "a stage in the intellectual and religious progress of humanity." Previous stages had been the revival of learning and the development of printing. The men who benefited from both, like Erasmus and Pico della Mirandola, had pilloried what was corrupt in the fifteenth-century Church long before Martin Luther. More people read the New Testament and realized by comparison with the apostolic assembly of the faithful how far the official Church had interposed its mediation between God and His sons. The medieval papacy, which had set itself in God's place, was as wicked and tryannous as the worst of Rome's emperors, and papal temporal power was the "unworthy means by which that rotten religion . . . stood in the way of godly Christian freedom and the conscientious application of a man's own wholesome perceptions."

Because Semler did not consider the Reformation a direct saving intervention of God in history, he minimized Luther's instrumentality and importance. He was merely one of many Reformers and it mattered little whether he was specially endowed or not. Nor was his doctrine of justification central to a movement whose object was to preach freedom of conscience and a renewal in moral life.

The theologian Semler had the same idea of human progress that is found in the pragmatic historians of the Enlightenment. Bossuet and Seckendorf had written history for the glorification of God. Voltaire and Hume, on the other hand, wrote history for the satisfaction of man. The pragmatic historian disciplined himself to study events as they happened. He preferred a detailed narrative with frequent digression to a selective and documented interpretation. As he worked his way through his data he looked for a trend that he could follow from its source all the way to his own age. He identified these trends with an infinitely wise providence, replacing the Christian theological understanding of history with the foremost ideas of the Enlightenment. Grace became humanitarianism, and salvation, progress.

It is ironic that Voltaire (1694-1778) chose to rely heavily upon Bossuet for his scattered remarks on the Reformation. That he also used Fra Paolo Sarpi is less remarkable. He offered very little by way of interpreting the events, and when he did he was superficial and slick rather than profound. In one place he compared the religious upheavals in sixteenth-century Europe with contemporaneous ferment in the Muslim world, but the effect was novelty not clarity.

In his essay on toleration he did spend a few pages on the causes of the Reformation. The Renaissance of the fifteenth century, he maintained, awakened many to complain against the obvious crimes that prevailed in the Church. Pope Alexander VI used the papacy, which he had purchased, to enrich his bastards; Pope Julius II stirred up hatred and disorder all over Italy with his wars; and Pope Leo X hawked indulgences to finance his costly pleasures. It could hardly be immoral for the Reformers to condemn such men pretending to be other Christs when they knew Jesus never levied a tax or sold an indulgence.

In the *Essai sur les moeurs et l'esprit des nations* he struck shallow ground. At the root of the reform movement was a monastic dispute over the profits from the sale of indulgences, "and this little squabble of monks in a corner of Saxony produced more than a hundred years of discord, fury, and misfortune for thirty nations." His observation on the Reformation in England also contains more charm than depth.

"England separated from the Pope," he wrote, "because King Henry fell in love."

Voltaire admired the Reformers' knowledge of the ancient languages and the ancient wisdom. They were responsible for freeing the human mind from the dead weight of barbarism. On the other hand he had little liking for their appeal to the emotion of the masses and for their ultimate reliance on brutality and force. Because they transcended reason Voltaire hated reformed doctrines as much as he did Catholic ones. He drew on the theological issues of the Reformation only to satirize them: the Reformation as a spiritual crisis was nothing more than the stupid antics of "Roman Catholics who ate God for bread, Lutherans who ate bread and God, and Calvinists who ate bread and did not eat God." Remarks like these must lead to the disqualification of Voltaire as a serious historian. He was unable to treat religious issues historically. The prophet of toleration was equally intolerant of Catholic and Protestant, and preferred to dispute their tenets rather than deal with them as historical data. We cannot look for historical precision in a man who quipped that all religion began when the first knave met the first fool. Catholic, Lutheran, Reformed—knaves and fools all—he held in equal contempt.

Although Voltaire wrote sparkling "universal" history that appealed to the literary and intellectual tastes of eighteenth-century Europe, he did little more than tack one fact onto another. Attaching little importance to continuity in history, he produced oversimplified explanations for complex historical events. The English philosopher and pragmatic historian David Hume (1711-76) had this requisite sense of continuity and was equipped to give a deeper explanation of the historical causes of the Reformation. In the course of his gigantic narrative, *The History of England from the Invasion of Julius Caesar to the Revolution of 1688,* he digressed to interpret the rise and progress of the Reformation and its theological issues; "or, what is more material," explained Hume in the language of the Enlightenment, "to trace from their origin those abuses which so generally diffused the opinion that a Reformation of the Church . . . was become highly expedient, if not absolutely necessary." This latter objective so occupied him that he never got around to the promised theological issues. Hume told much the same story as Voltaire, but he recognized that abuses in the Church of Rome were not the isolated causes of that "great revolution." Pope Leo X, humanist connoisseur of pleasure, resorted to the sale of indulgences ostensibly to acquire funds for the administration of the Church. A jurisdictional dispute between the Augustinian and Dominican friars who were parcelling out the indulgences in Germany was immediately responsible for the upheaval, but it was not the total cause. A series of circumstances and events converged to bring about the Reformation; not the least of these was the person and personality of Martin Luther who was able through his genius and appeal to direct the course of the movement. He condemned one error, the excesses in selling indulgences, and this led him to uncover another and then another. Hume used the eighteenth-century idea of progress analogically to interpret Luther's development into a radical reformer.

Behind the rapid success of the Reformation, Hume found the invention of printing and the humanist revival of learning. Printers wasted no time in getting the controversial and polemical literature of the Reformers published and circulated all over Europe. The men who read it had been newly awakened to learning, and therefore, with unrefined critical faculties, they wandered down the path that Luther and the others opened to them. As they read Scripture in their vernacular, they could determine how far the Church had strayed from its origin.

Hume cautions the eighteenth-century rationalist who might be tempted to acclaim rationalism the force that directed the Reformation. Philosophy had not yet matured and argument was impotent to dispel the superstition that held sway over the masses. Reason and reflection had little to do with a movement that depended upon the passions and violence of the masses for its success.

Hume was biased against the doctrine and structure of the Catholic Church, but he was neither as bitter nor as irreverent as Voltaire. The Church of Rome was a very powerful institution whose revenues, civil privileges, immunities, and sway over the people disturbed the welfare of the state. The Pope was not anti-Christ, but "a foreign potentate" who did not have the interest of the English nation at heart. The Church in Hume's interpretation of the Reformation, as in other enlightened opinions from the eighteenth century, was never more than a political monolith full of corruption. The achievement of the Reformation in ruining this power was a financial and political advantage for the state. The theological issues, spiritual anguish, and the supernatural were beyond the pale of reason.

William Robertson (1721-93), a Presbyterian clergyman, is

an exception to this last observation. Though enamored of both Voltaire and Hume, who left their unmistakable mark on his analysis of the Reformation, he retained his Christian sense of the supernatural. His treatment was also a digression—from his *The History of the Reign of Emperor Charles the Fifth*—but it was much better than Hume's.

Voltaire wrote that the Middle Ages deserved as little study as the quarrels of wolves and bears, and Robertson would agree. The age in which the Church of Rome predominated in Europe was very black for him indeed. The Catholic Church, he maintained, was an artificial fabric of lies and scholastic theology, a web of vain subtleties. The Reformation was the happy religious and political movement that liberated one part of Europe from the clutches of the Pope and weakened his hold on the other. It was responsible, said Robertson with Voltaire and Hume, for a radical change in "the sentiments of mankind." This signified the restoration of Christianity for the former, the advent of reason for the other two, and the end of the dark ages for all three. Robertson thought it the most fruitful revolution since the spread of Christianity.

The most important achievement of the Reformation, in Robertson's opinion, was the rejection of those doctrines founded on ancient prejudice, implemented by power and defended by crafty theologians. Only the direct intervention of God could have been sufficient to reverse the situation and set up its opposite peacefully and easily. In the first ages of Christianity God showed His favor through miracles and prophecies which prepared men to hear and embrace His Word. None of the Reformers claimed these charismatic gifts, yet the vigor and genius of the movement seemed to have been touched by the same hand that planted Christianity. This was illustrated, asserted Robertson, by the fact that the Reformation was embraced by men politically powerless in opposition to the political craft and power of Rome.

But in the course of her dealings with Luther, Rome showed neither sagacity nor certainty. Pope Leo X, one of the more skillful pontiffs, was inclined to regard the initial stages of the Reformation as an inbred monastic quibble between the Dominicans and Augustinians. When the unorthodox nature of Luther's tenets became more evident, Pope Leo oscillated instead of immediately taking a stand. Robertson guessed that had he censured Luther without hesitation, the Reformer would have lost his political support and might have lost his courage as well.

In his discussion of the rise and progress of the Reformation, Robertson followed Hume, but he saw the idea of evolutionary growth and extended it to the formation of reformed doctrine. If at the outset Luther had dared to challenge the authority of the Church directly, he would have brought the fullness of its wrath crashing down upon his head. Such effrontery was the farthest thought from his mind. Luther's doctrines evolved, one flowing from another, beginning with his opposition to the sale of indulgences all the way to his revolution against Rome. The doctrines of the Roman Church were so closely interwoven that discovering one error was like pulling a thread; in Luther's hands the whole fabric began to unravel. Luther was induced to question each error he uncovered more closely, and he bore his followers with him. He was successful because he proceeded without shocking his hearers; they were always ready for the next step. Robertson's explanation is superior to Hume's; he possessed a larger command of the complexity of historical causes. These matured and coincided in Martin Luther producing the upheaval.

While Robertson was a Churchman who wrote pragmatic history, Johann Lorenz von Mosheim (1693-1755) was a pragmatic historian who wrote Church history. Mosheim, the co-founder and chancellor of Göttingen University, was a prolific writer who authored no fewer than eighty-five works in ecclesiastical history. He indicated his alignment with the spirit and thought of the Enlightenment in the subtitle of his two-volume *Ecclesiastical History,* "in which the Rise, Progress and Variations of Church Power are considered . . ." It was a dull, tedious Latin narrative written for use in a university course.

Mosheim shared a dim view of the Middle Ages with Voltaire, Robertson and other representatives of the Age of Reason. A number of brilliant men at the beginning of the sixteenth century burst the medieval gloom with a sudden revival of learning, but it was not sufficient to stir the insensitive and corrupt "lords of the Church." This happy revolution of the human mind aroused love of truth and sacred liberty in the Church where ignorance had lingered for such a long time. It unfortunately stopped short of uprooting the evils altogether. The enlightened humanist readily lampooned the piggish monk, but he had not the courage to attack the source of abuse and excess—the Pope of Rome who had usurped his vice-regency from Jesus. The voices clamoring all over Europe wished only disciplinary reform in the papacy, hierarchy and clergy. When the question of root changes in the administration of the Church or the elimination of absurd and outdated doctrines was raised, they became silent.

The Reformers, on the other hand, did not stop short. The "Blessed Reformation," asserted Mosheim, was the "most glorious of all the revolutions that happened in the state of Christianity since the time of its divine and immortal Founder." A religious movement that started on a minor scale in Saxony and spread quickly throughout the world was the beginning of modern history, for it emancipated reason and brought Church power into decline. It had an influence on nearly all the political and religious revolutions through the mid-eighteenth century. The Age of Reason experienced and the future would continue to experience—"in a sensible manner"—the uncountable benefits the Reformation produced, along with the inconveniences it merely occasioned.

Mosheim did not subscribe completely to the enlightened skepticism toward revealed religion. Unlike Voltaire, he refrained from attacking dogma and showed signs of respect for the supernatural. He treated the theological controversy with detachment and calm, like a lawyer briefing a case. His handling of the spiritual issues, however, was less than profound; his method and mind reduced them to "mere verbal disputes."

Edward Gibbon (1737-94) relied on Mosheim for the brief consideration he gave to the Reformation in the *History of the Decline and Fall of the Roman Empire*. He proposed to place a value on the Reformation by studying the articles of faith "above or against our reason" through which it liberated Christian men. He was less able than Mosheim to discourse on history which involved theological problems.

Considered objectively, said Gibbon, the Reformers strike us as cautious and timid. They seldom shock us with their freedom of action. They embraced Holy Scriptures "with all their prodigies," and with the Jews defended them. Like the Catholics they were rigidly orthodox in their belief in the Trinity and the Incarnation. They did not scruple to damn all those who did not believe the Catholic faith when they recited the Athanasian Creed, but were reluctant to follow their reason and reject transubstantiation. In Gibbon's estimation Protestant belief in supernatural truth always remained a debit. "Many a sober Christian," he wrote, "would admit that a wafer is God rather than that God is a cruel and capricious tyrant."

Despite the Reformation's adherence to faith it has served the Church and the world well, liberating them from the idolatry of saint worship and other pious superstitions. The taste of the enlightened man for a religion cleaned up and rarified by reason led Gibbon to praise reformed liturgy. The worship of Christians was spiritualized and fathered a piety which did not debase man and was most pleasing to God. The Reformers, Gibbon asserted, did not intend this new freedom of Christians, but it came with the destruction of hierarchical authority and the doctrine of free individual interpretation of Scripture. The Reformers soon became as willing as the Catholic Church to crush freedom of conscience by persecuting the unorthodox, but they lacked the money and power of Rome. "The nature of the tiger was the same, but he was gradually deprived of his teeth and fangs." Gibbon was deeply scandalized by the execution of Servetus in Geneva and he censured Calvin's intolerance as contrary to natural moral principle and the Christian law of love.

Gibbon summarizes the attitudes of "enlightened" thinkers toward the Reformation. Where the achievement of the Reformation coincided with the goals of the Age of Reason, he praised it; where they conflicted, he censured. Freedom of conscience and freedom from a hierarchical church were dear to his idea of reasoned, purified spirituality. The Reformation's "narrow" adherence to faith and dogmas which led to the persecution of heretics contained its own folly and condemnation. Jerusalem had nothing to do with Athens; the Age of Reason put narrow-mindedness and intolerance aside, because unlike the radical Reformation it believed that what satisfied a child could not please an "enlightened" adult.

Gibbon was a much better historian than Voltaire or Hume, and had he not indulged himself in an attempt at combatting the theology of the Reformers he might have produced an acceptable interpretation of the Reformation. He failed, however, to live up to his own claim of objectivity. Leopold von Ranke (1795-1886), the giant of nineteenth-century scientific history, was one of the first scholars who could say he had written an objective account of European history in the early sixteenth century.

During the third centennial celebration of Luther's Reformation in 1817, Ranke allowed himself a few romantic meditations on the Reformers and their movement. The Reformation was a blessing to Germany and every nation; Martin Luther, whom the young scholar loved, was a genius who had restored the abuse-ridden Church of the Middle Ages to its scriptural purity. His scholarly creed that history must limit itself to a strict representation of facts, however narrow or unpoetic, would never again allow him such raptures. Nevertheless, in his later works, Ranke did not alter the kernel of his youthful observations.

The first two volumes of *German History in the Era of Reformation*, Ranke's masterwork, were published in 1839. His most important source was a ninety-six-volume edition of the proceedings of the imperial diet (1414-1613) from which he was able to reconstruct the development of Reformation period political institutions in Germany. He made this study the backbone of his work. Ranke believed that just as there was no human activity of intellectual value which originated outside of God, "so there (was) no nation whose political life (was) not continually raised and guided by religious ideas." He shaped his interpretation of Germany in the sixteenth century with this conviction, viewing the ecclesiastical and political events of the Reformation as one movement.

The structure of the Church at the end of the fifteenth century was an awesome but paradoxical combination of worldly and divine power, fanaticism and insipid scholarship, devout practice and brutality, religion and superstition. As a fruit of sustaining constant attack and frequently achieving conquest, it pretended not only to universal competence for all peoples, but also to control over the most intimate details of personal life. From the chronic conflict of the ecclesiastical and secular power, the Church had emerged victorious, bringing political disorder and impotence to Germany. Having won the day in the temporal order, the Pope dared to arrogate divinity to himself by usurping the place of Christ in His Church. Rome's legalists canonized the identification of the Pope's will with God's will; the Pope flaunted his victory in his court's pompous material display of power. Could any reasonable man, asked Ranke, have opposed the reshaping of this structure in which a reasoned faith was hardly possible?

Early attempts at Church reform had been abortive, and abortive, too, was the experiment of cooperation between the Emperor and the states. Abuses and greed caused opposition in both the religious and the political order. When the situation was approaching its worst, Martin Luther recaptured the core of evangelical Christianity. He unified and directed the movement, bringing all of Germany loosely together around him. Ranke let his nationalism inform his evaluation of Martin Luther: How much Luther could have done towards strengthening national unity, had he been able to oppose the Pope and nothing more!

Luther was well aware, said Ranke, that one age must carefully transmit its cultural heritage to the next. He accepted traditional doctrine insofar as it was not full of corruption or innovation. He was obliged to struggle both against the papacy and against the Reformers who had rashly exceeded scriptural norms. The Pope was out to recover what he had lost and the Reformers threatened to harm the secular and ecclesiastical order. Luther was, as a consequence, one of the greatest conservatives in history, whose aim had been not to overthrow the Reich, but to reform the Church and secure its new structure through cooperation with the state.

Ranke and the school of scientific history bequeathed a method and direction to Catholic Reformation scholarship which had been revived by the theologian Johann Adam Möhler (1796-1838). Möhler became a professor at the University of Tübingen in 1822, just as the Catholic Church in Germany was emerging from the effects of the Enlightenment. In 1825 the publication of his discourse on the unity of the Church initiated a decade of Catholic Romanticism that was supported at Munich by Döllinger and publicized by Görres.

Symbolik, which Möhler published in 1832, was a comparative study of the theological differences among the Churches based on an examination of their creeds. Möhler admitted to irenic motives in his preface and thought them fulfilled merely in the accurate and systematic presentation of differences in dogma. Only the naive would expect reunion in an age when ignorance and confusion had so blurred the distinctions among the confessions and even religious leaders did not understand the nature of faith. Reunion would not be acceptance of truth that is one, but a union in disbelief, a license for everyone to believe as he pleased. *Symbolik* was a vigorous tract which challenged the minds of young Catholic Germans and bore fruit in a rebirth of Catholic Reformation studies.

After the publication of *Symbolik* Möhler became a colleague of Johannes Joseph Ignaz von Döllinger (1799-1870) at the University of Munich. His frank conviction that Luther had been right on many points—the venal abuse of papal power for one—was not completely acceptable to Döllinger and was a source of irritation between the scholars.

Döllinger wrote *Die Reformation,* published at Regensburg between 1846 and 1848, as a response to Ranke's essay which he considered to be an apology for the Reformation. More theologian than historian, the Munich professor was not much interested in rehashing the proceedings of the imperial diets or in attempting a history of Germany in the Reformation era. He made it his object to investigate the spiritual development of Protestantism, a goal he would never completely attain. What he produced was a study of the religious and moral consequences of Reformation theology.

Döllinger did not see the Reformation as a sudden reaction against a tradition of decay in the medieval Church. Side by side with corruption there had been a tradition of ecclesiastical reforms that began with the monastic revival at Cluny and terminated in the Protestant Reformation. Luther did nothing more than enunciate and popularize the doctrine of justification by faith. The circumstances and crises of Luther's own personal spirituality, contended Döllinger, formed the basis of his justification doctrine to which he later gave theological expression. Döllinger cites evidence from Luther's translation of the Scriptures that he was at pains to find biblical certification for his conception of saving faith once it emerged from his own experience.

The Reformers had made the false assumption that the anarchy and confusion surrounding their initial revolt would be only temporary. They expected that the growth of a new piety and morality would stop the upheaval, but the opposite was the case. Döllinger presented contemporary quotations full of complaints about the relaxation of religious practices and common Christian charity. At first the Reformers had to warn their congregations about showing confidence in good works, but this concern soon disappeared with the general abandonment of morality. Even preachers of the word who frequently disobeyed the directives of the Reformers demonstrated the inherent weakness of the doctrine. It resulted ultimately in an irreverent attitude toward holy things and a popular uncertainty in matters of faith.

Johannes Janssen (1829-91) rounded out the rehabilitation of the medieval Church which Döllinger had begun. The first volume of his vast *History of the German People at the Close of the Middle Ages* appeared in 1874 and the eighth and final volume in 1891. He, with Döllinger, confronted Ranke's theses. Ranke interpreted the Reformation as a movement shaped and directed by its leaders, but Janssen, who was writing social and cultural history, found its source in the people. Ranke hailed the Reformation as a glorious moment when the German people were awakened to their political and personal freedom and the Church was restored to its original simplicity and goodness. Janssen, on the other hand, regarded the Reformation as a night during which rash men severed tradition and plunged others into disorder and religious revolution.

Janssen intended to show that, hardly an age of moral and intellectual disintegration, the fifteenth century had been rather a prosperous and vigorous period both spiritually and intellectually. Education, for example, both secular and religious, was enjoying something of a heyday. One sample of its finest fruit was the number of complete vernacular editions of the Scriptures published before Martin Luther's—fifteen in all.

Signs of degeneration appeared in Janssen's survey of the prosperity of townsmen and peasants. Wealth brought sister evils in her cortege: luxury, greed, immorality and usury. Janssen had little to say about the condition of religion because he was not writing an ecclesiastical history. He believed, moreover, that the Reformation was social and economic rather than spiritual and intellectual.

The later volumes of Janssen's history moved from grey to black. In the second volume he passed severe judgment on humanism as espoused by the "trifling and egocentric" Erasmus and "pagan" lesser lights. He carefully avoided saying much about Luther, but he was at pains to present circumstances of the early period in their worst possible light. The Church also received its due share of criticism. In the third volume he scrutinized and denounced the secularism of the German hierarchy. Janssen copiously documented the demoralization and degeneration in Reformation Germany, citing popular literature and evidence of abominable crimes and witchcraft, the moral being that the Reformation, not the Thirty Years War, brought social and economic ruin to Germany.

Janssen's *History of the German People* with its new understanding of the fifteenth century corrected the traditional Protestant story of decadence and anarchy. He made it impossible for scholars to bypass Catholic interpretation of the Reformation. On the other side of the ledger Janssen's selection of sources unfavorable to Protestants and his exclusion of data embarrassing to Catholics tainted his reputation as a first-rate critic.

Historiography has been kinder to Janssen than it has been

to the Dominican scholar Heinrich Denifle (1844-1905). His immense erudition and wide familiarity with the works of Martin Luther made his book formidable. Denifle wrote *Luther und Luthertum in der ersten Entwicklung* (Mainz, 1904) after a thorough examination of the sources in the Vatican and German archives. Unhappily, it would be misleading to imagine that he approached the documents with more objectivity than emotion. To say that he had an axe to grind would not be overstatement. Denifle made it his task to explode the myths which hallowed the name of Martin Luther. "He thrust through that stained glass window a fist as rough as Luther's own, and shattered it beyond repair" (Rupp). The self-righteous and steadfast Dominican attacked the fallen Augustinian with all the *studio et ira* that could be mustered.

Denifle took a darker view of the later Middle Ages than did Janssen. Out of the mass of evidence he had gathered he saw two currents emerge. One was rebirth and the other a current of disintegration. These two, parallel but in tension, corresponded to St. Paul's opposition of the spirit and the flesh. Martin Luther had at first immersed himself in the current of rebirth, but ended up as the leader of the strain of disintegration. The log in Luther's eye was the capital sin of pride and God added to it the condemnation of sensuality. Consequently, the Reformer became less and less a man of the spirit and more and more bestial, intemperate and finally unchaste. Denifle's thesis was that Luther, unable to cope with temptation and stripped of all moral restraint, projected his own depravity into his attack on the Church, and in particular into his attack on the monastic life.

The immediate Protestant reaction to *Luther und Luthertum* was outrage, and Denifle's rude, *ad hominem* rebuttals were not calculated to appease. Protestant scholars criticized him for suppressing evidence favorable to Luther and for committing factual errors. Catholic scholars, too, were reluctant to show signs of approval for his book. Historians must credit Denifle with a vast knowledge of the Middle Ages, which, combined with his experience in religious life, gave him an advantage over Protestant contemporaries. But for all his learning, the interpretation he gave Martin Luther and the Reformation was not true. He had concocted a monster who scarcely resembled a man. In doing so he brought on himself the condemnation of Protestant and Catholic alike. "The massive volume of 800 pages hurled at the memory of the Reformer is one of the most repulsive works in historical literature" (Gooch).

The Jesuit, Hartmann Grisar (1845-1932), took issue with
Denifle's interpretation on several counts. He showed that
evidence does not exist to bear out the Dominican's charge
that Luther was morally depraved. Luther's thought turned
around his concept of *concupiscientia,* but Denifle falsely restricted its meaning to sensual lust. Despite this attempt to
correct Denifle and burst a few of the traditional Catholic
myths about Luther, the Jesuit scholar came to harsh conclusions not very far removed from the Dominican's. Both
men concerned themselves with the *fall* of Luther; Denifle
traced his heresy to baseness, Grisar to his contempt for good
works.

Whereas the Catholic reformers wanted to restore the
Church according to its best traditions, Luther apparently
intended to level the whole ecclesiastical structure. Prudent
moral reform, which Jesus and the apostles had preached and
which the Church needed, could not come out of Luther's
aimless agitation. He had not even provided for the gross
immorality of the times. True reform could not result from
his urging the populace to subvert the Church or to revolt
from Rome.

Grisar had no taste for the tenor of Luther's Reformation, but he respected his diagnosis of the Church's sickness in head and members. "Luther's 'Reformation,'" he
wrote, "did not . . . consist merely in the overthrow of the
olden ecclesiasticism; it also strove to counteract much that
was really amiss." Grisar commended Luther for letting the
daylight shine on "the shady side of ecclesiastical life." For
centuries no one was brave enough to point up so insistently
the wounds of the Church. "He laid bare every regrettable
disorder, needless to say not without exaggerating everything
to his heart's content." We must thank Luther for pointing
out all that was reprehensible in the Church. Had he presented these wounds without hate and without using them to
stir up the people, we would be in his debt. Moved as he was
by the evil in the Church, Luther used his anti-papal preaching not to work for its eradication, but only to open the
way for his heretical theology. The moral reformation of the
Church was secondary for him and he did everything he
could to obstruct the orderly elimination of abuse.

Grisar's *Luther* would have had greater appeal had he
purged it of all slanders, subtle and simple. One chapter
entitled "His Single-handed Struggle with the Powers of Evil"
merely showed that Luther believed in the existence of the
devil. A further section, "Demonology and Demonomania,"

was purposeless, other than as a slander of Luther by frequently juxtaposing him and Satan. In another chapter he made the usual *ad hominem* criticism of Luther's vulgar sense of humor. "Here we have anything but the overflowing of a contented heart which seeks to look at everything from the best side and to gratify all," remarked Grisar after presenting a particularly offensive sample. He had not recognized the famous tale of seduction from Boccaccio's *Decameron* which Luther was quoting.

Lord Acton (1834-1902), a student of Döllinger, wrote his lectures on the Reformation without his teacher's explicit polemical intention. Acton was a Catholic scholar thoroughly trained in the principles of scientific history. His interpretation of the Reformation, formed by his Catholicism and his scholarship, was somewhat enlightened. He stood in the Catholic tradition with one foot outside the usual narrowness of Catholic historians of the sixteenth century. His observation that in the latter Middle Ages "discontent was deepest where men were best" is currently the well documented conclusion of Protestant scholarship. His survey of the immediate circumstances of the Reformation and his treatment of Luther probably sounded strange to Catholics accustomed to a more polemical approach. Luther's denunciation of the practice of indulgences, said Acton, fraught as it was with corruption and superstition, was not so strong as the criticism other Catholics were leveling against it. "He had no idea that he was not speaking in thorough harmony with the entire Church . . ."

The cleverness of Luther's Catholic opponents forced him to become more and more radical in his theological positions. Cardinal Cajetan put before him the bull of Pope Clement VI on indulgences, compelling the Reformer to oppose expressly what the Popes affirmed and not merely what they had been permitting. Luther had been forced to set his teaching over the Pope. Eck pushed him one step further and led him to reject the authority of the council that burned John Huss. Luther before the Diet of Worms is for Acton the "most pregnant and momentous fact" in the discussion. Luther had stipulated that he should be judged by Scripture alone and had not conceded anything, but "there was no question at issue which had not either been pronounced by him insufficient for separation or which was not abandoned afterwards, or modified in a Catholic sense by the moderating hand of Melanchthon." Lutherans dropped the doctrine of predestination and accepted the doctrines of good works and freedom of the will, tradition, hierarchical organization, the seven sacraments and the Latin Mass. "Luther," despite his refusal to recant at Worms, "it would almost appear . . . never became a Lutheran." The only doctrine he clung to, which did not find its way into the official Lutheran formularies, was that the Pope was anti-Christ.

Speaking of the influence of Protestantism on state policy, he asserts that the Reformation was an act of individual resistance and not a system. When the secular powers were engaged in supporting the authority of the Church, the authors of the movement were compelled to claim impunity for their opinions. Their language regarding the right of governments to interfere with religious belief resembles that of friends of toleration. Yet he concludes that Protestantism later set up intolerance as an imperative precept and as a part of its doctrine. It was only forced to admit toleration by the necessities of its position, after the rigorous penalties it imposed had failed to arrest the process of internal dissolution. While claiming that the civil and religious difficulties of his day were in a great measure due to the Reformation, he does not hesitate to indict the state that is Catholic *par excellence* as a byword for misgovernment, because the orthodoxy and piety of its administration are deemed a substitute for a better system.

The Protestant theologian and sociologist Ernst Troeltsch (1865-1923), although he diverted scholarship into new areas of research and interpretation, colored his treatment of the Reformation with a prejudicial hatred for the movement much as Denifle had distorted his for the sake of apologetics. Troeltsch was a professor of theology at the universities of Bonn, Heidelberg, and Berlin. He engaged in political activity to advance the democratization of the contemporary Lutheran Church, and consequently was unable to write the history of the Reformation with an open mind. He associated Luther and "Old Protestantism" with the rise of the absolute state and the state church, both of which he despised. He refused to admit that the Reformation had contributed in any real way to the rise of modern civilization.

Troeltsch set forth his interpretation in two monographs which were published in 1906: *Protestant Christianity and Churches in the Modern World* and *The Significance of Protestantism for the Rise of the Modern World*. He interpreted the Reformation from the standpoint of the interrelation of religion and culture. Christianity, in order to have an influence on a culture, must penetrate and unite with it. Protestantism was the shape Christianity took in response to the problems of the early sixteenth century. These were substantially the same problems, in Troeltsch's view, that had preoccupied the Middle Ages. As a result the Reformers, great conservatives rather than revolutionaries, formulated their theology and ecclesiology in medieval terms.

Early Protestantism, maintained Troeltsch, as distinguished from its altered modern form, was in essence a medieval ecclesiastical civilization analogous to Catholic Christendom. The individualism of the Reformation did not result in a Church without mediation. The certainty of the Protestant believer did not rely upon a hierarchical structure. His faith, although based on individual spiritual reassurance, was mediated through the divinely revealed word of the Scriptures. On this foundation Protestantism rebuilt the institution of the Church as an instrument of salvation. It rid the Catholic Church of a mediating priesthood and superstitions, replacing them with pure doctrine and soon became as doctrinaire, authoritarian and rigid as the Roman Church.

The Reformation, despite the fact that it came up with a new solution, preoccupied itself with the medieval problem of salvation, wrote Troeltsch. The asceticism and supernaturalized spirituality of the Reformation were not different from the medieval ascetic ideal, but more comprehensive in that they were transplanted from the monastery into the world.

Protestantism in Troeltsch's opinion was not the parent of the modern world. Despite fresh ideas the Reformation renewed and strengthened the ideal of ecclesiastical authoritative civilization. It inherited and accepted medieval preoccupations which suffocated whatever had already been achieved toward forming a free and secular culture. The Catholic revival elicited by the reform movement kept Europe medieval until awakened by reason two centuries later.

The most significant opponent of Troeltsch's thesis was Karl Holl (1866-1926), a professor of Church history at the University of Berlin. In 1921 Holl published a study on the thought and teaching of Martin Luther so well conceived and exceptionally new that a renaissance of Luther scholarship began with its center in his person and work. Holl maintained that religion exercised a creative influence on political, economic and cultural development. He made it his object in *The Cultural Significance of the Reformation* (1911) to specify where and how the Reformation shaped culture. Lutheran theology had given man a new conception of himself as an individual constrained only by his duty toward God and a new conception of the Church as a personal fellowship of love. In relating these new conceptions to German culture, Holl took issue with Troeltsch's assertion that the Reformation was a medieval carry-over.

Holl's success depended in part on the fruits of historical research which had uncovered new material on the young Luther and in part on his systematic analysis of Lutheranism. Holl showed the importance of Luther's recovery of the paradoxical concept of a biblical God who loves the sinner. Moreover, contrary to traditional interpretation which had little regard for Luther's theological ability, Holl maintained that Luther had given his new discovery a systematic theological development.

Paul Joachimsen (1867-1930), whose view of the Reformation represents the best fruit of modern Protestant historiography, stands between Troeltsch and Holl. Joachimsen more than other modern scholars was aware of the great debt Reformation studies owed to Ranke, and appropriately he was elected to supervise the German Academy's edition of Ranke's masterwork on Germany in Reformation (1925-26).

Joachimsen summarized his own opinions in his essay "Renaissance, Humanismus und Reformation." The Renaissance was the birth of an individualism that operated against the unity of the medieval feudal order. Its essence was the conviction that the reasoning individual could bring about a fundamental change in the world around him. The humanists gave the Renaissance a *Weltanshauung,* providing a basis for its individualism and rationalism. Petrarch, who opposed his aesthetic mysticism to scholastic theology, directed the Renaissance to strive after the "culture of the soul." Erasmus proclaimed the new ideal in his enlightened "philosophy of Christ."

The Reformation, the third agent in the disintegration of the Middle Ages, differed completely from the Renaissance and humanism. Luther, contrary to his intention, became a prophet of religious reform. The tension between what Luther intended and the actual history of the movement he began characterized the Lutheran Reformation. Luther's purpose was to establish that freedom of the Christian believer which he had achieved in his personal quest for salvation. His experience of faith was monastic in origin and had no relation to the urgent rejoinders during the late Middle Ages for a Reformation in head members. It was not elicited as a reaction against ecclesiastical abuses as were the convictions of Wycliffe and Huss. Luther's individualism, a search for a personal merciful God, was essentially different from the philosophical individualism of Erasmus and Petrarch. Luther found his theology of mercy in the Pauline doctrine of justification by faith in God's love for the sinner. Luther expressed his newly acquired understanding of faith in a biblical theology which he opposed to scholasticism, but he was not aiming at instituting an ecclesiastical reform. His only concern was to fulfill his duties as a preacher of the word. His theology brought him into opposition with the theory and practice of selling indulgences, thereby inadvertently beginning the Reformation.

Faithful to the scriptural understanding of Christian piety, Luther sought true Christian freedom, but his legions sought freedom from ecclesiastical, social, political and cultural oppression. The prophet, compelled by the circumstances of history, unleashed a political, social and ecclesiastical revolution and became the father of a new order. A movement which had begun on the level of a religious rebirth based on the inner conviction of the individual terminated in a newly organized Church which demanded strict theological orthodoxy of its members.

Luther's Reformation developed in this contradictory fashion because of its location in history. It was mixed with Emperor Charles V's political entanglements and with German internal tensions over the unity of the Empire. The movement was also in contact with the social revolution, but because of Luther's fear of rebellion, gave its blessing to social and political conservatism. Theologically, the Reformation absorbed and produced a new scholasticism that was inferior, in many respects, to that which it had opposed.

The work of Joseph Lortz (1887-   ), contemporary with Joachimsen's, represented a revolution in Catholic Reformation scholarship. The polemic of Cochlaeus, which had filtered down to the twentieth century through Denifle and is still resurrected in some dark corners of Catholicism, was laid to rest. Many Protestant scholars were delighted with Lortz merely because he had read what Protestants had written. His book, *Die Reformation in Deutschland,* is currently one of the most respected Catholic treatments of the subject.

"The Reformation," wrote Lortz, "arose out of the dissolution of the basic medieval principles." Although it rings of oversimplification, if properly unfolded, this statement could be a common denominator for the historical causes of the Reformation. After the eleventh century there prevailed a "movement of withdrawal from the Church," a revolution that originated in its spiritual center. The way was made straight for the advent of reform by a long series of events and ideas. At the far end of the series they were the long range elements that terminated in the Reformation and at the nearer end they were its immediate circumstances. Christendom slowly approached the point where separation from Rome did not appear to be unchristian. The people were prepared to say "yes" to the doctrines of the Reformers when they heard them.

Lortz gave the "movement of withdrawal from the Church" a threefold expression: the Reformation was the disintegration of Christian ecclesiastical unity in the West, it was an enunciation of thoroughgoing discontent with the condition of the Church, and above all it was the rejection of Catholic dogma. Each of these theses was one ordered insight into the complex of historical causes that brought about the Reformation.

In the first place strong crosscurrents began to rend medieval Christendom as early as the thirteenth century. One sign, according to Lortz, was the deeply rooted tension between Church and state, whose very relationship had been a manifestation of Western ecclesiastical unity. The bitter fruit of this disintegration was the multiple papacy of the Western Schism, a scandal which introduced doctrinal uncertainty into the daily lives of all Christians and prepared them for Luther's rejection of the papacy.

Secondly the Reformation was an enunciation of discontent with the condition of the Church. After the twelfth century this discontent was expressed by sons of the Church on every level in progressively louder voices and more radical terms. The demands for reform "in head and members," especially "in head"—the Pope and worldly Curia—planted seeds in men's minds which Luther harvested.

Principally the Reformation was the rejection of Catholic dogma. During the centuries before the Reformation the Church was marked by a lack of theological certainty which grew ever worse. Lortz partially documented this thesis by studying the nominalism of Occam, which, although still within the Church, was "no longer fully Catholic." It terminated, fatefully but understandably, in Martin Luther, who had been formed under the influence of Occam's school.

Die Reformation in Deutschland was not limited to the religious issues of the Reformation. Lortz produced an interpre-

tation of German history in the sixteenth century. He skirted
the pitfalls which Catholic scholars before him had not. He
was not concerned with making a judgment about whether
the causes of the Reformation were justified. He left that
polemic to the theologians. Moreover, he rejected a favorite
Catholic accusation that Luther was motivated to revolt by
moral depravity. In view of the lack of doctrinal certainty
throughout the Church, a condition evidenced by the reluctance of several universities and humanists to censure Luther's
teaching, Lortz held that it would be gross oversimplification
to charge Luther with these base motives. It is to Lortz's
credit that he acknowledged Luther's brilliance and originality. Although not much of what Luther taught was absent
in earlier theologies and ideas of reform, he presented a new
synthesis. Lortz paid "repeated tribute to Luther's creative
energy, to the vast, genial flood of his conceptions, uncoordi-
nated jumbles of paradox and insight, unrestrained and top-
pling over into subjectivism and one-sidedness which are for
him the key to Luther's error" (Rupp).

Not all Protestant scholars were pleased with Lortz's judgment on Luther's "subjectivism." *Die Reformation in Deutschland* has been classified as a part of the tendency of some
Roman Catholic historians to interpret the Lutheran Reformation as the origin of modern secular individualism. He is also
criticized for idealizing the cultural unity of medieval Christendom and then placing the blame for the divisiveness of
modern society upon Luther. In Lortz's opinion Luther was
too much of a religious personalist, trying to inject himself
into truth. This subjectivism inevitably resulted in the disintegration of the hierarchical authority of the Church, for the
personalist does not know how to obey. Lortz, say his critics,
rightly describes Luther's theology of faith as a personal
confidence in God's saving mercy, but he does not understand that this faith was not religious individualism.

More strongly criticized than Lortz for his treatment of Luther's subjectivism is the Catholic philosopher Jacques Maritain (1882-   ). In 1925 Maritain published *Three Reformers: Luther, Descartes, Rousseau*. This little book was not intended as an historical study, but rather as an investigation
of the spiritual roots of the modern world. The historical
information behind the study, however, was drawn largely
from Denifle and Grisar, and once or twice Maritain reached
back into the sixteenth century for an anecdote from Cochlaeus. Through his appeal among Catholics he has succeeded

in reviving popular acceptance of their conclusions. Pope Paul VI has translated this work into Italian.

Maritain's hatred for Luther is evident throughout the essay and is summed up at the outset of the book. He calls Luther "that enemy of philosophy." Maritain evaluates the quality of Luther's personal spiritual life, connects it with Luther's doctrine of justification and finds Luther's error in voluntarism—"the source of modern secular individualism."

Luther, in Maritain's view, seemed always to seek the sensible consolations that may accompany mystical prayer. He wanted to experience physically the life of grace. This desire disordered his spirituality and resulted in a "mystical egocentrism." "The human subject . . . became in fact for him of more concern than God." When Luther was denied the paradise of sensible consolation, instead of throwing himself on the mercy of God, he attempted to cover his anguish by distracting himself. He prayed only infrequently and laid himself wide open to the "malignant fevers of nature." Denifle said that Luther despaired of grace, giving himself over to sensuality, but Maritain held that Luther's fall was a spiritual and mystical one. It was summarized in his declaration "concupiscence cannot be conquered," which means, beyond the fact that concupiscence always revives, that man is powerless to overcome it. This dictum became the kernel of Luther's justification doctrine. Original sin thoroughly effaced goodness in man; he is saved by the merits of Jesus which cover over but do not eradicate his sin. Salvation is altogether external to man and man can do nothing for it.

Luther's notion of faith was mere human trust mimicking theological faith. He was unable to control himself and he transformed his personal weakness into universal theological truths. He relieved himself of a tortured conscience by despairing of works. "He is," observed Maritain, "an inverted Pharisee, a run-away victim of scruples." Because of Luther's egocentric projection of himself into eternal truth, Maritain calls him the father of modern individualism. He traces the modern dichotomy of the person and the individual—the spiritual and the material being—to Luther's egocentrism and doctrine.

Maritain devotes the rest of the essay to the presentation of further evidence linking Luther and individualism. Luther, he says, was almost wholly an affective man, a man of the will. This subjectivism went hand in hand with a "profound anti-intellectualism." Maritain quotes a few condemnations Luther hurled at various scholastic faculties as evidence that he hated all philosophy, not merely certain schools. He also reproduces Luther's most severe blasts against reason. He makes no attempt, however, to distinguish between a vilification of philosophy and reason themselves and Luther's vilification of their abuse. When reason, continues Maritain, is relegated to last place, then will is exalted. Voluntarism triumphs over intellectualism in Luther and makes him the father of modern individualism. Luther's hatred for reason fits in well with his doctrine of human depravity: reason had been vitiated by original sin. This was the source, continued Maritain, of two great ideas in modern philosophy—the ideas of radical evil and the primacy of the will.

How did the Reformation extend the voluntarist error into the modern mind? The Reformers themselves said that the essence of the movement was the exaltation of spirit against authority—"the interior energy of man . . . against dead ideas and lying conventions imposed from without." The Church and sacraments, imposed from without, interfered with the Reformers' concept of Christian liberty and separated man from God; "so for modern philosophic subjectivism, sensation and idea separate us from reality." Maritain does not assert that Luther formulated a creed for modern voluntarism. He does find Luther responsible for introducing the principle into his theology.

The interpretation which the English historian Philip Hughes (1895-   ) gives the Lutheran Reformation is similar to Maritain's. Msgr. Hughes has written popular histories of the Church and the Reformation which are widely read among Catholics and frequently used in undergraduate courses as textbooks. He put a distillation of his thought on Luther and the Reformation into the third volume of his *History of the Church.*

The controversy over indulgences might have been merely another of many great historical incidents, observed the Monsignor, had it involved a man who was less a genius than Martin Luther. His personal life exerted a titanic force on the whole movement. Msgr. Hughes intended his chapter to be an investigation of Luther's experience on the doctrines of the Reformation. His is a mixed historical, psychological, and theological study based mostly on nonhistorical works like Maritain's *Three Reformers* and Gilson's *Reason and Revelation in the Middle Ages.* He has taken over Maritain's conclusions and set them in the context of an historical narrative. Widespread political and ecclesiastical disorder in sixteenth-century Germany set the stage for the coming of "the great anarch." Luther epitomized, says Hughes, the decay and anarchy that characterized Catholicism in the sixteenth century. He presented as a solution for the Church's problems, a version of Christian teaching void of Christian significance. He put himself, man, rather than God at the center of religion. His doctrine separated spirituality from morality and led to the destruction of the hierarchical, sacramental mediation of the Church. "Luther as a Christian force was to prove sterile; there would not follow upon his activities any betterment of the moral lives of his disciples, any advance in learning, any new peace through social renewal." The effect of Luther's teaching was to divide Western Europe into two kinds of men, Protestants and Catholics, the point of difference being that in Lutheranism, "the very inversion of Christianity," man had dislocated and replaced God.

In Catholic opinion, Hughes says, this difference makes Luther a true "revolutionary" and shows that the religion of his Reformation is not really religion at all in the same sense that Catholicism is. Msgr. Hughes wrote this chapter nearly twenty years ago, before we were blessed with Pope John XXIII. Perhaps if he were to revise it anew he would mitigate the severity of his words. He has already modified his treatment of Calvin in the years between his *Popular History of the Catholic Church* and the *Popular History of the Reformation* (1947-56). In the first Calvin was a "French Lutheran refugee in Switzerland"; in the second he was a new Moses presiding over Geneva as the prophet had presided over the Israelites in the desert after their deliverance from Egypt.

Hughes' *Reformation in England* is a scholarly account based on wide familiarity with the sources. Protestant scholars find useful his exact study of the evolution of heresy in successive liturgical and dogmatic innovations. One Oxford historian called it "one of the rare books which it is almost an impertinence to praise." Protestant historians, however, are not universally pleased with the book's "special pleading." One, while praising Hughes' "sense of the tragic dilemma of the age," found the work much too loose a collection of documentary analysis, critique of Protestant historiography, and polemical evaluation of major developments to become *the* modern classic history of the English Reformation.

The genius of Martin Luther, central in Lortz's work, was also the point of departure for Gerhard Ritter (1888-   ), Protestant Church historian at Freiburg University. In his book *Die Neuegestaltung Europas in 16. Jahrhundert* (1941), he asks: Is it not puzzling that Martin Luther, whose faith and doctrine stirred up the Church at her foundations, was not denounced as a heretic in Germany? Ritter's answer, a discourse on the vigor of German piety, contains his interpretation of the Reformation.

Ritter asserted that religious life in Germany in the late fifteenth century was more intense than it was in the other European countries. Christian otherworldliness made itself felt in all forms of life. Surrounded by rank abuses such as pilgrimages to honor phony relics, German piety gave evidence of its flower in art and architecture, the multiplication of pious foundations, and the growth of religious orders. It is always a paradox, said Ritter, that the same people who are possessed of a genuine and rich spirituality complain in the harshest manner against the Church and her clergy. Irreligion does not explain why the Reformation happened in Germany and neither does clerical abuse, for the conduct of the Church's ministers was no more scandalous in Germany than it was in the rest of Europe. It is the love which a pious people had for Christ's Church that accounts for the bitter complaints. The Church, with her ossified structure for dispensing sacraments and her inability to respond to timely needs, could not satisfy popular German piety.

Art in Germany, Ritter said, shows how much the people wanted to replace the institution of the Church with a personal, immediate relation to God. Unlike the Italians they had little taste for splendid works that gloried in the Church as a mighty institution. Pictures of saints enjoying intimacy with the Lord were more to their liking.

The tendency to seek God as unmediated experience came into conflict with the Church's dispensation of sacramental grace which had become more and more bound up with legalism and external norms. Ultimately it resulted in a readiness to be rid of a priesthood that had already befouled itself with every kind of abuse.

Two factors, the vigor of German piety and the opposition to abuse in the Church, combined to give impetus to the revolution. The criticism of the clergy and Church did not remedy the situation, but merely patched it up here and there. The tendency toward direct contact with God struck the Church at her spiritual center. In Martin Luther both practical objections and a deep theological piety were present together for the first time. They made him a prophet of radical reform.

Pierre Janelle (1891-   ), Catholic historian, also built his

interpretation of the Reformation on the paradox that the
worst ecclesiastical abuses flourished in the midst of the
best spirituality. One of his theses in *The Catholic Reformation* (1949) was that the radical Reformation erred in its
attempt to purify the Church of disciplinary abuses through
a reform of doctrine. Reliable Catholic witnesses had so
thoroughly documented the deplorable state of the clergy
and Curia at the end of the fifteenth century that it was
an undeniable condition. In the eyes of the Reformers the
source of the Church's disfiguration lay in the corruption of
doctrine by superstitious accretions and the consequent death
of Christian morality. Once the corruptions were removed,
they thought, purified doctrine and a mitigation of severe
asceticism would restore the health of the Church. Were this
evaluation true and the roots of ecclesiastical abuse theological, then the fifteenth century should have been devoid
of genuine piety. This was not the case, for the century
before the Reformation, for all its decadence, was a period in
which piety, virtue and mysticism flowered. The survival of
abuse in an atmosphere of holiness demonstrated that the
need was for administrative and disciplinary changes rather
than for a theological reformation.

The Church's organization had been severed into autonomous blocks that functioned in opposition to one another,
disputing jurisdiction and possessions. Burdened with the
bribery that officials expected for their operation of the
juridical machine, enforcement of ecclesiastical law in this
entanglement of interests grew more difficult and complex.
As money became an increasingly important consideration of
the administration, moral degeneration set in. It was highly
unlikely that an officialdom enjoying the evil benefits of their
own system would initiate any administrative reform. Nor
did the new spirit of nationalism, which was a by-product
of the Councils of Constance and Basel, forward the cause
of reform, because it had little regard for the welfare of the
Church. The Popes were incapable of leading a Reformation,
for they were hopelessly entangled in Italian and European
politics. In order to preserve their spiritual authority, they
had to preserve their temporal domain. Had they not done
so, there might never have been a Catholic Reformation.

The Popes might have shown less concern for political loss
or gain and attempted a reform reckless of the cost, but they
had become so much a part of the world that they were incapable of appreciating the power and appeal of a spiritual
reform. The Renaissance had done more than merely erode

the personal morality of the Popes and curialists, it had destroyed their concept of their proper function. "For apostleship it had substituted 'policy' . . . the Curia had come to halo its privileges, its greed, its lusts with the sacred character of Christianity itself." If it were to make any progress the Catholic Reformation had to eliminate this self-centeredness of the Curia and restore the spirit of evangelical self-denial to the Church.

The Catholic Reformation began with a revival of the spirit of the Gospel. It relied for its advance neither on the medieval spiritual and intellectual outlook nor on that of the Renaissance, but rather on Christian humanism which filtered out of antique culture what would be of service in restoring the Church. This movement, epitomized in St. Thomas More, was suppressed during the religious wars, but it came forth through the Council of Trent and the Jesuits to again spearhead the Catholic Reformation.

Thus after four centuries of varied interpretation it remains clear that historians still dispute whether truth lies on the side of Protestantism or Trent, with Luther or with Loyola. Yet the question as to how the Reformation was possible must be conjoined with the equally perplexing query: Why did Catholicism remain? Perhaps the real cause of the wide spectrum of interpretation of the Reformation can be traced to the fact that its historians, like the men they portray, too often plead a cause, and generally those who plead causes do not write objective history. Such questions can be answered only by a realization that reform is an essential element in the very nature of Christianity, where perfectability and renewal are the key message of Him who by His coming renewed and continues to renew all things.

2

From individual to institutional reform

"Who will give me to see before I die the Church of God as in the days of old when the apostles spread their nets to take not gold or silver but the souls of men."

ST. BERNARD OF CLAIRVAUX

Gerhardt Ladner defines reform as the "idea of free, intentional and ever perfectible, multiple, prolonged and ever repeated efforts by man to reassert and augment values pre-existent in the spiritual-material compound of the world." For the Christian and his Church the notion of reform is a dynamic principle, essentially Christian in its source and development. Through the centuries of Christian history the idea of reform has been garbed in various expressions—rebirth, renewal, renovation, purification, return to the sources —but it has always been intrinsic to the mystery of Christianity itself: the death and resurrection of Christ.

The source of the Christian idea of reform is ultimately traced to the biblical themes of rebirth, regeneration, and conversion. It is St. Paul who applies them to the true life as the necessary foundation for sanctity. For St. Paul, rebirth in baptism is the beginning of man's restoration to the image of God proceeding through a process of continuous renewal. This reform idea is a facet also of the doctrine of the Church as the Body of Christ. Though perennial and essentially immutable, the Church nevertheless needs reform for her life and growth. At this point it is important to see the relation between the idea of reform and St. Paul's concept of the Church.

As Christ was the fulfiller of history, the Church was the center of history, the people among whom all life would be fulfilled. He interpreted the Church as a fellowship of eschatological hope and as a spiritual reality of mystical and sacramental salvation. In Galatians St. Paul finds the believers in Christ as now what formerly only the Jews claimed to be: "For through faith you are all sons of God in union with Christ Jesus. Baptized into union with Him, you have all put on Christ as a garment. There is no such thing as Jew and Greek, slave and freeman, male and female; for you are all one person in Christ Jesus. And if you are Christ's, then you are the offspring of Abraham and heirs according to the promise" (3, 26-29).

The Church is essentially one and universal because it eliminates everything that is opposed to unity and universality. Above all, St. Paul's conception, as seen in his Epistle to the Ephesians, is a spiritual one that transcends organization, rank, and privilege: "Thus you are no longer aliens in a foreign land, but fellow-citizens with God's household. You are built upon the foundation laid by the apostles and prophets, and Christ Jesus Himself is the keystone. In Him the whole building is bonded together and grows into a holy temple in the Lord. In Him you too are being built with all the rest into a spiritual dwelling for God" (2, 19-22). Later in the same epistle, St. Paul develops further the idea that the individual Christian and the Church are identified as one in the Body of Christ: "He is the head, and on Him the whole body depends. Bonded and knit together by every constituent joint, the whole frame grows through the due activity of each part, and builds itself up in love" (4, 15-16). Thus it could be said that the Pauline doctrine of reform was always applicable to the Church as a spiritual entity. In other words, the Church defined in terms of the people of God did not require the development of a hierarchical organization or a mature ecclesiology before the Pauline idea of reform would be actualized.

Though St. Paul does not anticipate the elaborate ecclesiastical organization of future centuries, he does assume the social nature and different levels of function within the Church. An illustration at this point can be seen in his discourse from Acts to the elders at Ephesus: "Keep watch over all the flock of which the Holy Spirit has given you charge, as shepherds of the Church of God, which He won for Himself by His own blood" (20, 28). The elders have only a subordinate authority and yet they watch over, inspect, and govern the faithful of Jesus Christ. Although they have been appointed and constituted officials, through the medium of man, they hold their authority from the Holy Spirit, from whom in the last analysis it is derived. Their charge is a local one and their jurisdiction restricted, yet they govern the Church of God because the Church is one and indivisible.

The worship and communal life of Christians in the early centuries was closely tuned to the Gospel and the teaching of Paul with its strong element of eschatological immediacy. They lived in an era of spiritual enthusiasm kept aflame by the certain expectation of the imminent reappearance of Christ. But the inevitable lessening of such feeling and the increasing differentiation of Christians from other groups, necessitated by the growing hostility of the surrounding world, gradually caused the emergence of definite institutional features of organization. It is their period in Christian history that future reformers continuously returned to and held up as the ideal.

As with St. Paul, the concept of the spiritual Church was closely related to the reform tradition in the Fathers. The sanctity of the Church was still manifested in the holiness of individual members even though the formation of the monarchial episcopate and formulation of doctrinal theology were beginning to play a greater role in the life of the Church. Only when the distinction between the empirical and ideal Church gains favor does the Pauline concept of a spiritual Church become modified. As the pressures from historical circumstances increase, the eschatological fervor declines.

The reform doctrine of the Greek Fathers, especially the Alexandrian school of the second and third centuries, conceived the possibility of man's return to a condition of integrity and innocence corresponding to that of Adam before the fall. This idea of a return to paradise was one of three major themes characterizing the Eastern reform tradition. The others revolved around the restoration of man to the divine image and the important element of eschatology.

Origen (d. 254) is the most significant of the Alexandrian theologians for the idea of reform. For him, spiritual reform on earth is bound up with eschatology so that, at the end of the world, all creation will be restored to its original dignity. God "will restore that state which rational nature possessed when there was no need of eating from the tree of good and evil." Origen understood the Church as the community of holy people whose lives are inwardly shaped by spiritual knowledge because they carry the Kingdom of God within them. Equally important, to certain medieval reformers, was Origen's notions of cyclic recurrence. The theory of alternating periods of decadence and resurgence applied in a Christian context would help shape the millenarian tradition in the Middle Ages and beyond.

The greatest of the orthodox continuators of Origen's thought, Gregory of Nyssa (d. 394) also assumed a close relation between eschatology and the possibility of terrestrial reform. Even on earth reform was the return to a spiritual Paradise in the soul and the recovery of the image-likeness to God: "The first making of man was according to the imitation of God's likeness . . . and the promise of Christianity is that man will be brought back to the original happiness. If then originally man was God's likeness, our definition will probably not miss the mark if we declare that Christianity is an imitation of divine nature." The mystical recovery of the lost resemblance to God, as envisaged by Gregory, is the most far-reaching reform conceivable for it amounts to nothing less than deification. It happens "continuously to him who participates in God, so that there is increase of ever better things for those who participate through the whole eternity of aeons."

The mystical reform ideas of the Greeks, as exemplified in Origen and Gregory of Nyssa, contained a potentially supra-individual significance which would extend to both the Church and the Empire of Byzantium. It was, however, a negative rather than a positive significance. This is seen in the triumph of Eastern monasticism where withdrawal from the world rather than penetration of the world was the principal feature.

Among the Eastern Fathers, John Chrysostom (d. 407) can be cited as an exception to the purely monastic trend insofar as he explicitly reapplied the scriptural principle of perfection to the entire Church. His was the conviction that, apart from marriage, the Christian who lived in the world had the same obligations as the monk. Thus he felt it was not impossible to reform the Christian society of his time and to bring about a fair measure of perfection in the Church as a whole. He held that "one man who burns with zeal is sufficient to set straight a whole people." To the whole Church of his day, not only to the monks, he held up as a model the age of the apostles, "when there was one soul and one heart in all."

The Western tradition, though not wholly independent from the Greek, gives the idea of reform a different direction. As early as the third century, both Irenaeus (d. 202) and Cyprian (d. 258) made attempts at formulating a more definite concept of the Church, grounded on the monarchial episcopate. For Irenaeus, the Church was a sacred institution which by virtue of apostolic succession possesses and preserves the divine truth and which administers divine salvation through the sacraments. In the Church "God has placed the universal operation of the Spirit; all those who do not belong to the Church cannot be the Spirit's participants . . . for where the Church is there is also the Spirit of God, and where the Spirit of God is there is the Church and all grace."

Cyprian went further and defined the "hierarchial" Church as the "mother" of every Christian on which he is dependent for his relation to God in Christ. The Church is constituted in the episcopate which is the bearer of the Spirit, the guarantee of Church unity, and the priestly mediation of sacramental salvation. Thus, "there is no salvation outside the Church."

Cyprian's idea of reform, somewhat separated from his rigid concept of the Church, concerned the problem of the relationship between truth and tradition. It was a problem bound up with the third-century controversy over the baptism of heretics. But the dispute was complicated by other simultaneous developments in Christendom, i.e., the weakness of many Christians in the great persecutions. In Cyprian's case it was the Decian persecution of 250 and the moral decline which accompanied the numerical growth of the Christian community itself.

Ambrose considered paradise as an altogether spiritual entity, existing in the rational part of the soul. Because of original sin, the Christian is in perpetual danger of lapsing from this paradise. It is in this sense that Ambrose speaks of a spiritual progress: ". . . the Lord came to reform the grace of nature, and even to increase it, so that where there was a superabundance of sin, there would be a superabundance of grace." Thus Ambrose's idea of reform goes beyond the Greek notion of mere return to pristine purity. He emphasized the fact that even the pre-eschatological reform by Christ of the Paradise of innocence in man's soul must result in a "superabundant" augmentation of natural grace: "In sum the primeval condition of the world and of all things has changed, so that it may be succeeded by the old age of a venerable mature faith. Let those who are disturbed about it blame the harvest because fertility comes late . . . Now our harvest is the faith of the minds, the grace of the Church is the harvest of the merits, which from the origin of the world flourished in the saints, but only in this last age spread among the peoples, so that all would realize that the faith of Christ has not stolen into unprepared minds."

In Augustine we find a synthesis of Western reform thought and a more obvious application of the reform doctrine to the communal aspect of the Church. His concept of the Church is initially a summary of the entire previous development of the Church idea. But he deepened this Church concept by the assertion that he only is a true member of the universal Body of Christ who practices the spirit of love thereby giving evidence of the illumination by the Holy Spirit and of the renewal of life by the grace of Christ. In other words, the Church is seen from two points of view: it is inwardly inspired by the spirit of love which Christ infuses into the hearts of believers.

The actual Church to which Augustine applied his theology was the state church of the declining Roman Empire. During Augustine's own lifetime, the Emperor Theodosius had declared Christianity the officially recognized religion of his realm. Earlier in the fourth century, the Church had been ostracized by the pre-Constantinian emperors as an enemy of the state. Now it became the cornerstone of public law and order. Conformity with its faith and discipline was now the guarantee of sociopolitical morale and unity, and reform ideology must be seen against the background of these conditions which prevailed throughout Christendom.

In relation to the Greek idea of reform, Augustine presents some fundamental differences. He insists on the superiority of Christian renovation over original innocence, always relating this notion to the trials and moral decisions of human life. If Augustine scrutinizes the simple image of a return to paradise, he does so with the belief that if God really was crucified as man, man could never be quite the same. Mankind "shall be renewed from the oldness of sin not into the pristine animalic body in which Adam was, but into a better one, that is to say, into a spiritual body." Christ has renewed us from the "oldness of sin" in order that we can rise above our animal state into a spiritual one. Even on earth God's elect receive a grace through Redemption which is above that possessed by Adam.

In his efforts against the Pelagian heresy, Augustine confronts two pitfalls which would subvert the Christian theology of reform. The first is centered in the belief that man can reform himself and the world on his own. The second is one of complacency under the illusion that trusting God means relaxing one's own efforts. Both have their origin in the traditional dichotomy between God's grace and man's free will. Augustine seeks a balance by stressing the role of the divine reformer, Christ, over that of man the reformer, and by insisting on the necessity of continuous reform in human life. "Though our outward man is corrupted, yet the inward man is renewed day by day."

Augustine, then, must speak of more than a return to the moral integrity of Adam in paradise. Reform is a creation in itself insofar as it is a process of formation rising from spiritual conversion. Man has been raised to a higher plane by regeneration in Christ, which became possible only through the Incarnation and Redemption, and is continued in an endless operation of reform until the ultimate return of all creation to God.

Perhaps the most far-reaching influence of Augustine's reform ideology is derived from his speculation on the communal nature of the Church. Though his concept is not an institutional one, his treatise on the City of God contains a definite ecclesiology. He wrote it in response to the shock which had been felt through the Mediterranean world after Alaric and his Visigoths had sacked Rome, "the eternal city," in 410.

The meaning of the term *civitas* keynotes the work as it conveys a mystical or scriptural equivalent of "society." Augustine's City of God is not placed in an historical or political context, as Eusebius did with his political theology of a Christian empire imitating the divine monarchy. Nor did Augustine attempt to anticipate the later medieval theorists with their notion of theocracy. Augustine's concept of the Kingdom holds to no earthly fulfillment but favors the transcendent theme of *Civitas Dei*, retaining its strong social and communal connotations.

Equally significant is the fact that Augustine preferred the "City of God" over the more obvious terms such as *Ecclesia* and *Corpus Christi*. His intention was to express a free and more spiritually oriented idea, especially since the Church transcends dogmatic or juridical definitions. Thus, all those who belong to the *Ecclesia* may not be included in the *Civitas Dei*: ". . . so also, as long as she is on pilgrimage in the world, the City of God has with her men who belong to the number of her enemies, men who are connected to her through the communion of the sacraments, but will not be with her in the eternal lot of the saints."

For Augustine, the historical Church is not identical with the divine order, but insofar as the communion of saints can be and is being realized, it is the City of God, "living sacrifice" and "living temple" of God. The institutional Church is thus viewed as the historical manifestation of the eternal order of love.

As the heavenly City, the *Civitas Dei* is beyond the scope of reform. Individual reform of Christians is the central concern of Augustine and the whole Western tradition. The citizens of the City of God, though on a pilgrimage, must again and again be corrected and renewed by divine grace if they are to persevere and remain members in grace. If Augustine wanted to indicate the permanent need of reform in the Church, he does so in terms of a group of men capable of reform. These are the members of the terrestrial *Civitas Dei* whose salvation will ultimately even "restore" and "replenish" the Kingdom of God: "For the things that are in heaven are reestablished when that which in the angels fell from heaven is made up through men; and the things that are on earth are reestablished when those same men themselves, who are predestined to eternal life, are renewed from the oldness of corruption."

Therefore a way of life must be made available which would serve as a type or sample of the City of God. It is here that Augustine points to monasticism as the ideal vehicle for Christian reform. He desired that at least some of the Christians comprising the terrestrial Church live in a milieu that would correspond as closely as possible to the heavenly City. By living the monastic life the Christian would gain an insight into the Church's essence. For those who would heed Christ's call to perfection, it would consist in giving all for Christ and joining the company of those who have already done so, the monks. They would be "a model to the believers by living before them and stirring them to imitation." Augustine believed that the monks had gone into the desert not only to seek a moral perfection unattainable in the world but also to lead on earth that radically Christian life of which the praise of God by the angels and saints in heaven is the great prototype.

Augustine's development of the relationship between monasticism and reform presents another essential contrast in Western and Eastern patristic thought. The attitude as it evolved from the Eastern Fathers tended to uphold the eremitic as the more perfect form. For both Augustine and Gregory the Great true monasticism was cenobitical, especially for the clergy who were gradually joining the monastic ranks. Augustine was convinced that the two highest forms of Christian life, monk and priest, should be combined into a unity of perfection. The formation of a quasi-monastic clergy would make concrete his desire for an earthly type of the *Civitas Dei*. Of added significance was Augustine's insistence on celibacy and communal property, two factors which were to appear perennially in the writings of the medieval reformers when emphasizing the spiritual nature of the priesthood. On these principles, Augustine was particularly adamant: "May such a one appeal against me to a thousand councils, may he set sail against me wheresoever he wishes, may he in fact be wheresoever he can: the Lord will help me so that, where I am bishop, he cannot be cleric."

The Western reform tradition, as represented chiefly in Augustine, does contain a major element on which there is general agreement in Greek thought, namely, renewal and reform on the personal level. To carry reform beyond individual and communal sanctity had seemed to be unnecessary. The idea of Church reform as we know it was alien to Christian antiquity and does not become a reality until the age of Gregory VII. It is clear, however, that in their efforts to promote a restoration within the precincts of orthodoxy, the medieval reformers drew abundantly from the vast repertory of personal renewal ideas found in the Fathers. It is also not surprising that the same ideas should already have played a prominent part in the rise of monasticism. For here was a reaction against and a compensation for the dangers threatening a now officially recognized and increasingly secularized Christianity.

Of even greater importance was the legacy of Augustine's ecclesiology. He provided future reformers with a pattern of thought which was to inspire them to judge the historical Church in the light of its eternal destiny. They would always look to Augustine's concept of the eternal Church, the City of God, which transcended all limitations of time and place and comprised within itself all who, filled with the Holy Spirit, are motivated by the love of God and man.

As monasticism developed into the vital force behind the growth of Christendom in the early Middle Ages, the principals of Augustinian reform theology remained intact. Throughout these "Benedictine centuries," the idea of reform was considered in terms of the restoration of the image of God in man. Here was a continuous link which tied the old and never lost tradition of Christian renewal to the ideal of personal and communal sanctity. There were many instances of monastic reform, all with the same object, to restore the monasteries to their proper function and specific duties, namely, pure observance of the rule. There was no thought of reforming the world at large, or even the Church and secular Christendom. Such a goal would be achieved indirectly, once the monasteries had regained their spiritual health and could sanctify the surrounding world by their spiritual influence.

Cluny is the model of a great reform movement aimed exclusively at correcting abuses which had weakened the monastic edifice. It had no intention of initiating or leading a widespread reform of Christendom. Instead it held up the monastic ideal and the reformers were determined to demonstrate its superiority through a rejuvenation of rule and members. Regarding monasticism as the highest life, engrossed in the task of its own reform, and in the struggle to maintain autonomy, Cluny had little attention to spare for the secular Church. This outlook is illustrated in Cluny's attitude of neutrality toward the lay investiture struggles of the tenth and eleventh centuries.

But the ideal championed by the Cluniac movement outlasted by far the greatness of Cluny herself. She left a legacy, often referred to as "spiritual materialism," which was transmitted to the secular Church. The Gregorian reformers were quick to see the initial success of Cluny as a potential panacea to cure the defective spirituality in Christendom. A particular example and one that became permanent was the imposition of the monastic Office on the secular clergy, despite the fact that there had never been any necessary connection between the Office and the priesthood.

Until the eleventh century the papacy, when it did entertain thoughts of reform, held to the patristic norm. In fact there were various reasons why it could not have been any other way. One was the broad definition of Christendom allowing for wide episcopal powers, lay influence, and a minimum of centralization. Secondly, the papacy was often corrupt itself, especially in the hands of ambitious Roman families. And finally, the Popes were tied to a subservient position under the Carolingian theory of sacred kingship.

But the eleventh century soon saw a radical change in the orientation of the medieval Church. With the election of Leo IX, Christendom was set on a new course led by a series of reforming Popes and dominated by the figure of Gregory VII.

Gregory's idea of the Church was essentially a spiritual one. Yet he had to apply it to a complex feudal society which had long confused the Church's true function. To reform herself and carry on her divine mission, the Church must have "freedom" and this is what Gregory set out to accomplish. For Gregory the emancipation of the papacy from its dependence on the Empire and the separation of the spiritual authority of the bishop from his secular obligation as a member of the feudal hierarchy called for a reconstruction of the whole order of ecclesiastical administration and jurisdiction. It was clear that moral reform was not enough, that the axe must be laid to the root.

Gregory's concept of "right order" in Christendom demanded a re-evaluation and reorganization of society, both ecclesiastical and secular. By rejecting the monastic axiom, "withdrawal from the world," Gregory interpreted the Church's vocation as a mandate to remake not only the individual but Christendom as a distinct entity. For the first time reform became the official policy of the Roman Church.

For those who saw this interpretation as unprecedented and unfounded, Gregory pointed to St. Cyprian's principle that truth is superior to custom. If custom is not in conformity with the truth and truthful tradition, then it must be *reformed*. The revolutionary implications of this principle were obvious to the Gregorian reformers who proceeded to exploit it to the fullest extent. Perhaps the most important objection to the Gregorian idea of reform came from men who could not reconcile the Church's vast accumulation of power with the simplicity with which she had been founded. Could the Church become a mighty organization and still remain the Bride of Christ? Was there not a real danger of forfeiting her essentially spiritual nature? These questions were summed up by St. Bernard's judgment of the papacy in his own time: "You are the successor of St. Peter, not Constantine."

Much of the opposition to the Gregorian movement came from supporters of the monastic ideal. The conflict was manifest during the reign of Paschal II. Paschal stood as the personification of the ascetic ideal against the Gregorian party in the Curia which was determined to extend Rome's influence and power. As a deviation from the Gregorian type, Paschal presented a serious threat to the religious and political aims of the Curia. With an otherworldly disposition, he was devoted to the monastic and ascetic ideals of poverty and charity. For Paschal the Church was sufficiently established to allow the papacy to turn its attention away from the problem of lay interference and assume the task of producing a thorough moral reform of the entire Christian community. Unlike Gregory, Paschal did not see a relation between both problems. Thus his agreements with the French and English kings in 1111, by which the Church would forfeit her temporal possessions, signified an abandonment of Gregorian policy. Where Gregory sought the freedom of the Church as a means of asserting her authority, Paschal hoped to offer the Church's secular wealth in exchange for her liberty.

The fierce opposition to Paschal's plan by the Curia and the French and German bishops was obviously justified inasmuch as the Pope's solution was naive and would leave the Church's position to the mercy of lay control. Yet by attacking Paschal the Curia laid open to public scrutiny the bureaucratic machine which had emerged from the Gregorian movement. What was intended to be an administrative agency of the papacy had assumed more power than the Pope himself. Paschal's defeat revealed to the ascetic wing of the Church that the pursuit of power, not moral reform, was the main goal of the curial party.

Reformers like St. Bernard learned much from the events of Paschal's reign. It was apparent that if a genuine moral reform was to be realized under papal direction, the Pope himself must be freed from subservience to curial ambitions. The Curia's very concept of the papacy, which conceived the Church's power in purely material terms and sharply distinguished the practical from the ideal in Christianity, would be a source of continued friction with the spiritual reformers of the twelfth and thirteenth centuries.

St. Bernard had a clearer insight into the purpose of the Gregorian reform than many of Gregory's successors. He saw it as a plan for uncompromising spiritual reform based on the assumption that the monastic-ascetic ideal could be applied to the whole of Christendom. The rise of the new "orders" of monks like the Premonstratensians and his own Cistercians led Bernard to pursue the problem of reform through a revised brand of monasticism. Its idea of a return to the apostolic life and poverty of the early Church was to characterize every major movement for the next two centuries. Confronted with corruption in Rome and worldliness of prelates throughout Christendom, Bernard was convinced of the necessity for self-renunciation as the key to reform.

Despite his high regard for the papacy, Bernard found it stifled by the centralism of the organization around it. Against the corruption of the Curia and the preoccupation with worldly power which made the Pope the successor of Constantine rather than Peter, Bernard turned to the reformer's ideal of the prophetic and apostolic mission entrusted to the Vicar of Christ. Like Gregory, Bernard believed in the Vicar set over the nations to destroy, and root up, to build and to plant, "a mission that suggests the heavy labor of the peasant rather than the pomp of a ruler. For if you are to do the work of a prophet you need the hoe rather than the scepter." In Bernard's eyes the secularizing tendencies of the papacy had produced a hopeless confusion between the spiritual and temporal functions of the Church, to the detriment of the former.

His view of the spiritual authority did not fall short of the extreme conception of Gregory VII. He refers to the *plenitudo potestatis* of the Pope and the two swords, material as well as spiritual, belonging to the Church. But he was emphatic that this power must be used for spiritual purposes only, and the idea of the Pope as a ruler is abhorrent to him. The Pope has a *ministerium* not a *dominatio;* the church is the mother not the *domina* of all the churches. Bernard is especially vehement against the increasing absorption of the Pope in the pomp and secular cares of his office.

Bernard's reform doctrine was similar, perhaps unwittingly, to those whom he opposed, especially Arnold of Brescia, and to the later lay movements. His zeal for evangelical poverty was related to his dream of a purified Church and made him the proponent of ideas which could easily lapse into Donatism. His criterion for obedience lay in the character of those in authority. The authority which Bernard upheld as divinely instituted was that of the Pope, by no means that of the Curia. In condemning abuse, he appealed to the rule of conscience whereby the casuistic canon is swept aside and issues are judged by the demands of conscience. Since the Curia was corrupt, allegiance is abolished. It was clear to Bernard that insidious elements controlled the Curia and that so long as these elements prevailed, reform was impossible.

The spiritual framework of Bernard's reform is further demonstrated in his idea of the Church. He defined it as being much more than the clergy since it consisted of the whole army of baptized members of which the humblest can have an immediate vision of God and experience His love. Christian fellowship obliterated all human distinctions and united all believers in the bond of charity. In the Church every man had his place and the peasant, who enjoyed neither rights nor liberty in the feudal system, could claim the rights of spiritual citizenship. Thus surrounded by the flagrant abuses afflicting the Church, it is conceivable that nothing could have held Bernard's allegiance except his spiritual conception of what it was as founded by Christ.

The reform efforts of the new monastic orders found an able apologist in Bishop Anselm of Havelberg. As a diplomat for the papacy and the imperial court, Anselm was a vigorous participant in the ecclesiastical and political affairs of the early twelfth century. He was chosen by the Emperor Lothair III to head the important embassy to Constantinople in 1135 where he was to discuss with the eastern emperor the possibility of taking concerted action against Roger II of Sicily. While in Constantinople Anselm was invited by the Patriarch to debate the questions which currently caused disagreement between the Eastern and Western churches.

Fifteen years later, in 1150, Pope Eugenius III asked Anselm for a written account of the debate in order to aid new discussions that were being carried on in Rome. Anselm presented his reflections to the Pope in a work called the *Dialogi,* which contains both an account of the Constantinople debates and Anselm's reform ideology.

As an apology, the *Dialogi* had a twofold objective. On the one hand it is a defense of the new religious orders which had risen in the first half of the twelfth century, especially the Premonstratensians of which he was a member. On the other hand, Anselm wants to justify the development of the Church over the centuries, including certain Roman doctrines such as the filioque and papal primacy which were attacked by the Eastern bishops as heretical inventions. In Anselm's view both charges stem from a single premise, namely, that the Church was being subverted by innovators. This he attributed to a false notion of the Church herself and he seeks to refute it by a theory of history and the economy of salvation.

Many who resisted the reform attempts of the twelfth-century monastic orders claimed that change or diversity in Church practice led to a weakening of the faith. For Anselm this was a position that denied the possibility of progress, both in the Church as the chosen people and in the individual's growth in grace. Both are the same in essence, continually renewed, and perennially youthful.

By the term Church, Anselm means "the body of the elect from the time of Abel down to the last man to be saved." It is the Holy Spirit by "which the Church lives, and from his life-giving source she has her unity and oneness." Under the Spirit the "one body of the Church" progresses in one continuous movement from Abel to the last judgment. The great figures of the Old Testament like Abel, Noe, Abraham, and Jacob all held the same faith but used different modes of sacrifice. Without having a clear understanding of the faith, they were like men seeing from afar, saluting Christ who was to come and waiting for the grace of the longed-for promise. By faith they "were in unity with the Christian

Church and are part of the New Jerusalem envisioned in the Apocalypse. Thus Anselm contends that divine wisdom saw fit to gradually unfold the full development of the faith and its practices. He suggests the image of the *plebs sancta* moving from a state of idolatry to the law and finally to the Gospel.

How then does the Church progress and renew herself under the New Dispensation? Anselm cites the example of the patristic era when the doctrine of the Trinity was formulated. Here was a crucial tenet of the faith not explicitly stated in Scripture but grasped only after a sufficient understanding of the Father and Son. For Anselm it is "the divine physician measuring out all matters of faith according to the strength of the believers."

But it is mainly through speculation on the Apocalypse that Anselm hopes to demonstrate that Christian history is one of permanent reform and renewal. From the time of Christ he distinguishes seven ages of the Church, derived from the seven seals of the Apocalypse, which provide the framework for his theory of progress.

The first seal represents the first coming of Christ when "the multitude of believers increased in the Lord, and daily the Church of God shone with the power of miracles and the number of believers." The second seal opens to the Church of martyrs from Stephen to the end of the Roman persecutions "when the peace of the earth was taken and sword of persecution laid upon the Church." When the persecutions ended, "laws were passed for the peace of the Church, kings rushed to baptism, princes of different provinces received the faith of Christ, the whole world honored the Christian name and venerated the Cross. Churches sprang up and the hierarchy grew, expanded, and branched out into the whole world." From the third seal the Church grows in wisdom as she overcomes the onslaught of heresy in a brilliant age of Fathers and councils.

With the fourth seal Anselm takes a hard look at his own times and labels it an age of hypocrisy. Yet he sees the Church blessed with certain "valiant men, lovers of truth, and renewers of religious life." In the lives of Norbert, Bernard, and the Cistercians, Anselm sees a manifestation of the Holy Spirit stirring and exciting the dormant souls of the faithful by the example of those who search after perfection. "And it is the marvelous dispensation of God that new religious life should be renewed so that it can fly to more sublime contemplation and gaze at the light of the true sun."

With the fifth and sixth seals, Anselm comes to the last age before Judgment. He explains the great earthquake in St. John's vision as the persecution under anti-Christ. It is the most severe of all since it will be perpetrated in Christ's name. Many will be confused, not knowing what to believe. The great men will succumb to worldly pleasures and the unlearned will fall away from the Church. "In those days the use of the sacraments and Christian worship will recede from view." No longer will they be available to the faithful. When the seventh seal is broken, anti-Christ is destroyed and the world reaches its end as Christ returns in glory. The elect enter into divine contemplation where the truth of all the figures and sacramental signs used throughout the ages is clearly revealed.

Anselm's justification for the idea of reform contained some key elements that appear throughout the twelfth and thirteenth centuries. Most prominent was his theory of progress and his excursion into the boundless areas of scriptural exegesis. Even more significant, the *Dialogi* may be seen as a depository of the spiritual ideals many of his contemporaries applied to the Church. It was by his very broad concept of "Church" that Anselm was able to see new developments as part of a continual, progressive movement of reform within the Church. Finally, Anselm's speculation on the Apocalypse touches on a theme of major importance for the twelfth and thirteenth centuries, namely, a new revival of eschatological fervor in Christendom. Unlike the Parousia of the primitive Church, the new wave of expectation brought promises of an imminent new age, not warnings of the last days. The sources of the new movements center around the mysterious figure of Joachim of Fiore.

Joachim, born in 1135, was a native of Calabria, and, except for his travels, spent all his life in southern Italy. Around 1160 he joined the Cistercian order. His life as a monk was spent both as an abbot and a hermit, though it was the latter which he preferred. The fact that Joachim lived in Calabria, and had travelled in the East, is significant for the understanding of his thought. He dwelled in the midst of a hybrid civilization in which Catholic Europe, the Byzantine East, and Islamic Africa were all strangely mingled.

Joachim's teaching was centered on the Trinity and his unique interpretation of history. Through an inspiration he received, sometime between 1190 and 1195, Joachim was convinced that he had found a key which, when applied to the events and personages of the Old and New Testaments and especially the Apocalypse, enabled him to perceive in history a pattern and a meaning and to prophesy its future stages. He viewed the course of history as an ascent through three successive stages, each presided over by one of the Persons of the Trinity. The period of the Old Testament was primarily the age of the Father; the period from the time of Christ down to Joachim's own time was that of the Son; and the third and completing period was the age of the Holy Spirit. Though his link between the Old and New Testaments was traditional, Joachim introduced a unique interpretation by seeing in the New Testament a figure of a third historical age yet to come.

The three ages represent a spiritual progress. Truth is revealed dimly in the first age of the Old Covenant, more clearly in the second age of the New Covenant, and fully and finally in the last age of the Holy Spirit. This third epoch would be one of pure love, joy, and freedom when divine knowledge is directly revealed to all men. For Joachim it will be the new kingdom of the Spirit and the last revelation of God's purpose on earth and in time. The three stages grew from each other and the end of each is marked by change and upheaval. The rites and sacraments of each age pass away for they are but types of the better things to come. Even the Mass will disappear as the Paschal Lamb had disappeared.

The Church, in Joachim's idea, was not so much a static and monumental temple, but a tabernacle accompanying the journey of the Chosen People through the desert, "pitched here one night, but to be dismantled with tomorrow's dawn and pitched one stage further on." Joachim's third age called for a new order of men who would comprise a spiritual Church of the future. The old clergy and the old Church, especially in his own time, had shown themselves incapable of molding and guiding the "new man" to become perfect in love and spirit: "The signs as described in the Gospel show clearly the dismay and ruin of the century which is now running down and must perish. Hence I believe that it will not be in vain to submit to the vigilance of the believers, through this work, those matters which divine economy has made known to my unworthy person in order to awaken the torpid hearts from their slumber by a violent noise and to induce them, if possible, to a new kind of exegesis to the contempt of the world."

Consequently the institution of the papacy and clerical hierarchy is limited to the second age. This implies a radical revision of the doctrine of apostolic succession, perhaps in terms of a gradual abolition of the clerical office giving way to a universal reign of contemplatives. In any event, there could be no role for a dominant and highly organized hierarchy in an age when the power of interpreting the Bible would be granted to all the elect. Joachim did, however, regard the ecclesiastical order of his time as favorable to the new age but as playing no part in it. In fact, he himself submitted all of his extant works to the Popes for approval and continuously protested his loyalty to the Church. His interpretation of the angel of the Apocalypse, "the one sent to renovate the Christian religion," only meant that a messianic leader was to appear, "whosoever it will be." His mission would be to bring about a spiritual renovation for the sake of the kingdom of Christ, revealing but not abolishing what had been veiled in mystery.

Much of what was subversive in Joachim's thought came not from his own conclusions but from the rigorist wing of the Franciscan order. The large amount of writings, attributed to Joachim, whether authentic or apocryphal, played a major role in the growth of eschatological fervor during the thirteenth and fourteenth centuries. Every wild dream of the reign of anti-Christ, of the last persecution of the faithful, of the downfall of the papacy, of the rise of a purified Church, of a new millennium found expression in some prophecy credited to Joachim of Fiore.

Even before the fall of the Western Empire, the emperors, by endowing the Church with great wealth, had made it the greatest landed proprietor in the world. This wealth, which enabled the Church to survive the great migrations and invasions relatively unscathed, was increased century after century by legacies and offerings from princes and the rich. Moreover, at least from the twelfth century onwards, the papacy itself was again decidedly worldly. Popes tended to be primarily statesmen and administrators. The greater circulation of money and the revival of trade enabled the papacy to develop a fiscal system on a continental scale, operated by an elaborate and highly trained bureaucracy. By such means it was able to fight purely political battles by purely political means and even to buy allies and wage wars. It was also able, as a great monarchy, to maintain a court of unparalleled splendor.

There had always been individual voices who protested against the accumulation of wealth in the Church. Poverty, often interpreted as an evangelical precept by the Fathers, was one of the guiding principles of both Western and Eastern monasticism. Though Augustine did not require his clerics to take a vow of poverty, he believed that "to no one . . . is it lawful to have anything of his own." Like the Church in the Acts of the Apostles, all property was to be held in common. In the Rule of St. Benedict, there is explicit legislation for the practice of poverty. "If he has any property, let him either first bestow it on the poor or by solemn deed of gift make it over to the monastery, keeping nothing for himself as knowing that from this day forward he shall have no power even over his body." That this legislation was perpetually abused by Benedict's heirs is a well-known fact, but the witness it bears to the tradition of poverty in Christian history remains intact.

Though it had much popular appeal in the twelfth century, poverty as a means of reform always lacked sufficient direction and unity. It enjoyed only sporadic and uneven degrees of success and constantly bore the stigma of heresy. The tragedy which befell Arnold of Brescia, Peter Waldo and others is indicative of many genuine reform movements. But orthodox or not, the various branches of the poverty movement shared a common ideal. All believed that Christian perfection lay in the renunciation of temporal possessions, since this was the example of Christ and His disciples. Consequently the poverty movement would always be characterized by a fierce protest against the Church's wealth and luxury. They could never reconcile the poverty of the primitive Church with the pomp and power of the ecclesiastical organization in their own day.

One of the first attempts at disentanglement had been undertaken by Pope Paschal II. Though his plan failed, the power of its suggestion did not. It provided a measure of inspiration for the Lombard communes who by the early twelfth century were achieving some degree of liberty from both Pope and emperor. It is the midst of the communal movement that saw the rise of Arnold of Brescia (d. 1155) to prominence. Little is known of Arnold's early life except that he was a native of Brescia and may have been a cleric. Also, he is known to have been a close associate of Peter Abelard; Arnold's condemnation by the Lateran Council of 1139 occurred in the same year as that of his more famous friend. The decree of the Council gives some idea of Arnold's activities involved with the communes. According to this decree Arnold "spread among the vulgar pernicious doctrines and filled their ears with impious words. The sacred laws, he said, did not sanction clerical possessions; the monks and priests had no right over the land; nor should the abbots relegate to themselves temporal power which belonged to the princes of the earth; government was the prerogative of the elected representatives of the people alone. Offerings and tithes should be tendered only for the needs of the body, not for their own pleasure. He condemned without restriction the lives of the priests . . . the splendor of their vestments, their lascivious joys and the relaxed manner of the monasteries." In 1137, with the Bishop of Brescia in Rome, the townsmen with Arnold's party took over the city and ruled it under the "two-consul" system. The coup was short-lived, however, and Arnold was forced into exile through pressure from Rome.

In 1145, Arnold re-established his leadership in the communal movement, this time in Rome itself. The city had undergone a popular revolution which had almost succeeded in overthrowing the papacy. With the new Pope, Eugenius III, Arnold and his party arrived at an uneasy peace. But it was not long before the continued corruption among the Roman clergy forced Arnold to renew his protest. In Arnold's eyes the possession of wealth and temporal dominions by the Church were both a negation of Christian ideals and a betrayal of Christ's teaching. For the clergy to covet worldly goods amounted to apostasy from their sacred calling. Moreover, he held that possession of property by the clergy was a barrier to salvation. Otto of Freising quotes him as saying: ". . . the clergy who hold property, the bishops who enjoy regalia and monks who have possessions cannot attain salvation. All these things pertain to the secular rulers and should by their beneficence be given to the clergy for their use."

Arnold continually looked to Pope Paschal's attempt to free the Church from her feudal bonds. But the hope that the papacy itself might initiate a definite program was doomed to disappointment by the mediocre and worldly Popes who followed Paschal. Not even Bernard, Arnold's archenemy, or his protégé, Eugenius, could check curial ambitions for temporal affluence.

In the Roman republican movement, Arnold found what he felt was the means to purify the Church. He hoped to free Rome permanently from all priestly rule, to reduce the clergy to a condition of apostolic poverty and limit to strictly spiritual functions the bureaucratic machinery of the Curia. With Eugenius out of the city, Arnold and his party gained control. "While dwelling in Rome . . . he won the city to his side, and preaching all the more freely because the Lord Pope was occupied in Gaul, he built up a faction known as the sect of the Lombards. He had disciples who imitated his austerities and won favor with the populace through outward decency and austerity of life. . . . ," writes John of Salisbury. But both the republic and Arnold's reform scheme were doomed to ephemeral lives. Pope Eugenius returned to Rome in 1149 and began to play the rebellious commune against the authority of the Emperor Frederick Barbarossa. The death of Eugenius in 1153 did not check Arnold's decline because the new Pope, Adrian IV, continued his predecessor's policy. Finally, through imperial intervention, Arnold was captured and hanged in 1155.

In some ways Arnold of Brescia shared a common fate with other medieval reformers. While his message had popular appeal, he struggled in vain to inspire ecclesiastical institutions with the will to reform. Instead, his program was crushed by that same combination of Pope and emperor which he sought to dissolve.

Despite Arnold's defeat, the closing decades of the twelfth century witnessed the growing popularity of the poverty movement among the laity. The earlier efforts at reform, however admirable, left the mass of people untouched. Yet with the ever-present antagonism of the clergy and the absence of sound direction, it was almost inevitable that these new movements tended to develop independently of the institutional Church.

Perhaps the best illustration of a potentially genuine movement driven from orthodoxy more by circumstance than conviction was the Poor Men of Lyons founded by Peter Waldo. Waldo (d. 1217) was a typical middle-class figure from the city of Lyons. His personal history and religious development is known only through thirteenth-century chronicles seldom sympathetic to the Waldensian movement. He is said to have experienced a conversion on hearing the legend of St. Alexis who had abandoned his riches for the sake of poverty. Waldo promptly did the same and thereby embarked on a mission which was to have ramifications for the next two centuries.

Waldo's action, about the year 1173, immediately stirred the imagination of the Lyonese and his example attracted imitators, particularly among the lower, uneducated classes. Waldo's followers, preaching in the streets and public places throughout southern France, discoursed on poverty and called men back to the evangelical ideal. It is certain that the original aim of Waldo and his followers was conceived in a spirit of protest against corruption and negligence among the clergy. But their impulse toward evangelical poverty and their eagerness to preach the Gospel was met with suspicion by the hierarchy. Although the Waldensians justified their mission to preach by the necessity of explaining the Scriptures, the Archbishop of Lyons sought to silence them, especially since they were laymen. In response to the Archbishop's prohibition, Waldo said, "Judge you whether it be lawful before God to obey Him who has said, 'Go ye into all the world and preach the Gospel to every creature.'"

Banished from Lyons, Waldo journeyed into Italy to appeal his case to the Pope. He arrived in Rome about 1177, on the eve of the Third Lateran Council. He did secure the approval of Pope Alexander III and the Council, but just five years later the new Pope, Lucius III, condemned the group in words recorded by Bernard Gui: "Therefore we lay under perpetual anathema . . . those who falsely call themselves . . . Poor Men of Lyons. . . . We include, in the same perpetual anathema, all who shall have presumed to preach, either publicly or privately, either being forbidden, or not sent, or not having the authority of the Apostolic See, or of the bishop of the diocese." Since preaching was a crucial factor in Waldo's mission, the papal decree was a turning point for the movement. Waldo claimed that every Christian, layman or priest, was a depository of the Holy Spirit with the right of expounding on Holy Scripture. As the moorings which bound them to the Roman Church were cut loose one by one, the Waldensians drifted away from orthodox doctrine. They came to deny purgatory, indulgences, and prayers for the dead. They denounced all lying as grievous sin, and refused to take oaths. All were inventions of the ecclesiastical institution which had abandoned the spiritual character of the early Church.

The fate of the Waldensians provided an important lesson for both the papacy and the later mendicants. Under Innocent III (d. 1216), the papacy began to realize that men inspired by enthusiasm for evangelical Christianity could not be suppressed, and that multitudes would hear and follow those who were obeying literally the commands of Christ.

When one turns from the Waldensians to the Franciscans, he is immediately struck by the parallel in the careers of the two founders. Though younger than Peter Waldo, Francis (d. 1226) was a member of the same economic class and attracted by the same idea. As Waldo was inspired by the legend of St. Alexis, Francis was struck by the words of Matthew's Gospel: "Going therefore preach saying: the kingdom of God is at hand. Do not possess gold, nor silver, nor money in your purse: no scrip for your journey, nor two coats nor shoes, nor staff, for the workman is worthy of his meat. When you come into a house salute it, saying, peace be to this house."

The ideal of evangelical perfection had the same appeal for thirteenth-century Italy as it had for twelfth-century Lyons. Before long, a group of like-minded men had gathered about the youthful maverick. Although Francis did not contemplate the founding of a religious order, the old monastic organizations which he knew had a restricted apostolate which influenced fewer and fewer of the growing urban populace. Like Waldo before him, Francis demanded little more of his followers than a dedication to evangelical ideals. According to St. Bonaventure's account, Francis "perceived that the number of the Brethren was gradually increasing and wrote for himself and for his Brethren a Rule for their life, in simple words. Herein the observance of the holy Gospel was set as the inseparable foundation, and some few other points were added that seemed necessary for a consistent manner of life."

This, the primitive rule of the Franciscans, was the one Francis submitted to Pope Innocent III in 1209. The journey to Rome is another intriguing parallel in the career of the two religious innovators. But if Waldo and Francis followed similar paths to the papacy, their receptions were very different. Alexander III was willing to approve Waldo's way of life—except for preaching. Pope Innocent hesitated at sanctioning the absolute poverty adopted by the small band from Assisi. Surprisingly he showed less reluctance in general regarding the permission to preach. Only one or two of Francis' adherents were clerics, but Innocent ingeniously salvaged the letter of the canon which forbade laymen to preach. He ordered that "all lay Brethren that had accompanied the servant of God (Francis) wear narrow tonsures, that they might preach the word of God without hindrance."

In terms of reform, Francis and his followers were closely attuned to the revival of eschatological expectancy in Christendom during the twelfth and thirteenth centuries. Francis believed that he had been called to follow Christ's poverty so that he might be free to herald more effectively His coming Kingdom: "I am the herald of the great King." He was doubtless aware of the various prophecies, like Joachism, which foretold the imminence of the Last Days. Francis looked to God's Kingdom as to a power already working in the Friars' lives and impelling them to an exercise, in their own day, of the ultimate ideals of the future. But he looked even more expectantly to the coming of that final realm which would completely transcend the present. He writes of the coming "Kingdom of God": "Thy Kingdom come that Thou may reign in us by grace and may make us come to Thy Kingdom, where there is the clear vision of Thee, the perfect love of Thee, the blessed company of Thee, the eternal enjoyment of Thee." Francis here does obeisance to the double sovereignty of God. One reign is by grace in the visible world through the function of Christ as mediated by the saving, sacramental Church. The other Kingdom is the realm perfect and transcendent. The one is visible within the framework of the existing world while the other is supernatural and within the cosmic frame of reference.

Francis prepared his friars for participation in both kingdoms, or rather for life in both phases of one Kingdom. Their status in the existing world was necessarily one of pilgrimage and exile. In this manner only could they enjoy deliverance from the fleeting present and attachment to the abiding future. True friars, contemptuous of all worldly affairs, would pass without danger from the temporal to the eternal. They could claim the coming kingdom because they were not fettered by the existing order. Francis' ideal was simple: "the followers of most holy poverty, having nothing, loved nothing, and therefore had no fear of losing anything."

Poverty and the Kingdom were linked from first to last in the thinking of Francis. Poverty was the special means which his unique followers were to employ in announcing the coming of the Kingdom. Francis may at certain times have questioned the reaction of the Church to his way of Gospel poverty. But he never doubted that the Church would ultimately and inevitably defend that special renunciation in the friars which was likewise Christ's will for them. He did not hesitate, therefore, to pledge his loyalty to the Church, to her Pope, and to her institutional procedure. The Second Rule contains this passage: "Brother Francis promises obedience and reverence to the Lord Pope Honorius and to his successors canonically elected and to the Roman Church . . . Let the clerics perform the Divine Office according to the order of the holy Roman Church."

Francis sought, finally, to subordinate his life and brethren to the historic Church as to the authoritative guardian of his Christ-inspired poverty. The Pope was to be asked "to assign them one of the cardinals of the Holy Roman Church to be governor, protector and corrector of this brotherhood, so that being always subject and submissive at the feet of the same holy Church, grounded in the Catholic faith, we may observe poverty and humility and the holy Gospel of our Lord Jesus Christ, which we have firmly promised."

By the year 1223, when the Second Rule was approved by Pope Honorius III, the Franciscan brotherhood was definitely a religious order. Some years before his death Francis was forced by illness to relinquish his leadership of the Order. He did, however, try to see to it that the principles of poverty, itinerant preaching and manual labor were retained and incorporated into the revised Rule, although in other respects he had to compromise.

Those who claimed to be Francis's spiritual descendants were to meet with little success. With the death of the founder, the Order was torn between two factions, the Spirituals and the Conventuals, which constantly competed for control. It was the Spiritual wing which revived the Joachimite prophecies and attempted to tie them to the message of Francis. Rejecting the alleviating distinction between strict precepts and flexible counsels, they made a radical attempt to live a Christian life in unconditional poverty and humility. To them the clerical Church was indeed at its end and their mission was to transform the Church into a community of the Holy Spirit without hierarchy or sacraments. The rule of St. Francis was to them the quintessence of the Gospel. The driving impulse of their movement was, as with Joachim, the intensity of their eschatological expectancy with regard to the present epoch as a state of corruption.

While the message of Francis still remained within the framework of traditional eschatology, the Spiritual Franciscans became revolutionaries by interpreting their founder, themselves and the events of their times as the fulfillment of Joachim's prophecy. They thus became involved in severe conflicts, first with the rival aspirations of the Dominicans, secondly, with the messianic ambitions of Frederick II (1215-50) and, finally, with the Church.

In 1254 a young Franciscan in Paris, Gerard of Borgo San Donnino, published the *Introduction to the Eternal Gospel*. The treatise expressed publicly and in writing thoughts that had long been incubating in the minds of Joachimites and Spirituals in Italy, southern France and Spain. Gerard interpreted Joachim's prophecies in a manner very favorable to his Order and considered them to be the new gospel of the age of the Holy Ghost. "Now will all images cease and the truth of the two Testaments stand revealed." The dispensation of the old Church was drawing to its close. The new era would start in 1260, and those already inspired by the Spirit to become members of the new Church of the Holy Ghost could rejoice.

The fact that the *Eternal Gospel* was published in Paris is significant. It came at a time when the conflict between the mendicants and the University was reaching a crisis. The secular professors immediately snatched at this golden opportunity for making a *cause célèbre*. Here was proof that the mendicant orders were infected with heresy. In 1255 Gerard and his writings were condemned and the following century saw a constant persecution of the Spiritual faction of his Order.

Pierre Olivi (d. 1298) stands as a representative figure and somewhat of a spokesman of the Spirituals' dream. After joining the Franciscan Order at a very young age, Olivi's career was filled with controversy, especially as leader of the Spirituals in Provence. In his own commentary on the Apocalypse, Olivi produced all the chief ideas that had been associated with Joachim of Fiore. He firmly established St. Francis as the Messiah of the new age, but regarded his mission as the renewal of the life of Christ on earth rather than the proclamation of any new doctrines. Olivi believed that the Franciscan Rule bore the same sanctity as the Gospel, yet would be rejected by the "carnal Church" just as Christ's teaching was scorned by the Jewish priesthood. The great crime of the Church had been the denial of the twin doctrines of poverty and the *usus pauper*, and the persecution of those who adhered to them.

Olivi declared that the purification of the Church depended on the separation of the faithful from the "carnal Church" just as the early Christians had withdrawn from all contact with the synagogue. This separation would be manifest in the complete renunciation of possessions and strict practice of evangelical poverty. In his *Commentary*, Olivi continuously alludes to a great persecution when the power of anti-Christ is at its height. It is here that he assigns St. Francis a messianic role, for he would rise from the dead and lead his faithful followers to their final triumph.

The ultimate defeat of the Spirituals and the rejection of their poverty ideal was inevitable. Their brief taste of victory upon the election of Pope Celestine V in 1293 afforded small satisfaction to the Spirituals. The pontificates of Boniface VIII

(d. 1303) and John XXII (d. 1334) sealed the fate of the movement by their support of the moderate wing of the Franciscan Order.

The triumph of the papacy under Innocent III over the Hohenstaufen emperors proved to be an unfortunate victory. On the one hand, the Church's new position as temporal overlord of Europe served to extend the alienation of the reformers who had sought to restore the Church to her genuine spiritual character. On the other, the collapse of the secular pillar upon which the arch of the medieval order rested, the decline of the universal imperial authority in the West and the resultant rise of democracy and nationalism, weakened the spiritual pillar, the universal papal authority. The long and bloody war of the Sicilian Vespers (1282-1302) climaxed the drastic decline of papal prestige and exposed the shallow ideals of the Crusades. The attempt of Pope Boniface VIII to revive the papal monarchy was followed by a long period at Avignon in which the papacy fell under the complete dominance of the French kings.

Against this state of decline the great poet Dante (1265-1321) provided an articulate voice, "the voice of ten silent centuries" according to Carlyle, which echoes many of the ideals of the reformers. Dante had been deeply involved in Florentine politics, and because he belonged to the discredited pro-imperial faction he was permanently exiled from that city in 1302. The fact that papal intervention had much to do with the defeat of Dante's party left a lasting bitterness in the poet's attitude toward Rome.

As an exile in France, Dante spent many years brooding over the reasons why both Church and empire had failed to maintain the right order within their respective realms. With the *Divine Comedy* he assumes a sense of mission to proclaim his apocalyptic vision of the coming redemption. He is the defender of the much persecuted Franciscans, hounded down by the Popes of Avignon because they clung to their ideal of poverty. Dante's chief target is the *Ecclesia carnalis*, the curial Church, now become the French king's whore, corrupted by the ambitions of the Popes and by the intemperate ideological claims of the canon lawyers.

Dante's constructive purpose was to set Christendom on the right road to the apocalypse. In the last days the Church would be refashioned into a Church of the spirit. In the *Paradiso* Beatrice, symbol of light and the incarnation of this Joachimite-Franciscan vision of a spiritual Church, he proclaims its victory by her triumphal entry into Paradise.

For Dante the Church is the mystical Bride of Christ, absolutely pure in nature. To ensure the union of the Church with her divine Bridegroom, God has sent her two guides, Francis and Dominic. In the *Paradiso*, Dante adopts the view that the two Orders founded by Francis and Dominic are in practice interchangeable since they envisage the same ideal. In Canto XI he clearly supports the Franciscan cause, their notion of poverty and concept of a spiritual Church. Using the figure of Thomas Aquinas, Dante gives a eulogy to Francis in which he emphasizes his devotion to poverty:

"Henceforth assume that Poverty and Francis/ Are the two levers in my narrative . . ./ That father, that great master, went his way/ Together with his bride and family/ Who now had girded on the humble cord;/ No cowardice of heart oppressed his brow,/ But with a carriage worthy of a king,/ He told his stern resolve to Innocent/ And gained from him approval for his order."

Dante's admiration for Dominic is equally high and further demonstrates his agreement with the original objectives of the mendicant movement. Thus Dominic is a worthy companion for Francis since both endeavored to steer the bark of Peter safely into port:

"For this man was a patriarch to us./ Hence, whosoever follows his commands,/ Will load himself with priceless merchandise./ But now his flock is greedy for strange food,/ So that perforce it only can be found/ Scattered in many pastures growing rank./ The farther that his sheep thus stray from him/ And wander off afield, so much the more/ Return they to the fold devoid of milk./ There are indeed those which fear danger/ And follow close the shepherd—but so few/ That it takes little cloth to make their copes."

For Dante, God gave Francis and Dominic to the Church with one and the same end in view, namely, that they should revive its respect for its spiritual nature and its contempt for worldly things. But he frankly admits a rejection of this mission by the Church and within the two orders themselves. Wealth and temporal power are the principal pursuits of the churchmen. In Canto IX he found: "For of the shepherd it has made a wolf. This is the reason why the Gospel and the great Doctors are forsaken, and men no longer study aught but the Decretals . . . It is with this that the Pope and Cardinals busy themselves. But the Vatican and the other places in Rome, which were the graveyard of the army that followed Paul's steps, will soon be purged of this adult-ery."

Dante's sympathy for the ideals of the Spiritual Franciscans is manifested again in his treatment of Joachim of Fiore, "whose spirit was endowed with prophecy." He held the Calabrian abbot to be a prophet who exalted the purity of the spiritual order and who foretold an era in which the clerical order of the visible Church would be reabsorbed into the spiritual Church. Such a final "desecularization" of the Church was in strict accordance with Dante's political passions. His belief in the mutual independence of the temporal and the spiritual orders, of the Church and the Empire, dominate his thought. In the *Inferno* he speaks of the Hound, the savior of Italy, "who shall come to make her (the She-wolf, symbol of greed) die of grief. That Hound who shall not feed upon the land of riches, but on wisdom, love and valor." On earth this new era, the "second Easter" of mankind, will be ushered in by the descent into Italy of the emperor.

Dante's notion of a savior for Italy envisions someone who will come to conquer greed and injustice. But the greed and injustice of whom? In the *Paradiso* he suggests the ambitious Pope John XXII, who by his political aims has laid waste the vineyard of the Church in whose cause Peter and Paul died. The Church spiritual has been abandoned by those "who ought to be at your devotions and let the emperor ride in the saddle." For Dante the most monstrous injustice of his day was precisely the papacy's usurpation of the empire. Like the tyrant who puts power to personal use, the cleric who puts revelation to a temporal use commits the supreme crime—the betrayal of the Holy Spirit. It is that "most heinous of crimes, the abuse of the Spirit's intentions," he reports in *On Monarchy*.

The failure of the reform movements at the close of the thirteenth century was accompanied by a more rapid decline of the fortunes of the medieval Church. From Dante onward the reformers grew more radical and increasingly antipapal, nurtured by the recurring crises of the fourteenth and fifteenth centuries. The ideal of the spiritual Church, clearly exercising its spiritual duties, which existed in the minds and faith of the reformers, seemed all but rejected by the hierarchical institution. There would be no new age of the Spirit nor would the Church return to the evangelical poverty of its birth. Despite itself, medieval Christendom was a mixture of the sacred and the profane and its loyalty to a spiritual mission could not overcome the onslaught of secularization.

Contrary to the intention of Gregory VII to be free from secular influence and control, his efforts to exert the full spiritual powers of the papacy further entrenched the Church in the role of a temporal force. The subsequent confusion between spiritual and temporal roles in medieval Christendom provided a common theme of protest for reformers from St. Bernard to Dante. Their goal was to restore and preserve the ideal of a spiritual Church. In the case of Joachim of Fiore this ideal represented the Church of the future, a fellowship of love and direct revelation. His eschatology, however, was placed in time, specifically the thirteenth century, and implied radical changes in the organization of the Church. After Joachim millenarian reform movements were bound to incur quick reaction from Rome. The persecution of the Spiritual Franciscans, champions of the Joachimite prophecies, demonstrated this reaction.

The poverty movement had as an ideal the primitive Christian community and its practice of renunciation. In the case of Arnold of Brescia the aims were limited somewhat to the twelfth-century Italian communes and their political and economic ambitions. The mendicants represented a more popular manifestation of the growing discontent over the Church's temporal affluence. They cherished an ideal of the Church that was inspired by the laws of apostolic poverty. Thus by granting official approval to the Franciscans and Dominicans, the papacy under Innocent III displayed a degree of sympathy with mendicant principle. But the subordination of the mendicant zeal to ecclesiastical politics, by which the friars became a kind of papal corps, prevented the movement from achieving significant reform goals.

Perhaps the one complaint that links all the medieval reform movements was against an over-institutionalized Church. Ever since the Hildebrandine reform the papacy had acquired a growing bureaucratic machine. As the center of power shifted to the Curia, institutionalism became a permanent mark of the Church. The formulation of canon law and the development of a papal diplomatic corps were just two examples of this institutional trend. The reformers' concept of the Church went beyond the bounds of feudalism and was essentially biblical. They were more impressed with the community of early Christians filled with eschatological fervor. In light of their ideal, the medieval Church obscured its identity and frequently betrayed its mission.

Although internally weakened by the residence in Avignon, the papacy continued to maintain itself as the dominant spiritual power in Europe. Yet there was a definite shift in the tone and purpose of reform efforts. Relying on Aristotelian political theories, papal writers came more and more to identify reform with a strengthening of the corporational side of the Church. Critics of the Pope's absence from Rome were silenced by indications that since the Pope was the Church it mattered little whether he resided in Rome or Avignon. The Mystical Body of Christ was where its head was: *Ubi Papa ibi ecclesia.*

Confronted with innascent nationalism the papacy reasserted its claims to spiritual and temporal absolutism in even more fantastic terms. It is one of the strange ironies of history that those who argued the case for papal plenitude of power were the very agents of its undoing. This usurpation of episcopal prerogatives had of course not gone unchallenged. Already in the twelfth century voices were raised that saw in the rise of the papacy as a world power a threat to the unity of Christendom. The anonymous author of the York Tracts denied the primacy of the Pope by asserting that to claim one church as superior to another was to divide the Church. The bishops, he wrote, were representatives of Christ and hence liable to no one. Papal mandates and decrees were not the will of God, nor was obedience to the Pope the unifying bond of Christendom. Rather unity was to be found in oneness of faith and baptism in Christ. He argued that if one examines the commands issuing from the Bishop of Rome he will find that they neither contain the will of Christ, nor harmonize with evangelical and apostolic doctrine. St. Peter was not constituted as a judge over the other apostles, rather each apostle was equal to Peter. There is no scriptural basis for the primacy of the Roman Church; each individual church represents Christ insofar as Christ is recognized as the Son of the living God. The Roman primacy rests solely upon human claims, the most important of which is that Rome was at one time in the distant past the capital of a now defunct empire. If primacy is to be awarded according to such arguments, it should be bestowed upon the Church of Jerusalem, the mother of all churches.

The cultured Bishop of Alba, Benzo, also strongly attacked the monastically inspired centralization of ecclesiastical authority under Hildebrand. In Benzo's eyes the Pope's function is that of a head of the priesthood and nothing more. By assuming the role of a universal monarch the Pope has become the anti-Christ, a false and diabolical monk. If the order of the Roman Empire is to be re-established, then the Pope must submit to the emperor. Historically it has been the emperor's duty to protect and govern the Apostolic See. In speaking of the election of Hildebrand to the papacy, Benzo becomes especially vitriolic. It is inconceivable that the most important official in the priesthood should have been elected by monks. He refers to the electors of the great "reforming Pope" as fugitives from the Rule of St. Benedict.

During the same century a work entitled *Liber de Unitate Ecclesiae,* probably written by the provost of Aachen, Gottschalk, also sharply attacks the Pope's usurpation of power. The author contends that by disregarding the essentially limited authority given to St. Peter, Hildebrand disturbed the peace and unity of the Church. The Petrine power to bind and loose was not as comprehensive as the successors of Peter maintain. Hildebrand has further violated the apostolic command, "Fear God and honor the king," since the king's power issues directly from God. The ideal Pope is the one who admonishes by using the work of God rather than binding laws. The Church is essentially a *congregatio fidelium,* a spiritual fellowship bound together by charity, peace and love. It is a moral force in which the Pope may possess teaching authority but no jurisdiction in the sense of coercion to obedience. This remonstrative tract was discovered by Ulrich von Hutten in the early sixteenth century and found a wide audience during the first years of the Reformation.

By the fourteenth century opposition to papal claims had become more than the isolated vituperations of disgruntled bishops. The humiliation of the papacy at Anagni and the imperial claims of Louis of Bavaria gave rise to an increasing stream of propaganda that supported with incisive logic the view that the Pope had become the living image of Christ. The decretalists reasoned that papal power was of such magnificence that it could not possibly be the subject of human scrutiny. Although a terrestrial body, the Church had a mystical being in Christ and was the Body of Christ with His spiritual personality. The terrestrial representative of Christ's personality was the Pope, and as Christ was the Church the Pope was seen as the Church on earth, the head of society, outranking all other men.

Boniface had gone so far as to claim that he was the vicar not only of Peter, and of Christ, but of God Himself.

He had proclaimed that "for every creature it was absolutely necessary for salvation to be subject to the Roman Pontiff." His famous bull *Unam Sanctam* thus implied the identification of the Church with the supreme pontiff. The papal publicist Aegidius Romanus expressed the identification more graphically when he stated that the Pope, Christ, and the Church are all fundamentally the same thing. As the vicariate of Christ the papacy is Christ and the Church, the head and the whole, on earth.

The monk Augustinus Triumphus carried this claim to its extreme theoretical development in a work published in 1328, *Summa de Potestate Ecclesiastica*. For this papal propagandist the Church was the indivisible universal body of all Christians, embracing the religious, social, and political elements of society. It was a Christianized version of the Roman Empire. In the Pope, as representing the Church, lay all power, and all spiritual life proceeded from him as from the head to the members. As the vicar of Christ, the Pope was both head and body of the Christian commonwealth. The Pope could be considered the Church because in him were found the power of the keys to the grace of salvation and through him all were given supernatural life. True membership within the Church necessarily involved membership in the Pope, and all Christians formed the body of the Pope.

The purpose of papal plenitude of power was the creation of right order in the Church and the preservation of this order from whatever might disrupt it. This comprehensive ordering was understood as the expression of a divine plan and could be carried out only under papal direction. The Pope alone was able to take abstract principles of faith and transfer them into codes of law for the administration of a political society. He alone could allocate individual functions as they were needed, ordering society according to the divine plan entrusted to him. The Pope was the head, heart, and soul of the Church. As the heart he pumped faith and life-giving blood into the Christian body, as the soul he vivified the body in every way, and as the head he gave guidance without which the body would lose all sense of direction. He also describes the Pope as the source from which all rivers of power and faith flow into society, the font from which flow those waters that irrigate the universal church. The power of the Pope is the essence of the Church and is identifiable with it.

Augustinus shows that the distinctions between temporal and spiritual merely describe two aspects of one all-inclusive power over the laity and clergy. Since the Church is one, the power of the Pope is one and is hence temporal as well as spiritual. Kings are but a part of the all-inclusive Church and temporal power comes to them through the Pope. All temporal power is included in spiritual power. Every ruler received his authority from Peter and his successors and is subject to the Pope, accountable to him.

These claims to papal supremacy were, of course, buttressed by the official protocol of the papal court. Assuming all of the trappings of the deified emperor they adorned themselves with robes of imperial purple; their tiaras were topped with a golden crown and in processions they were preceded by imperial banners. Papal coronation had eclipsed consecration in importance; he was "the prince," "the true emperor." The Church had all the appurtenances of an *ens politicum*. The Pope was the successor of Marius and Caesar; Peter was *Consul Caesarque*. While the defense and consolidation of extreme temporal and spiritual claims preoccupied the papacy, two voices were raised that were to shake the institution to its very foundations.

William of Occam and Marsilius of Padua, although not reformers in a doctrinal sense, must be considered as important agents in that movement which envisioned a new planting of the Church in terms of a curtailment of those extreme views that identified the *corpus mysticum* with the papacy. It is important to note that both men launched their attack on the papacy at a time when it was perfecting those fiscal policies that were to make it the greatest financial power in Europe. It was a period when every spiritual favor, every privilege, every ecclesiastical appointment exacted a fee. It was a time when, as Tawney rightfully remarks: "Men felt with considerable justice that the papacy was too little interested in the business of saving souls and too much concerned with that of extracting money from its constituents." Papal power, founded upon moral authority, had come more and more to base its prerogative on a fiscal system. The evil consequences of attempting to induce into an institution an elaborate system of financial support for which it was never intended are obvious enough. Nothing else could possibly have done more to corrupt the spiritual character of the hierarchy.

Some historians exaggerate the flight of the English Franciscan William of Occam to the court of Louis of Bavaria by claiming that it marks the beginning of the medieval papacy's disintegration. It must certainly be considered as the final chapter in the long struggle between imperium and sacerdotum that began with the investiture strife. Although more renowned as the inceptor of nominalism and as a participant in the contest between the Spiritual Franciscans and Pope John XXII on the question of evangelical poverty, Occam laid the foundation for all later denunciations of papal extremism. He launched his attack on these papal claims in his *Dialogus,* composed between 1333 and 1338. The work is basically a treatment of the Pope's relationship to ecclesiastical law. For Occam the Church is to be understood as a community of believers whose basic structure is outlined in the primitive Church of the apostles. It is a society governed by law and reason that cannot be changed by individual Popes. Rejecting the claim of canon lawyers as true interpreters of the Gospel he urges a return to a theological understanding of the Church. Thus the Pope as a legislator may approve doctrines that have already been accepted by the universal Church, but he may in no way create new articles of faith. "No truth," he writes, "is catholic unless it has been divinely revealed, either by its being inserted into the Scriptures or because it has become known through the certainty of the universal Church."

Hence it is wrong to assert that the Pope possesses the plenitude of power in temporal affairs. Placing him above all positive law in temporal matters is tantamount to reducing Christian law, the law of liberty, to a binding custom of slavery. All who bear the Christian name then become the slaves of the Pope. Everyone, kings, princes and laity, could be deprived of their possessions by the Pope, and the result: interminable dissension and strife. Such an interpretation of papal power would produce greater servitude than did the law of Moses. Therefore the power possessed by the Pope must be purely spiritual. It is a power that derives in part from Christ and in part from human legislation. Most of it is received from canons that have been enacted by general councils and it is evident that the councils did not derive their authority from the Pope but that the Pope derives his from them. Whatever coercive power the Pope possesses he does not hold immediately but mediately, not from Christ but from the faithful. In the matter of temporalities Christ gave to the successors of Peter only the right to demand what was necessary for their sustenance and the fulfillment of their official duties. Whatever power the Roman pontiffs possess beyond this they have obtained as the result of human action, rights tacitly granted or proceeding through the impotence, negligence or malice of other men.

Occam was also of the opinion that a Pope could and actually had fallen into heresy, as was true with the College of Cardinals, or even the majority of the faithful. From this flows his interest in the idea of a general council as representing all of Christendom in an emergency situation. Anyone, he maintained, even a woman, had the power to convoke a council without the permission of the Pope. In the event of a schism, a particular council could be summoned without papal assent to decide who was the true papal claimant. This precedent had already been established by the bishops who assembled to judge Pope Marcellinus for idolatry and condemn John XXII for simony. Should a Pope deviate from the faith he would lose his office by that very fact, and hence it would be absurd to deny that the emperor, whose power was from God alone, could not depose a Pope in heresy. He maintained that the choice of the Pope actually rested with the entire body of the faithful, especially with the clergy and people of Rome. His election by the College of Cardinals was nothing more than the exercise of delegated authority, justified by its usefulness and thus revocable in case of an emergency.

In a later work entitled *De Imperatorum et Pontificum Potestate* he placed his denial of papal plenitude of power on the authority of the Scriptures. "When Christ established St. Peter head and prince of all believers, He did not give him such fullness of power that he could regularly and by his own right do everything which was not contrary to divine or natural law, but assigned definite limits to this power, which were not to be transgressed. That He did not give him such fullness of power in temporal matters is proved by both authority and reason. For the Apostle says in the second epistle to Timothy: 'Let no one fighting for God involve himself in secular affairs that he may please Him whose favor he has won.'" Although Occam accepted the monarchal authority of the Pope over the Church as necessary for securing the salvation of souls and the government of the faithful, he maintained that the Pope's power was ministerial rather than dominational in that it was to serve only the spiritual needs of the faithful. The Popes, he claimed, had over-extended the rights they falsely attributed to the Petrine commission. St. Peter did not possess the plenitude of power and hence it was foolish to believe that his successors had an all-inclusive and unlimited power to bind and loose in both temporal and spiritual spheres. Occam saw the main trouble in the Church arising from the fact that the Roman pontiffs had left their own province of operation and stretched out their hands to what was not rightfully theirs. The "whatever you bind" in the Petrine commission had to be understood with limitations and exceptions.

Far more revolutionary in his denunciation of the medieval Church was the former Chancellor of the University of Paris, Marsilius of Padua. In 1324 he wrote his monumental work the *Defensor Pacis* and two years later was forced to flee like Occam to the court of Louis. The book was denounced in a papal bull of 1327 and Marsilius was declared a son of perdition and the fruit of malediction. For Marsilius the Church is a purely spiritual and sacramental community, its members united in a common faith and sharing of sacramental rites. Like the state it is dependent upon a meshing of various parts and functions. Relying heavily on Aristotelian concepts of the state, Marsilius attacked the sharp dichotomy of the papalists between lay and cleric. Each cleric or layman was a citizen with inherent rights to participate in those affairs that affected society as a whole. The important question was not whether a person was ordained but whether he was a citizen using his reasoning powers in matters affecting his religious belief. A quantitative increase in the governing of the Church will bring about a qualitative improvement. The choice of laymen to serve in councils will permit their superior intellectual and moral qualities to offset the ignorance and selfishness of certain of the clergy. As a multitude of persons the Church really demanded no supreme leader, but it was advantageous to have an arbiter in matters of theology. Practical government should be relegated to local bishops and priests, and religious sanctions such as excommunication and suspension ignored, since the priesthood has no coercive power.

For Marsilius "coercive jurisdiction over all men, whether priests or laymen, the appointment and approval of persons, and the institution of all offices belong to the authority of the faithful human legislator and certainly not to any individual priest or college of priests as such." The Roman Bishop's position in his system is that of an administrator executing the wishes of the general body of Christians. A representative council of all Christians would be the supreme authority in the definition and prescription of secular and religious matters as well. The principal authority (mediate or immediate) to determine the meaning of ambiguous statements in Holy Scripture belongs only to a general council or to those to whom it has been delegated by the corporation of faithful Christians. In regard to the ritual of the Church nothing which binds men to obedience under penalty, either in the present life or the life to come, can be established by any individual man of whatever dignity or rank he may be unless it meets these conditions: (1) it be derived through the immediate or delegated authority of a general council; (2) it be intervened by a decree of the chief faithful human legislator or of a prince ruling by its authority.

Marsilius finds little charm in the concept of the Church as a self-governing body able to legislate in its own behalf. Supported by arguments from Aristotle and the Scriptures, Marsilius demonstrates that papal claims and ecclesiastical jurisdiction are actually a perversion of the idea of the state as an autonomous body. It is the Popes, he says, who have attempted through the canonists to make the Church a competitor with the state; the Popes who are responsible for the violent deaths of thousands of the faithful. In disturbing the peace of society with excommunications and interdicts they have given rise to hatred, contention, moral corruption and all sorts of crime. Devastated cities, abandoned churches and pillaged countrysides are ample evidence of the consequences of papal greed for power. The papacy has been the real cause of civil discord in every kingdom where it has been able to make entry through its claim to plenitude of power. In a final analysis the Church, when viewed by Marsilius, can never be the perfect society envisioned by the medieval canonists for the simple reason that the assumption of the temporal sanctions necessary to enforce its laws is contrary to the spirit of the Gospel. Hence, it is more an association of believers who find their true unity in the state. The chief task of the Church is to serve the state by creating those moral and spiritual conditions that will facilitate its work: the happiness of mankind established in peace.

In spite of the ban on their works, Occam and Marsilius exerted a profound influence over the reform movement of the following two centuries. Occam's role in the Reformation is more commonly ascribed to his nominalistic philosophy. Nominalism was, according to present-day Catholic opinion, the chief factor in the breakup of Christendom. Luther is described as an ossified Occamist. Grisar contends that Luther arrived at his radical doctrines concerning grace and redemption under the influence of Occam and a more recent author attributes the evils of the sixteenth century to nominalism "with its barren and spectral extrinsicism." Yet the new concept of the nature of spiritual power, developed in Occam's treatment of the papacy, did more to change men's view of that institution than his theological writings on the absolute omnipotence of God. Nor has Marsilius been spared the accusation of pre-Reformation Protestantism. The Louvain theologian and imperial statesman, Albert Pighius, traced to him Luther's doctrines on the nature of the Church. The Catholic historian Philip Hughes recently found in the *Defensor Pacis* "the first full outline of the ideal and scheme of religious organization that later ages would know as the distinctive form of the Church of England as by law established."

In their insistence that the layman belonged to the Church no less than the clergy, Occam and Marsilius merely reiterated what had been a constant complaint since the post-Hildebrand clericalization of the Church. What gave their arguments a greater cogency was the absence of the mystical analogies employed by the earlier defenders of the lay thesis. These two men couched their arguments in cold logic. The hypothetical schism that they imagined became a reality two generations later, and the question of reform began to focus on the very nature and constitution of the Church that needed reforming. Then the question of how gave way to that of what; the challenge was levelled at the essential structure of the Church. The problem ceased to be one of reviving the observation of rules found in ancient decretals. The defense of the Church's superstructure behind juridic and legalistic pronouncements was abandoned. The laity had for too long been limited to a passive role that confined their more sensitive awareness to the providential call of history and thwarted their mission to intensify the creative effort of Christian thought. It would therefore be incorrect to regard all advocates of that reform based upon a diminution of papal temporal involvement as harassed or excommunicated clergy.

The most persistent critics of curial corruption in the years immediately before the Great Schism were not only from among the laity, they were women. Brigitta of Sweden sets the tone of these criticisms in one of her revelations addressed to Gregory XI. She speaks of a vision in which she beheld the Pope standing before the throne of the heavenly Judge who rebuked him with the following words:

"Why is your daring and presumption so great against Me?

Your mundane Curia is plundering My celestial court. In your pride you have deprived Me of My sheep. You have unlawfully confiscated the goods of the Church which are Mine and the goods of the subjects of the Church to give to your secular friends. You are robbing the poor for the sake of the rich. Your audacity and presumption are far too great. What have I done to you, oh Gregory! I permitted you to ascend the supreme pontificate and foretold to you My wishes and the great reward they would offer. How have you repaid Me for all My benefits? Why have you ruled in your Curia with such great pride, insatiable cupidity, lust and horrible simony? You have robbed Me of innumerable souls, for almost all who come to your Curia you cast into the fires of hell, insofar as you fail to attend to the things that pertain to My court although prelate and pastor of My sheep.

"The fault is your own because you have failed to consider wisely what is to be done for their spiritual salvation and what is to be corrected. Although I could with justice condemn you for these things, yet I continue to admonish you for the salvation of your soul to return to Rome, to your See, as quickly as possible. Return not with your customary pride and worldly pomp but with humility and burning charity. And once you have returned, extirpate and root out all vices from your Curia. Put far from you the counsels of your carnal and worldly friends and humbly follow the counsels of My spiritual friends. Rise up and manfully recover your strength. Begin to renovate My Church which I acquired with My own blood. Bring it back in spirit to its primitive holy state, for what is now venerated is a house of shame rather than holy mother Church."

Catherine of Siena was even more forceful in her denunciations of the Curia. She informed Gregory that the stench of the papal court was equalled only by the putrefaction of hell itself. Through immoral lives the clergy had been put to shame by the virtues of the laity. In a prophetic voice she told his Holiness that God was allowing to take place by force what should have been carried out by charity. The Church would be deprived of temporalities in order to show that God wished it to return to that primitive state of poverty, humility, and meekness that characterized it when the clergy attended to nought else than the honor of God and the salvation of souls, caring for spiritual things instead of temporal, In 1377 she wrote the Pope: "God wills and demands that you, according to your power, should take your dominion from the hands of demons. Set yourself to freeing the holy Church from the foul smell of her ministers; weed out these stinking flowers; plant in their place sweet-smelling ones, virtuous men who fear God." Although she foretold of the coming schism within the Church there was a note of optimism in the prophecy: ". . . *sequeturque post haec tanta reformatio Ecclesiae sanctae Dei et renovatio pastorum sanctorum, quod ex solo cogitatu exult spiritus meus in Domino.*" Flacius Illyricus traces the Reformation of the sixteenth century to this medieval mystic's amazing forecast.

3 Conciliarism as reform

"*Christendom has no longer any leader whom it respects or is willing to obey; the titles Emperor and Sovereign Pontiff are for it no longer anything more than names without reality and those who bear them are in its eyes only vain images.*"

POPE PIUS II

Historians will probably never arrive at a final agreement as to the immediate cause of the Great Schism. The accounts of those who were present at the fateful election of Bartolomeo Prignano differ radically. In the *Declaration* drawn up by the rebellious cardinals some months after the event there are apparent contradictions in their explanation that the hostility of the Roman mob forced the election. St. Vincent Ferrer, the ardent supporter of the Avignon Pope Clement VII, claimed that Prignano was merely nominated, not elected as Pope. He asserted this was done in order to placate the Romans who clamored outside the gates of the conclave for a Roman Pope. St. Catherine of Siena urged the crowned heads of Europe to the support of the Roman Urban as the truly elected head of the Church and certainly her personal contact with Urban must have given her sufficient reason for supporting his claim. The celebrated canonist Baldus de Ubaldis, although aware of the condition of duress claimed by the cardinals, still concluded that Urban was the legal Pope. Regardless of whether the election of Bartolomeo Prignano, Archbishop of Bari and former member of the Curia at Avignon, was valid or invalid, or whether the validity was a question of law or of fact, what happened on the 8th of April in 1378 set in motion a series of events that were soon to plunge the whole of Europe into one of the greatest religious crises it had ever experienced. More importantly these happenings were to bring into sharp focus the long neglected need for reform in the head and members of the ecclesiastical body that was rent by schism.

The month following the election the majority of the cardinals, ostensibly to escape the inclement weather of Rome, departed for Anagni, scene of the unhappy encounter of Boniface with the agents of Philip the Fair seventy-five years before. Two months later, on the 9th of August, the assembled cardinals startled the Catholic world by solemnly announcing that the election of Prignano was null and void and that Christendom lacked a spiritual head. On the following September the 20th they elected Cardinal Robert of Geneva, a relative of the French King, as Pope Clement VII. Excommunicated by the Roman Pope whom he termed the anti-Christ, he retaliated by creating his own College of Cardinals and moved to the papal residence at Avignon.

The cardinals who revolted against Urban explained their action by pointing out that in choosing him as Pope they had acted under duress. There is certainly evidence that the personality of Urban, his arrogance, his fiery temper, his determination to remain in Rome, away from the fleshpots of Avignon, and especially his intentions to reform the Curia were all factors in his abandonment by his former colleagues. Yet in a broader sense the schism that this move created was due to a number of other causes. It has been customary to ascribe it to the antagonism that had grown between the Italians and the French in their desire to control the central administration of the Church. Some historians trace it to the conflicting ideologies that had developed within the governing body of the Church. Was there to be absolute rule as opposed to a limited and constitutional oligarchy? Was the College of Cardinals merely an advisory and electoral group, or did it constitute the real governing body of the Church, with the Pope merely as an executive officer? Was the Pope an absolute monarch or was he a functionary whose sole office was to carry out the commands and recommendations of his counsellors?

Since the pontificate of Alexander III, antagonist of Frederick Barbarossa, the College of Cardinals had exercised the exclusive and uncontested prerogative of electing the supreme head of Christendom. Succeeding Popes had confirmed their position as integral agents in the machinery of ecclesiastical government. They were allotted a considerable portion of the papal revenues, notably the *servitia communia* or those benefice taxes imposed upon most of the ecclesiastical provinces and monasteries in western Europe. Canon law had come to consider that a failure on the part of the Pontiff to consult with the cardinals in matters of important Church legislation would render such legislation null and void. They were compared to the seventy elders of the Old Testament with whom Moses was wont to take counsel. In the corporational legalism of the medieval period it was considered that although the Pope was head of the Roman Church, the cardinals in conjunction with him formed the Apostolic See.

Yet if the schism was due to a constitutional development that considered the Pope as only one integral part of the governing body of the Church, it must be noted that a deep-rooted lack of respect for the sacral nature of ecclesiastical government also played an important role. The corruption that had characterized the papal court at Avignon, the luxury and immorality that made it the scandal of Europe, had considerably weakened the sublime purpose of both the cardinalate and the papacy. The root-cause of the deteriorating situation that produced the schism was to be found in the abasement of the papacy itself, its secularization, its preoccupation with fiscal matters, and its glaring lack of spiritual ideals. Unlike earlier schisms in the West, which were caused at least indirectly by the interference of secular powers, the Western schism was traceable to the inherent weaknesses and malformation in the governing apparatus of the Church.

Hence it is not surprising that, as the schism spread throughout Christendom, dividing the faithful not only along national lines but turning Christian against Christian within the same dioceses, monasteries and parishes, some means should be sought for restoring peace and union from other than either the cardinals or the contending Popes. The vituperous charges and defamatory statements that the rival Pontiffs hurled at one another gave little credence to the claim that they were the truly elected vicars of Christ. Serious doubts concerning the divine origin of the papacy, as we have seen, and particularly incredulity toward their claim of supreme spiritual authority in the Church, had for many decades been debated among scholars and ranking churchmen. With every Christian now excommunicated as being a follower of one or the other of the papal claimants it is not difficult to see how the ordinary citizen began to entertain similar doubts with a subsequent breakdown of respect for spiritual authority at all levels. What aggravated the situation even more was the fact that now instead of one group of papal tax collectors, many dioceses and provinces were plagued with two. We get a description of the moral breakdown of the clergy from an anonymous French prelate who laments the neglect of divine services and speaks of the papal collectors who devastate the land and excommunicate or suspend those who do not justify their demands: "Judgment is given in favor of those who pay the most. The loss of ten thousand souls is easier borne than the loss of ten thousand shillings. The study of the Scriptures and theological professors are openly turned to ridicule. Bishops do not hesitate to sell licenses to priests authorizing them to keep concubines. Priests blaspheme the names of God and the saints and hurry to the altar from the embraces of prostitutes."

As recalcitrant Popes succeeded one another with seemingly little intention of reforming the Church or bringing a close to the schism, it became apparent that neither persuasion nor military force, means hitherto applied in similar situations, would be of any avail. The ills were too deeply rooted in the very makeup and nature of the organization that demanded mending and reforming. The gravity of the situation and this impasse produced a confluence of reform idealism with a theory of government that is historically termed conciliarism.

Once considered traceable to the teachings of Marsilius of Padua and William of Occam, the doctrine is now known to have evolved from the corporate ideas of government that were developed by thirteenth-century canonists, particularly Huguccio and the fourteenth-century Dominican, John of Paris.

Faced with the dilemma of two Popes whose claim to absolute authority kept them above judgment by any other power, and a college of aristocratic cardinals whose oligarchical orientation would allow submission to none outside their own ranks, conciliarism appeared as the only solution for bringing peace, order and reform to the Church. Since the abuses in the Church were blamed on the extravagant claims of the papacy, effective reform could be achieved only through a limitation of papal authority by means of a general council representing the entire Church, in short, through conciliarism. What had been for several centuries a hypothetical situation envisioned by canonists had now become an unhappy reality.

It is not surprising that the first advocates of reform conciliarism should be found among the German theologians who taught at the University of Paris. Anti-papalism had a long history in the Empire and the final phase of the investiture struggle, the conflict between Louis of Bavaria and John XXII, was still a living memory. Moreover, in contrast to the spirituality of the Latin world to the south with its rigid judicial theological overtones, the peoples of the North, the Germans in particular, had throughout the entire medieval period leaned more toward a mystical and personal religious development. The great Rhenish mystics Suso, Taule, and Eckhart reflect this tendency as does the *Devotio Moderna*. These factors contributed to a widespread belief in the North that any reform of theology had to begin with a return to the ancient truths of the early Church. These had to be made intelligible to the laity and the laity should be given a greater voice in the affairs of the Church. The Church required a horizontal as well as a vertical dimension.

Henry of Langenstein and Conrad of Gelnhausen, German theologians at the University of Paris, are considered the first proponents of conciliarism as a means of reform. Both were expelled from Paris because of the anti-papal stand they took during the early phases of the schism. In 1379, Gelnhausen composed a tract which he sent to the monarchs of France and Germany advocating a general council of the Church as the sole means of healing the schism. The *Short Letter* (*Epistola Brevis*) stressed the fact that the papacy exists for the Church, not the Church for the papacy. In the absence of any legal apparatus adequate to deal with the dire situation created by the schism it recommends that *epikeia*, the interpretative principle of legal equity, be adhered to in order to solve the disorder. A few years later, in 1381, Langenstein developed this theory still further in his famous *Letter on Behalf of a Council of Peace* (*Epistola Concilii Pacis*), expatiating on the ideas proposed by Gelnhausen.

The German theologian begins his tract by emphasizing that the present schism is due to the sins of the people: "The ministers of the Church seek after the things of the world and despise the things of the spirit, they set their minds on the laws of the world and the formulating of legal writs, and have not proficiency in the word of God with which to kindle men's souls. The regulations of spiritually minded men of former times, deserving our attention, are obliterated by the negligence of their successors. To them the antiquity of the Fathers, so discordant with the works of darkness, is invariably displeasing, while the novelty of their own inventions, vying with the law of God, has given them pleasure. For in this way lawsuits are perpetuated and a thousand deceits committed in the city of God. It is simony that sells benefices, that confers bishoprics. It is money that secures indulgences, absolutions, dispensations, and confirmations. It is avarice with its exactions that ruins bishoprics, that impoverishes monasteries. In a word it is avarice, kindled by its own lust, that does everything, that perverts all."

The schism, he continues, is opposed to the very laws of nature: "The present contentious schism is not merely in opposition to divine and human law. It has even tried to break the inviolable law of contradiction, since positive law seeks to assert that the statements of the cardinals are true, while they themselves make contradictory statements with, as it were, equal testimony of the truth. Who could be surprised if this wretched schism, the progeny of contradiction, the monster of monsters, the begetter of strife, the enemy of all things, when it has destroyed the lawful courses, confounds everything? This schism is entangled in much equivocation, is troubled by finely drawn distinctions. It is rending the seamless robe of Christ, bringing confusion to the ecclesiastical order, dispersing the universities, propagating heresies and errors, and offending the people of God in a thousand ways. Even more terribly, it deforms by its base grotesqueness the Bride of Christ."

He then goes on to point out that the papal disagreements actually provide an opportunity for Church reform: "Although the face of flattering fortune is turned away and we are oppressed by adversity and enveloped by the wiles of the Devil in the confused intricacies of the present schism, let us not believe that those who are suffering such things are alienated from Christ, but rather hope that we, when we have been *reformed* through this opportunity, will be restored to Him in a better condition."

Langenstein then explicitly states his solution in terms of a general reformatory council: "I believe that this schismatic iniquity which is hindering the action of divine grace by its venomous germs can be terminated in three ways. The first is that all who are aware of being a party to the above-mentioned crimes take it to heart and through penance reconcile themselves with God. The second is that throughout the universal Church supplication for divine mercy be made publicly in fasting, weeping and prayer. Finally, when preparations have been made for the grace of the Holy Spirit, a general council should be called in the name of Jesus Christ to purge His Church from the evils and various excesses all too common at this time. After these causes have been removed the council must tear up from the very roots the present division in the city of God which this begriming and monstrous schism has produced. Here is a way of peace, a way often walked by our fathers before us, a way of salvation. The record of past events, which reaches modern men, ought surely to move Christian kings and princes to undertake with the greatest enthusiasm the way which is pleasing to God and demand its execution without delay. History informs us that formerly, in the past emergencies of the Church, provincial and general synods of bishops were in the providence of God frequently called, through the same devotion, patronage, and encouragement of kings. They faithfully submitted themselves, their litigations, and the correction and emendation of their laws to the holy judgment of the councils."

After disposing of arguments as to why a general council should not in the present condition of the Church act as the supreme legislator, the German theologian goes on to list the more important abuses that have corrupted the government of the Church of the day, and proceeds to describe the deplorable state of the clergy that has resulted. Since these observations present a comprehensive and detailed catalogue of the defects of the late medieval Church we quote the entire passage:

"What benefit or what usefulness does the magnificent glory of princes and the superfluous pomp of prelates and cardinals, unmindful that they are but men, confer upon the Church? Is it not detestable that one person should hold two hundred, another three hundred, ecclesiastical benefices? Is it not true that the divine worship is thereby curtailed, that the churches are impoverished and deprived of capable men and doctors, and that evil examples are given to the faithful? What does the fact that the cardinals were elected from one nation only, or, as it were, from one country, mean? Amongst them there ought to be some from every kingdom and from all tongues. Is there with Christ a distinction between Greek and Latin, French and German, Spanish and Hungarian?

"Why is it that today one person—would that he were moderately well educated—holds four, five, six or eight benefices, of not one of which he is worthy, in which eight could be supported who would apply themselves to teaching, prayer, and the offices of divine praise? Consider whether today the poor of Christ shouldn't be eating the patrimony of the Church rather than horses, dogs, birds, and the excessive households of the ecclesiastics. Question whether a portion of this patrimony shouldn't provide a suitable means for increasing the divine worship and for the conversion of the infidels, or pious works of this nature. Why is it today that the places of divine worship (such as monasteries and

churches of the venerable martyrs, at Rome and elsewhere),
owing to what has been said above, and to the negligence
of the clergy, are deserted and in ruins? Judge if it is even
right that the books of the churches, and the like, are sometimes sold, and castles and houses mortgaged to pay to the
collectors the exactions imposed by the bishops on the clergy.

"Why is it that today all make for the hub of Christendom,
which abounds with rich benefices and which is, so to speak,
a center of quiet, while the parts of the Church on the periphery, where the ungodly walk, have been neglected and un-
visited? Why is it that these places, where faith is weak and
virtue imperfect, where schismatics abound and infidels make
their attacks, have been left vacant and unattended by the
doctors, who should have been appointed and sent there?
Indeed, in these places there is need of prelates, doctors, and
masters more experienced in the law of Christ, and in more
laudable and effective polemics. Why is it that the sword of the
Church, excommunication, is now so lightly drawn to its
own contempt and thrust so cruelly against the poor for a
small matter such as debt or the like? Why is it that one
legal process over an ordinary affair now lasts for many
years? Why is the excessive prolongation of the lawsuits—the
despoiler of the poor—not done away with in a seemly manner? Why is the means of earning a living from their own
property not mercifully given to converted Jews? Instead they
are compelled to live in extreme poverty, driven to apostatize
and to accuse Christians of ungodliness. Why is it not ordained that Jews must not remain among Christians unless
they earn their livelihood by becoming servants to the Christians, by cultivating the fields or working as mechanics, and
not by practicing usury, which for themselves is committing
sin and for Christians means being looted? What is the meaning of the fact that the canons of certain cathedral churches
put on boots and short tunics—the clerical habit being put
off and the military assumed—and engage with each other
in jousting? That even the bishops lay aside their copes,
surplices, and books, take up arms and, fully equipped, fight
in the fields like secular princes?

"Why is it that some prelates place their administrative
authority, secular and spiritual, in the hands of certain powerful and avaricious tyrants for a certain sum of money, to
the detriment of the Church, the subversion of justice, and
the oppression of the poor? Why is it that today, bishops, abbots, and monks, rather than being ministers of Christ, are
fiscal officers, laboring with all their strength for the world

in the courts of princes, of secular justice, or of parliaments? Why are all bishops, prelates, and parish priests now appointed through the Pope rather than natives of the countries, who are known and better qualified, so that men who are strange in manners, speech, and customs may not be appointed to ecclesiastical dignities, while clerics, renowned in life and doctrine, are made subject to them? Why is it that now the government of the Church is being entrusted preferably to men totally ignorant of spiritual matters, who from boyhood have devoted themselves to worldly and argumentative sciences, such as law, the study of which by the priests is prohibited?

"Is it not true that the Church is being governed according to the world and not rather contrary to the way of the world, for it is written, 'Be not conformed to this world'? There are many other abuses such as these. Open your eyes and see if any nunneries have today become prostitutes' houses. If any monasteries, consecrated to God, have become market places and taverns. If any cathedral churches have become dens of thieves and robbers. Make a careful examination and see if anywhere the priests have committed illicit intercourse, having concubines under the pretext of maidservants. Judge whether such a variety of images and pictures in the churches is suitable and whether it does not turn many simple people to a kind of idolatry. See if the large number and variety of religious orders is proper. Consider carefully if the military orders are carrying out their duty. Do they uphold the priesthood, guard the practices, the faith, the rules, and canons of the Fathers? Investigate whether it is beneficial that there should be such a large number of immunities and such granting of privileges to certain people and such complete exemption from the discipline of the ordinaries.

"Is it proper that, notwithstanding the excessive number of the saints, Urban V and Brigitta of Sweden, and Charles, Duke of Brittany, should be canonized? Is it seemly that the festivals of certain new saints should be celebrated more solemnly than those of the chief apostles? Is it right that the earlier and more stately churches of the saints should be deserted and in ruins, owing to the taxes exacted by the collectors or the cardinals, and then sometime afterwards new little chapels built to their memory, or, as it were, to their glory? Think whether it is right that the stupid should be in command, and the wise in subjection; that the youths should be the masters and the old men servants; that the ignorant should discuss the difficult questions and the wise not dare to speak; that grooms should be advanced to positions of preferment and students of the Scriptures disregarded. Inquire if any apocryphal scriptures, hymns, or prayers have been introduced in the passage of time, either through zeal or ignorance, to the detriment of the faith. And correct these. Settle the differences of opinion concerning matters such as the conception of the renowned Virgin and similar subjects. Reform unjust laws and customary practices.

"Is it not true that unjust laws are to be met with in Saxony, which elsewhere have been attacked by the theologians? And what practice of Christians could be more damnable than this: the clerics and the laity, prelates and princes, everywhere are so mad as to celebrate the most holy night of the Nativity of Christ in playing dice—not in contemplating the heavenly mysteries? Is it not true that in Livonia the practice has grown up of not giving the sacrament of the Eucharist to any of the peasants? Is it not true that here one may find that one husband has two wives living, and a matron several husbands? What need is there to mention more? Inquire of the bishops who come to the general council from any province about the conditions of the people and all the vicious practices and pernicious rites that have been introduced on some occasion or other into the churches.

"Because of these evils now mentioned and similar ones, reform all ranks of the Church in a general council or command that they be reformed in provincial councils, that thus the Church may, with the help of God, be restored and the house of God purged of all impurity, vice and error."

Nor were these severe criticisms of the central government of the Church limited to disgruntled university professors. The Bishop of Worms, Matthew of Cracow, penned a work in 1404 entitled *Concerning the Filth of the Roman Curia* in which he followed the general lines of Langenstein and Gelnhausen. He stresses the point that the granting of benefices by the Pope is in direct contradiction to ancient laws and urges that this right be restored to bishops. The Pope, he maintains, is the steward rather than the proprietor of the benefices and his right to dispose of them is circumscribed by canon law as well as by the very purpose of the benefices, the edification of the faithful. However evasive and subtle may be his explanation, whenever he grants benefices for the payment of money, he commits the sin of simony. Whoever either gives or receives an ecclesiastic office for money is guilty of serious sin. To reason that papal taxes and annates are necessary for the Pope's financial needs is equally open to question. In fact the neglect of convening councils is the very cause of the financial vicissitudes of the papacy. They are the just judgment of God because the Roman Church has determined to rule without reference to other Churches.

Dietrich of Niem, a former member of the Roman Curia, was no less critical of the institution he knew so well. In a dialogue that he published in 1410 entitled *Ways of Uniting and Reforming the Church (De Modis Uniendi ac Reformandi Ecclesiae)* he points out that neither reform nor reunion can possibly be achieved unless the authority of the Pope be limited. He begins the work by making a distinction between what he considers the Universal Church and the Apostolic Church:

"As you well know, the Universal Church is made up of various members of Greeks, Latins, and barbarians who believe in Christ, of men and women, of peasants and nobles, of poor and rich, constituting one body, which is called Catholic. The head of this body, the Universal Church, is Christ alone. The others, such as the Pope, the cardinals and prelates, the clerics, the kings and princes, and the common people, are the members, occupying their various positions. The Pope cannot and ought not to be called the head of this Church, but only the vicar of Christ, his viceregent on earth, this only while the key does not err. In this Church and in its faith every man can be saved, even if in the whole world a Pope cannot be found, the reason being that upon this Church alone has the faith of Christ been grounded, and to this Church alone has the power of binding and loosing been handed down. For suppose there were no Pope, but only one faithful person: even then the power of binding and loosing would be available. In this Church are the seven sacraments and our entire salvation. This Church has never been able to err, according to current law, never been able to fail, has never suffered schism, has never been stained by heresy, has never been able to be deceived or to deceive, and has never sinned.

"The other is called the Apostolic particular and private Church. It is included in the Catholic Church, and is made up of the Pope, the cardinals, the bishops, the prelates, and the churchmen. It is usually called the Roman Church, whose head is believed to be the Pope; the others are, however, included in it as superior and inferior members. This Church may err, and may have erred, may deceive and be deceived, may suffer schism and heresy and may even fail. This

Church is seen to be of far less authority than the Universal Church, as will be pointed out below. It embodies the instrumental and operative functions of the keys of the Universal Church and exercises its power of binding and loosing. It does not have and, in good conscience, cannot have greater authority or power than that which is granted to it by the Universal Church. These two Churches, therefore, differ as genus and species, since all of the Apostolic Church is Catholic, but not the other way around."

After discussing the historical foundations of the conciliar theory and indicating: "Ancient histories record that all schisms formerly arising in the Roman Curia were terminated through the Roman emperor and kings with their consent and support," he reiterates the basic theme of conciliarism: "A holy general council which represents the Universal Church cannot concede to any private individual, by whatever dignity he may be adorned, even to the Pope himself, the authority and power of granting dispensations from, or changing and interpreting in any other way the statutes of a holy council. Although on the face of it the rights of the canons may seem to say the opposite, the proof is nevertheless evident. The Universal, as has been said, is a power superior to the Pope."

The work then continues with a criticism of the fiscal abuses which he sees arising from an exaggerated notion of the papal office, and a recommendation of how these are to be abolished:

"Let the prelates of the Church arise and offer to God a sacrifice of justice, and let them deign to remove completely all these plunderings, thefts, and robberies of the Roman *Curia*. They cannot remain or be enjoined to the detriment and danger of the Universal Church, since they are contrary to the real nature of the Mystical Body of the Church, as has been said, and to every just order and harmful to all the spiritual blessings of the Church. In that very *Curia* you will find a thousand officials for the procuring of money from benefices, but probably you will not be able to seek out one for the preservation of virtue. There, every day the conversation is of castles, land, cities, different men of arms, and money. Rarely, if ever, is mention made of chastity, almsgiving, justice, faith, or holy living. Thus what used to be a spiritual court has become worldly, diabolical, tyrannical, worse in morals, even in civil actions, than any secular court.

"From thence proceed all these and many other evils such as heresies, schisms, and scandals and those all-engulfing reservations and financial constitutions which the Pope together with his cardinals have wished to be preserved and maintained. This taxation of churches and monasteries, the payment to the apostolic camera and the College of Cardinals of firstfruits, of the half of the income of the lesser benefices, and of money for obtaining in that court apostolic letters—even the general and special taxation and reservation of churches, monasteries, and benefices—for the greater part originated in the *Curia* while it remained in Avignon. For no cardinal was able to maintain the regal status of that time unless he were daily supported by great sums of money from whatsoever part these came. Further, should the Pope ask: What will be the purpose of this convocation? Is it not for the defense of the faith? Surely it cannot be for the restriction of my power, or for the bringing about of my resignation?

"O Pope, if you fully understand what I have said, if you are a Christian, if you have compassion, if you grieve for the common good of the Universal Church, (you will agree that) a council of Christians is to be called for the accomplishment of all these things. For if you are good, if you are holy as you are called, if you place any value upon holiness, you must fight to the death for the sake of justice. What justice can be greater, what can make your good life better, your holiness and your reputation greater, than that you, realizing that because of your papacy and because of your unfettered power the common good of the Universal Church is perishing and being destroyed, and the faith diminishing, the Church being cast under the feet of tyrants, her liberty suppressed, monasteries and churches destroyed, and the consciences of the faithful endangered—(what greater) than that you resign the papacy and allow your usurped power to be diminished?"

Niem then directs his attack on the Petrine commission: "The Pope cannot ordain or decree anything in the Church beyond what is and has been granted to him in the first place by Christ Himself and then by the Universal Church. We do not read that Christ conferred upon him the power to dispense and distribute benefices, dignities, bishoprics, farms, and lands, nor do we read that this was even done by Peter. He only handed on to him the particular power mentioned in Matt., ch. 16, which He bestowed even on the last bishop in the world, namely, 'Whatsoever you shall bind on earth will be bound also in heaven,' that is, by penance, and 'whatever you shall loose,' etc., that is, by absolution and indulgence, but only while the key does not err. However, in the course of time, as the devotion for the modern emperors and kings and the Christian faithful increased, churches sprang up in various parts of the world which in diverse ways were in need of government. Therefore certain powers of dispensing certain benefices were entrusted to the ordinaries, so that the patriarchs and cardinals were appointed by the Pope, the primates by the patriarchs, the archbishops by the primates, the bishops by the archbishops, the abbots and the other dignities by the ordinaries. Afterwards—this has been touched upon several times previously—as intolerable pomp, avarice, and ambition increased among the Pope and cardinals, they began little by little to reserve benefices.

"Since, because of the lack of councils, no one opposed their evil deeds, they have successively by open robbery reserved every benefice in the world, thus depriving without cause the bishops and ordinaries of their power, authority, constitutions, and rights, being unmindful that the occasion for wrongs ought not to proceed from the very source of rights. If the rights of each individual bishop are not preserved, what else happens than that the ecclesiastical order is frustrated? The Pope does not publish rights, nor say, 'I do not consider that an honor to me, in which I recognize that my brothers, the ecclesiastical prelates, lose their honor.' Why, therefore, in modern times does the Pope so strangely forget the ancient ways and attempt to usurp practically all the rights of his brothers by making a thousand regulations in his chancery for obtaining at all times ready money in abundance? 'Indeed when justice has been removed, kingdoms are nothing but great robberies. . . .'

"Judas once sold Christ for thirty pieces of silver, but our ecclesiastical superiors every day sell Christ and his Church a thousand times not merely for thirty pieces of silver but for hundreds and for thousands. And when they have sold (a benefice) to one and received the money, again they take it from him and offer it for sale to another. Those who receive and procure churches and benefices in this way and make payment for them according to the tenor of these constitutions, knowingly and deliberately commit simony, sin mortally, and are bound wholly to renounce those churches, benefices and positions so obtained and are disqualified from holding other benefices, as the Pope is not able to dispense, through simony, in the Church of God. . . .

"It is because the prelates of our time are dumb dogs, not able to bark, that these diseased constitutions and reservations strive to occupy the place of laws and rights to such an extent that it is horrible to say how many evils arise from them. For those who are of the households, of the cardinals, at one time murderers, uneducated, uncanonically ordained cooks, grooms, or muleteers, are through these chancery rules able to hold dignities, and canonries in cathedral churches; but those who are either Masters in Arts or Medicine or Bachelors in Canon or Civil Law, by no means are able to enjoy such grace. From this it is patently evident how, by these reservations, the virtuous and the educated are excluded but the ribald, the unlettered, the assertive, the evil-tempered, and the doers of evil are promoted. Now all who receive promotion under cover of these reservations are in a state of damnation and sons of death, unless they wish to do penance and completely relinquish the benefices which they have received in this way for 'they enter not by the gate but climb in some other way.' "

Niem concludes his work by listing recommendations which he feels will regenerate and reform the Church:

"Before everything else, let there be a reincorporation and reintegration of the members of the Universal Church. Let one who is approved and agreed upon by all, of praiseworthy life and respectable manner of living be appointed the one universal and undoubted shepherd in the way I have said.

"Also, let there be a certain limiting and moderating of the excessive power of this one shepherd, which has greatly deprived and diminished the rights of the other former prelates; a reformation and renewal of the ancient laws, decrees, and customary procedure of the primitive Church; such statutes and ordinances made concerning the Pope as well as the cardinals that hereafter schisms will no longer arise or continue.

"Then, make provision for monasteries, churches, and benefices with stipulation that they in no way be given *in commendam* to any cardinals or prelates unless they are poor, in order that they may reside personally in them as rectors with the charge of souls. Abolish the abuses, indeed the violence, the open robbery, and extortions of the apostolic camera and its diseased constitutions, censures, excommunications, and deprivations. Revoke the granting of *commendae,* the incorporating and uniting of churches, the erection of monasteries into parish churches, the holding of two or three incompatible benefices under the covering of dispensations, and the other abuses that have been committed during this time of schism, contrary to God and conscience. Provide for the universities lest in them doctors and masters be promoted (too) easily.

"Finally: let such persistent attention be brought to bear on all other matters that God may be glorified, the holy Universal Church pacified, and the entire world and Christendom saved, to His honor and praise who with the Father and the Holy Spirit lives and reigns blessed forever. Amen."

One cannot read the writings of this sincere man without recognizing his burning conviction that the private interests of the Curia had deprived the entire church of justice. In spite of the boldness of his attack, he died in 1418 as a canon of the church of St. Salvatius in Maastricht, unmolested by ecclesiastical authority.

The theologians of Paris, Langenstein and Gelnhausen, as well as Bishop Dietrich of Niem, are generally classified as publicists in the conciliar movement, that is, authors who voiced a more popular and, as it were, emotional appeal for a return to the practices of the early Church as a means of putting the house of the Lord in order. In a sense, all three represent the deep-rooted grievances of the German Church. One must not conclude, however, that the position of the papacy was entirely immune from attack either from the legists or from the Italians, who were generally extreme advocates of papalism.

Francesco Cardinal Zabarella, one of the outstanding Italian canonists of the period, comes to almost identical conclusions as do the Ultramontanes, in his efforts to heal the schism. In a little known tract entitled *On the Schism (De Schismate)*, he devised a system of conciliar government based upon earlier canonistic writings. His arguments were drawn from the glosses of the commentators on the decretals and revolved around the quasi vacancy of the papacy created by a duality of claimants. Should the Pope err or fall into heresy, it is the duty of the Church to elect a new Pope. Should a dual election occur, the true Pope is to be the one whom the universal consensus of the faithful acknowledges. Zabarella transposes the Aristotelian idea that the government of the state rests with the congregation of the citizens on the idea that the government of the Church is founded upon the congregation of the faithful. He points out that although canon law states that the Pope is superior to a council, the present situation involves not only the Pope; the very life of the Church is at stake, and hence a distinction must be made between the Pontiff and the Apostolic See. The Pope may err, but never the Apostolic See. The schism, since it is an obstacle to the faith itself, transcends ordinary legal procedures effecting the papacy. Because the present situation also involves a division between the Pope and the cardinals, the only solution lies in the voting of a general council representing the entire Church.

He supports his arguments by pointing out that this concept is neither a novel nor a revolutionary one, but one traceable to the Scriptures. The Apostolic Church gives evidence of conciliar rule in the synod of Jerusalem as described in the Acts of the Apostles. Nor, he proceeds, was Peter ever granted the plenitude of power, as the papalists claim. Only in subsequent centuries did Peter's successors, imitating the rule of the secular princes, fail to convoke periodic councils, and it is to this failure that much of the evil presently confronting the Church traces its source. Those who have erroneously ascribed this fullness of power to the Pope would have already destroyed the Church were it not for the assistance of the Holy Spirit.

For this Italian cardinal Christendom was one vast corporation over which the Pope exercised authority in the same way as the director of any other corporation. The Pope's authority was therefore a limited and derivative one whereas the plenitude of power attributed to him by the papalists resided in the whole Church, *tamquam in fundamento*. According to this view the Pope could only exercise those powers that the Church as a whole had conferred upon him, and he was never permitted to exercise any power to the detriment of this conferring body. His power and authority were limited by a general council not only in matters affecting faith and the condition of the Church but also in the matter of ordinary jurisdiction exercised by the episcopacy. Zabarella particularly attacked the Avignon tradition of centralization of ecclesiastical control. All bishops, as successors of the apostles, exercised a divinely ordained authority which the Pope was bound to respect.

Throughout his works on the schism, the Cardinal constantly stresses the fact that the general council alone has the authority to pass judgment on the Pope and to restore unity to the Church. Yet, as with the other conciliarists, he sees the dilemma that arises from the question of who shall summon the council. Keenly aware that the earlier councils of the Church were summoned by the emperors rather than by the Popes, he cites the particular example of the disputed election of Pope Symmachus in the fifth century, and of the council summoned by Theodoric to decide the true claimant. It is now, as in the past, the emperor who must convoke a council if Christendom is to be healed.

As events developed, it was the German Emperor Sigismund who finally set in motion the machinery that was to end the twenty-year schism by convoking a general council at Constance in 1414. It is interesting to note at this point that historically the eight ecumenical councils of antiquity were all summoned by the Roman and Byzantine emperors. For centuries historians have debated whether or not these early gatherings were convened with the previous assent of the Bishop of Rome; however, documentary evidence points quite clearly to the fact that they were not. Of the 220 bishops present at the first council held in Nicaea in 325, not a single one represented the West. The Council of Constantinople, convened by the emperor in 381, was not attended by the Pope or his representative. The Council of Ephesus, called by the Emperor Theodosius in 431, was also noticeably lacking in representation from Rome, although the Pope did send two bishops and a priest to the second session. In one of the largest assemblies of the early Church at Chalcedon in 451, the West was represented by only three bishops and two priests. The later recognition of these early councils by the papacy does not possess the character of formal approval, and in fact the ecumenical character of any council cannot be traced to comprehensive legislation on the part of the Popes.

The Council of Constance has been described as the watershed that separates the modern from the medieval world. Its conciliar decree, as the culmination of the medieval constitutionalism, has been termed the most revolutionary document in the history of the world. These claims are, perhaps, exaggerated, for conciliarism reached its apogee at the Council of Basel a generation later, and certainly the essential characteristics of the medieval period endured for another century. Nevertheless, the Council of Constance is remarkable in that it brought into open conflict the dissension on the theories of Church constitutionalism that had been smoldering for over a century and provided a testing ground for the reform ideas that reached even farther back into the Middle Ages. It was the first of three ecumenical councils which took place within the territory of the Holy Roman Empire, the other two being the Councils of Basel and Trent. It is significant that this Council witnessed the final flowering of that equilibrium between the sacerdotum and the imperium that had formed the framework of the moribund Christian republic. The Emperor Sigismund's aim to renovate the Empire and to restore it to the prestige it enjoyed under the Ottonian and Salian kings was evidenced in more than the theatrical enfeoffments that offered the assembled prelates relief from the boredom of the council proceedings. Some historians trace the origin of electoral Brandenburg and hence of modern Germany to the political activity of Sigismund at the Council.

For the Church historian, the Council is unique in that a day-by-day account of the proceedings, written by a layman, Ulrich von Richental, is still extant. It is thus possible to read the account of what happened here as it appeared to a layman who was actually present. The transformation that took place in the sleepy little town on Lake Constance, on the present border between Switzerland and Germany, is recorded with vivid detail. The influx of over seven thousand of Latin Christendom's great in a colorful panorama of feudal pageantry is set forth with all the enthusiasm of the medieval burgher. No detail is too small to escape the eye of citizen Richental—the fluctuating market prices, the housing problems, the splendid retinues of the great prelates, and the pathetic execution of John Huss.

In a proclamation addressed to the whole Christian world, on October 30, 1413, Sigismund, King of the Romans, announced that "the most reverend fathers in Christ, the lords Anthony, priest of the church of St. Cecilia, and Francis, deacon of SS. Cosmas and Damian, cardinals of the Holy Roman Church and legates of the Apostolic See, and the noble Manuel, knight of Constantinople, being possessed of full power from our most holy lord, Pope John XXIII, and his sacred college of lords as stated in their Apostolic brief, have conferred and consulted with us at length, and have finally chosen with our council and consent the city of Constance in the province of Mainz as the place for the assemblage of a general council." Failure on the part of the rival Popes to arbitrate the division of Christendom, in Rome in 1389 on the part of Boniface IX and at Avignon five years later on the part of Benedict XIII, had forced the cardinals of both obediences to call a council in Pisa in the spring of 1409. Since neither of the rival Popes would condescend to stand in judgment before the assembled cardinals and bishops, a new Pope, the Cretan Peter Filarghi, was elected and took the name of Alexander V. He was succeeded by Baldassare Cossa, and as Cardinal Fillastre remarks, "It is said that the election was corrupt, and certainly it was so as regards the merits of the man elected." The new Pope took the name John XXIII. After failing to convoke a new council in Rome, he was finally persuaded by Sigismund to summon an assembly at Constance. He was convinced that the new council would confirm him in office and depose the other two Popes. Events were to prove otherwise.

Since it had become apparent that the Pope would depend upon the vote of the "poverty-stricken" Italian episcopate for the confirmation of his position, the council fathers decided quickly that all voting would be conducted by nation rather than popular suffrage. Originally, four nations were to be represented, France, Italy, Spain, and Germany; however, the Spanish delegation did not arrive until 1416. The fathers also decided that all three Popes would either be deposed or would abdicate voluntarily. This decision provoked the secret flight of John XXIII from the city in March of 1415. It was John's hope that his sudden departure would wreck the entire council. Again the diplomacy of Sigismund in persuading the fathers to remain in Constance saved the day. However, the Pope's flight occasioned the final implementation of the conciliar theory. Despite opposition from the College of Cardinals and the Italian prelates, the northern nations formally declared the superiority of a council to the Pope in the celebrated decree *Haec Sancta*. The decree was officially proclaimed in the fifth session on April 6, 1415, and reads as follows: "This holy synod of Constance, constituting a general council, lawfully assembled to bring about the end of the present schism and the union and reformation of the Church of God in the Holy Spirit, in order that it may achieve more readily, safely, amply, and freely the union and reformation of the Church of God, does hereby ordain, ratify, enact, decree, and declare the following. First, it declares that being lawfully assembled in the Holy Spirit, constituting a general council and representing the Catholic Church militant, it has its power directly from Christ, and that all persons of whatever rank or dignity, even a Pope, are bound to obey it in matters relating to faith, and the end of the schism, and the *general reformation* of the Church of God in head and members."

A cursory examination of the famous document may shed some light on its more immediate significance. The expression "represent" as taken in context had neither a dogmatic nor a judicial meaning. Rather it strongly implied the immediacy, the vicarious presence of the Church in its more primitive sense as the assembly of the elect of God, the biblical *plebs sancta*. The extreme monarchical views of the papalists as fostered by Aegidius Romanus and Augustinus Triumphus, who identify the Pope with the Church, as well as the entirely spiritual notion of the Church more recently advocated by Wycliffe and Huss, were avoided in the text of the decree. Nor is the Church, as here envisioned, the purely democratic institution advocated by Marsilius of Padua and Occam. Although the Church is led by the Holy Spirit, in her external and organizational form she is directed by the assembled council with its episcopal makeup. The corporate nature of the Church as composed of body and members is explicitly stated. Perhaps the most important feature of this famous decree is that it not only emphasizes the importance of the episcopate, but that it also silently rules out the theory of the majority of the cardinals that they constituted the governing body of the Church. The authoritative pretenses of this aristocratic-oligarchical body had actually perpetuated and prolonged the schism, and they, perhaps more than the Pope, were the real obstacles to both reunion and reform. It is noteworthy that Cardinal Zabarella refused to read the proclamation and that the French Cardinal Pierre d'Ailly opposed it, as did most of the other cardinals. Consequently, it was officially announced to the assembly by the lowly Bishop of Posen. Thus, at least for the moment, the council had triumphed over both monarchical as well as oligarchical notions of the institutional Church.

Once the authoritative position of the council had been clarified it proceeded to the important issues that perturbed Christendom almost as much as the schism—the heresies of John Wycliffe and John Huss.

The case of John Wycliffe had been called to the attention of Pope Gregory XI before the outbreak of the schism. Wycliffe, a professor of theology at the University of Oxford, had advocated a complete overhaul of the nature of the Church. Tracing the ills of Christendom to the Church's preoccupation with wealth and temporal power, he based his reform upon a return to biblical simplicity, according authority to the Church only insofar as the Scriptures allow. The Church, as the assembly of all the predestined, is invisible, and hence formal membership in the external, institutional ecclesiastical body is no guarantee of salvation. In a revolutionary work, published in 1379 and entitled *On the Power of the Pope,* he disavowed the papacy as a divine institution. In the case of Peter, the primacy was a matter of character, faith and, above all, love for Christ. Therefore, as far as Peter's successors are concerned, wherever these qualities are lacking, the successors cannot be called Vicars of Christ. What distinguishes Wycliffe's doctrine from the radicalism of both Occam and Marsilius of Padua, upon whom he clearly depends for many of his ideas, is his rejection of the idea of transubstantiation. In one of his final works, *De Eucharistia,* written after he had been expelled from Oxford, he urges a return to the practices of the primitive Church and to the testimony of Augustine, Ambrose, and Anselm in exposing the idolatry of eucharistic worship. For Wycliffe, the consecrated elements of bread and wine were merely efficacious signs of the body and blood of Christ and to worship them was a return to paganism. Although some twenty-nine of his propositions were condemned by the English hierarchy and the Pope, Wycliffe died unmolested in his parish at Lutterworth in 1384. By that time his doctrine of the spiritual Church was refined to the point of teaching the priesthood of the laity and the refection of the sacramental system, as well as the denouncement of the Pope as the anti-Christ.

To what extent the Czech professor of theology, John Huss, was influenced by Wycliffe is still debated by historians. However by the time the Council was convened at Constance, John Huss, former rector of the University of Prague, had become the acknowledged leader of the Czech reform movement. His relentless attacks on the immorality and simony of the clergy and his doctrines on the spiritual nature of the Church had resulted in his excommunication. Although he shared many of the beliefs of Wycliffe, he did not, as the English theologian had done, deny the doctrine of transubstantiation.

Although there was an exchange of Wycliffian ideas between the Universities of Prague and Oxford as a result of the marriage joining Richard II with the daughter of the Emperor Wenzel, there is strong evidence that many ideas similar to those of the English reformer had been in ferment in Bohemia for several decades. A return to biblical Christianity and the abolition of the juridical Church had been advocated by Mathias of Janov and Conrad Waldhauser long before the works of Wycliffe were disseminated in Prague.

The vivid description of Huss's trial and execution at the Council of Constance offers an example of the tragic fate that awaited those who so openly attacked the abuses of the Church at this time. It shows also how deeply rooted, at least in the popular mind, was the opposition to freedom of conscience on the part of both the Church and the state. Here is how the citizen Richental describes it:

"When the Council came to Constance and began to hold sessions, it was decided to condemn the unbelief and extirpate the heresy in Bohemia. A summons was sent to Huss and Jerome to appear before this court, and they were put under excommunication. But they ignored the order and refused to obey the ban and sentence. So the Council wrote to King Wenzel of Bohemia, asking him to perform a service for the Christian faith and send the two to Constance. They requested our lord King of the Romans to write his brother about the matter. He did this and still they would not yield. Then, our lord, the Roman King, assured John Huss safe-conduct to and from the Council and gave him a sealed document to this effect. The King sent with him an escort.

"King Wenzel then sent him honorably to Constance. His escort consisted of Lord Wenzel of Duba and Lord Henry Latzenborck with more than thirty horsemen and two wagons. Huss had a wagon for himself and his chaplain and when they arrived at Constance, they stayed at the Pfister house on St. Paul's Street.

"Having rested for a day or two, Huss read Mass in his bedchamber near the living room and many people from the neighboring building came to see him. He said Mass the same way as our own clergy do. But when our lord Bishop, Bishop Otto of Constance, heard of it, he sent his vicar, Master John Tenger, and his official, Master Conrad Helye. The two envoys asked Huss why he was reading Mass, since he well knew that he had been under the Pope's ban for a long time and was now under the Council's ban. He answered that he recognized no ban and would celebrate Mass so long as he was in the state of grace. Then the Bishop forbade the people to hear his Mass.

"When he saw by this and other signs that they were planning to trap him, he attempted to escape on the Sunday of Oculi, after saying his Mass. He took a loaf of bread and a bottle of wine and hid in Latzenborck's wagon, for he knew that they were to leave the city and pick up hay and fodder that had been purchased in another village. But when the knights came to their dinner, they asked for Huss and when he could not be found Latzenborck informed the burgomaster and the alarm was sounded. The burgomaster immediately issued orders that the city gates should be closed and that everyone should be ready to set out in search of him on horseback and foot. But soon Huss was discovered and the people were told to go home.

"At the stroke of one in the afternoon, Lord Henry Latzenborck took Huss and his chaplain on horseback and brought them to the upper court of the palace, to see Pope John. Then Huss reminded them of the safe-conduct guarantee that he had received from the King and that therefore they should not put him into prison. Latzenborck replied: 'You must set yourself right, or you die of this.' Thereupon, Huss leaped from his horse and tried to hide among the Bohemians, for more than eighteen thousand people had come to see Huss brought before the Pope. When the Pope's guards, who were carrying silver staves and drums saw this, they caught and locked him in the palace, while letting his chaplain escape. While Huss was being held at the palace, our lord King wanted to help him for he felt that it would be a disgrace if the promise of safe-conduct were to be broken. But he was told by the learned men that there could be no law by which a heretic had safe-conduct and, when he heard their severity, he let it be. Then Huss was taken to a special monastery of the Preachers and closely guarded. And every day the most learned theologians went to him and tried to persuade him to abandon his wicked beliefs.

"Then, on Monday after the Holy Day of Easter, Jerome came secretly to Constance with one of his disciples and no one was aware of it in the multitude. He posted a placard, saying that he knew Master John Huss had taught and preached the truth and that their charges against him had been made out of enmity. If Huss were really guilty, he would not be defending him. As soon as he had posted the placard, he left the city. Then I and many others were asked where he had gone, but no one knew. Six days later, word was spread that he had lodged at Gutjar, on St. Paul's Street. In his panic to leave the city, he had left his sword and returned to the Bohemian forests where he intended to remain.

"But as one scholar seeks another, he went to the house of the parish priest who by chance had invited all the clergy to dinner, and Jerome went. At the dinner, he began to tell how he had been at the Council of Constance, which might well be called a school of Satan, the Devil, and a synagogue of all iniquity, and how he had documents in possession, sealed with seventy seals, to show that Master John Huss and he had passed excellent examination and no scholar could confute them. He spoke much evil of the Council, so that the clergy was terrified and decided secretly to inform the lord of the place. He answered that they must wait until the next morning. In the morning, the lord and his men took him prisoner and said: 'Master, yesterday you said something of the Council. I must find out if it is true or not and take you to Constance.' On the twenty-first day of Easter, he brought Jerome to Constance and put him under strong guard at the castle of Gottlieben in a special dungeon. Learned men rode out to see him and found him much more expert than Huss. So many learned men went to them both and they promised to abandon their wicked beliefs and denounce what they had taught. At this news, many were glad and lauds were rung.

"Then a session was held and it was decreed that they should be kept in Swabia, in whatever monastery or city they chose, and that each should have enough for his livelihood but that neither should ever return to Bohemia. Also they must write to Bohemia in their own hands and with their own seals that their preaching had been false and that no man should henceforth listen to it. All this they were quite willing to accept and abide by, except the order to write to Bohemia. They would not humiliate themselves. They said: 'We will not take this sin upon ourselves, to lock many away by our words from the Kingdom of Heaven whom we have brought hither by our teaching.' The account may all be read in Latin.

"I now return again to the Council and how it dealt with those two and what took place and how our lord King departed to go to other kings and lords and how he came back again. On the Saturday after St. Ulrich's day, July 8, 1415, there was a session. Our lord King was present and Duke Louis of Bavaria-Heidelberg and many other temporal princes and lords, and the session was held at six in the morning. Master John Huss of Bohemia, the heretic, was brought in and the reverend devout Master John Dachery, rector in divinity at the High School in Paris, preached to him of his wicked heresy. And Huss was confuted by holy divine teaching from Holy Writ, proving the articles which he preached and taught were truly false heresy and that the sentence passed on him was just.

"Since he was a consecrated priest, he was first degraded and his consecration stripped from him. Lord Nicholas, grandmaster and lord Archbishop of Milan, two cardinals, two bishops, and two bishops-elect stood up and dressed him in a priest's habit and took it off again with prayers and divested him of his office. But he only mocked at that. When that was done, they pronounced sentence upon him, that he was a heretic and must be punished for his iniquity. Then they delivered him over to the civil justices, requesting our lord King and the civil court not to put him to death but to keep him imprisoned.

"The King then said to Duke Louis: 'Since I am one who wields the temporal sword, take him, dear uncle, Duke Louis, our Elector of the Holy Roman Empire and High Lord Steward, and deal with him as a heretic in our stead.' Then Duke Louis called to Hans Hagen, the advocate of Constance, who was advocate on behalf of the Empire and there present, and said to him: 'Advocate, take him, under the joint sentence of us both, and burn him as a heretic.' The advocate then summoned the soldiers of the town council and the executioner to take him away to be burnt but forbade them to remove his gown, purse, money, knife, stockings and shoes. He wore two black coats of good cloth and a girdle with small ornaments on it and two knives in one sheath and a leather purse which might have contained something. He had a white miter on his head, on which two devils were painted, and between them was the word *'heresiarch,'* which means archbishop of all heretics.

"They led him out of Constance with more than a thousand armed men, and the princes and the lords also went armed. Two servants of Duke Louis guarded him, one on his right hand, and one on his left. He was not in fetters, for they walked close behind him, and they called me, Richental, to go with them. Before and behind him were the soldiers of the town council and they took him out through the Gelting Gate. Because of the immense throng that had gathered around them, they were forced to make a path through the meadow, by Richman's dower house. The men in armor grew still more numerous, about three thousand, in addition to the unarmed men and women. At the bridge by the Gelting Gate they had to keep back the mob and compel them to pass in file for fear that the bridge might collapse. They led him into the middle of the small outer field. On the way out, he uttered only the prayer: *'Jesu Christe, fili Dei Vivi, miserere mei.'* When he came to the outer field and saw the pyre, and the wood and the straw, he fell three times on his knees and cried aloud: *'Jesu Christe, fili Dei Vivi, qui passus es pro nobis, miserere me.'*

"They asked him if he wished to confess and he answered:

'I would gladly, but there is no space here.' For now he was surrounded by people. They made the ring wider, and then I asked him if he wished to confess. There was a priest there, called Lord Ulrich Schorand, who had authority from the Council and the bishop. I called this Lord Ulrich, and he came to Huss and said to him: 'Dear lord and master, if you will renounce the unbelief and heresy for which you must suffer, I will gladly hear your confession. But if you will not, you yourself know well that the spiritual law forbids us to perform any divine service for a heretic.' And Huss replied: 'I do not need it. I am no mortal sinner.' Then he began to preach in German, but Duke Louis would not permit that and ordered them to burn him. The executioner then quickly bound him in his gown to an upright stake, set a stool under his feet, piled wood and straw around him, scattered a little pitch over it, and lighted the fire. He began to cry out terribly but was soon burned.

"When he himself had been entirely burned, the miter on his head was still intact. The executioner knocked it down, and it burned also. Then the worst stench arose that one could smell, for Cardinal Pancratius had a mule that died of old age and was buried there, and when the heat went into the earth, the stench arose. All the ashes that were left, they threw into the Rhine."

The cruel execution of this sincere reformer, whose personal life was blameless and whose guaranteed safe-conduct was obviously violated, was to haunt would-be reformers for the remainder of the century. It was doubtless in the mind of Luther when he was summoned, also with an imperial grant of safe-conduct, to the Diet of Worms. More importantly it added fuel to the religious rebellion in Bohemia, and for decades to come central Europe was plunged into a bloody conflict between Slavic and German elements on the eastern boundaries of the Empire. Huss was immediately hailed as a martyr and a national hero and is still looked upon by many as the important precursor of the sixteenth-century Reformation. A century later Erasmus remarked that the Council may have burned Huss, but it had failed to conquer him. At Luther's request Huss's major writings were edited by Flacius Illyricus. Jerome of Prague was executed a year later and his heroism in the face of death drew the praise of the worldly humanist, Poggio, who described Jerome as one of the most outstanding individuals he had ever encountered.

The cause of reform was to suffer a not unsimilar fate.

The northern nations, convinced that Church unification without needed reform would frustrate the whole purpose of the Council, demanded that immediate legislation be enacted to cleanse the Church. They felt, and rightly so, that, were a new Pope elected, there was a strong possibility that he would postpone legislation in the direction of reform and turn instead to the restoration of the papal states. There also existed the well-grounded fear that the Italian prelates present, many of whom were exasperated by the duration of the Council, would return home once a new Pope was elected. A re-establishment of the papacy, more than reform, was indeed the overriding objective of the Latin episcopacy at Constance.

Due largely to the efforts of the English delegation, the Council finally agreed that the matter of reform should be given priority treatment. Yet the decrees that were issued proved to be, in the final analysis, of a compromising nature. In the thirty-ninth session of the Council, in October, 1417, five reform decrees were published, the most important of which was the decree *Frequens*. The text of this decree reads as follows: "The frequent holding of councils is the best method of cultivating the field of the Lord, for they root out the briars, thorns, and thistles of heresies, errors, and schisms, correct abuses, make crooked things to be straight, and prepare the Lord's vineyard for fruitfulness and rich fertility. Neglect of general councils sows the seeds of these evils, and encourages their growth. This truth is borne in upon us as we recall times past and survey the present. Therefore by perpetual edict we affirm and enact that, henceforth, general councils shall be held as follows: the first within the five years immediately following the end of the present council, the second within seven years from the end of the council next after this, and subsequently every ten years forever, in places which the Supreme Pontiff, a month before the end of the previous council, with the council's approval and consent, shall name, or failing him, the council itself shall appoint and designate. Thus there will always be a certain continuity. Either a council will be in session or one will be expected at the end of a fixed period. This period the Supreme Pontiff, on the advice of his brethren, the cardinals of the Holy Roman Church, may shorten, in case of emergency, but he may on no account prolong."

The decree then goes on to describe measures to be taken in case of a dual election of a Pope. It is manifestly the aim of this decree to establish within the framework of the

Church's constitution a permanent instrument of conciliar control. As a compromise, its purpose was to subject the central apparatus of the Church to periodically convened assemblies, which would keep in check the claims of the papacy as well as insure reform. In short, it gave the general council the same powers as those of a modern state. It envisioned the same type of parliamentary control over the Pope that was emerging in Europe in terms of the heads of the National states being subjected to popular sovereignty. No reform of the Church could be achieved unless this control system were incorporated into the government of the Church, for there was no other practical way to curtail the centralization of the papacy. That it would actually "cultivate the field of the Lord" and "make the crooked things to be straight" was, however, illusory.

July of 1417 had seen the deposition of Benedict XIII, Pedro de Luna, who, as the sole survivor of the fateful election of 1398, still claimed to be the legitimate Pope. Holding out in Peñíscola in what he termed Noah's ark, he finally passed away in May, 1423. Overcoming the opposition of the Cardinalate, who insisted *de jure* on the exclusive right to elect a new Pope, the Council ruled that the balloting should be effected by both nations and the cardinals, that is, by six representatives from each nation together with fifteen cardinals. Odo Colonna, a creation of Innocent VII and later a follower of John XXIII, was finally elected on November 10, 1417, and took the name of Martin V.

Any hopes that Martin would carry out his promise of reform were soon dissipated when it became apparent that his notion of reform was the re-establishment of the papal states. It is true that he did issue a number of general reform decrees the following March, but they had little effect upon the deeper abuses that were hastening the complete breakup of the Church in the West. Dealing, for the most part, with fiscal matters—exemptions, revenues, tithes and dispensations—Martin's decrees reflect the depth to which the papacy was still involved in financial affairs. The last decree, which recommended greater dignity in clerical garb, seemed a ridiculous climax to a four-year-old effort toward a renovation of the Church.

Martin was too much of a diplomat to openly revoke the decree voicing the superiority of the Council over the Pope. It would have been folly to have thus condemned the very body that had elected him. Nor can it be historically proven that the celebrated prohibition to appeal to a general council that Martin issued in the Consistory of May, 1418, was intended as anything more than an appellation against the Poles in their litigation with Falkenberg. The new Pope did, however, adhere to the decree *Frequens* and summoned a new council to meet in Pavia in 1423. On the grounds that it was too poorly attended, he moved it to Siena and then dissolved it. By the end of his pontificate, nepotism and political involvement with the territorial aims of his powerful family, the Colonnas, had distracted him from any real interest in the reform of the universal Church. Martin's successor, Eugene, was no better qualified to lead a reform of the Church.

Eugene's monastic upbringing—he had entered the Canons of St. Augustine at an early age—and the nepotism that launched his own career in the Church characterized his pontificate. Ill health and constant harassment from the condottiere of the Colonnas plagued the unfortunate man during the early years of his pontificate. Before his death Martin had summoned a Council to Basel, and one of Eugene's first acts was to confirm this convocation in keeping with *Frequens*. He attempted to follow his predecessor's advice of foiling the assembly by transferring the council to Bologna. The maneuver only antagonized the assembled prelates and, in its second session, the Council reiterated the superiority of the Council over the Pope. In its third session in April of 1432, it firmly informed the Pope that, unless he retracted his "act of dissolution," the Council itself would provide for the needs of the Church according to justice and the inspiration of the Holy Spirit. Threat of another schism became apparent when the Cardinal of Capranica, who had not been present at the election of Eugene, appealed to the Council, claiming that his absence from the conclave of 1431 invalidated the Pope's election. All but six of the cardinals abandoned the Pope and panic swept the Curia in Rome. To complicate matters, Sigismund sided with the fathers at Basel. Eugene attempted the stratagem of filling the Council with bishops of his own appointment, but this maneuver resulted only in a threat, on the part of the assembly, to depose the Pope if he did not agree to its decisions within two months.

The occupation of much of the papal states and finally the fall of Rome itself to the Pope's enemies forced Eugene to flee to Florence where he spent the next nine years. As Eugene's difficulties increased, the success of the Council in introducing reform measures became more and more apparent. In November of 1433 the Hussites were reconciled with the Compactata of Prague, under an agreement that allowed Communion under both species, free preaching of the Gospel, public penances, and the return of confiscated properties to the Church. The autonomy of the National Church for the Czechs was an accomplished fact. In December the Pope withdrew his decree of dissolution and declared Basel a legitimate assembly. The reform decrees, providing for such matters as regularly convened provincial and diocesan synods, liturgical changes, the restriction of papal interference in ecclesiastical appointments, and clerical concubinage, are a remarkable testimony to the spirit of renewal which characterized this last really ecumenical gathering of Western Christendom.

By autumn of 1433, seven cardinals, five archbishops and thirty-four bishops, as well as over three hundred representatives of religious orders and universities, were supporting the Council. A program of reform was not the sole occupation of the Council. Debates and discussions on Mariology led to the definition of the dogma of the Immaculate Conception, although the perennial enemies of this traditional medieval teaching, the Dominicans, termed the Council a synagogue of Satan whose firstborn was this definition. The Council also assumed many of the offices generally associated with the Curia: they sent their own ambassadors to various countries, settled litigations, and even granted dispensations from impediments to marriage.

Paradoxically enough, it was a question of reunion with the Oriental Church that caused the final break between the Council and the Pope. At Constance, representatives of the Eastern Church had pressed for reunion with the West: Manuel Chrysdoras, agent of the Byzantine Emperor in the West, had accompanied John XXIII to the Council in 1414. The fathers at Basel had been in negotiation with the Greeks for some time and had sent ambassadors to Constantinople in the fall of 1435, an action that resulted in an agreement between the Patriarch and the Emperor to send delegates to Basel. However, due to difficulties, many of them fiscal— Basel was finding it difficult to act as the supreme spiritual moderator of the West without adequate finances—and reports of deteriorating relations between the Pope and the Council finally convinced the Greeks to negotiate with the Pope rather than the representatives of Basel.

In offering a better plan for reconciliation, and thus winning the Greeks to his Council at Florence, Eugene finally undermined the prestige of the hostile fathers at Basel. There is little doubt that the extreme radicalism, the over-democratizing of the Church, and, above all, its threat to elect a new Pope were vital factors in the failure of Basel. More than anything else, the election of Amadeus of Savoy, a layman, as Felix V, the last antipope in the Church's history, turned the crowned heads of Europe away from the assembly. Yet, the triumph of the Pope over the conciliarists, as well as his reunion efforts with the Greeks, were Pyrrhic victories. In obtaining the support of the secular powers in Europe, the Pope initiated a policy of power politics that was soon to plunge the papacy into one of the darkest periods in its history. The establishment of a national state in Italy, dominated by the Vatican, became the ultimate goal of his successors. The reunion with the Greeks, although announced in July of 1439 with great rejoicing in the famous bull, *Laetentur Coeli,* proved a bitter disappointment. It was never accepted by the majority of the Greek clergy. Most of them preferred the power of the Turkish turban to the tiara of Rome. The tolerance offered by the former was in many respects more realistic than the dogmatic rigorism tendered by Rome. The bull of reunion was formally rejected by the Greek Patriarch Scholarius in 1472. Not only had the curialists failed to unite the Church, but for centuries thereafter the Council of Florence was held up by the Greeks as a model of papal oppression and of how not to heal the Church.

In the minds of many in the West, the Council was also a model of how not to reform the Church. Few historians will deny that Eugene's successful opposition to the Council of Basel checked the impetus for reform within the Church and contributed greatly to the growing conviction that if reform was to come, it would not come from the papacy.

Throughout the remainder of the century sporadic efforts to reform the Church through a general council continued. Unfortunately, however, the threat of convening a council independently of the Pope became a political weapon in the hands of papal adversaries. The Emperor Frederick III carried on a secret correspondence with Louis XI in an effort to force concessions from Sixtus IV. In 1461 the German princes at Nuremberg demanded that a new council be convened in order to reestablish the legislation of Constance and Basel which they rightly claimed had been cast aside. Podiebrad of Bohemia made several abortive attempts to convene a general council in 1460 and again in 1467 and was excommunicated for his efforts. In France the King continued to threaten the Pope with a council in 1476 when it was suggested that a council convene at Lyons. Again in 1478 the Pope was formally summoned by the French King to convene a council that would reform the Church and take measures for defense against the Turks. In March of 1482 Andrew Zamometič, a Dominican who had been named Archbishop of Kraniá, called upon the Christian princes of Europe to assemble in council in order to prevent the ruination of the Church by Sixtus IV. The Pope was accused of heresy, simony, shameful vices and of conspiring with the Sultan. Again in 1511, five members of the College of Cardinals in collusion with other members of the Sacred College convoked a council in Pisa. The King of France and the Emperor both threw in their support for this assembly. The Council however was dominated by the French and its radicalism lost it the support of the Emperor.

It is interesting to note that conciliarism played an important role in the English Reformation. One of the strongest weapons of Henry VIII in his propaganda campaign against Rome was the *Book of Nine Articles,* which declared that a general council was in the sense of the Council of Basel superior to the Pope and the court of last instance in matters of faith. During the period (1533-34) a treaty was concluded between England and Lübeck that bound both parties to repudiate the Bishop of Rome on the basis of conciliarism. Thomas More understood the Church as the *ecclesia omnium fidelium,* representing the multitude of Christian men, good and bad, forming a "common known," i.e., visible company on earth. For More the most important sign of a true Church was its unity. His views were anything but curialistic. The Church was not the Pope and his cardinals, but all Christian nations who were not separated from the common corps of Christendom. More held it possible that a Pope, for instance Clement VII, might be deposed by a council. In 1498, the reforming Dominican Savonarola undertook an attempt to summon a general council with the assistance of the Emperor in order to depose Alexander VI whom he declared was no longer a Christian and as such had ceased to be Pope. During the same year the King of Portugal threatened to convene a council in order to purge the papacy of nepotism, simony and immoral practices.

Perhaps the strongest call for a council that would succeed in reforming the Church where Constance and Basel had failed was voiced by men of the cloister. The Carthusian monk, Jacob of Jüteborg, wrote: "The reform councils have made it abundantly clear that the doctrine of the Pope's supremacy is only a shield behind which the Italians and their party shelter themselves from reform. Even if the Pope were a man of good will, the resistance which the people around him offer to reform is such that one may boldly affirm that a reform of the Church cannot be brought about by the Pope alone. It demands an effort by the whole Church gathered in council. Everything must be done to ensure the execution of *Frequens*. By this means the wound inflicted on the Church by Eugene IV may perhaps be healed." Two Camaldolese monks, Quirini and Giustiniani, presented Leo X at the Fifth Lateran with a *libellus* which thoroughly castigated the superstition of the clergy, the degradation of the monasteries and the inconsistencies of canon law, evils that they laid at the feet of the Popes who had surrounded themselves with money-making adulators and made Rome a center of shameful revelry. The only hope for a reform of the Church was to be found in a regularly convened council. The Pope's answer to the suggestion was to add to the prohibition of an appeal to a council a condemnation of the theory of conciliarism itself. To add insult to injury the Curia forced a re-issuing of the infamous bull of Boniface VIII, *Unam Sanctam*. At the same gathering the Augustinian monk, Aegidius of Viterbo, warned the cardinals that judgment must be made in the house of the Lord and that men must be changed by holiness rather than holiness altered by men. Six months after the unsuccessful Fifth Lateran Council terminated, another Augustinian monk in far-off Saxony was to prove that time had run out and papal indifference to reform would be paid for at a heavy price. Judgment was indeed being made in the house of the Lord.

4 Two reformers who failed

> "In the eyes of religion we are all the same. But humanly speaking Christ on earth is an Italian, and you are Italians. You cannot be led astray by patriotism as are those from the other side of the Alps."
>
> ST. CATHERINE OF SIENA

Two figures tower above all others in the century that witnessed the abortive attempt to reform the Church on a basis of conciliarism: the pious and practical chancellor of the University of Paris, Jean Gerson, and the subtle and versatile curial Cardinal, Nicholas of Cusa. An examination of their writings and basic doctrines can perhaps help to dispel the popular notion that all reform efforts during this period were aimed at preserving and protecting the rights and privileges of the Church rather than making the doctrine of Christ more acceptable to the changing structure of late medieval society. Neither has enjoyed the honor and prestige that the Church has granted to lesser personalities—Cusa because of his attack on the prevailing Aristotelian system, Gerson because of his identification with conciliarism and especially with Gallicanism. Yet there is little doubt that if the reforms advocated by these men had been considered, the tragedy of a separated Christendom might well have been avoided.

Unlike contemporary conciliarists, they probed more deeply into the spiritual nature of the Church as the *congregatio fidelium*, as the extension of Christ in time and eternity. More representative of the Augustinian tradition, they added a mystical dimension to the *Corpus Christianum*. Both were deeply influenced by the *thelogia negativa* of the neo-Platonistic and Victorine schools. Both envisioned God as capable of being known only through a higher form of cognition, beyond the rational categories of finite man. For both the Holy Spirit was the soul of the Church. Each had little use for the canon law defense of the rights of the papacy when these rights led to the destruction rather than the building up of universal Church.

Jean Gerson (Jean Charlier) was born in 1362 in the village of Gerson-les-Barby in the Diocese of Rheims, the eldest of twelve children, two of whom entered the service of the Church. After the usual preparation in Latin studies with the Benedictines in Rheims, he matriculated at the University of Paris, entering the College of Navarre in 1377. As a native of Champagne he was registered in the faculty of arts as a member of the French nation.

The College of Navarre, founded by the wife of Philip IV some sixty years before, had been the prototype of the collegiate movement within the universities that later developed at Oxford and Cambridge. Although not as famous as its sister institution, the Sorbonne, the College of Navarre, particularly its theological faculty, dominated the University of Paris, under whose direct patronage and government it functioned during the conciliar epoch.

It was, in a certain sense, the breeding ground of the *via moderna* or what is generally termed Occamism or nominalism. Gerson's education was greatly influenced by such well-known nominalists as Henry of Oyta, Pierre d'Ailly, and Henry Langenstein. Therefore, any attempt to evaluate him as a reformer must be made within the context of this extremely important theological movement of the late Middle Ages. Generally discredited as the root cause of the decadence in late medieval thought, nominalism has recently been shown to have been more a theological movement than a metaphysical or philosophical school. It was, perhaps, one of the most solvent elements in the breakdown of scholastic theology and has thus been variously described as "the utter corruption of Christian thought at the end of the Middle Ages," as a "caricature of the true content of Catholic truth," and as "the baleful influence of the Middle Ages."

In spite of whatever may have been its shortcomings as a system, it must be judged on the basis of its aims during the fourteenth and fifteenth centuries. These were to cleanse the concept of God and hence theology itself from the accretions of pagan philosophy. It was an attempt to stem the disruptive forces in the realm of religious thought resulting from the application of Greek metaphysics to the revealed truths of Christianity. To emphasize the absolute omnipotence of God, it stressed the impossibility of deductive theology (regardless of methods) to anthropomorphize the Almighty. It was in many respects an evangelical reaction against the influence on Christian thought of the necessitarian doctrine of Aristotle. As a movement, it led the way to a reform of theology conceived more as a discipline of faith based on tradition and more closely aligned to the tradition of the early Fathers. It was a reaction, therefore, against the attempt on the part of contemporary theologians to reduce the God of revelation to a sterile and isolated metaphysical principle, a prime mover, a remote first cause. As Gerson was to emphasize so often in his later attacks on scholasticism, there was too heavy a reliance on pagan philosophers. Such, he writes, was the error of Origen, who drank too freely from the golden cup of Babylon.

Hence as a movement it was characterized by a strong sense of the immediacy of the divine and the absolute sovereignty of God. As such it exhibited a strong element of individualism and voluntarism. Sin, for the nominalist, is not involved in the nature of man himself, but only in his relationship with God; for the nominalist there is no direct proportion between God's reward and the status of man. He is in no way obliged to reward man. He is, as Occam states it, no one's debtor. Man's will, not God's grace, determines an act's merit. The concern of the nominalists with this question of justification was in a certain sense intended to safe-guard the orthodoxy of St. Augustine, the *Doctor Gratiae*, from the inroads of Pelagianism let loose again by the Scotists and their followers. The preoccupation of Gerson with a more universal notion of the Church as expressed in his conciliarism and his concern for a more practical mysti-cism (especially for the laity) are reflections of the strong nominalistic elements in his reform theology.

Some of the more partisan of Gerson's Catholic biogra-phers have attempted to refurbish the image of the great the-ologian by stressing that although he may have been a nominalist in his philosophical outlook, he was definitely a realist, some would even say a Thomist, in his theological position. Such a judgment fails, in the first place, to perceive nominalism as a basically theological movement. It must be judged, therefore, not on a basis of philosophical or logical characteristics, but rather on its concept of God and reve-lation. In his attitude toward revelation Gerson exhibits one of its most prominent features, an emphasis upon Christ as a biblical figure. Like all nominalists he restricts Scripture to factual information. *"Omnia Christi actio instructio nostra est."* For Gerson a good theologian is a man versed in the Scriptures—*"theologum nominamus bonum virum in sacris*

litteris eruditum." Nor can Gerson be readmitted to the scholastic camp on a basis of his allowing the Dominicans to
return to the University of Paris during his chancellorship.
This he did, he tells us, not because he wished to justify
their aberrations but because, out of Christian charity, he
wished to give them a chance to prove themselves. As a
recent authority on late medieval theology (Oberman) has
clearly indicated, Gerson, like Pierre d'Ailly and William
Occam, attacks prevailing scholastic theology because of its
divisiveness. His criticism of party strife and disunity cannot be identified with a criticism of nominalism.

By the time he received his doctorate in theology in
1395, Gerson had risen to a position of prominence in the
university as well as in the service of the Church. In 1384,
he had been appointed Procurator of the French Nation and
two years later was sent to the papal court at Avignon, as a
member of a delegation petitioning the condemnation of the
Dominican, John Montesono. Ecclesiastical preferment was
assured him through the patronage of the Duke of Burgundy,
as he was appointed almoner to the Duke and given a benefice
in the collegiate church of St. Donation in Bruges in 1383.
In 1395, he succeeded Pierre d'Ailly as chancellor to the
university. Few men had taken over this important position
in a more turbulent period in its history. The schism had
forced the withdrawal of many of its faculty, particularly
those from the German Empire. The university itself had
become the sounding board of all Europe on the question
of solving the schism. In January of 1394, the faculty had
voted in favor of a plan whereby both claimants would
abdicate, a plan foiled by the obstinate refusal of Pedro de
Luna to step down from the papal throne.

Although Gerson later became one of the most outspoken
advocates of the conciliar theory, he remained aloof from
the political aspects of the question of papal obedience during this phase of the schism and directed his efforts toward
the reform of theology in the university itself. The reform
of education and the improvement of morals were to occupy
him more than any proposed reform of the institutional
Church. After a period of time in Bruges, during which he
became, as a pastor of souls, keenly aware of the crying
need for a reappraisal of the Church's pastoral apparatus, he
returned to the university convinced that no reform of morals
would be possible unless the educational methods of the
Church were radically altered.

He launched his attack upon the prevailing method of

teaching theology in two well-known documents, one addressed to the students of the College of Navarre and the other to the theological faculty of the university. He reiterated his aims in a series of sermons entitled *Against Vain Curiosity in Faith* delivered in 1402. The objective of both his letters of admonition to the students and faculties and of his preaching in the parish church of St. Jean en Brève in Paris was the same: a radical change in theological direction. He constantly complained of the lack of piety and unity in theological education. Entirely too much time is wasted, he says, on useless discussion that has absolutely no bearing on religious doctrine. More interested in the subtle and complicated terminology of scholasticism, teachers have lost the ability to express the simple truths of Christianity. Debates, rather than the acquisition of knowledge, have become the preoccupation of the faculty of theology which has become the laughing-stock of the other faculties. To counteract this parody of theology, he recommended that students of theology direct their interests to the more important aspects of revealed religion: the question of creation, the Incarnation, the sacraments, and the commandments. The prime requisite of all learning, he points out, is the virtue of humility. It is pride that has produced the lamentable state of present-day theology and that has goaded the philosophers and theologians on to a dangerous curiosity in matters of faith. For the student, one thing is necessary: a humble recognition of the inscrutability of the divine. "Do penance and believe in the Gospel" is the constant slogan that he repeats to his clerical audience.

The true function of philosophy is to demonstrate that there is one God, the ruler of all things, who has given being and life to all. An over-subtle investigation into matters concerning which the human mind, unaided, can have no true knowledge is the source of vanity. Like Occam, Gerson endeavors to liberate theology from man-made concepts by illustrating that both faith and metaphysical tradition demonstrate that God is completely unique in the highest form of uniqueness. There is no need, therefore, to divide His completely unified essence into metaphysical forms, quiddities, ideal reasons, or a thousand other figments of the imagination. Like Occam, he also feels that the Scotists have been the chief offenders in this matter. The followers of Scotus have already filled up so many codices with formalities, signs, and modalities that it would take a lifetime to read them, let alone understand them. For Gerson, an over-speculative interest is one of the chief dangers to Christianity. The Scotists in particular have attempted to analyze the Divine Being in terms derived purely from reason, and in so doing have cluttered up the purity of revelation with a bewildering array of merely logical terms. The complexity of the vocabulary required for such a process has rendered the practical explanation of the deposit of faith impossible.

To those who defend these constantly evolving systems by arguing that they are not appreciated because their critics have grown old and flabby in the art of rationalizing, Gerson answers that if a new type of logic is required to understand them, then why waste the time in teaching any method of logic? This insatiable quest for proposing the truths of revelation in increasingly complicated formulas gives rise to a constant search for new and different doctrines. It is an endless striving for novelty that leads to the neglect of what is essential for man's salvation. The innovators have, by introducing metaphysical forms or ideal reasons into the Deity, destroyed the free and simple God of faith. To borrow too heavily from paganism is contrary to the penitence and the humility that faith demands. For Gerson, one is not a theologian simply because he has mastered dialectics. In scorning the Bible and the Fathers of the Church, present-day theologians have failed to take cognizance of the warning of Augustine that theology, unlike philosophy, is not unrestricted. It has its own rules.

As practical recommendations, he urges that the teachers of theology avoid disputes on matters in which they are not grounded. They are urged also to refrain from branding as heretical doctrines that may be beyond their comprehension. Here again he strikes out at the members of the mendicant orders who he feels are the chief culprits in the disruption of theology. They do not teach according to the content of Scripture but according to the traditions of their own orders. The Franciscans are entirely enslaved to the erroneous doctrines of Scotus, and the Dominicans to the teachings of Aquinas. He recommends that one central school of theology be established, a single *studium generale* for the entire Church or at least for all of France, so that just as there is one faith, and one head in spiritual matters, so there may be one single theological font from which all may be uniformly nurtured.

The reform of the university was in a certain sense preliminary to the reform programs that Gerson envisioned for the clergy and the religious, as well as for the laity. Unlike the contemporary reformers Huss and Wycliffe, however, who tended to base their reforms upon inflammatory denunciations of the evil of the clergy, Gerson followed a more positive course by advocating an improvement of existing conditions. He begins with a much needed reform of the episcopacy, attacking the practice of appointing and consecrating unworthy bishops more interested in the temporal than the spiritual concerns of their diocese. He points to the usurpation of temporal power by ecclesiastics, and their occupation with mundane affairs, as one of the chief abuses in the hierarchy and therefore one reason for the lowly opinion in which the clergy are held.

In a sermon he delivered at the Diocesan Synod of Rheims in 1408, based on the theme of the good shepherd who lays down his life for his sheep, Gerson outlined a program whereby the prelate should fulfill his pastoral duty in the preaching of the Gospel. His function is threefold: to instruct the faithful, to set before them the example of a good life, and finally to rule his diocese directly and in a spirit of charity.

One of the abuses most frequently deplored by Gerson was that the bishops of his day had almost completely fallen away from their obligations to preach the word of God. There was a tendency among many of them to look upon instructing and exhorting the people as something fit only for members of religious orders and indigent theologians. He further urges that in every diocese special care be taken to train men properly for the ministry of preaching and that a compendium of instruction be drawn up to insure that a minimal knowledge of doctrine be given the people. As far as giving a good example, Gerson contends that they might begin by ridding themselves of all those faults that are contrary to the state of perfection. They must see to it that the poor and sick are taken care of, and their servants must avoid extorting money from the needy. There must be no sale of spiritual benefits. The number of censures attached to sins must be reduced, since the punishment of the faithful with excommunication is one of the abuses that scandalizes them most frequently.

Finally, he insists, there must be a reduction of whatever smacks of pomp and display. The chief virtue of the episcopal state was its humility. If the poor see the bishops following less lavish manners of life, they will be better able to bear their own poverty. Gerson's third episcopal reform is a reorganization of the government of the diocese. To insure a more worthy administration of the sacraments, great care should be exhibited in the selection of candidates and the practice of visitation of parishes should be reintroduced. This is the hinge upon which the reformation of the Church must swing; *"Hic est cardo totius reformationis ecclesiae."*

In his efforts to reform the lower clergy, Gerson stresses once again the need for humility and penance. "Do penance and believe in the Gospel" is his constant exhortation. He often compares the evil priest of his day to Judas Iscariot. It is true, he says, that Judas was the direct opposite of a good priest, yet there were too many clerics of his day who were enslaved by the same vice as Iscariot, especially those whose very entrance into this state was motivated by the hope of temporal gain. Any cleric who did not live up to the doctrine he preached betrayed Christ just as much as did Judas. They did worse, for Judas betrayed the mortal body of Christ but they betrayed the immortal body of Christ in profaning the Eucharist. Gerson explains the duty of doing penance in terms of the support the clergy receive from their benefactors.

Perhaps the most cogent argument in Gerson's plea for a reform of the secular clergy is found in the role he attributes to them in the hierarchical structure of the Church. Although he develops this theory within the context of explaining the preeminence of the secular clergy over the religious in the matter of perfection, it nevertheless demonstrates the importance he places upon the diocesan clergy as the instruments of reform. In championing the parish priests, Gerson begins with the principle that they are the immediate successors of the seventy-two disciples. Although this truth is not directly formulated in the Scriptures in so many words, it is implicitly contained in the Gospel narrative of the mission of the seventy-two, particularly in the tenth chapters of Matthew and Luke. It was thus understood and explained by the Fathers of the Church. In their commentaries, they showed how Christ, in sending out this group, wished to establish a permanent institution of evangelical laborers, distinct from the College of Apostles, but destined to work with them for the salvation of the kingdom. Christ likewise conferred hierarchical power on the group of aides whom He called "the Church," promising that whatever they should bind or loose on earth would be bound and loosed likewise in heaven. And, as early commentators say, not only the apostles but also the seventy-two disciples constituted this group. Hence it was that Pope Damasus declared that there were two orders among the disciples of Christ; the twelve and the seventy-two. Just as we recognize the major prelates as the successors of the apostles, so we must acknowledge the parish priests, the minor prelates, to be the successors of the seventy-two.

Hierarchy, therefore, he defines in the abstract as the power to further the divine work of salvation conferred by Christ on the apostles and disciples to the end of time. Considered under this aspect it includes a twofold power, the power over the real body of Christ, the Eucharist, and power over the Mystical Body of Christ, the Church. The second type of jurisdiction is held by the parish priests, and in spite of its inferiority, it is as truly an essential part of the hierarchy as the episcopacy or even the papacy. The jurisdiction is held by the parish priests as "ordinary" in the fullest sense of the word. Like bishops, they, too, have been mystically wed to the Church and are by divine right the spiritual shepherds of the children she confines to their care. Between them and their flock exists a mutual obligation, on the one side of service and self-sacrifice, on the other of respect and obedience. Chief among the duties which Christ imposes upon them is that of preaching and hearing the confessions of their parishioners. The parish priest receives his commission to preach from the Gospel, not from papal bulls.

By reason of their divine institution, their fundamental rights are inviolable. That is why, for instance, ecclesiastical superiors must be extremely prudent in conferring jurisdiction on religious, monks and friars. Still another consequence of their divine foundation is the right to deliberative suffrage in general councils. This, too, is evident since if they belong to the essential hierarchy of the Church, *a fortiori*, they have a right to participate in the assembly which represents the Universal Church.

Gerson argues that, therefore, the secular clergy are superior to the members of religious orders whose state is not properly called a state of perfection, nor a life of perfection, but rather a way of perfection. A clearer understanding of Gerson's attitude on this point is illustrated by his conduct during the revolt against the *Bulla Mendicantium,* issued in 1409 by Pope Alexander V. John Gorel, a Franciscan, had asserted that those entrusted with the care of souls have as such no right to preach or hear confessions, because their office was instituted only by ecclesiastical authority and not by Christ; on the contrary, these works are proper and essential to the vocation of the Friars inasmuch as they were obliged by rule to perform them—and the Rule confers a

more basic right than the ordinances of Pope Dionysius instituting the parochial office. He solicited a bull in favor of
the mendicants from Alexander V who published the
Regnans in Excelsis in which he defended the religious orders
and imposed canonical penalties of the severest kind on
those who would continue to defend a contrary doctrine.
The University of Paris was commissioned to execute the
bull but refused to do so, saying that it had been extorted
from the Pope without the knowledge and consent of his
cardinals. Gerson, leading the opposition, delivered a sermon at the university summarizing his views. The rights of
the parish priest, he declared, are as inalienable as those of
bishops, because both offices are of divine institution. The
office of parish priest is an essential element in the constitution of the Church; therefore, prescriptions even of the
Holy See which would tend to curtail its primary function
in favor of any humanly instituted societies are necessarily
devoid of force.

Although Gerson admired the efforts of certain religious
toward spiritual perfection, he insisted that the religious orders are not, properly speaking, a state of perfection, and
that the title "religious" belongs to them only in a secondary
or applied sense. His reason for opposing the word "religious"
as applied to the regular clergy was based on the obvious
fact that there is only one true religion—that founded by
Jesus Christ. Gerson later developed this idea in his tract
On Religious Perfection, where he protests vigorously against
the Dominican Garbon's claim that vows of religion are the
fullest expression of Christianity. Written at Constance, it
takes a strong stand against the public profession of the
three vows, which Garbon insists are the essential elements
of Christian perfection. Here Gerson explicitly states that
the Christian religion should alone and by itself be properly
termed religion. (*"Sola Religio Christiana est proprie, vere et
autonomatice dicenda Religio"*). The Christian religion in
no way obliges observance of the evangelical counsels and
one can observe its mandates most perfectly without vows.

Controversies on the merits of religious life were distasteful
to him because they smacked of the hypocritical wranglings
associated with the Pharisees. It would be far better, he said,
for religious and parish priests to help one another carry
their burdens, instead of quarreling about who is in the
more perfect state. After all, whoever is in the superior state
of perfection is not by that fact himself more perfect; we
shall be judged not on the excellence of the vocation we

followed, but on our personal sanctity. Finally, every Christian, whether priest, religious, or layman, is in a state of perfection by virtue of the fact that he has embraced the Catholic religion.

We have already seen the proposed change in theology and contemporary methodology at the university which Gerson regarded as the fundamental means of reform in this area. What the ecclesiastics and religious of his day needed in addition to improved education, however, was an intense interior life. He was keenly aware that only when its clerics were men of virtue could the Church hope to eradicate the abuses which dishonored the clergy and precluded their influence on the faithful. It was to this end that he inaugurated a series of courses in which he treated the nature and excellence of contemplation not only from the speculative but likewise from the practical viewpoint. He stressed that true perfection is attained when both the contemplative and the active life are conjoined. For a priest who joins his solicitude for the temporal needs of the faithful to his mental prayer will double his existence. The excellence of this is to be seen in the fact that it more closely resembles the life of Christ on earth. He went about, the Scriptures say, not only preaching the Kingdom of God, but also healing the sick and doing good; but at night He would separate Himself from the crowd and spend the hours in prayer. Since Christ came to give man the example of how to live, it is evident that a life modeled directly on His will be the most perfect.

As with the reform of the clergy, the call to repentance was uppermost in his exhortation to the laity. "Do penance and believe in the Gospel" is the recurring theme of his sermons, and the sum total of all his preaching is the love of God. Without the love of God all exterior acts of devotion, all penances and visions are as nothing. Knowledge itself is dangerous unless it is prompted by love. In his estimation, the simple country people stood on a higher level of spirituality than the scholars. To all he held out the idea of the two standards, the love of God and the love of the world. He besought all to turn with full heart to God, and he assured them that they had only to ask for mercy to obtain it.

The means for spiritual advancement that he suggests are prayer, self-study, humility, and submission to the guidance of a spiritual director. Prayer would lead them to the contemplation of the life of Christ and in His sufferings they would find solace from their own feelings. Self-scrutiny was to make them distrust their own ability and to act as a check over the desires of the heart and the demands of the senses.

In order to present the layman with a simple means of attaining a closer union with God, Gerson wrote *The Mountain of Contemplation*. Composed in 1397, it was perhaps the most typical and certainly one of the most widely read of Gerson's mystical works. He begins by recalling how Denys reminded Timothy that none of those who were inexperienced, that is, who were swollen with philosophy, who led bad lives, and who attacked what they knew nothing about, could come to a knowledge of mysticism, but simple people could, if they had faith, rise to a union with God. The tract is composed of forty-five short chapters and contains a prologue wherein Gerson distinguishes two tendencies in the mystical life, the speculative and the affective, and points out that whereas knowledge is necessary to the ascent, it is, above all, humility that must be the basis of the realization of contemplation. Love, not reason, opens the door to contemplation. And the simple soul that accepts the truths of faith and seeks to please God has a better chance of arriving at a knowledge of God's nature than the scholar who, without a grain of affection, seeks to delve into the mystery of the divine. Those who wish to attain the heights of the mountain of contemplation must first of all give up worldly affection. They must be content to progress slowly and by stages. A three-fold mode of progress is necessary: penance, solitude, and perseverance. None can prepare himself for this journey until he has been purged of all worldly and carnal affections.

To illustrate the complete abandonment that must characterize the soul seeking to lose itself in the divine love, Gerson draws the picture of the man of the world pulled into the throes of an illicit love affair, how his whole being is drawn into the thought of his beloved. He goes on to tell how he loses self-respect, becomes deaf to advice and the threats of future judgment. Waking or sleeping he has no other concern and nothing can keep him from his love. Just as this worldly love dominates his every concern, even that of God Himself, so must the true love of God possess the soul. Anyone with such a love may be said to be dead to the world because it no longer has any charm for him. Following this duel between the love of the world and the love of God the soul must seek the silence and solitude that even a break with the material world would not deter. It is an inner purgation that will lead the soul to higher contemplation because there is a gradual disillusionment with itself.

In his works on practical theology Gerson constantly keeps in check any tendency to put too much value upon the external, *ex opere operato,* element of devotion. His mysticism was something that would not lead to physical raptures or extraordinary favors, but would lead to what all Christians are seeking: the making of themselves pleasing to God. Just as Gerson holds that perfection is open to all regardless of their status in the hierarchical structure of the Church, he insists that mystical union is not the unique prerogative of the learned but open to everyone. Humility and obedience are the indications of the call to a closer union with God. Private devotion is not to receive a priority above one's station in life. Emotional and intellectual heresy are to be thus avoided. A middle way between the hidden secrets of the contemplative and the purely disciplinary code of the theologians is the ideal to be striven for. Here again, as in his attack on formalism in philosophy, Gerson demonstrates that there is no incompatibility between nominalism and mysticism. Mystical theology is for him superior to scholastic theology because the latter theologizes with the mouth rather than with the heart.

One of the difficulties in attempting to evaluate the reform work of Gerson is that his appreciation for the degradation of the Church of his day was so profound that his efforts extend into the entire structure with a profundity that defies categorizing. His reform of theology, his popularization of mysticism, his struggle to recover and secure Church unity, his constructive moralizing sermons, all have such a character of discretion and prudence and such an element of circumspection as to defy analysis. The zeal that characterized his entire reform program was modified time and time again by a deep appreciation of human weakness. When appraising the weakness of the clergy regarding celibacy, he defends them rather than expose them to the tyranny of the money-seeking agents of the bishop. He once wrote the Archbishop of Rheims that nowhere under heaven was there greater tyranny than that which flourished in certain curial ecclesiastics and especially those in Rheims. A reform of the Church for Gerson consists less in removal of individual incidents of misuse of ecclesiastical authority than in the suppression of every legal enactment which supports these misuses, especially when they are of such a nature that the change of time and custom has rendered them untenable. The neglect of the study of the Scriptures had, in the eyes of the Chancellor, brought about a preponderance of legislation. A belief that all power was based upon temporal possession and jurisdiction had occasioned an almost complete secularization of the Church.

In order to explain what ecclesiastical legislation was necessary for salvation and what was not, Gerson composed one of his most famous works, *On the Spiritual Life of the Soul*. The book attempts to delineate that law whose transgression destroys the spiritual life given in baptism by the Holy Spirit and makes a man unworthy of eternal life. He feels that ignorance in this matter is the cause of many disturbances in both the ecclesiastical and the temporal areas. This he blames on the excessive zeal of the canonists who have made of the light yoke of Christ and the law of liberty, a yoke of iron and a heavy burden pressing upon the necks of the Christians. The law of the Gospel had been replaced with a multiplicity of decrees and regulations entirely foreign to the mind of Christ. Christ had aimed solely at elucidating those rules that were necessary for salvation. The consequence of this proliferation of man-made laws was that many laws that were purely ecclesiastical came to be looked upon as divine legislation and as having the same cogency as Scripture. For many the inability to obey all of them led either to despair or to a complete rejection of all law. There is a certain irony in his remark that if such a superman as Adam, who had but one single command to obey, failed to fulfill it, how shall we who are placed among innumerable such commands escape. The accumulation of non-pertinent legislation, equated with divine law, has the dire effect of reducing divine law itself to ridicule. The poor Christian is so hemmed in and surrounded by these unreasonable laws that he loses hope of ever fulfilling them and is lost in a labyrinth of confusion. The identification of spiritual and temporal legislation has been, in the mind of Gerson, the root cause of the confusion reigning in the Church. It was chiefly responsible for the schism and the separation of the Greeks from the Church. The punishments leveled against violations of man-made laws had increased in direct proportion to the lessening of respect for divine law. To remedy this situation, Gerson proposes a new evaluation of the nature of law. Ecclesiastical regulations concerned with temporalities are not, properly speaking, spiritual laws. A law cannot be called divine simply because it is deduced from the principles of divine law. Hence it is a mistake to suppose that every precept of Scripture is necessarily a part of divine law. The only scriptural statements which can be pronounced with certainty as being divine law are those which must be believed in order to attain the goal of beatification.

With regard to ecclesiastical laws, he distinguishes the legislation of the apostles and immediate disciples of Christ, and that of those who come after them in apostolic succession. There is ample evidence that the authority of the primitive Church was greater than the power of Pope or council, and hence it is folly for the canonists and the papalists to attempt to change these traditions. The superior inspiration of the primitive Church seems to form the basis of Gerson's proposals for a change in the constitution of the Church. The foundation for his conciliarism is in a certain sense based upon the conviction that canon law in itself has no inseparable connection with divine law and may, therefore, like any other part of positive law, be modified and superseded when circumstances require. This is the very root of his idea of reform. For Gerson, the basis of Church unity is found in the perfectibility of the Church through the ecumenical council, since the council exhibits an instinctive creativeness in preserving itself.

In a tract entitled *On the Unity of the Church,* the body of which he composed in 1409, he stresses the notion of equity or interpretive law as a means of reforming and uniting the Church. As Gerson views it, not the Pope but Christ is the true head of the Church. "Essentially the unity of the Church always remains in Christ, her spouse, for Christ is the Head of the Church in whom all are one according to St. Paul. If she does not have a vicar, as when he is dead, corporally or civilly, or because it is not credibly to be expected that obedience will be conferred any longer on him or his successors by Christians, then the Church, by divine as well as natural law, which no positive law properly hinders, is able to assemble in a general council representing her in order to procure for herself one undoubted vicar. This action can be taken not only on the authority of the cardinals, but even with the help and cooperation of any prince or other Christian. For the Mystical Body of the Church, perfectly established by Christ, has, no less than any civil, mystical, or truly natural body, the right and power to procure its own union. It is not in accordance with the absolute and immutable law, divine or natural, that the Church should be unable to assemble or unite without the

Pope, or anyone of a particular rank or association, when death or error may occur at any time. Hence right order and the law of reason demand at least some kind of vicarious leadership, although it should not be in any way based on canon law or papal decretals."

He argues further: "The unity of the Church in one undoubted vicar of Christ, who is to a certain extent unessential and mutable, must in no way be hindered or deferred on account of the contention of two men or their supporters over the papacy if these seek to maintain their position on the strength of charges drawn from positive law, and on various pleas and complaints, such as that they have suffered deprivation, and must, therefore, before all else be reinstated. To aid the council it is expedient that churchmen should forget what is behind and strain forward to what lies ahead. For according to Augustine, greater attention should be given to finding out how the Church is to be delivered from this exceedingly deep pit than how and through whom it fell into it."

Accumulated laws must not be a stumbling block to the council and must not defeat the ends they were created to serve. The unity of the Church in one vicar of Christ does not require for its attainment a literal observance of the outward terms of positive law, or of ordinary processes in summonses, accusations, denunciations, or similar matter. A general council may proceed summarily, and with the good and important principle of equity. It shall have sufficient judicial authority to interpret all positive laws, to adapt them for the sake of accomplishing union more speedily and more advantageously, and, if need be, to abandon them if they run contrary to the peace and well-being of the Church.

As far as the authority of the Pope is concerned, Gerson explains its monarchical nature in terms of its historical development. The Pope's powers were originally given to all the apostles and disciples, but as the number of the faithful increased, the power was ceded to the Pope with the consent of the faithful for the sake of a more convenient rule. However it is a mistake to conclude that the papacy is above other authority. The Pope or the cardinals may err, but the Church, and the council as its representative, remain the infallible repositories of truth.

As head of the French delegation at Constance, Gerson was looked upon, after Sigismund, of course, as the great light of the Council. Certainly he was its most respected orator. Unhappily his identification with the French crown in the Burgundian-Armagnac dispute and in the condemnation of the tyrannicide theories of the Franciscan Petit lessened his influence at the Council. His involvement in the litigation between the Poles and the Teutonic Knights, and his defense of the Brethren of the Common Life against the Dominican Grabon also served to soon alienate him from many of his earlier supporters.

The final position of Gerson on the limitation of papal power is expressed in an appeal he wrote to Pope Martin V. Soon after his election he pleaded for recognition of the conciliar theory which was responsible for the Pope's election and stated that no individual, not even the Pope, could declare any doctrine to be heretical. Papal decisions in matters of faith are neither permanent nor irrevocable. They are in fact no different than the opinions of other theologians in so far as they bind under pain of sin. However, out of respect for the papacy, the faithful should respect such decisions unless they are contrary to the Scripture or the decrees of a council.

Gerson never returned to Paris. His attack on the House of Burgundy and the uprising against the Dauphin made residence in the city where he had spent the greater part of his life unsafe. After a brief sojourn in Germany and Austria, he returned to Lyons. There, after composing a number of works on mystical theology, he passed away in 1429.

Few writers influenced the reform of the century more than this chancellor of the University of Paris. Luther considered him to be a greater help in the spiritual realm than such saints as Jerome, Augustine, Ambrose and Aquinas. He referred to Gerson as the "great comforter" and attributed to him more than to any other spiritual writer the gift of calming troubled consciences. Gerson's approach to the problem of spiritual temptations, and his sober distinction between what is mortal and what is venial sin were to the mind of Luther the chief reasons for his condemnation by the papacy. Both men were preoccupied with a deep desire to gain assurance of their final salvation; both were convinced that it did not rest with good works. Each believed in the primacy of faith in Christ's salvific act. In his denunciation of the flagellants at Constance Gerson voiced what Luther was to make the basis of his theology—the gratuity and uniqueness of Christ's salvation, *"Christus autem ex gratia sua voluit nos misericorditer salvere per sanguinem suum* semel *effusum."*

Melanchthon refers to him in both the *Confessio Augustana*

and the *Apology*. Erasmus, who calls him *"doctor expertissimus,"* quotes him extensively in his works, particularly in his *Enchiridion* and his *Ichthuophagia*. The Franciscan, Gaspar Schatzgeyer, was dependent upon him for his doctrine of Christian liberty, and the Catholic apologist, Georg Witzel, admired him to the point of calling himself the German Gerson. John Geiler, often called the Savonarola of Germany, frankly admitted his dependence upon the writings of the great Chancellor in the reforms that he attempted to introduce into the diocese of Strasbourg at the close of the fifteenth century. John Wimpfling, rector of the University of Heidelberg on the eve of the Reformation, spoke of him as the man who had shown Popes and prelates how to reform the Church by following a *via media*. His was a method that made the road to salvation accessible to all, avoiding the pitfalls of blind assumptions and making light the yoke of Christ (*Jugum Domini leve esse contendit*). It is significant that nine complete editions of Gerson's works were published at Cologne, Strasbourg, Basel, and Paris between 1483 and 1521.

Often hailed as the inaugurator of modern philosophical thought, Nicholas of Cusa, as a metaphysician, a scientist, and a papal diplomat, stands out among his contemporaries as probably the most original thinker of the fifteenth century. Even the vast periphery of his scientific and philosophical achievements astounds the modern reader. As a philosopher, astronomer, physicist, and humanist, he represents medieval man already plunged into the social, economic, and religious flux that was his century. As a metaphysician he perfected an intellectual system whose profundity and subtlety provides a unique relationship to both the philosophy of the Middle Ages and that of modern times. His emphasis on the quantitative rather than the qualitative, on the transrational rather than the rational, mark him as a pioneer in the breakthrough that was to produce the prevailing ideologies of man in the western world. As an astronomer he anticipated the discoveries of Copernicus and set the stage for the tremendous reappraisal of the universe that was to culminate in the discoveries of Kepler and Newton. The impetus theory as well as the entire field of dynamics was explored by him. Von Humboldt, like Regiomontanus and Campanella before him, found in him a precursor in exposing the new cosmology. Few of the advocates of religious tolerance in the sixteenth century escaped his influence. Bodin, Postel, Costellio, and d'Etaples all indicate a dependence upon him for their theories on religious pluralism.

Nicholas of Cusa occupies a unique position in the intellectual history of late medieval society. Not only his social and political works but also his philosophical writings give evidence of trends that on the one hand demonstrate his scholastic background and on the other indicate his emancipation from the metaphysical necessitarianism that was so much a part of the latter. The diversity of his thought does not, however, result in mere ambiguity or contrast, but rather it gives rise to a system which, while retaining the inner consistency and rigor of the schoolmen, far surpasses them in cosmological and anthropological perspective. He was perhaps more than any other in his age the symbol of that grand endeavor that sought a conception of the universe that would allow a reharmonization of the discordancies that heralded the modern era. Yet it was as a reformer, a man dedicated to the renewal of the Church, a renewal that was with and through Christ, that Cusa left his deepest marks on the pages of history.

Born in the Mosel Valley in 1401, he received his early education at the hands of the Brothers of the Common Life in Deventer, and later studied at the universities of Heidelberg and Padua. After receiving a degree in canon law from the latter university in 1423, he continued his studies at the University of Cologne until his appointment to the entourage of Cardinal Giordano Orsini, papal legate in Cologne. The appointment launched the young cleric into a career of ecclesiastical politics which was to make him one of the most important figures in the Church's futile efforts toward reform during the fourth and fifth decades of the fifteenth century.

Sent to the Council of Basel as a legal representative of Ulrich von Mandensheid in a litigation involving the bishopric of Trier, he soon attracted the attention of all Europe through the publication of his first great reformatory work *De Concordantia Catholica*. This remarkable document has often been described as the most original product of the conciliar theory. In reading the *Concordantia* one immediately detects the Platonic influence so strong in his writings. Cusa was one of the first northern Europeans to have a firsthand knowledge of Platonic philosophy.

As Plato desired the reform of the actual Athenian city-state according to a pattern laid up in heaven, so Nicholas of Cusa sought a reform of the Church in the light of the celestial model. Following the Pseudo-Dionysius, Cusa envisions the Church as a divine cosmos from whose Head,

Christ, grace flows into humanity through the channel of the hierarchy. The earthly Church, the ecclesiastical body, must incarnate the heavenly pattern if she is to be worthy of the bride without spot or wrinkle. The pattern laid up in heaven is the very nature of the Godhead itself: diversity in unity or triune unity. In the created order, but still in the realm of spirit, the angelic hierarchy is modeled upon this pattern. The angelic order is therefore the norm for the hierarchical structure of the Church on earth. The Church is, as it were, the epiphany of the invisible order. The Church itself is the triune unity: the Church triumphant, the Church sleeping, and the Church militant. She consists of sacrament, priesthood, and faithful, and each individual within her reflects this theme of triangular diversity within unity, for hers is a composite of spirit, soul, and body.

The hierarchy is the depository of the priesthood in which the Pope, the bishops, and even simple priests participate. This must be considered against the fact that men are by nature free, and hence it is only with their consent that ecclesiastical laws may demand their obedience. For if by nature men are equally strong and equally free, the true and determined power of one over the others, the ruler having equal natural power, could be set up only by the choice and consent of the others, just as a law also is set up by consent. It is in view of this consent of the subordinates that the bishop represents his diocese and the council, the entire Church.

In outlining the chief elements of the Church's constitution, he emphasizes the principle that the Pope and the bishops are equally successors of Peter, and are therefore invested by divine right which is essentially the same authority. The gradation of powers in the Church refers to their use or execution, and this gradation is the result of an enactment of positive law, although it is accompanied by divine concurrence. The authority of the Pope therefore rests not only upon Christ's institution when He constituted Peter as the principle of unity, but likewise on a transmission by the Church embodied in the cardinals who elect the Pope. The Pope therefore may not properly be called a universal bishop. Like Peter, his primacy is that of an administrator. He takes precedence over the others for the good of the whole body. Aware of the falsity of the Donation of Constantine, the forgery upon which many of the legists still based their extreme claims, Cusa feels that the doctrine of the Pope's plenitude of power over the entire Church is a discovery of base adulators. Supreme power, as well as infallibility, belongs to the general council, which in turn derives its authority directly from Christ, while it represents at the same time the unanimous agreement of all Christians. Hence the council is above the Pope and may depose him, or reform him, not only when he falls into heresy, but for any other misdemeanor.

Although the council must be convened by the Pope, it is not dependent upon him. Its decisions do not demand papal confirmation. On the contrary, they are binding upon him so that he can only dispense from them in particular cases. The difference between conciliar canons and papal decrees consists precisely in that the former have already secured the assent of the Universal Church, whereas the latter still demand it. The decrees of the councils therefore constitute an insuperable barrier to papal legislation. In order to forestall the misuse of papal power for the future it is necessary to create constitutional securities by giving wider authority to the College of Cardinals. The cardinals should be chosen with the consent of the bishops from all the various nations. Both the rights of metropolitans and those of patriarchal councils should be restored.

The *Concordantia* thus contains all the principles of the conciliar theory, and all the demands of its earlier adherents, the superiority of the council over the Pope, its right to correct him, the subjection of papal legislation and administration to the canons, the need of guarantees against misuse of the primacy, and a return to the laws of the ancient Church. The speculative mold of these ideas results in a conception of the Church as a divine cosmos in which God's will and man's freedom are interlocked. Harmony will result only when each part of the whole is functioning in the light of its particular pattern, i.e., when each member of the Church is fulfilling the obligation of his vocation within the total complex of the Church's vast life. We see here the heart of Cusa's reform thought: the restoration of all things to conformity with their archetypes.

Cusa's abandonment of his extreme anti-papal views after 1436 may have been prompted by the lack of leadership he perceived in the Council of Basel. The tumult and disorder that resulted from this over-democratized assembly, where laymen and uneducated clergy clamored for equal voice, must certainly have driven him toward the more moderate position of the papacy of Pope Eugene. One of the participants of the later sessions of Basel remarked that even if the devil himself had proposed legislation here, it would have been accepted with a majority vote. Fearing a schism would result from this unbridled use of conciliarism, he left the Council for the Pope. There is evidence also that Eugene's concern for reunion with the Greek Church was also a factor in his joining the papal force. As matters developed, it was Cusa who, along with the Archbishop of Tarentaise, was selected by the Pope to negotiate with the Greeks in Constantinople on the preliminaries that were to confirm their decision to attend the new council summoned by Pope Eugene. Although he abandoned the anti-papal party at Basel, Cusa never quite relinquished his conciliar thoughts, spending the rest of his career in an untiring effort toward Church reform and reunion. In 1441 he pleaded the papal cause before the Diet of Mainz and was instrumental in having Emperor Ferdinand III and the majority of the electors submit to the Pope.

Again in 1450 he was sent to Germany, Bohemia, and the Low Countries by Pope Nicholas V as a special delegate entrusted with the difficult task of introducing reform into the anti-papal area. He was commissioned to preside over local and provincial councils, to visit and reform the monasteries, and regulate the abuses arising from the plurality of benefices. Perhaps one of the greatest obstacles to his reform efforts in the Germanies at this time was the fact that they were associated with the proclamation of a special jubilee indulgence. He proclaimed the indulgence in Salzburg, Brandenburg, Hildesheim, and Utrecht. Yet a definite spirit of hostility was in evidence throughout this vast area. There was a widespread feeling that the whole business was but a pretext to raise money. In some places the clergy seized part of the indulgence money and refused to turn it over to the legate. Nonetheless Cusa carried out his reform with determined effort. In the city of Hildesheim he deposed the Abbot of St. Michael's who had obtained his office by means of simony and was openly opposed to the Cardinal's reform. In Minden he published a severe edict against concubinage among the clergy. When the edict failed to produce any change, he caused a decree to be affixed to church doors threatening any beneficed ecclesiastic who took back his concubine, or kept her elsewhere, with the loss of his income and exclusion from public worship, and the entire city of Minden was to incur an interdict reserved to the Holy See.

In his own diocese of Brixen he followed a similar pattern. Some of the synodal decrees that he issued between 1453 and 1457 give an idea of the problems that confronted the zealous Bishop. There are repeated enactments aimed at the improvement of clerical morals. The clergy are to avoid taverns and gambling, and extravagance in wearing apparel. They are urged to instruct the people in the basic truths of the faith, the sacraments, and the commandments. Almost all of the synodal decrees speak out strongly against the superstitions associated with the lives of the saints. Cusa is particularly vehement in his attack on the superstitions attached to the cult of St. Blaise, and he recommends the abolition of those feasts in the liturgical calendar which have no scriptural foundation, such as the octave of the Epiphany and the feast of St. Valentine. Prayers and Masses for the purpose of averting storms, epilepsy, cattle plague, and so on, are to be eliminated from the divine service.

Cusa's reform of the laity is aimed at recalling the people to the purity of the Gospel message and away from the corruptions of belief and superstitions, practices due in a large degree to the anxiety which gripped late medieval Christianity because of the widespread belief that the final end was near. In reading Cusa's reform one is forcefully struck with the earnestness of the man who has spent his entire ecclesiastical career in attempting to reform the Church. One perceives almost immediately the constant stress he places on Christocentrism.

An examination of Cusa's writings indicates the wide range of his reformatory objectives. Unlike Gerson, whose reform of theology is a plea for a return to a more simple knowledge of the scriptures, Cusa, in his *De Docta Ignorantia,* proposes a complete overhauling of the theological system. Rejecting the system of Aristotle, which he claims seeks for a victory in words alone and only increases the distances between God and ourselves, he attempts to go beyond the limits of discursive reasoning and to envision the Trinity with the soul as well as with the mind. He feels that the dogmas of Christianity possess a suprarational element that transcends the principle of contradiction. By placing the concept of the divine in a mathematical rather than an analogical framework, he seeks to avoid what was the basic defect of scholastic theology—circumscribing the divine with the finite. Taken as a whole his proposals in the realm of speculative theology continually emphasize a more immediate orientation to revelation and especially to the Christological doctrines of John and Paul. The prologue of the Johannine Gospel runs through his theology from beginning to end,

combined with the Pauline insistence on the unique emi-
nence of the humanity of the Logos in His role as Mediator.
To this end he applies the acuteness and analytical ability
of his mind in terms which, because of their mathematical
precision, avoid the ambiguities of traditional scholasticism.

It is not his intention to substitute speculative faith for
divine revelation, but rather to bring into clearer vision what
is contained in the mystery, the depth, and width of Scripture. In developing his system he avoids the fruitless strife
between the various schools that had reduced the theology
of his day to ridicule, and having skimmed off the cream of
traditional theology, he refreshed it with a blend of his own
genius. The end result is a picture of Christ which, although
less logical than the traditional one, is nonetheless more
personal and pervading.

His *De Docta Ignorantia* has been described as a remarkable attempt to plunge the soul into a mystical drowning
where the contradictions of the philosophers disappear in a
triune God who unfolds rather than causes. The concep-
tualized theology of the day, with its stress on interdetermin-
ing analogies proving that a number of perfections existed
prior to both God and creatures, destroyed the whole notion
of the eternity and the infinity of God. Cusa feels that the
dogmas of Christianity relating to facts and happenings of
spiritual experience have a supralogical or suprarational character and are above the law of identity and contradiction. He
constantly asserts that the superlative is the basis for all
comparison, and God alone is the superlative.

The originality of Cusa's thought does not consist so much
in that he achieved a different result from his predecessors
in the realm of Christian philosophy, but that he arrived at it
through a different route. To reduce Aristotelian arguments
that are at most approximates of metaphysical proof to
absolute arguments was as inconsistent to Cusa as it is to
many present-day non-Thomistic philosophers. They achieve
results that are not only complicated and questionable but run
the risk of increasing the gap between God and the soul.
As with Anselm and Eckhart before him, the question that
Cusa proposed to answer is not whether God exists. Whatever references there are to God's existence in his writings
are not to be interpreted as an analogical proof for this
existence. They are intended rather to enrich the concept of
God with greater color and life, and in strengthening it to
increase one's belief. They are attempts aimed at clarifying
and defining the notion of God. The Thomistic tradition,

aimed at establishing through causal relationship a simultaneity between God and creature, ran the risk of circumscribing the divine with the finite, since the very notion of cause is limited by its creatureliness. Faced with the problem of model existence and univocal concepts, Cusa avoids the subterfuge often used to overcome this dilemma. The basic failure of Aristotelian metaphysics is its inability to go beyond a mere rational knowledge of God. Cusa's philosophy thus takes on an anthropomorphic character in the person of Christ who represents as a human being the most sublime image of God because He is, at the same time, the essence and equivalent of the Father and thus the pre-image of all creation.

It is a view of Christ that comprehends the great wealth and beauty of the visible world here below as well as the beatitude to come. It is a view more congenial to a generation swiftly changing its attitude toward the universe from one of self-defense and escape to one of conquest and development: "The earth itself is formed so as to reflect the image of the divine power." The reforms that Cusa proposed were, therefore, an attempt to establish a penetrating and harmonizing diversity within the divine power, a vital organic unity. For both the Church and the empire, harmony will be achieved only as the result of having each part of the whole function in the light of its particular pattern. The heart of Cusa's reform both individually and collectively is the restoration of all things to conformity with their archetypes. It is basically a restoration that is Christoformal, that is, remade into the image of Christ. It is a restoration of each segment of society to its *prima forma*. It is a rededication of all creation to the figure of Christ, wherein the disparate elements of Cusa's time achieve diversity in unity and unity in diversity.

Perhaps one of the most remarkable of Cusa's reforms was the *Reformation Generalis* which he presented to the College of Cardinals at the request of Pope Pius II in 1463 as a member of a newly created reform commission. A brief examination of this document will give some idea of the intensity with which Cusa returns to the etymological meaning of the word *reformare* as a basis for personal and institutional renewal. To his audience of cardinals, Cusa began by stressing the need of reform for those who are the eyes of the body, because if they be in darkness, one can hardly expect the other organs of the body to be enlightened. He points out that man is created for God Himself and that the only true and sure way of knowing God is through His Son; he stresses the Word of God as the light of the world, and hence the center of the Church. Christ came and chose His disciples from the world and built His Church on those faithful to Him, which Church is nourished and lives by His doctrines and spirit, and in which He will remain for all time. The Church is therefore a union of the faithful of which Christ is the Head. Christ is the rock upon which it is built. He who lives and moves in this unity is assured of salvation, for he alone has the words of eternal life. We are all much like Christ, each in his own way, in order to be made partakers of God in the kingdom of eternal life and coheirs with Christ the only Son. Cusa insists repeatedly on this identification with Christ. It is impossible for man to attain to the kingdom of immortality unless he puts on the likeness of Christ the Lord. We have taken the place of the apostles so that we might clothe others, he writes. The entire purpose of Holy Scripture is to enable us to become imitators of Christ. Christ alone is the Mediator in whom all that is required for eternal life can be found, and without whom there is no hope of everlasting happiness.

The cardinals have taken the place of the apostles in order to cover others with the garb of Christ. Hence, the apostle, as when Christ is speaking, says: "Be imitators of me, dear sons, as I am of Christ." The first requisite for this transformation is docility, and here again the docility is exemplified by Christ. "For I have given you an example that as I have done, so also might you." Christ is the form of our virtue; our victory over the world stems from and is united with our likeness to Christ. Those who desire to reform all Christians, then, are to propose no other model for imitation than Christ from whom Christians receive their name. All efforts ought to be toward a restoration of the innocence of baptism so that when Christ appears in the glory of God the Father, we will be like Him. We will be of His likeness, which likeness is alone found in the Kingdom of God to which we journey.

The Mystical Body is the framework in which Cusa develops his reform program. In the Church there are various functions for different members. The eyes he compares to the cardinalate. It is their function to visit all the members of the body and see that no rottenness adheres to them. The eyes are the light of the body. "However it is known that at this time the Church has almost entirely fallen away from the light and has become enveloped in shadows because the

eyes which ought to be its light have fallen into darkness."
Since the eye which sees the stains of others cannot see its
own faults, it is necessary for it to submit itself to others
who visit, correct, and cleanse it. In this way Cusa proposes
that the "eyes" of the Church submit to correction themselves, and proceed to carry the reform to the members of
the Church. Hence the reform must begin at the very top, in
the Curia, and then spread throughout each province of the
Church. The Pope himself must undergo this scrutiny. The
substratum of the fourteen rules that Cusa then proposes
is that the visitors or inspectors see to it that all are led to
that pristine form which they put on when in baptism they
became Christians.

The chief abuses which the visitors are to eradicate in
ecclesiastical officialdom are to be determined to the extent
that the particular official departs from the significance of his
duties with the canonical name he holds and is a liar and
unworthy of Christ. Much of the work of the visitors is to
determine whether absenteeism and plurality of benefices
are not the cause of the scandal that is weakening the force
of religion. Special care must be taken for the reform of
hospitals and convents of women: convent inmates, having
solemnly vowed themselves as spouses to Christ, must cease
being the cause of scandal and the wrath of God; and among
the hospitals, the alms that are given them for the poor
must not be deceptively misused. Care is to be taken that
religious relics be examined to determine their authenticity,
and the display of so-called bleeding hosts is to be prohibited. In those regions where reports of miracles are attributed to either relics or miraculous hosts, they should be
regulated or suppressed by ecclesiastical authority under pain
of severe punishment. These practices are more often than
not motivated solely out of avaricious gain, and the deception employed by the greedy clergy has an evil effect on
religion. It is sufficient for the faithful that they have
Christ truly present in their churches in the sacrament of
the Eucharist. Relics may be venerated, but it is Christ,
who is the Head of all the saints, whom one should really
venerate.

The reform also inveighs against the practice of public
usury, sorcery, and incantations, and then reiterates that the
visitors are to do nothing more, in essence, than lead back
the officials of the Church to the duties and obligations to
which they have sworn themselves in taking the oath of
office.

Then, the document of reform voices the manner in which the Pope himself is to undergo the scrutiny of the visitors. Taking the various titles of the vicar of Christ, Pope, patriarch, archbishop, bishop, and priest, each is held up as the key to determining his proper function as the father of fathers. He is the principal on which they are founded, the superintendent of bishops, as well as of the divine flock. As the servant of the servants of Christ, he must conform above all to the sanctity of Christ. If the Pope glories in all of these titles, he must endeavor to comply with what the names he bears signify, and by his action to be what he professes to be. The Pope must be judged as to whether his person, his family, his Curia, and all that pertain to papal dignity and office, are in conformity with the ideal, and he must accept the judgment passed upon him with a gracious heart. Nor are the visitors to hesitate in passing severe judgment on the Pope; for although the vicar of Christ, he is also the minister of Christians, and although the father of fathers, he is also the servant of servants. When they see him endowed with the highest and holiest dignity, they must view him also as a sinful and weak man, the greatness of whose office, according to the Gospels, consists not in the domination, but in the edification of the Church. Whatever, therefore, is a source of scandal rather than edification must be amended. The tract then turns to the reform of the College of Cardinals, and lists three conditions that must determine their conformity to their calling: the zeal of the house of God, freedom and confidence in their capacity as advisors, and, finally, good example of well-regulated lives.

The very designation "cardinal" indicates that they are the firm hinges of the Church on which all disturbance and commotion is steadied, all fluctuations stabilized. As a group they represent the consensus of the entire Church, and hence their office of choosing a pastor for the Church. Him to whom they consent, the Church as represented in them also consents. They ought, therefore, to convene each day as legates of the various nations in a miniature council, and as parts and members of the Mystical Body, i.e., of the holy, Roman, apostolic, and catholic Church. Hence they must be men pleasing to God and of mature judgment, since their office is to cooperate with the Supreme Pontiff toward the edification of the Church. In order to keep the Church free of commercialism, they must be appointed to this dignity on a basis of their own merits rather than through favoritism.

To insure freedom in advising the Pope with honesty, they

must remain above national or family interests, and be paid a determined salary. Finally, since they must edify the entire Church through the example of their daily lives, they must cut down their retinue of servants and hastily reduce the number of benefices they hold, and dress in a uniform manner. A final recommendation urges the expulsion of hangers-on, displaced prelates, and undesirables, particularly curial courtesans, from the College of Cardinals.

Many of the ideas contained in this document were introduced into the discussions of the Council of Trent almost a century later when it had become obvious that no reform of the Church was possible without a thorough cleansing of the Curia.

More important than Cusa's reform of theology and his recommendations for a modification of the Church's constitution was his growing concern for a more universal Christianity. A failure to introduce practical reforms into his own diocese of Brixen, the continued spread of the Hussite wars, the refusal of the Greeks to approve the Union of Florence, and above all the fall of Constantinople in 1453, had convinced him that the whole content of the faith demanded a new dimension if it was to restore, effectively, all to Christ. The Church, commissioned to preach the Gospel to all nations and races, had become in the course of centuries identified with a limited area and a small group of Europeans. To the mind of Cusa, if she was to recapture her original ecumenical purpose, and to follow the mandate of Christ in preaching the Gospel to all nations, a new orientation was necessary. The Church had managed to adapt herself to the late Empire and to the world of feudalism. She had greatly contributed to the expansion of the eleventh and twelfth centuries in both cultural and political leadership, but in the fifteenth century she had failed to accommodate herself to the new trends in economics, science, and government that were reshaping Europe.

Hence Cusa in his *De Pace Fidei* attempts to present the basic truths of Christianity in a way that will transcend the dialectical limitations that had rendered traditional Christianity unpalatable even to the western Europeans. In a sense he anticipates the tremendous expansion that the age of discovery was to usher in during the century after his death. This was an expansion that brought the European Christians into contact with new and different cultural patterns.

Cusa wrote his famous tract on religious pluralism soon after the fall of Constantinople. There is no doubt that recollections of his visit to the God-guarded city on the Golden Horn as a member of the papal commission sixteen years before were in his mind when he wrote of the catastrophe that now made more necessary than ever some sort of religious universalism. The work is actually set within the framework of a dialogue between representatives of the world's great religions as Cusa knew them. Although it is developed in the same close and blunt style that characterizes his earlier works, its very directness seems to voice the earnestness of its author in pleading for a faith that would unite rather than separate mankind.

There are three fundamental concepts on the basis of which his Christianity of the future becomes intelligible: human knowledge, human societies, and the characteristics common to all religions. With regard to human knowledge, Nicholas begins by establishing that all intellects naturally desire the truth. This is a desire which never fails and through which we can know with certitude wherein our happiness lies. Concerning the truth, we can at least *a priori* know that it is the maximum, that is, an absolute beyond which nothing can be thought of or can exist; it is the absolute maximum, and we may therefore identify it with God. Now, evidently the human mind cannot be the measure of the truth because this presupposes what it seeks and is not, and hence only truth itself can be the measure of truth. And if the mind is not the truth, it is therefore finite. But between the finite and the infinite there can be no proportion and the distance always remains infinite.

But we must not despair of human knowledge altogether since we also know that the mind has a resemblance to God. This resemblance indicates the distinction of human knowledge in comparison with God: truth actually exists in the divine mind whereas the human mind possesses only images. The earth itself is "formed so as to reflect the image of the divine power," and we may therefore expect an accurate, although limited and finite knowledge of God. It is in the actual predication of our knowledge to God that these limitations become most apparent because such names are derived from creatures, thereby being finite, and as a result cannot properly be predicated to God; and since our knowledge always remains finite, we are forced to conclude the necessity of a "negative theology" in which we deny God finite perfections in order to ensure Him the infinity that we realize He must have although we cannot know. God is truly above every name we are able to understand and formulate, even that of

"Being." Through this reasoning the true condition of human knowledge is grasped. The object of this knowledge is therefore to recognize this ignorance; to recognize that Wisdom itself is "higher than all knowledge, and utterly unknowable and unspeakable." As with Dionysius, to recognize this condition of human knowledge is the greatest wisdom and is itself absolute precision.

Beyond Cusa's theory of human knowledge, to understand *De Pace Fidei* it is also necessary to relate this to his conception of God and reality. God is the maximum and truth in itself, and from His absolute infinity Cusa successively reasons to His eternity and unity. This initial conceptualization of God as the maximum must always be kept in mind as it often constitutes the unspoken premise of Cusa. Also of interest in his idea of God in Himself is that Cusa thought he could demonstrate that it was necessary that God be "unitriune," a Trinity, a point to which we shall have to return.

A second characteristic derived from the principle of the absolute maximum is Cusa's famous and often misunderstood doctrine of the coincidence of opposites. This theory should not be presented simply in terms of human knowledge since such knowledge is derivative of the actual fact in reality and only occasionally and dimly apprehended in our minds. In the abstract consideration we see that the maximum must equal the minimum since both are infinite by definition, although this is not readily grasped by reason. But it is only when understood as resultant upon the concrete fact of God's existence that Cusa's meaning and intention can be adequately understood, because God is the infinite actualization of all that is simply and absolutely possible. Within God's providence all things, even the non-possible, are reconciled; within His being all finite beings receive their being and become intelligible. For the fact is that without God nothing could exist, and all beings exist only insofar as they exist in Him.

Nor is it possible to arrive at any absolute perfection. This perfection is true of individual creatures—they are "finite-infinity," i.e., are God but finite. Now otherness is not possible between God and things, but it is nevertheless not necessary that all things be one and God. Individual existences participate in God in differing degrees, each in the fullness of its particular limited form. Whereas God is simplicity, individual creatures are distinct due to the degrees in which they possess this simplicity. If they are simple and perfect in their own right they cannot be other than God, but be-

cause their perfection and simplicity differ according to the
variety of limited forms they are not each other.

There is a specific character of human societies throughout the thought of Nicholas of Cusa fundamental to the universal religion he intends to describe in *De Pace Fidei*, i.e.,
the organic nature of society. His political and ecclesiastical
theory is always based on internal harmony rather than imposed authority. In society men are bound together by common agreement in the natural law of reason, and the Church
is analogously the union of the faithful in the love of Christ.
Societies, encompassing as they do great multitudes of people,
"cannot subsist without great diversity." Nicholas always finds
the analogy with the organic body most appropriate for expressing his notion of social unity and organization. Within this framework no one element could adequately account
for the entire social structure, and upon none was the unified
body exclusively dependent. However it is possible that a
multiplicity of factors be indispensable to that particular
form of organization. Consequently each part of society had
a limited but necessary function which could be effectively
accomplished only in conjunction with the other parts. However, the whole body and its end or goal is always foremost
in Cusa's mind, and is superior to the individual components.

Nor was this an inflexible structure; rather, wherever necessary for the good of the entire body, Cusa could compromise
its individual elements and yet retain the ultimate *raison
d'être* of that society. From this point of view conciliarism
was merely one particular form which this over-all view
could engender, and probably the most immediately evident;
but others have not thereby been excluded. If it were not for
this general concept of society, with all its toleration of
variety and flexible harmony of coordinated processes, it
would never have been possible for Cusa to have envisioned
the universal Christendom of the *De Pace Fidei*. And in this
respect he is totally medieval since to him this unified Christendom was still an attainable reality, and yet he is at the
same time free from the typical Scholastic rigorism and lack
of toleration because no truly human social elements could
be basically alien to the forthcoming Christianity.

More immediately determining religious concord are Cusa's
theories concerning all religions in general. As we have seen,
the human mind naturally desires and inclines toward truth.
On the strength of this hypothesis Nicholas concludes that
all men have a knowledge, however indeterminate, of the
infinite God, and that at the heart of the worship of all

nations there is a recognition of God as the maximum. The verity of this conclusion may be ascertained by an investigation of the nature of wisdom itself. To love wisdom, as the philosopher purports to do, presupposes the existence of an absolute wisdom. A contrariety of cults and rites does not deter from this essential fact of all religions; and therefore it is their particular manifestations and not the religions themselves that are in contradiction. Each religion presupposes this basic worship and knowledge of the unique God, and since this is essentially the same fact in each, Cusa's task rests more in charity than in polemics or dogmatics. Such conclusions are perfectly consistent with the philosophic principles of Cusa. This theory forms the basis of a specifically Christian revelation of God's authority, as one would normally expect. This characteristic of all religions is the common denominator on the basis of which Cusa intends to establish the harmony and unity of all religions. It rests on human reason rather than direct revelation.

But even this natural phenomenon does not fully explain the foundation upon which Cusa proposes to reconcile religious diversity with the fact that God informed each nation with its own prophets, each of them truly revealing God's laws. In obeying its own religion each nation has been obedient to the Creator. God Himself is thus responsible for the diversity of religious worship. The divine commands, brief and intelligible to all, have been revealed to all by God. Nicholas in no way denies the superiority of the Christian revelation, but he merely asserts that God has made known elsewhere the minimal ordinances by which human life shall be governed. Here again is compelling evidence that all religions are basically in accord with each other since "the truth is but one . . . and the diversities ought now to give up their place to a single orthodox faith." For Cusa, therefore, rather than undermining the Christian faith, these conditions actually serve to facilitate the reception of Christianity by all nations.

How then, we may inquire, has religious oppression and discord resulted when both the persecutor and the persecuted were obedient to the creed and will of God? Cusa replies that it is the "law of our earthly human condition that a long habit (e.g., customs of worship) become second nature to us, and dissension occurs when one community opposes its faith against the faith of another." This brings us now to consider the essential ideas in *De Pace Fidei* in which Cusa seeks to demonstrate the possibility of a religious concord, not by changing the faith of non-Christians, but on the basis of that "same faith which is everywhere presupposed."

In *De Pace Fidei* Nicholas of Cusa indicates three principal ideas which through Christianity will become acceptable to all nations, and upon which Christianity is exclusively dependent. These minimal requirements for Christian peace are Christ, the Trinity, and the Church. Upon these principles alone, and particularly the first two, rests the entire structure of *De Pace Fidei;* but, as is usual within the thought of Cusa, these principles acquire an especially distinct meaning.

According to the Cardinal all knowledge is but preparation for faith in Christ. Depending solely upon human means, we are forced to recognize the difficult situation of human knowledge, and with this realization the necessity of Christ becomes apparent, or at least acceptable to the human mind. It is necessary to remember that in Cusa there is an unequivocal superiority of the intellect over the will, and it is therefore to be expected that the role of Christ be presented as essentially one of knowledge. In fact, the entire philosophic structure of Nicholas is conceived as the indoctrination by means of which we are able to fully grasp the ultimate significance of Christ. Christ is therefore the keystone binding together the diverse elements of his system. With Christ the doctrine of learned ignorance, rather than being destroyed, is fulfilled, and achieves its purpose of freeing man's intellect of its finite boundaries.

Moreover, Christ is not merely a convenient supernatural solution extrinsically imposed; but rather belief in Him is necessary for all knowledge. In faith all things are included, and understanding is nothing other than the unfolding of faith. It is therefore evident how thoroughly the complete system of Cusa is imbued with the Christian faith. But there is a similar faith that seldom has the explicit form we find in Christianity, and it is Cusa's intention to explicate the real and hidden meaning of that faith which is common to all men, and to show how it is actually a faith in Christ.

To establish this faith Nicholas again insists on the premise that the intellect naturally desires truth. The philosopher then shows how all people, "despite all their diversities, presuppose a single reality called Wisdom." This absolute Wisdom is identified with the Word, or Principle. Hence, merely to profess the existence of a science of wisdom, as all nations have done, is to believe in a single absolute reality which is also the Word.

After having reached agreement on the Trinity, Nicholas

again returns to Christ, first as the Reason or Word which is the creative power of the Trinity (the Logos), and then more importantly, the Incarnation. Prescinding from the actual fact, we may observe that human nature above any other is most suited to be joined to the World. The situation of man between the highest and lowest realities thereby makes this union of God and man most convenient since, due to his duality of composition, man participates in both the material and spiritual worlds.

Nicholas begins by asserting that this human nature was truly and fully human, and always remained so. And since we also know this union must be the maximum, the two elements unified will therefore be perfect and absolute in itself, and consequently we must understand this union to be personal. However, if, as the Koran claims, the humanity of Christ had received only the greatest grace ever bestowed upon man, then a more perfect union would still be possible. And the Koran itself teaches that in Christ human nature is raised to God in the highest manner possible; hence this union or adhesion must be in the order of nature and not merely that of grace. If the union is such that none greater can be conceived, then it must be a personal, indissoluble union, the only limits being the nature involved. This adequately satisfies the hesitations of non-Christians as to the possibility and type of Incarnation, but we must delve deeper to realize the full significance of this fact.

The real importance of Christ is to be found in His capacity as Mediator. The need of redeeming man from the state of original sin is not at all thereby diminished by this emphasis of Cusa, and, in fact, this restoration of human nature and its liberty of choices is presupposed. But even here, as in the case of faith, Nicholas immediately concentrates upon the importance of Christ in relation to the human intellect and knowledge. And by stressing the function of Christ as Mediator, an office ever remaining present and individual to each person throughout history and not merely an historical fact accomplished once and for all, Cusa thereby impresses the personal reality of Christianity as a vital and organic force throughout all ages.

Only with great difficulty and admixture of much error can man's knowledge transcend from the limited natural world to that of infinite reality to which it ultimately aspires. By original sin man is even more thoroughly restricted to earthly knowledge. If, therefore, only such transcendent knowledge perfects man, Christ as the Mediator is necessary for human perfection since through this union of God-man all things, especially man, are related to God. This union, absolute in itself, effectively bridges the gap between God and man, and, because human nature is a microcosm of the whole universe, Christ Himself, in addition to being absolute power, is the perfection of creation and the universe. To man in particular, the basic function of the Mediator, through His humanity, is to unite the human intellect to the divine reality and knowledge by means of which humanity subsists in the divine and achieves immortality. Hence, Christ as the "humanization of the Word," having made this Word concretely attainable to man, represents not only the necessary restoration of man, but is also the means whereby man attains perfection in the divine life and knowledge of it-self—"the plenitude of divinity and grace." This mediatory function of Christ is important in the light of his previous philosophic principles, i.e., God as the maximum and in Him the coincidence of opposites, and through these princi-ples we may better understand the importance placed on Christ as the Mediator by Cusa.

The entire structure of Cusa's system of knowledge and reality rests on his principles of God as the maximum and the resultant corollary of the coincidence of opposites in Him. Through these principles, actually different aspects of the same reality, Cusa succeeds in establishing a basis of knowledge at once including God and nature and insuring the stability of human knowledge. As the maximum Christ is important because in Him "we have the most important activity of the maximal power of God." Not simply human nature, but the absolute perfection of that nature is to be found in Christ. Without Christ, man on his own could only achieve endless approximations of perfection; no matter what man's condition was prior to the Incarnation, Cusa im-plies that it is nonetheless only by means of this mediatory function, in itself being the maximum of both limited natures, that man can concretely apprehend the maximum reality. Hence, in Christ the maximum is most fully actualized be-cause it involves both God and nature, and because man, through Christ, attains his maximum, the ultimate antithesis between God and nature is finally transcended without deny-ing the distinction of finite essences. Since Christ is in Him-self both the perfection of the universe and the absolute God, over and above His role as Mediator He is also the maximum in itself. Therefore not only through Christ, but in Christ as well, does man realize the maximum, and consequently, if faith is necessary for learned ignorance and divine knowledge, the maximum faith can and must exist in Christ only.

Furthermore, the principle of the coincidence of opposites also receives its ultimate significance in Christ. If Christ is the absolute maximum, then we already know that in Him the absolute minimum (infinite) must likewise exist, because despite the limitations of human nature and its powers of apprehension, the two must be coincidental in reality. This is most important when we consider the humanity of Christ; since the reality of Christ, and the infinite reality within Him and mediated by Him, is within the grasp of man, he therefore now has a tangible apprehension of the actual fact of the coincidence of opposites. As a result, Cusa does not restrict faith to simply a knowledge of the maximum, but within faith the maximum is equal to the minimum. In this way the consistency of Cusa's system is insured and his doctrine of learned ignorance is transformed from an hypothesis of vague speculation to actual (or experientially attained) knowledge without denying the superiority of negative affirmations to the maximum.

The second constitutive element of Christianity insisted upon by Nicholas of Cusa in *De Pace Fidei* is that of the Trinity. Two aspects of his doctrine have important bearing on *De Pace Fidei:* the conception of the Trinity in Itself, and Its intelligibility from reason alone; and the Trinity in relation to the universe.

To begin with, Nicholas of Cusa purports to demonstrate the necessity of a "triune" God, without a direct reference to Scripture. The unspoken premise is always that God must be the Maximum—unity, eternity, infinity, etc. Considering God in Himself, and because there exists an observable diversity in nature, we therefore know that God must be the absolute unity because this is necessarily prior to diversity. Then in like manner observing inequality, we are brought to realize that God must be equality of some sort and thereby imply distinctions. Finally, in noticing division in nature we may likewise conclude that there must be connection in God. But since each of these absolute qualities must be eternal also, we are forced to recognize that there may be only one divine essence fully possessed by each.

Although this is his most simple and intelligible statement of the Trinity, the one which exhibits the greatest logical consistency, it fails to indicate the essence of Cusa's thought on this his most important problem. When we consider God in Himself, the most fundamental reason why He must be a Trinity is that we know Him to be love, and at this point the influence of Augustine becomes predominant. "Thou art, then, that infinite love, which cannot seem to be natural and perfect love without a love, and one lovable, and a bond between them." It is primarily due to His nature as love that God need be a Trinity, and although this is most difficult to formulate, it is toward this insight and belief in God as love that Cusa's Trinitarian doctrine tends, and it is finally this alone which he seeks to render intelligible.

But one fact in our theologies of the Trinity must never be forgotten, according to Cusa: as at all other times the names affirmed of God come from our knowledge of creatures. Cusa therefore conceives the possibility of several sets of names for the Trinity, each having their own particular reasons, limitations, and usefulness. The terms—Father, Son, and Holy Spirit—however improper, are convenient; nevertheless, Cusa thinks our most appropriate names are unity, equality and synthesis, because of their unsurpassed simplicity.

Furthermore, the Trinity, as all other elements incorporated into Cusa's system, has a distinctive significance in addition to its usual meaning. The real importance of the Trinity is not exhausted by the consideration of It in Itself, and there are further conclusions reached by Nicholas from the same principles and always remaining within his initial framework of thought. This principally is indicated in his idea of the relationship of the Trinity to the cosmos or universe, and to man as the most important part of this universe.

In the mind of Cusa the Trinity is necessary for, and explains the entire structure of the universe. God must not be worshipped merely as Redeemer and Mediator; but, as the Trinity, He must further be realized to be the principle of the universe, and necessarily (from the composition of the world) a unitriune principle. From God the Father the universe results since possibility descends from eternal unity, that is, from His omnipotence non-being receives being, which being can only be the same as God Himself. Nevertheless, this is not the Platonic theory of emanations—a theory Cusa rejects explicitly. The Son, as the principle of equality in the Trinity and the universe, "is the limiting principle which gives determination to probability." The infinite equality is therefore the explanation of multiplicity and plurality. These first two principles are responsible for the existence of matter and form, according to Cusa, but this is not yet sufficient for actualization of the universe. There is also need of a connecting principle relating matter to form, potency to act, or possibility to necessity. The Holy Spirit is therefore the infinite connection or synthesis uniting the previous two principles in a spirit of love and finally bringing about reality. "As a result, the absolutely simple principle of all things will first be three in one"—potency, act, and nexus, by means of which the absolutely contracted unity is created. To Cusa the entire universe is nothing other than the cosmological manifestation of the divine Trinity, the final explanation of which must terminate in this Trinity.

There is also a particular relationship of the Trinity to the human person forming one aspect of his doctrine in *De Pace Fidei*. It is most fitting that the intellect, constituting man's highest faculty, should be the image of God. Thought in itself gives birth to understanding or wisdom, from which issues forth the loved one. This conceptualization by Cusa, even while recognizing his debt to the previous Christian tradition, is important and distinctive because he centers his attention on the bountifulness or fecundity resulting from the spiritual soul's image of the Trinity. Therefore the infinite creative power exists and is "universally creative" through the creature, and through this bountifulness, and depending upon their participation in it, the world and the creature exist in the best possible way. This is the final aspect of the fundamental notions involved in the Trinitarian doctrine of Cusa and explains why the Trinity, the most difficult of all Christian beliefs, received such thorough consideration in the *De Pace Fidei*.

The third and final element of *De Pace Fidei* is the role which Cusa intends the Church to have in this universally accepted Christianity. Under this principle comes Nicholas' treatment of justification, the sacraments, and other constituents of the visible Church, or his omission of these points. One is first impressed by the fact that anything in *De Pace Fidei* related to the Church is ostensibly consonant with his conciliarist principles, although Cusa's own practical activity had radically altered his loyalty by this time. Nowhere do we see him contradicting his previous theoretical position; in fact, it is possible to show how the implications of his "ecclesiology," if it can be called that, are basically consistent with his earlier position, although *De Pace Fidei* is a different approach to the subject than *De Concordantia Catholica*.

In *De Pace Fidei* Cusa proposes that "all diversities of religion ought now to give up their place to a single orthodox faith," but one that in no way entails the assertion of one faith over another. Rather, Cusa's entire effort is to show how all religions are ultimately grounded in the same faith and that this common core of belief, regardless of its explicit formulation, is actually faith in Christ. But there is also a further importance of faith in the thought of Cusa, one more orthodoxly Christian. St. Paul, appropriately enough, assumes the leading role in the dialogue, and proposes to teach that "salvation of all souls does not come from good works, but from faith." But this is not an indeterminate faith in an unseen God; on the contrary, Cusa carefully establishes the necessity of faith in the Christ Incarnate—Redeemer and Mediator. In Cusa's mind, therefore, this religion of the future is not a vague, meaningless compromise; instead he seeks to enliven every element or principle he considers necessary with real belief in and dependence upon Christ. Consequently, "the plenitude of divinity and grace lives in this spirit of Christ and it is in this plenitude that all those who will be saved receive the grace that salvation has merited." Then Cusa's foremost task was to instill into the heart of all nations faith in Christ, and this actually does seem to have been his intention. Such is the faith which alone is at the foundation of this universal religion; it does not depend on any good works, but in fact meritorious deeds naturally emanate from it.

Once Cusa succeeds in implanting the basic faith in Christ, he has little concern over its local manifestations among which he recognizes the probability of diversity. In the final consideration, his concept of the sacraments is reducible to a particular expression of faith which seems to be most universally applicable.

Concerning the less important elements of the visible Church, Cusa is even more indeterminate and unwilling to enforce, Catholic (Western and Roman Christianity) customs on other cultures. Wherever possible, and if a greater good would result, uniformity of rites of worship is desirable. But as a practical psychologist, Cusa recognizes the importance of a concession in secondary matters once the basic faith has been received. Christianity, divinely inspired and harboring the divine Word, is not dependent upon any particular rites or cult, but proposes to cut across and transcend this variety. A toleration of rites is therefore permissible if it is confirmed in the peace and love which is the law of faith. In fact, a diversity of modes of worship may at times be encouraged since it may be a means of augmenting devotion, zeal, and diligence.

Nowhere does Cusa become involved in the problem of authority in the Church, which may warrant the suspicion that his earlier ideas in theory had never really been relinquished. His idea of the Church always remained the "union of the faithful and loving in Christ." It was this faith and love, not the institutional Church, that was the message and Gospel preached by Christ; and the success or failure of the religion envisioned in *De Pace Fidei* will ultimately depend upon the strength of this bond of union.

It was Cusa's aim to restore a Logos, Christ, who was neither a legalized fiction nor a fiscalized dispenser of salvation. The Word is organically related to the whole of reality and harmony in an organic structure such as cannot be achieved unless each element or organ fulfills its own particular function with respect to the whole. Both Empire and Church were lost in speculation on human and spiritual needs. The Church's great error at a time when speedily evolving institutions were causing confusion was that it rationalized itself out of critical involvement by withdrawing into the stratified hierarchy of an earlier period. It was a withdrawal that produced a false ascetic distance, instead of an awareness of temporal needs. Based upon a limited notion of humanity, it was a failure to realize that man has a horizontal as well as a vertical dimension. The answer to the complexities of the fifteenth century was not legal subordination, but rather the spirit of cooperation and toleration flowing from the conviction that any organism, political or ecclesiastical, is composed of interests that must be conditioned by mutual dependence. Whereas Augustine meant to warn his readers against the earthly city, Cusa wants to save and improve it by extending the whole concept with more vitalized notions of Christ's humanity—"This humanity, being maximal humanity, embraces the total power of the species and is so much the source of being of each man as to stand far closer to him than ever could brother or friend. For the maximal of human nature so works that each man adheres to Him by formed faith. Christ is that man in perfect union while man's individuality remains untouched."

Thus Cusa finds his fundamental conception of humanity embodied in the idea of Christ. The humanity of Christ becomes the bond of the world and the highest proof of its inner unity; for it is Christ's humanity which bridges the chasm between the infinite and the finite, between the creative first principle and the created. Cusa, following the Pauline teaching that in Christ "everything which is in heaven and on earth is united," holds that if every man is a microcosmos, then Christ is the same in a maximal way, and, therefore, the completion and the goal of the universe and of mankind. Cusa addresses his works to the Renaissance man with his awareness of this microcosmic condition. He speaks to the urbanite father rather than to the men of the university with their "school" partisanship. His reforms are aimed at the world of the technician, the engineer, the artist, the merchant. The *idiota* or the "layman" is the spokesman in his dialogue on wisdom and on cosmology; his *De Docta Ignorantia* is a kindly bypassing of the theology of the schoolish, and his *De Pace Fidei* is a silent appeal for tolerance without reference to organized religion. Cusa was aware of the implication that "in the late medieval period the concept of *civis* came to take the place of both lay and cleric; the citizen did not bear the overtones of a complementary concept but stood alone and on his own feet."

The religious universalism that he fosters in this new approach is remarkably lacking in the juridic and formalistic concepts that the layman found oppressive in the over-organized religion of his day. It is a universalism that is accessible to the world of mathematics, of natural science, of physics. It presents a new and dynamic approach to the meaning of history, and only a deified humanity will accomplish this.

The *causa causarum* of the failure to put Christ in proper perspective was the inability of the dominant theology of the period to adapt itself to a more Incarnationalist viewpoint. As in the field of science so in the area of systematic theology the closed and completed structure of the universe theorized in the framework of Aristotelian metaphysics possessed a finality that was making it moribund. The discovery of the historical Aristotle by the Paduan philosophers had given rise to serious doubts as to the compatibility of the Stagirite with Christianity. Late medieval theology had turned away from the earlier emphasis on the triune nature of God so evident in the patristic writings, and as Hoffman points out, it was Cusa who turned once again to this central mystery of revelation. The assumption that the humanity of Christ ceased to exist after his death is evident in speculation that identified the divine law with a prime mover and that envisioned God as a far-away sovereign only causally related to His creation. If Christ had been overlegalized by canon lawyers, theologians had diminished His mediating role by accommodating Him to the metaphysics of Aristotle in a manner that obscured His vital role in all creation and creative activity. To reduce grace to a *habitus* or to express the revealed mysteries in hylomorphic terms ran the risk of creating a barrier between God and man. Cusa, convinced that doctrines lose their vitality unless they affect the souls as well as the mind, unless they move society as well as individuals, attempts to show the Trinity as a revelation that goes beyond a mere rational or metaphysical conceptualization. He endeavors to make divine revelation more accessible and intelligible.

Cusa spent the last years of his life in alternating attempts at introducing his reforms into his own diocese and applying his diplomatic experience and talent toward a final effort at reconciling the dissident Bohemians. Yet here as elsewhere his ideals were to come to naught in fruitless struggles with recalcitrant religious and insolent clergy supported by Hapsburg imperialism and Czech nationalism. His lifelong endeavor to achieve organic unity out of multiplicity and to lessen the tensions that were rending the Church Universal by putting the Logos, the life of the world, in a more democratic and catholic framework, by giving Christ both a horizontal and vertical dimension, was illusive. The ills that sapped the strength of the West had advanced too far and too deeply. There was little hope for reform from a Curia that had surrendered universalism to conformism and that was concentrating its efforts on those methods of statecraft that Machiavelli was later to extol; a Curia that had, so to speak, turned itself inward upon itself.

There is a note of bitterness and defeat in what Cusa wrote to his former friend Pius II during those years. "If you face up to the truth, I must inform you that I like nothing that takes place in this Curia. Everything is corrupt. None performs his duty. Neither you nor the cardinals have any real concern for the Church. Where is there observance of the canons, or respect for law? What concern is there for divine worship? Everyone is preoccupied with ambition and avarice. Whenever I speak to a consistory on the question of reform I am ridiculed. I am no longer of any good here. Permit me to withdraw. I can no longer put up with what takes place here and as an old man I require rest."

There was even less hope for the *renovatio imperii* where nascent nationalism had conspired with a particularism to threaten Christendom from within as the Turk was threatening it from without. The new social classes, the merchant, the artisan, the scientist—those to whom he addressed his writings—were gradually absorbed into elite groups only to perpetuate an aristocratic Europe wedded to absolutism for centuries to come.

Above all the religious forces, the spiritual dynamism, upon which Cusa had based his metastasis, had been exhausted to a point where a more radical, a more revolutionary movement was needed to revive them. He was no revolutionary, as d'Etaples eulogizes him: *"Venerentur igitur omnes, et detrahatur nemo."* The faith informed with charity, so much the foundation of his synthesis—his aim for a better rapprochement between God and man, among men, between man and the universe—was singularly lacking. Cusa died in Umbria in 1464 and his body was taken for burial to his titular church in Rome. His heart was buried in the Church of St. Nicholas in Cues.

Cusa, like Gerson before him, had based his reform on a plan that envisioned a Church no longer dominated by the temporal and spiritual claims of the papacy. The restored papacy of the late fifteenth century had little sympathy for men who criticized its Machiavellian policies. In addition both men were regarded in Renaissance Italy as revolutionary scions of the barbarian North. The Leonine identification of the papacy with civilization, and the aims of Julius II to liberate Italy from the barbarians, did little to enhance these two men or their ideals in pre-Reformation Rome. Pius II had disliked Cusa's concern with German national interests and once described him as "a German too devoted to his nation." Gerson had become identified with the strong Gallician element in France which was on the ascendency after the Pragmatic Sanction of Bourges. The strongest invective of the Italian Cardinal Cajetan against Luther was to accuse him of being a "Gersonist." He informed Luther that all followers of Gerson are damned just as Gerson himself is.

Perhaps the real reason for the failure of Gerson and Cusa to bring their reforms to fruition was the fact that both of them were too deeply involved in the system they attacked. Both were guilty of pluralism. Gerson's Flemish benefice and his incumbency of the church of St. Jean-en-Greve in Paris were hotly contested by other claimants. Cusa held five church positions before he left the Council of Basel, and was to double this figure during the course of his life. His final years were clouded with litigations concerning his rights to the Bishopric of Brixen. Yet there is much truth in the observation of Will Durant: "Had there been more Nicholases, there might have been no Martin Luther." Had the effort of both Gerson and Cusa to modify the constitution of the Church by putting it in a more Christological framework prevailed, the radical reform of the next century might well have been avoided.

5
A community no longer dominated by charity

"If Christianity had remained what its Founder made it things would have gone differently, and mankind would have been far happier, but there is no plainer proof that this religion is falling to pieces than the fact that the people who live nearest to Rome are the least pious of any."

MACHIAVELLI

There can be little doubt in view of what transpired at Constance and Basel that the government of the Church in the fifteenth century faced an unresolved crisis. Yet perhaps of even greater significance than the struggle between the curialists and the conciliarists, and perhaps even obscured by that struggle, was the disturbing disquietude that was so much in evidence in the realm of practical piety during this period.

Historians have debated for centuries whether Catholicism in the late Middle Ages faced an inner religious crisis. If an interest in the externals of religion is any criterion of the spiritual temper of an era, then the late medieval world gave every indication of a renaissance in the realm of popular piety. Seldom before in history had the things of the spirit so permeated the everyday life of the populace. The recent invention of printing and the discovery of a cheaper method of producing paper had coincided with an increase of literacy among the laity to make the fifteenth century a golden era of devotional literature. Hymnals, Books of Hours, and *Biblia pauperorum,* or illustrated Bible stories from the Old and New Testaments, were widespread. The clergy benefited from the new invention with the introduction of *pleniaria* and *postilla,* books of sermons which were used during the Mass service. No household of the upper classes was without a copy of such pious treatises as *On the Art of Dying, The Snares of the Devil, The Road to Heaven,* or *The Imitation of Christ.* By the first decade of the sixteenth century, the Bible had gone through over fifteen editions in the vernacular in

Germany and numerous translations, in spite of local ecclesiastical prohibitions, had appeared in the Low Countries, England, and France. Although the construction of cathedrals had ceased in the previous century, Western Europe was dotted with private chapels and chantries whose patrons vied with one another in providing them with ornamentation and decoration.

Sermons delivered by municipally appointed preachers from the mendicant orders attracted huge crowds of the faithful in the larger cities of the Empire. Confraternities outdid each other in colorful processions and foundation Masses for their deceased brethren. It was impossible to traverse the great commercial arteries of Europe along the Rhine and through the Alpine passes without encountering thousands of the faithful with the staff and the traditional cry of the medieval pilgrim: "We travel for the honor of God." They flocked to the tombs of the apostles in Rome, and the wealthier travelled to the scenes of the birth and passion of Christ in the Holy Land.

Yet it was a piety which like the theology of the period had succumbed to formalism and desiccation. In a sense, it was a reaction against the monastic idealism of an earlier religious culture. Piety had become a matter of urgency and pathos. In a sort of anguished uncertainty, the people clutched in a childish frenzy at whatever external they could identify with temporal and spiritual security. The very elaboration and multiplication of devotional practices led many to lose sight of what underlay them. There was a strange mixture of faith and irreverence, ceremonial usage and immorality.

If on the surface the fifteenth century gave indications of a renewed interest in the things of the spirit, it was an interest that was pervaded by a morbid preoccupation with death and suffering. Rarely was anyone denounced for failure to communicate at Easter. Devotion to Our Lady had reached a higher pitch than in any previous period. Men still received ashes on Ash Wednesday, kissed the pax at Mass, crept to the cross on Good Friday, remembered the dead on All Souls Day, and joined in the Corpus Christi processions. Yet there was too much of what Gerson described as *imaginatio melancholica*, "a melancholy imagination." It was a religion of fear. In art the central themes were the sufferings of Christ, the Last Judgment, and the dolorous Virgin. The paintings of Grünewald and Bosch reflect an almost brutal realism in delineating sufferings. The "danse macabre" was a constant reminder to the faithful of the imminence of death and the swift passage of wordly honors, as were the sepulchral effigies that portrayed the dried-up bodies of the royalty of France and England. Much of what was intended to stimulate a consciousness of the spirit was reduced to an appalling profanity. As Huizinga remarks, "The tendency to embody in visible forms all holy concepts exposed them to the danger of hardening into mere externalism." It led to a craving for the sensible. People turned to the representing objects, rather than to the depths of the mysteries represented. Preachers were preoccupied with the theme of sin and the grim face of death waiting for the moment of merited punishment. There was an emphasis on the horrors of hell and the sufferings of the damned. Their sermons were filled with descriptions of burning trees on which hung the souls of those who did not attend church services, vultures gnawing at men's vitals, venomous serpents stinging the unholy, boiling lakes, frozen fens, heated ovens, and vile dungeons. Scripture, when quoted, was completely torn from its living historical context. Its personalities and their sayings were distorted and mutilated into passive conveniences for moral dilation. Everywhere the emphasis was on the negative side of man's salvation, his sins and punishment.

The writings of the thirteenth-century Franciscan, Jacobus Mediolanensis, were widely disseminated during the fifteenth century, and we garner some ideas of their spiritual tone from the following passage: "O happy temptation, which compels us to fly to God's embrace. O Sweet Lord, who dost permit us to fly higher and thither, and dost always give Thyself as a safe refuge, that we may dwell with Thee forever. And always have this for a general rule: whenever you wish to bend God deeply toward you, bear in your heart the wounds of Christ, and sprinkled with His blood, present yourself to the Father as His only-begotten Son, and He will most sweetly and most fully provide for you. Turn to Christ, and humbly pray Him, that since it is not meet that He be wounded anew, let Him furbish you wholly with His blood, and so clad in the purple, you can enter into the palace. Think deeply on these wounds every day, they will be to you a refreshment and solace. And doubt not that if you imprint them well upon your heart, no temptation will weigh upon you."

Indicative of the spirituality of the laity during the fifteenth century is the remarkable autobiography of the Englishwoman, Margery Kempe. Although an abnormal woman, sensitive and at times hysterical in her religious enthusiasm, she nonetheless portrays the piety of the age as almost completely centered in the sufferings of Christ: "And there at Leicester she came into a fair church, where she beheld a crucifix that was piteously devised and lamentable to behold, through beholding which the Passion of our Lord entered her mind, whereby she began to melt and dissolve utterly in tears of pity and compassion. Then the fire of love kindled so quickly in her heart that she might not keep it privy, for, whether she would or not, it caused her to break out with a loud voice and cry marvelously and weep and sob full hideously, so that many a man and woman wondered at her therefore." While visiting the holy places in Jerusalem she appears to be affected in the same manner: "Then the friars lifted up a cross and led the pilgrims about from one place to another where our Lord had suffered His pains and His passion, every man and woman bearing a wax candle in his hand, and the friars always, as they went about, told them what our Lord had suffered in every place. And the foresaid creature wept and sobbed so plenteously as though she had seen our Lord with her bodily eye suffering His passion at that time. Before her, in her soul, she saw Him verily by contemplation and that caused her to have compassion." Not all of the laity however were possessed of the same sincerity of this English mystic. In Germany the fame of Anna Laminit of Augsburg, a visionary who claimed to take no food other than Holy Communion, and to have frequent visits from St. Anne who had presented her with a blooded crucifix, attracted huge crowds including the Emperor himself. Huge sums of money were given to her for distribution to the poor. The Duchess Kunigunde invited her to the ducal palace in Munich where she was finally exposed as a fraud and expelled from the city. She was later apprehended and executed in Switzerland on charges of kidnapping.

Curiously associated with this morbidity in popular piety was the increased interest in witchcraft and sorcery. In 1484 Pope Innocent VIII, at the urging of the two German Dominicans, Henry Kraemers and Jacob Sprenger, issued a bull, *Summis Desiderantes,* against the growing menace of diabolical possession. The two Dominican Inquisitors published a work three years later entitled *Malleus Maleficarum* which became the handbook for discerning the symptoms of those allegedly in league with Satan. Thousands of innocent victims were executed during the next two centuries on the basis of the almost incredible criteria contained in the atrocious work. It was not until the seventeenth century, thanks to the philosophy of the Enlightenment and the efforts of the German Jesuit, Friedrich Spe, that the specter of incubi and the Sabbatal iniquities gradually vanished in Europe.

The mingling of fraud and duplicity with piety transcended almost every aspect of religious life. There was no city of any size that did not boast the possession of some relic that gave it creditation in the vast network of miraculous shrines that criss-crossed Western Europe. The city of Cologne, surpassed only by Rome itself as a center for relics, enshrined the remains of the Three Kings in its magnificent cathedral. The bones of St. Ursula and her thousand martyred companions were buried in the Church of St. Gereon. Aachen, the burial place of "Saint" Charlemagne, contained the outer garments of the Blessed Virgin and the blooded cloth on which the severed head of John the Baptist had been carried. A contemporary chronicler informs us that over eighty thousand visitors a day had come to see the seamless robe of Christ displayed periodically in its cathedral. Turin guarded an even greater treasure, the Holy Shroud. In Spain, the tomb of St. James of Compostella and the resting place of the Holy Grail at Montserrat were centers for a flourishing pilgrimage trade.

The collection and translation of relics also reached a ridiculous stage during this period. The King of France, Charles V, is recorded to have given Cardinal d'Ailly some of the ribs of his ancestor, St. Louis, following a banquet at Paris. The Order of the Golden Fleece in Burgundy possessed a reliquary which contained, among other remarkable items, a considerable part of the crown of thorns, the lance that pierced Christ's side, the tablecloth used at the Last Supper, and pieces of the tablets of the Law that Moses had broken. The Emperor, Maximilian, participated in the translation of the remains of St. Simbertus, carrying part of the Saint's head in somber procession. The castle church in Wittenberg contained over five thousand relics, among which were: thirty-five fragments of the true cross, milk of the Virgin Mary, a piece of the burning bush of Moses, and 204 parts of the bodies of the Holy Innocents of Bethlehem. An indulgence of more than 1443 years could be obtained by venerating these relics.

Closely associated with the veneration of relics was the constant increase of feast days. Already in the twelfth century, Potho of Prüm had sensed dangers inherent in this monastically inspired practice, and had protested the multiplication of holy days. Why, he argued, was it necessary to

seek out occasions to worship God when this is His constant due? He deplored the fact that days which the Fathers
of the Church had purposely left free were now dedicated
to recently canonized saints. In spite of century-old warnings
dioceses and monastic orders continued to vie with one
another in establishing new saints' days. Nicholas of Clemanges attacked the practice in the early part of the century by
pointing out that the ritualistic innovations brought about
by the increase of holy days produced only confusion and
instability. He particularly scorned the practice of ecclesiastical authorities of tracking down and punishing those who
failed to observe the feast days. He considered the practice
similar to the incident in which Christ took the Scribes and
Pharisees to task for tithe hunting while neglecting the essentials of the law. The multiplication of feasts not only
lessened the value of holy days and fostered indifference
toward them, but it also took men's minds away from the
principal mysteries of Christianity. The new hymns and prayers demanded for such occasions were often from apocryphal
writings or the imaginations of the composers while the Scriptures were entirely omitted. Through an overemphasis on
the lives of the saints, a genuine distaste for the Scriptures
arose. According to Clemanges this situation was not entirely the will of the people, for the majority of the faithful
seemed unwilling to have the saints venerated to such a degree that God's worship was neglected. Nor were the laity
unaware of the temporal advantages that the increase of feasts
afforded the clergy. The transfer of the relics of a particular saint to a church dedicated to him generally called for the
institution of a new feast in his honor. The relic enhanced
the reputation of the church and increased its revenue. The
monks at Salisbury, for example, noticing that the central
tower was in need of repairs, petitioned and obtained the
canonization of St. Osmund, thus assuring sufficient offerings
from the faithful. The monks of the monastery of St. Augustine in Canterbury petitioned Pope Innocent VI to raise
the status of St. Augustine so as to have the church "made
attractive by suitable honors."

Especially open to criticism were the superstitious rites
associated with the veneration of saints. St. Julian was called
upon in hope of finding a night's lodging, usurers implored
the Blessed Virgin in obtaining higher interest from their
loans. Housewives turned to St. Sith for aid in finding lost
keys. St. Roch was the guardian against the plague, and on
his feast day herbs were blessed and mixed with fodder

against contagion. In many cases the feasts were actually a travesty of Church services. For example, on the feast of the Boy Bishop or the Feast of Fools, the clerics wore masks at the office, danced in the choir in women's apparel, and sang in a dissonant fashion. The practice of making feast days, for practical purposes, second Sundays not only hampered the economic life of the period through frequent and enforced idleness, but also was a constant source of immorality because of the license and disorderly conduct it occasioned. In Breslau the townspeople petitioned the Bishop to reduce the number of holy days which were making it impossible to follow their trades. The *Gravamina* of the German nation repeatedly denounced the plethora of holy days as a burden upon the farmers who could scarcely find time to harvest and store their crops.

Perhaps even more detrimental than the excessive devotion to the saints was the extreme and oftentimes superstitious veneration given to the consecrated Host. Among other causes, certainly this practice can be traced to the general trend after the thirteenth century of not permitting the faithful to communicate under both species—Pope Leo the Great inveighed against this practice, attributing it to Manichaean doctrine. Consequently the laity were no longer allowed to carry out the command of Christ: "Eat and drink." In a sense this was an outgrowth of the practicality that had always dominated Christianity in the West. Baptism by immersion had under the influence of practical-minded Rome given way to that of infusion. It was a more convenient rite, but it lost the striking symbolism of dying and rising again unto new life as seen in the earlier rite and spoken of so eloquently by the Fathers. The same may be said of the practice of private penance. The penitential system of the early Church with all its ritual in the liturgical cutting off of the sinner from the life of the Church, and the liturgical restoration of the penitent had a symbolic force that legal-minded Rome excluded by cloaking the sacrament with all the trappings of a secret tribunal. Receiving Communion under both species was looked upon as a special privilege of the clergy and sometimes the nobility. If this practice paved the way for envy, contention, and apparent inconsistency for the educated, it lent itself even more readily to the conviction in the minds of the unlettered that the Host was the end-all of the Christian religion in the devotional sphere.

Although there are many instances of the extremes to which this undue enthusiasm for the real presence had led, the case of the "bleeding Host" of Walsnach illustrates how deeply entrenched this practice had become. During his reformatory mission in Germany in 1451, Cardinal Nicholas of Cusa had openly denounced the abuses associated with the exposition of the Eucharist, and had focused his attack on the little Brandenburg village of Walsnach which was attracting crowds from all over Northern Europe because of its claim to possess a number of miraculous Hosts. Some years earlier the parish church had burned down and three Hosts covered with blood had been found among the ruins. Preserved in a crystal reliquary, they soon became the object of widespread devotion. A new church was constructed and what had been an obscure crossroads grew into a town of international repute. In denouncing the practice of worshipping the Hosts Cusa wrote: "The faithful take the red color of the Hosts for the blood of Christ, and the priests do not merely tolerate but actually encourage the belief because of the money it brings them." Cusa's protests to Rome remained unheeded. In 1471 and again in 1500, the Holy See issued new indulgences to the faithful who would visit the Hosts and pray for the intentions of the Holy Father.

Walsnach was not an isolated example of the cult of "bleeding Hosts." An overemphasis on the doctrine of the real presence led many of the faithful as well as the clergy to view the sacrifice of the Mass as an actual renewal of the passion of Christ and a new expiatory shedding of His human blood. Primitive milling processes often produced wheat that was contaminated with bacteria (bacculus prodigiosus). The chemical reaction caused by the minute organism produced in the wheaten bread a secretion that resembled blood. This phenomenon substantiated in many instances the legends relating to sacrificial miracles. One of the most celebrated of these tells of a German priest who while celebrating the Mass in Bolsena was afflicted with doubts concerning the real presence. Blood suddenly issued forth from the Host and flowed so copiously that it saturated the corporal cloth. The cloth is preserved to this day in the cathedral of Orvieto. In 1405 the parishioners of the little church of Bois-Seigneur-Isaac were startled to find a corporal used to preserve the Blessed Sacrament reddened with blood. It was immediately placed in a silver reliquary and venerated by the faithful for generations to come. More often than not these stories were associated with alleged sacrilegious abuses of the Host by the incredulous Jews. This was particularly true in those areas where anti-Semitism was strong. In many cases the crime of stabbing or dissecting the Host was said to have taken place in synagogues on Good Friday afternoon. A celebrated case of alleged Jewish desecration of a Host took place in Brussels at the end of the fourteenth century and the unhappy victim of this unfounded accusation was burned at the stake. The church of St. Gertrude commemorates the sacrilege to this day.

Needless to say, the scholastic theologians of the time, always anxious to apply the categories of Aristotle to strange and mysterious phenomena, wrote copiously on the problem. Unable to satisfactorily explain the Incarnation in terms of Aristotelian metaphysics, they turned to a dialectical explanation of transubstantiation and the multilocation of Christ's body. Thomas Aquinas embodied nothing in his doctrine on transubstantiation that would actually lead to a belief in the tales of Christ's carnal presence. He explained this phenomenon by pointing out that it was not the real flesh and blood of Christ but rather a miraculous symbol. The Franciscan theologians on the other hand were inclined to believe that what appeared in the Eucharistic miracle was the real flesh tissue of Christ. Duns Scotus reasoned that if the miracles were to be taken as true testimonies of the real presence, it must be the reality that appeared in them and not merely representative signs as Aquinas supposed. Others of this school felt that it was within the power of the glorified body to appear to the non-glorified eye either entirely or partially. Therefore, although the blood seen flowing separately in the eucharistic miracles could actually be Christ's, it would be so only apparently, but not actually separated from His invulnerable body. Here in typical scholastic fashion they made proper distinctions. If the blood appeared for only a short time, it could be the blood of Christ; but if it remained permanently as in reliquaries and in venerated corporals, it was another substance miraculously produced as a symbol.

The mendicants also argued on the relative amount of devotion to be paid to relics of blood which had issued from the miraculous Hosts. The Franciscans were in favor of giving it the same divine adoration given to the Host at Mass. The Dominicans, Cajetan among them, held that the honor paid them should be the same as that given to relics of Christ's clothing.

Since a great deal of theology on the Eucharist of the Middle Ages is traced to the eleventh-century controversy of Berengar of Tours, it might be well to look for a moment to the problem that arose out of this early doctrinal conflict. The questions raised centuries earlier by this theologian were still perplexing divines of the late Middle Ages. Wycliffe, for example, based his rejection of traditional Eucharistic beliefs on what he called "a misunderstanding of the condemnation of Berengar and his antagonists, Lanfranc of Bec and Alger of Liège." Many of the reformers of the sixteenth century followed to a certain extent his rejection of the theory of the conversion of the elements. Following what he considered to be the more primitive doctrine of the Eucharist as explained in the symbolic interpretation of Augustine, Berengar formulated his doctrine in his principal work *De Sacra Cœna*. Relying on the principle that the Holy Scripture is the sovereign source of authority and the voice of the Holy Spirit, he interprets the Eucharist in a figurative sense. If Holy Writ is interpreted in a physical sense, he writes, it no longer nourishes but destroys, since there is in the Gospel a letter that kills. Applying this reasoning to the Eucharist, Berengar points out that the doctrine of substantial conversion as advocated by his adversaries led to the absurdity of a sacrament being a symbol both of the body of Christ and the blood of Christ at the same time. According to the error of Lanfranc and the monk Paschasius, he complains, "There is nothing on the altar after the consecration but a little portion of flesh and blood." It is repugnant to Berengar that the little portions of Christ's flesh are broken by the hands of the priest and torn by the teeth of the faithful. Christ's body cannot be cut into sections because it is incorruptible. Even if it were not cut up into sections and were actually present on the altar, one would encounter a million bodies of Christ in the world, which is also contrary to both reason and Scripture. The entire doctrine of the real presence thus becomes grossly materialistic.

For Berengar the bread and wine become a sacrament through the consecration, but are termed the body and blood of Christ only because they are sacraments, that is, signs of the body and blood. While they remain the material things that they were, they acquire a new value, that of the body of Christ. Before consecration the bread and wine are devoid of religious significance. Through consecration they acquire the value of a means of salvation. Drawing an analogy from the Incarnation, he explains that the Word made flesh assumed what it was not, without ceasing to be what it was. So the bread consecrated on the altar does not lose its proper nature, but acquires a divinely increased dignity and worth. Through the physical reception of the bread and wine, made a symbol of Christ crucified through the consecration, the thought of the believer is borne toward Christ and is absorbed in Him. The effect of this contemplation provides the faithful person with the strongest motives to imitate the virtues of Christ and to regulate his life according to the example of the crucified Savior. The visible sacrament becomes a means of stimulation to awaken in the mind the remembrance of the Incarnation of Christ. Berengar was condemned in 1050, but in 1079 at the sixth Council of Rome he made a revocation and accepted a profession of faith that affirmed the real presence. Yet from that time on, and perhaps influenced by the Albigensian heresy, the focus of eucharistic speculation was on the "person" of Christ rather than the mystery of the Eucharist. It gave birth to an excessive longing to see what was hidden behind the eucharistic veil.

Many of the legends traceable to this overemphasis were still current in the fifteenth century. There was for example the story of the abbot Arsenius, who while saying Mass saw an angel over the altar ritually slaying a child and pouring his blood into a chalice. Thereupon the angel divided the members of the slain child to correspond with the division of the Host by the priest. Late medieval art also reflected this overrealistic interpretation of the Eucharist. The precious blood was often pictured flowing from the wounds of the crucified Christ into a chalice held by a priest. Other paintings depicted Christ being ground in a mystic wine press with His blood flowing forth from the bottom of the press into a chalice.

In addition to exaggerating the material aspect of the consecrated elements, the late Middle Ages also witnessed a flowering of Mass theology that engendered a superstitious confidence in the temporal and spiritual benefits of the Eucharist. With the spread of monasticism, the practice of saying Mass privately became a norm for the regular as well as the secular clergy. In most of the monasteries it was looked upon as a private devotion. What had in antiquity been an act of public worship in which the Christian community gathered together to hear God's word, and by the eucharistic meal to seal the new covenant, gradually became a dramatization of the passion and death of Christ. Eucharistic theology had come to regard the sacrament entirely under the aspect of *persona*. It was a consideration of the Mass that was destined to obscure the all-important truth that although Christ is present in the Eucharist, the presence is by mode of substance and of sign. It tended to encourage a childish imagination which represented the eucharistic Christ as a normally visible personage, accidentally concealed from sight by an obstacle. To facilitate this image of the eucharistic Lord, various formulas were devised which, nursed by allegory, fitted in with the popular eagerness to contemplate the Christ of history and His earthly appearance. Since the language used in the service was no longer intelligible to the faithful, they came to look upon it as a theatrical performance not entirely different from the morality or mystery plays that were frequently associated with the great feast days. The Mass was no longer a service that enfolded the mystery of Redemption in its totality. Emphasizing the death and passion, it neglected the implication of the Resurrection, the communication of grace to mankind, and the consummation of all things.

The central act of Christian worship had lost sight almost entirely of the liturgy as the proclamation of God's word to all Christians to do and to become what the word of God proclaims. The disintegration of the Roman Mass during the Middle Ages and how it became increasingly misunderstood by both the clergy and the laity is a historical fact no longer to be doubted. The earlier Christian view that considered the Mass as a token of man's gratitude to God and an act of reverence was entirely overshadowed by the notion of a sacrificial oblation. The Mystical Body, once a liturgical term applied to the Host and indicating the unity of redeemed mankind, now referred to the judicial body that was the Church. The *verum corpus* in contrast was now become the object of a private and personal devotion centered on a repeated miracle.

Even the vestments worn by the priest had come to symbolize some aspect of the passion. The chasuble represented the cross, the alb signified the gown given to Christ after the scourging, and the amice symbolized the crown of thorns. The movements of the celebrant also took on this suffering symbolism. As he moved from the epistle side of the altar to the Gospel side, the priest dramatized the journey of Christ from Pilate to Herod. The washing of the hands at the beginning of the offertory signified Pilate cleansing his hands before the Jews. The paten was held under the corporal to signify our Lord's self-debasement; the priest bowed his head at the Memento to signify Christ's death; the *Nobis Quoque* was read with lifted voice, symbolic of the captain of the guard; and at the end of the Canon, five crosses signified the five wounds. In holding his hands over the chalice and in stretching out his arms, the priest portrayed Christ suffering in the garden and on the cross. The elevation could only mean the raising of Christ on the cross. The dramatic nature of the whole service is confirmed in the expression still common today, "to hear Mass."

In addition to obscuring the real meaning of the Mass by emphasizing it as a reenactment of the drama of Calvary, the medieval Church fostered an attitude toward the consecrated elements that tended to isolate them from the context of the liturgy. The Host and the chalice were elevated by the priest, and the elevation rather than the consecration and the offering was considered the high point of the service. Detailed directions were issued as to the procedure to be followed in the event of a Host being dropped upon the ground or the precious blood being spilled. They were enforced with heavy penalties. Theologians speculated on the defects and dangers that might affect the consecrated Host. Most missals contained pages of instructions on a pattern to follow should the Host suddenly appear as a child or as living flesh. An entire ritual was evolved for the washing of the corporal and the finger towels. The Christians in Greenland were wont to worship the corporal whenever Mass could not be celebrated. The laity were not allowed to carry viaticum to the dying, and it was considered sacrilegious for a layman to touch the chalice.

Gazing upon the sacred Host at the elevation became for many the very essence of the Mass devotion. In many cities, the populace ran from church to church to see the elevated Host as often as possible, believing that rich rewards came from such practices. There were incidents where lawsuits were started in order to insure a more favorable view of the altar. Michael of Hungary, a well-known preacher, complained that many of the faithful waited outside the church until the Sanctus bell had rung, rushed in for the elevation, and then rushed out as quickly as they had come in. Condemned prisoners on their way to execution were allowed to look at the Host in the monstrance, but not to receive Communion. Fortesque informs us that in England, if the priest did not elevate the Host high enough, the people would cry out, "Hold up, Sir John; heave it a little higher." Berthold of Regensburg, the fourteenth-century Franciscan preacher, urged his listeners to focus their attention on the elevation of the Mass. "At the elevation of the Mass, the priest appears to say three things to you: see the Son of God who for your sake was thus lifted on the cross; see the Son of God who will come to judge the living and the dead; see the Son of God who for your sake shows His wounds to the heavenly Father." Some theologians recommended that the congregation greet and worship the body of the Lord in prayerful song. Suggestions that the Host be elevated more than once during the Mass were however voted down on the grounds that Christ had died only once. Certain priests were known to receive larger stipends for holding the Host up longer during the elevation.

Although both Gerson and Nicholas of Cusa had repeatedly denounced the extravagant promises attached to the Mass on the ground that they were misleading the people into a form of Judaism and promoting superstition, the fifteenth century witnessed an increase of what the reformers of the sixteenth century were to call a "blasphemous fable" and a "monstrous doctrine." The daily slaying of Christ as described in the sermons and devotional books of the period naturally fostered a belief that the Mass was a cure-all, a panacea for all mankind's ills, spiritual and temporal. With the passage of time, the Mass, having been stripped of its communal character, was looked upon as a private commodity to be disposed of at the will of the celebrating priest. That the Mass procured graces for the living and the dead was a belief among early Christians. Yet the popularizing of this aspect of the rite led to abuses that were violently denounced, and rightfully so, by Calvin, Luther, Zwingli, and most of the sixteenth-century reformers. The fruits of the Mass, as they were called, had over the centuries become classified in terms of a well-ordered scale of applied values: *fructus specialis, fructus specialissimus, fructus ministerialis.* A corresponding system of stipends, or required offerings, had also evolved whereby the varying fruits of the Mass were applied to the person supplying the stipend. Beginning in the thirteenth century, the compilation of the fruits of the Mass gradually took on all the earmarks of Aladdin's lamp. Urged on by the preachers of the mendicant orders especially, the people were led to believe that attendance at Mass would assure them of whatever spiritual or temporal requirements were necessary in this life or in the life to come. If the Mass had been paid for by a particular individual, then this assurance was all the more final.

Attendance at Mass was a sure guarantee against sudden and unprepared-for death. It was a protection against blindness, starvation, and bodily injury. In most cases the authority of an apostle or a Father of the Church was called

upon to substantiate the claims. Thus, for example, St. John
and St. Gregory were quoted as saying that after hearing
Mass a man's digestion would improve. St. Augustine is
credited with saying that during the time one hears Mass
he does not grow older. St. Luke and St. Paul attest to the
fact that if a pregnant woman hears Mass on the day she
gives birth to her child, she will suffer little pain. A man's
departed relatives do not suffer when he attends Mass. And
finally, for every Mass said, one soul is freed and one sinner
is converted.

Closely associated to the seemingly endless fruits of the
Mass were the even more complicated formularies of votive
Masses for the dead. Arranged in a well-defined series and
calculated to being specified results in the afterworld, they
not only satisfied the faithful as to the fate of their departed
loved ones, but they also constituted a substantial source of
revenue for the clergy. Traced to a legend according to which
St. Gregory read thirty Masses for a deceased monk who had
violated his vow of poverty, whereupon the monk appeared
in a vision announcing his release from purgatory, the arith-
metic of Gregorian Masses became quite complicated and we
assume quite lucrative. Special value was given to Masses
celebrated in a series of 3, 5, 6, 7, 9, and 30 times. Other
series were worked out in terms of 41, 44, and 45. All
were assured that once the series was completed, the soul
would be freed from pain without delay, *liberabitur sine
mora*. Since a High Mass was more lucrative than a Low
Mass, an ingenious means was devised whereby a choral group
was able to accommodate a number of sung Masses simultaneously. The so-called "boxed Masses" were arranged in such
a way that when the priest had advanced up to the offertory, he moved to a side altar where he read the rest of the
service silently, while another priest intoned a new High
Mass at the central altar. Many priests were wont to celebrate
Masses that were termed *missa bifaciata missa trifaciata*
wherein they recited the variable orations of the Mass a given
number of times and thus fulfilled a corresponding number
of intentions at one Mass.

What was perhaps an even greater evil in the late medieval
Church than the opiate of cumulative and unreasoned piety
was the growing rift between the laity and the clergy. The
participation of the lay folk in the splendorous and often
dramatic celebrations of the Church year had become vicarious. They supplied the financial assistance to build and
adorn numerous churches; their stipends paid for the cele-

bration of Mass, but they were deliberately excluded from open participation in divine cult. Pope Boniface VIII sounded the keynote to the growing dissension between the clergy and the faithful when he wrote: *"Clericis laicos semper infestos esse manifestum est."* (It is clear that the laity are always vexatious to the clergy.) An interesting indication of this separation of the priest and the people may be seen in the Canon of the Mass where the name of the emperor or king was no longer included. Where his name was still found in the ancient missals, it was in most cases scratched out. Even the church architecture of the period demonstrated this unfortunate separation. The so-called "rood screens" that were originally constructed in the churches in which monks chanted the office, now began to appear in parish churches as well. They were structures separating the choir from the nave of the church, and then developing into a wall cutting off the choir completely from the view of the faithful. In many larger churches, a second altar was set up in front of this screen where a second, abbreviated service was conducted for the laity. The high altar, which in the early churches was usually on a raised platform between the presbytery and the nave, was now moved further and further back into the apse, thus increasing the distance between the service and the people. In compensation, a number of side altars, already necessary for the large numbers of Mass priests, were set up, thus completing the destruction of genuine community worship.

Hence the liturgy, no longer understood in its sacramental depth, became the mechanical prerogative of the clergy. The real mystery of Christ as a present reality and a leaven needed to permeate and vivify the congregation gave place to a magical parcelling out of the fruits of redemption by a commercialized clergy. Forgotten was the notion of the Redeemer as living eternally in His humanity. Forgotten was Christ, the God-man, the Head of the Mystical Body who through the Holy Spirit animates the whole organism of the Church.

Little wonder that the faithful, compelled to live on a few fragments of the tremendous message of the Gospel, were duped by the clergy into believing that salvation was a purchasable commodity controlled by a select few. Little wonder that they slowly came to realize the distressing insufficiency of the organized Church.

If popular piety, in spite of its apparent vigor, was moving ever farther from its Christocentric moorings the official

Church also found itself sinking deeper into a morass of confusion and disquietude. It was faced with a crisis from within that a mere strengthening of its juridic structure failed to solve. Whereas the medieval Church had been shaped in response to the social and economic exigencies which the fall of the Empire in the West and the influx of new Germanic peoples had forced upon it, now confronted with the break-up of feudalism, it had failed to properly assess the new social classes that were emerging. Men were everywhere beginning to question the sacral institutionalism that had developed out of the medieval synthesis. The institution that had accommodated itself to the problems arising out of the general illiteracy and disrespect for authority that followed upon the Barbarian invasions failed in many areas to perceive that this condition no longer existed. Both respect for organized secular authority so evident in nascent nationalism, and the emergence of an educated laity had given the world of the late Middle Ages a new dimension which no longer demanded the protective and paternal idealism fostered by the Church in an earlier period. Above all else, the Church was no longer a community distinguished from all others because its members were motivated by a mutual love for one another and for the entire human race. This failure to adjust gave rise to a tenseness within the Church that confirms the opinion that before there was a cleavage in doctrine and belief there was a deterioration of Christian charity.

A new concept of faith was needed because its first fruit, fraternal charity, was sadly lacking. It was this lack, more than any other cause, that gave the post-schismatic Church all the strained symptoms of an uneasy truce between those who placed salvation in membership in an organization, and those who identified it with the love of one's neighbor.

It was a tension that in a certain sense merely reflected a general condition pervading the entire superstructure of the ecclesiastical edifice. At almost every level of the official Church there were growing signs that if the message of Christ was essentially one of fraternal charity and mutual forbearance, there were very few who were giving it a serious hearing. Strained relations between the higher and lower clergy, tensions within and among the religious orders, and, above all, an increased anti-clericalism on the part of the laity were everywhere in Europe reaching a breaking point. Although it was a breaking point that could be traced, at least on the surface, to a systematic reduction of the means of salvation to economic expediency, it was also a crisis that was caused at a deeper level by a deterioration of the very quintessence of Christianity, the love of God, and the love of one's neighbor for His sake. A preoccupation with rights and privileges rather than with spiritual needs and evangelical values had ossified from top to bottom much of the external apparatus of the medieval Church.

In an age when the education and recruitment of the clergy follows a rather well-defined pattern, has in fact become almost stereotyped, it is difficult to picture the wide gap that existed between the higher and lower clergy in the late medieval period in terms of social standing and education. Since the absorption of the Church into the feudal system during the eleventh and twelfth centuries the role of the bishop had undergone a radical change. From what was originally an elective office in which he acted as the head of the congregation, its teacher, pastor and minister of the sacraments, the bishop now assumed many of the responsibilities of the hereditary feudal lord.

The heavy emphasis in the feudal system on the importance of land tenure demanded of the episcopal office many of the duties generally associated with the administration of property. There was a blending of temporal and spiritual powers that gave the bishop the appearance not only of a prince of the Church but of a feudatory of the king and the emperor. From the reign of Louis the Pious, bishops and abbots in the Empire were required to commend themselves as vassals to the king, and their office was regarded as a benefice. As far as the oath of fealty was concerned there was no distinction between bishops, counts, and royal vassals. Later the Ottonian Emperors built their hopes for a renovation of the Empire upon a group of prince-bishops whose loyalty to the crown was guaranteed by their lack of dynastic aspirations. Otto I, for example, had placed his brother Bruno within the framework of the imperial government by appointing him Duke of Lorraine, although he was already Archbishop of Cologne. This precedent was followed for centuries thereafter throughout the Empire with the end result that Germany became covered with episcopal principalities.

Nor did the investiture struggle do away with the policy of making bishops agents of the state. The Concordat of Worms in 1122 was at most an unsatisfactory compromise. Although the Emperor renounced the right of investiture by crozier and ring and accepted, in theory at least, the freedom of episcopal elections, this did little to lessen the enfeoffment of the episcopacy. It was, in fact, a final triumph of feudal principles over the Church. Henceforth, bishops were chosen from cathedral chapters composed exclusively of the nobility. Their chief qualifications lay in their ability to carry out the affairs of state. The electors of the Holy Roman Emperor included the prince-bishops of Mainz, Cologne and Trier, and the incumbents of these important sees held important offices in the imperial household. In fact the vast network of ecclesiastical territories in Germany was held together as much by the ducal claims of its spiritual leaders as it was by the common interests of religion. The Bishop of Würzburg in the twelfth century had made himself the duke of much of neighboring Franconia and he had been imitated with varying degrees of success by the bishops of Bremen and Halberstadt.

Various concordats with the Holy See in other parts of Europe had given papal sanction to this dual capacity of bishops. We have the extreme example of this duality of office in the case of a French bishop who could observe strict celibacy insofar as his episcopal office was concerned, but at the same time, as a baron, claim the hereditary rights of his children. In the papal states there is ample evidence of the feudalization of the episcopal office. The ancient oath of office as prescribed by the *Liber Diurnus* was replaced by a new form. The profession of faith of an earlier period gave way to an oath of fealty. The older form, which had demanded from the bishop assurances of vigilance in matters of the faith and devotion to the Holy See, now became an administrative oath of office in which the word "faith" was no longer mentioned. After the thirteenth century, bishops were required to swear that they would not sell, give away, pawn, reinfeudate, or otherwise alienate property belonging to the diocese without the permission of the Roman pontiff. The non-alienation of Church property took on a greater significance than the protection of faith and morals.

In many dioceses in Germany the children of the nobility were made abbots and abbesses of the richer monasteries. Duke Alexander of Zweibrücken stipulated in his last will and testament that all of his sons and daughters, with the exception of Duke Louis and his wife, were to enter the service of the Church. The Prince of Saxony besought the Pope in 1476 to provide that no person be appointed to the Cathedral Chapters of Meissen, Naumberg and Merseburg unless he were a member of the nobility. The Chapter in

Breisgau demanded that no candidate for the episcopacy be considered unless both parents were of noble blood. When the Bishop of Bremen, Henry of Schwarzberg, died in 1496, a citizen of the city, one John Rohde, was elected as his successor only on the condition that the fourteen-year-old Prince Christopher of Braunsberg be named his coadjutor. The situation was a little different in England and France.

Though supported from the revenues of the Church, the hierarchy in England dedicated themselves almost entirely to the service of the state. The king paid most of his ministers out of episcopal revenues. In fact, of the twenty bishops functioning in English dioceses between 1376 and 1386, thirteen held high secular office in the royal court. Both the lower clergy and the laity envisioned their bishops at best as judges who passed sentence on the legality of their benefices, marriages, wills, and property rights. Rather than a pastor of souls, cloaked with the highest dignity of the priesthood, the bishop had become for many a highly paid functionary whose chief concern was the protection of his own rights and privileges. His episcopal ring signified his marriage to Church property rather than to the Church. He held a judicial office that replaced the preaching of the Gospel with a concern for the preservation of legal entities. A fifteenth-century writer aptly remarks that in England three things are necessary for the making of a bishop: "the will of the king, the will of the Curia, and the payment of large quantities of money to the latter." The last three bishops of Brixen prior to the Reformation were all active in the military affairs of the Tyrol. It was recorded, not infrequently, that the only time many bishops ever celebrated Mass was on the day of their consecration. What education in theology they received was for the most part training in the legal sciences. A degree in canon law was, after noble birth, the essential prerequisite for advancement up the ecclesiastical ladder. The general indifference of the bishops of the sixteenth century to contemporary theological problems can be explained in part by an absence of any academic background that would make them aware of the gulf between popular piety and belief.

Perhaps an even greater cause of discord between the episcopacy and the lower clergy was the practice of absenteeism and the accumulation of benefices. Since a benefice was looked upon as a profitable possession, a financial asset easily separated from the duties attached to it, it was common practice for bishops to turn over the administration of their diocese to vicar generals or to a titular bishop, the latter usually drawn from among the regular clergy and subject to the vicar general. In England, many of the bishops spent their entire lives at the royal court in London. The Archbishop of York during the early fifteenth century, John Kemp, is recorded to have visited his diocese only every ten or eleven years and then only for a few weeks. The primatial see of Aragon, Valencia, was ruled for over eighty years by absentee Borgia bishops. The Archbishop of Saragossa from 1478 to 1520 was an illegitimate son of King Ferdinand and was succeeded by his own son. Of the eighteen cardinals created by Pope Sixtus IV in 1471, four were non-resident bishops; and at the conclave of 1492, eleven out of twenty-three members of the sacred College were absentee bishops. Cardinal d'Este, Archbishop of Milan, did not visit his archdiocese once between 1520 and 1550. Cardinal Wolsey held the archbishopric of Winchester and the wealthy abbey of St. Albans, but visited neither. In addition, he secured the deanery of Wells and half a dozen other prebends for his illegitimate son. It can hardly be assumed that such a state of affairs inspired any filial devotion among the lower clergy for their apostolic leaders. A fact that rendered the situation even more intolerable was its condonation by the papacy. Typical of the papal attitude was the view of Pope Honorius III, who reasoned thus in explaining the system to the Archbishop of York. "Since those who faithfully serve the Apostolic See, as the head of the Universal Church, are held to give useful service, as it were, to all the members, it is right that they should be honored with suitable benefices; lest otherwise, if they had to serve at their own cost and were defrauded of special revenues, they might be slower of service."

The Bishop of Hereford, Roger Otery, explained his pluralism by pointing to his constant efforts to reform the morals of the clergy, efforts that required placing his diocese in the hands of substitutes. "And it is laid down in the sacred canons that a good and industrious and literate person can govern two or even ten churches better than another can govern one; and both he who resides and he who does not reside are understood to serve the altar, so long as they live a good life and expend well the income they derive. And I say also that by the custom of the English Church it was and is the used and approved custom, from time out of mind, and tolerated by the Roman Church, that the bishops and other patrons of the said realm of England can provide their well-deserving clerks with benefices, especially sinecures, up to any number, without any contradiction or offense to the Holy See."

Nor did absenteeism affect the episcopacy alone. Most parishes were in the hands of pastors or vicars who seldom resided in them but relegated them to hired curates who celebrated Mass and administered the sacraments for a well-defined salary. Dispensations granted to rectors of parishes by the Curia were even more frequent than to absentee bishops.

In many areas the unbeneficed clergy were far more numerous than those with a benefice. It is not surprising that these often uneducated and underpaid curates relied upon simoniacal practices to support themselves. Practically every one of the sacraments was dispensed for a stipulated price. In the case of Extreme Unction, for example, if the sick person recovered there was an additional charge. Throughout the late Middle Ages the practice of setting up chapels or chantries, as they were called, for the celebration of foundation Masses increased exceedingly. The wealthy families as well as the guilds and fraternities often erected their own chapels so that they might later be delivered from the fires of purgatory. The chantries were usually independent of the parish church, for the chantry priest was paid a salary out of a sum of money donated specifically for his service as a Mass celebrant. Neither the priest nor the Masses he read were part of the congregation. In many cases the chantry priests were so numerous that they organized into small communities or colleges. These ecclesiastical corporations had little to do with the care of souls. Aside from saying the founded Masses and the office of the dead the chantry priest's day was completely unoccupied. The ecclesiastical equivalents of landless laborers, they often demanded higher pay. Enforced idleness led them to all types of moral turpitude. The multiplicity of the "Mass priests" resulted, in fact, in the creation of a clerical proletariat. In the church of Newark-on-Trent in England there were no less than thirty perpetual benefices. The parish church of John Eck in Ingolstadt, in addition to the regular curates, supported fifteen Mass priests. The small city of Breslau supported more than 400 Mass priests. Cologne, with 40,000 inhabitants, had over 6,000 clerics. Even the mild-mannered Melanchthon spoke of Cologne's "papal rabble, the bastard breed whose dirty, lascivious, infamous lives are before the eyes of the whole world." In Hamburg there were over 450 secular priests although the total population of the city was only 12,000. The cathedral in Meissen supported over 90 clerics, including canons, altar priests and vicars.

An even greater scandal involved the accumulation of benefices. Bremen's Archbishop was the Bishop of Verdun, the Bishop of Osnabrück and Bishop of Paderborn. The Archbishop of Mainz held the same office in Magdeburg and Halberstadt. John Eck, in a letter to Pope Adrian VI, complained of one prebend hunter who, although he held over thirty parishes, had no desire to preach or even to take orders.

If the accumulation of benefices and absenteeism were sources of the laity's growing anticlericalism, the scandalous life of both the lower and the higher clergy in the area of sexual morality was equally a cause for animosity. The question of clerical celibacy was perhaps the greatest dilemma confronting the Church throughout the Middle Ages. Its relevancy to the Reformation of the sixteenth century can be measured by the fact that no single issue involved the lower clergy more intimately. Its rejection often sealed their determination to abandon the ancient faith. It still remains the standard explanation in certain areas for the rise of Protestantism. Many Catholics today seriously believe that Luther left the monastery to get married and that the Reformation was caused by the unwillingness of priests to keep their vows.

Since the Hildebrandian reform of the eleventh century had enforced the ideals of monasticism on the whole of Christendom, legislation that had been sporadically enforced against clerical marriage during the earlier centuries gradually became the universal law of the Western Church. That the prohibition of clerical marriage was a means of preserving Church properties from hereditary transmission and a safeguard against the establishment of a dynastic ecclesiastical aristocracy cannot be denied. Yet it would be fanciful to assert that the forced imposition of chastity upon the clergy was an unmixed blessing. It is of interest to note that its chief advocates, from Peter Damian to Innocent III, were most prominent in asserting the supreme temporal authority of the papacy. It might also be observed that those divines who forced the legislation were men in their late sixties and seventies. Bernard of Clairvaux unconsciously forecast the result of enforced continence when he preached, "Deprive the Church of honorable marriage and you fill her with concubinage, incest and all manner of nameless vices and uncleanness." The unavailing but constant efforts of local and provincial synods to enforce clerical celibacy and the recurring lists of its violation are sufficient proof that nowhere in Europe was celibacy universally accepted. In the thirteenth century Pope Alexander IV openly proclaimed that licentious clerics were the cause of the burdensome evils under which the Church was groaning. He asserted that "through them the name of God was blasphemed throughout the world. It was an unchaste priesthood that had polluted the sacraments, caused a loss of reverence on the part of the laity for the Catholic religion and deprived them of the benefits of divine service."

Paradoxically, though, the law of celibacy was not so much concerned with the question of a priest's chastity as it was with his remaining unmarried. In 1213 the Archbishop of Lund had inquired of Pope Innocent III whether a man who had two concubines was ineligible for orders and was told that concubinage did not stand in the way of ordination. Little wonder that the faithful balked at the inconsistency of a law which condoned immorality but deprived the clergy of the benefits of the matrimonial state. Nor is it surprising that they paid little heed to admonitions of those who themselves were leading notoriously immoral lives.

The knowledgeable Pierre Dubois, antagonist of Boniface VIII, comments shrewdly on clerical celibacy in his famous *De Recuperatione Terrae Sanctae.* Quoting Aristotle's dictum that first movements are not within our power of control, he argues that in the presence of the desired object scarcely anyone can in any way resist the power of concupiscence. "The resistance of a few is less likely to replenish the celestial fatherland than the lack of resistance on the part of many is likely to injure it. If only the holy fathers—before they set those snares which they did with good intent when they multiplied sins beyond the teaching of the Old and New Testaments—if only they had seen clearly then as they do now those snares which they set voluntarily and the many damned by them." Referring to St. Paul's warning: "To avoid fornication, let every man have his own wife, thus living chastely," he adds: "The Apostle makes no exception when he says every man (*unusquisque*) because he who says all (*omnes*) by so saying excepts nothing. The holy fathers, who were frequently old or decrepit, and could therefore easily avoid fornication, and abstain from all association with women, said, 'We vow perpetual continence,

and we decree that all who are to be advanced to holy
orders shall make and observe a similar vow.' Under penalty
of mortal sin they prohibit the attainment and reception of
holy orders to those who enjoyed intercourse with wives
and spurned such men." "It is also true however," he continues, "that they do not reject secret fornicators, adulterers,
incestuous persons, and those who by words profess themselves continent, but in actual practice are the very opposite,
embracing false pretense and hypocrisy. Indeed, prelates today know very well that they frequently admit to orders this
type of person. All who are advanced to orders vow continence and demand that it be observed by others. Yet the
obvious fact is that very few practice this and they thereby
proclaim themselves to be those whom the Lord described
when he said, 'The scribes and the Pharisees have placed
themselves in the chair of Moses.' "

The reform literature of the fifteenth century is filled with
earnest pleas from prominent churchmen that the papacy
abolish clerical celibacy. The earlier works of William
Durandus suggesting the discipline of the Greek Church
which allowed married clergy were often quoted. Cardinal
Zabarella suggested at the Council of Constance that since
concubinage among the clergy was so deeply rooted they
be allowed to marry. The Carmelite preacher Thomas Con-
necte recommended the restoration of clerical marriage as
the only cure for the evils that beset both the clergy and
laity. However, his pleas were of no avail, for in 1432 he
was apprehended and executed in Rome for denouncing
the abuses of the Curia.

The Emperor Sigismund also recommended the example
of the Greek Church to insure an amelioration of priestly
morals. Cardinal Nicholas of Tudeschi declared that clerical celibacy was neither essential to ordination nor commanded by divine law, hence, the matter should be left to
the discretion of the individual. Aeneas Sylvius, before his
election to the papacy, held that many who were damned
in the celibate state would be saved if a married priesthood
were allowed. In Paris, in 1484, one Jean Laillier presented
a doctoral thesis to the faculty of the Sorbonne defending
the position that a clandestinely married priest required no
penance, that Eastern priests permitted to marry committed
no sin, and that the present law was traceable to the decretals of Gregory VII who exceeded his authority in imposing them. The affair was referred to Innocent VIII and Laillier recanted. Innocent himself has been accused by certain

historians of issuing decrees that authorized clerical concubinage in Rome. There is evidence of a litigation involving
the same Pope and the incumbent of St. Albin's in Normandy
who claimed that he had been given papal permission to
marry. Innocent VIII made no secret of the fact that he had
a number of children. The Augustinian Giles of Viterbo
writes that he was the first of the Popes openly to make a
show of his children and to arrange their own marriages
in the papal palace. Clerical concubinage was so common
in Paris that a local synod debated whether fornication was
a mortal sin. But even in light of all this there was no area
where a relentless adherence to past legislation was more in
evidence than in enforced clerical celibacy.

One of the reasons why the Church authorities were
reluctant to abolish celibacy was that it was a lucrative
source of revenue. The fines imposed on "married" priests
were paid periodically to the bishop as were payments toward the quasi legitimization of their children; in many
cases where the sons of clergy were given parishes the property reverted to the bishop who had legitimized them. There
was a popular saying among the clergy of Switzerland:
"Why should I save for the bishop today, for tomorrow I
may die. And then the bishop will inherit what I have.
I would much prefer to drink day and night and thus occasion frivolity (*Ad quid congrego ego pro episcopo hodie
vel castrina morior et sic volo die noctuque libere et nihil
congregare, et sic levitatem occasionantur*)." One writer es-
timates that in the diocese of Constance alone an average
of 1,500 illegitimate children of priests (*Pfaffenkinder*) were
born each year.

Writing some years after the religious fronts in Europe
had begun to solidify, the irenicist George Witzel wrote of
celibacy: "It seems foolish that Church unity should be
destroyed on account of a matter concerning which Christ
issued no commands, nor which the apostles handed down,
nor which the Fathers taught, nor finally is in no way harmful to faith and morals. Why not follow the doctrine of
Augustine in this matter? There is certainly a great deal of
anxiety today over the fact that the clergy take virgins
and wives into their rooms and make them prostitutes. I
think that we ought to choose the lesser, and certainly
more tolerable, of two evils and permit clerics to have one
virgin wife. For if the 'sacrificers' be separated for life
from the companionship of women, this would constitute
sufficient reason for one not to give himself to the loathsome

shackles of orders. Here again is a problem. For if the present plan of the bishops is to connive with the clergy and ignore their clandestine concubinage, then it goes without saying that religion will perish. No matter how we look at it, there is no doubt that this matter is fraught with danger. As the matter stands now, the canons of the Church are at variance with one another. Certainly the late Pontiff, Aeneas Sylvius, was cognizant of the danger involved in deciding for or against clerical celibacy. John Faber, the renowned speaker of the Gospel, pondered the problem seriously before speaking of a married priesthood and in his work entitled *A Doubt Concerning the Taking of a Wife,* he spoke quite openly and hid nothing. Those who imposed a canon against the honor of marriage could not have foreseen that through celibacy so much debauchery would take place in the Church. Nor is it likely that Pope Calixtus, were he alive today, and witnessing the impurities of those who ought to be the light and salt of the earth, would promulgate such a restrictive law."

Erasmus, in his colloquy on *The Virgin Opposed to Marriage,* expresses a widespread conviction when he says of the celibate clergy: *"Patres vocantur ac frequenter efficiunt, ut hoc nomen vere competat in ipsos"* (They are called fathers, and they frequently accomplish literally what the name implies).

Clerical celibacy was in many respects the final phase in the molding of a sacerdotal caste system that came to identify the Church with the clergy rather than with the entire body of believers. It formed an inseparable barrier between the layman and the clergy. Even a cursory glance at the literature of the medieval period shows how it tended to denigrate the married state. The oftentimes nauseating denunciations of marriage by the monks and clergy read like the rantings of a sick mind. In the opinion of St. Paul and the early Fathers the institution of marriage was a great mystery that symbolized the union of Christ and His Church and was, hence, something sacrosanct and eminently holy. Yet for many a clerical celibate, marriage was at most a cure for concupiscence. Spiritual and ascetic writers invariably mingled their mystic exaltations of virginity with sordid denunciations of matrimony. The pious obscenity addressed to Heloise by Abelard on the superiority of virginity over marriage is hardly an isolated example of such neurotic diatribe. Nor can it be denied that the reluctance of the Church to ameliorate the sufferings of the poor caught up in the economic changes of the late Middle Ages are traceable to a policy that placed married life on a lower scale than that of celibacy. One seeks in vain in medieval literature for a positive theology of marriage or of the Christian family.

Equally responsible for the gulf that separated the higher and the lower clergy was the almost complete lack of formal education among the latter. Although it is customary to think of the medieval universities as the strongholds of clerical learning, less than one percent of the parochial clergy held academic degrees. Most of them acquired what little theology they knew from a few months' residence in a parish as an apprentice. It is not difficult to imagine what a sorry state of learning centuries of this inbred training must have produced. The Dominican, Ulrich Egelberth, a preacher of Strasbourg, sums up in his *Summa de Summo Bono* what he considers the educational requirement of the typical Mass priest: "Insofar as he is obliged to say Mass he must be able to pronounce correctly the words and have at least a literal understanding of what they mean. Insofar as he is the administrator of the sacraments he must know the form and matter of the different sacramental rites. Insofar as he is a teacher he must know the fundamental articles of belief. Insofar as he is a judge, he must know the difference between serious and venial sin, and the various kinds of sin. Since many are ordained only to say Mass they do not require a knowledge of these latter matters."

From the manuals of instruction that were written during the fourteenth and fifteenth centuries we can garner some ideas of the points of theology that were stressed by parish priests whose duties extended beyond the mere recitation of Mass. Most of these manuals were inspired by the legislation of the Lateran Council of 1215 which made annual confession to the parish priest and annual Communion obligatory for all Christians. Confessors were expected to cross-examine penitents on their knowledge of religion as well as of the species of their sins. Hence, the correct use of the sacrament of penance is the dominant theme of most of the instructions. The confessional had replaced the pulpit for all practical purposes. Rarely is mention ever made of the intelligent preaching of the word of God. The Ten Commandments, the seven capital sins and the creed are the chief areas in which a minimum knowledge is required. Lists of sins and types of excommunication attached to reserved sins, divided and subdivided in mathematical fashion, take up the major part of the works. There is no reference whatsoever to dogmatic questions, grace, merit, or the nature of virtue. The corporal works of mercy are seldom mentioned.

There is advice to be given to expectant mothers who are enjoined to suckle their own children. The problems of marriage and sexual morality are dealt with in great detail. In one manual entitled *The Eye of the Priest* there is a long consideration of the pros and cons of marriage. Traditional arguments from the sayings of St. Jerome, Theophrastus, and the Stoics are produced to prove that the wise man does not marry. All the drawbacks of marriage are listed: it impedes the study of philosophy and a man cannot equally serve both his books and wife. A horse, an ass, an ox, a dog or any other animal can be tried out before it is bought, only a wife had to be taken on good faith. Whether it is better to marry a beautiful or an ugly woman is answered by pointing out that although it is irksome to have an ugly wife whom no one wants, this is to be preferred to having a beautiful wife whom everyone is chasing after. On the whole, an ugly wife will bring one misery. To keep a poor wife is difficult, to put up with a rich one is a torment.

In the *Manuale Sacerdotis,* written by John Mirk in the early fifteenth century, the ideal priest is "the priest of God, whose soul is in His hands always and (who) knows that he is hired to celebrate every day. The priest lives justly when he renders what is his due, when in return for the salary which he receives from him he pays back spiritual commodities, not only by celebrating every day for him one single Mass, but also in other spiritual services, as for instance the seven penitential psalms, the fifteen gradual psalms, devout litanies, offices of the dead and similar spiritual things." The general impression of the manuals of instruction is that the priest is little more than a hired functionary, employed to say Mass or instruct the faithful with a series of dry and stereotyped exhortations that mutilated the beauties of revealed religion almost beyond recognition.

Nicholas of Clemanges sums up a general impression on the lack of education among the lower clergy when he remarks in his work *De Ruina Ecclessiae* (*On the Ruin of the Church*): "What can one presume to say about their illiteracy and learning? Although they may stumble syllable by syllable over the words, they have no grasp of what the words mean. How can we possibly educate them?" Much of the satirical literature of the early sixteenth century is filled with ridicule of the unlettered clergy. Ulrich von Hutten, in his *Roman Trinity* (*Trinitas Romana*), attacks the poorly educated clergy and taunts a typical cathedral rector in Regensburg who had recently received a doctor's degree in Rome for money: *"Ille in nulla arte doctus, tantum emeret titulum hunc."*

The most common complaint against the clergy in this matter was their lack of knowledge of the Latin they were required to use in the liturgy and in the administration of the sacraments. Yet, as the general public felt that the mechanical ability to say Mass was the chief requisite for the priesthood, there was little demand for an educated clergy. The reform councils' concern for higher education among the clergy was limited to a scaling of payments in terms of the academic requirements for important benefices. It was only early in the sixteenth century, under the impetus of humanism, that any serious attempt to educate the lower clergy was undertaken.

Any consideration of the Church's relationship to education in the late Middle Ages must consider two powerful forces of the age: the increasing laicization of education and the growth of humanism. There is much truth in the view that as long as the monastic spirit prevailed in education the formation of a large educated laity was all but impossible. Though clerks multiplied, learning perished with them and each successive generation had to start anew from the scions of the unlearned. However, during the later Middle Ages many of the educational functions formerly performed by the monasteries had been taken over by schools and universities, and gradually lay influence had the opportunity of making itself felt more fully. The growth of lay influence was sometimes opposed by the churchmen to the extent that in some cases the ecclesiastical authorities even objected to the teaching of other than strictly religious material in the schools. As early as in the thirteenth century there were disputes as to how far the song schoolmaster might teach the elements of grammar, and in 1357 Bishop John Grandison of Exeter complained that the schoolmasters in his diocese took the boys away from reading matins and the hours of the Virgin.

Although it is difficult to overemphasize the influence of the Church on education in the Middle Ages, it is a gross exaggeration to maintain that only clerics could read and write. Recent research has shown that we must modify the view of almost total illiteracy of the laity in the Middle

Ages. In the late Middle Ages municipal schools (and consequently increased lay education) followed the growth of towns and the communal movement. Town governments established new schools and often struggled with the bishops and other ecclesiastical authorities for freedom from Church control of these schools. Even where church schools were fairly adequate town governments sometimes preferred to set up schools of their own. Sometimes the town wished to check the over-multiplication of individual schoolmasters and their rivalry for pupils. For example, Ferrara in 1443 decreed that no one should open a grammar school there without first obtaining consent of the municipal governing board. One scholar goes so far as to say: "It would appear that the thirteenth century made a closer approach to popular and social education than the sixteenth."

The tendency toward lay control was one of the most important trends in fifteenth-century education. In England such agencies as lay endowed chantries, guilds and foundations by wealthy individuals such as Eton were responsible for this tendency. Usually (but not always) the schoolmasters were still in holy orders, but even this practice was opposed in a few instances. An important factor is that the clerics in these new-type educational institutions were not necessarily attached to a cathedral or monastic establishment, and consequently were free from their jurisdiction. The creation of schools by wealthy and influential citizens who placed their management in the hands of agencies other than chantry and stipendiary priests constituted a radical change in the medieval educational structure. For example, in 1430 a London grocer at his death left certain revenues to the rector, vicar and churchwardens of the Sevenoaks Church in Kent County: ". . . to find and maintain forever one master, an honest man, sufficiently advanced and expert in the science of grammar, B.A., by no means in holy orders, to keep a grammar school in some convenient house within the said town of Sevenoaks . . . and to teach and instruct all poor boys whatsoever coming there for the sake of learning, taking nothing of them or their parents or friends for teaching and instructing them . . ." The phrase "by no means in holy orders" is especially significant; it seems a point of departure from the almost universal practice of employing only teachers who were priests, clerks or in some kind of holy orders.

The guilds were also important not only in providing education for the poorer classes but in expediting lay con-

trol of education. In the middle of the fifteenth century the
Trinity Guild of Deddington and the Trinity Guild of Chip-
ping Norton both demanded of their priests the duty of
teaching any of their children who desired it. The same
tendency is evident in the action of the town of Bingham
in 1439 asking leave of Henry VI to found a college to train
grammar schoolmasters. Moreover, the successive headmas-
ters of York Cathedral Grammar School were laymen.

Nor was the expansion of lay education limited to England. The printing press doubtless increased secular subject
matter, and burgher families of Paris, Tours, Lyons and
Antwerp were often active agents in the growth of lay
education. Moreover, patrician families of Augsburg and
Nuremberg made southern Germany a center of culture.
The secular influence in education made itself felt especially early in Italy. In many towns so-called Latin schools
grew up, and it is significant that these schools did not
depend on the Church, but rather on the municipality or on
private enterprise.

The northern universities retained for a longer period a
much stronger ecclesiastical bias than those of Italy, but in
the fifteenth century the northern institutions were to an
increasing degree being frequented by lay students seeking
training for secular rather than clerical careers. The growing demand for higher education is indicated by the number
of new universities founded between 1450 and 1517 for the
most part by secular authorities. However, it was in the
Italian universities that lay influence was strongest. There
the revival of Roman civil law and the study of medicine
gave the layman a prominent place in institutions of
higher learning. This growth of lay participation in secondary and higher education helped to produce a new educated class in European culture. It was from this group,
more than any other, that the call for Church reform arose.

The anti-clericalism occasioned by the economic burden
that tax exempt Church properties placed upon the medieval
city must also be added to the causes that contributed to the
tension between the official Church and the laity. Crowded
conditions in many of the cities and the constant rise of
prices due to crop failures and the depreciation of money
fostered an attitude dangerously critical of the wealthiest
institution in Europe. The Church, especially in Germany,
was the richest landowner in Christendom. It is estimated
that one-third of the real estate of the Empire was in its control. Legacies and bequests increased the ownership from

year to year. In many of the larger cities ecclesiastical establishments, cloisters, convents, and friaries occupied as much as one-fourth of the business district. Often entire market places were in their control; the city council of Freiburg wrote the prior of the Augustinians in 1495 complaining that the financial burden placed upon that city by tax-free monastic holdings was a greater threat to its economic security than expenditures for war or imperial taxes. In Goslar, the citizens complained that the Franciscans obstructed the security of the city by building their monastery along the city walls and thus allowing the ramparts and fortifications to collapse. In Halle the Dominicans erected a convent that diverted the city's sewage system and imperilled the health of the inhabitants. In Essen a group of nuns dammed up the river in order to supply their own fishponds with fresh water and ruined the local milling industry. Municipal records at the end of the century are filled with complaints against the wealth of the mendicant orders.

Equally oppressive to the citizenry was the fact that many of the religious orders were deeply involved in competitive business practices where their free labor and methods of mass production created monopolies. Monastic breweries, wineries, mills and bakeries were commonplace. More often than not the breweries operated by the religious also maintained their own taverns. They were immune to city ordinances and frequently were open to business on Sundays and feast days. Their immunity to local laws made them places of refuge and sanctuary for the undesirable elements of the populace.

The textile industry presents another area where a monopoly by religious orders of women, especially the Beginnen, created an unhappy situation. The manufacture of cloth articles by the sisterhoods generally tended to drive the local products from the markets. In an age when cloth manufacturing was an important aspect of the economy of each individual locality, one can understand the seriousness of the competition.

To these grievances one must also add the numerous privileges enjoyed by the clergy. They were exempt from the municipal taxes, they were not obliged to bear arms, and although frequently apprehended for crimes, were to be judged in their own courts. On the other hand, the ordinary civilian was constantly irked by the tax he was forced to pay to the diocese for dispensations from marriage impediments, permission to eat certain forbidden foods, and the lifting of other ecclesiastical penalties; missing Mass on Sunday or eating meat on Friday were misdemeanors that entailed a fine. A popular saying of the time was *"Quicumque secure et impune vult vivere, fit clericus"* (Whoever wants to live safely and without punishment becomes a cleric).

The case of the drummer of Niklashausen is a striking example of how social unrest, apocalyptic fanaticism and anti-clericalism combined to inspire a violent uprising against the Church in the diocese of Würzburg. Hans Boheim, a native of Helmstadt, had for years entertained the villagers of Niklashausen in the Tauber valley not far distant from Würzburg with his drum and bagpipes. A shepherd by profession, he underwent a sudden conversion during the Lent of 1476; influenced no doubt by a recounting of the fear-inspiring sermons preached a generation previous in that area by the Franciscan preacher, Giovanni di Capistrano, he burned his musical instruments in front of the parish church and announced a new crusade for the righteous. The program, not unlike that of many another visionary before and since, had been outlined by an apparition of the Blessed Virgin. She had appeared, he claims, and informed him of the approaching of the end of the world. Unless mankind mended its ways and came to Niklashausen to venerate the statue of the Virgin in the local church the catastrophe would be postponed no longer. The Tauber, and not the Tiber, was now to be the central distribution point for God's grace. Whoever came there would be absolved from all sin, and whoever died there would go immediately to heaven.

The local pastor, not entirely adverse to making the town a famous pilgrimage spot, at first encouraged the young mystic and allowed him the use of his pulpit. Crowds from all parts of Germany flocked to the place, in some cases as many as 70,000. As the movement gained momentum, Boheim's preaching took a definite anti-clerical turn. Soon he was denouncing the gross immorality of the clergy, their avarice, their concubinage, their tithing. It would be, he said, easier to make a Christian out of a Jew than out of a priest. God had been too long outraged by the behavior of the clergy, He would tolerate it no longer. The day of reckoning was at hand, when the clergy would be happy to hide their tonsure and to escape their pursuers. A wrathful God had withdrawn His support from the clergy and soon there would be no more priests and monks left on the face of the earth.

The killing of a cleric would be looked upon as a most meritorious act. A fearful punishment awaited them if they dared burn him as a heretic, for it was they who were the real heretics. He called upon his hearers to refuse all payment of taxes and tithes. Henceforth, the clergy should be made to give up their many benefices and live from meal to meal on what their parishioners chose to give them.

The situation in the diocese of Würzburg was especially conducive to such an explosion. For generations its prince-bishops had exasperated the people with increasing taxes, not a small amount of which went to the support of their mistresses and hunting parties. The incumbent bishop, Rudolph of Sherenberg, was notified by the primate of all Germany, Archbishop Deither von Isenberg of Mainz, to call a halt to the movement. By this time it had taken on all the aspects of a social revolution. Boheim was now proclaiming a communist state wherein tributes of all kinds would be abolished. There would be free use of wool, pasturage, and hunting for all. No rent or services would be owed to any lord, no taxes or duties to any prince. All would live together as brothers, all would enjoy the same privileges and liberties. The time had come when the princes and the lords would have to work for their daily bread. "The Emperor is a scoundrel and the Pope is useless." Fantastic rumors were circulated claiming that paradise had literally descended upon the area of Niklashausen where infinite riches were lying about to be gathered up by the faithful. Crowds swarmed around the prophet crying, "O man of God sent from heaven, have pity on us." They chanted, "To God in Heaven we complain, Kyrie eleison, that the priests cannot be slain, Kyrie eleison."

Finally the Bishop sent a squad of horsemen to Niklashausen and carried the prophet off to the episcopal palace. In spite of the threats of a large crowd of pilgrims to storm the city, he was secretly judged and sentenced as a heretic. Along with two of his companions he was burned at the stake in the city square and his ashes were thrown into the river. The offerings left at the church of Niklashausen were confiscated and shared between the Archbishop of Mainz, the Bishop of Würzburg, and the count on whose territory the church stood. Pilgrims, although threatened with excommunication, continued to flock to the church although it had been closed and placed under interdict. In 1477 it was burned to the ground by order of the Archbishop of Mainz.

Anti-clericalism bred by resentment of clerical privileges was not limited to Germany. The case of the London merchant Richard Hume gives some idea of the anti-clericalism prevalent in England during the early decades of the sixteenth century. Hume had lost a case in an ecclesiastical court against a priest who had taken the burial sheet from his deceased child as payment for funeral services. He had then taken the case before the Court of the King's Bench charging the cleric with a violation of praemunire. Thereupon the Bishop's officials had him arrested on trumped-up charges of harboring heretical books. He was found hanged in the Bishop's prison and it was alleged that he had committed suicide. A popular uprising forced the king to intervene in the case and return the murdered man's confiscated property.

The religious orders present another area where a failure to live up to high ideals, coupled with an increasing rivalry among themselves, gave the laity ample reason to question seriously their alleged call to Christian perfection. The older orders had long since lost the rigor and austerity that had marked their activities during the twelfth and early thirteenth centuries. The dietary rules which formed such an important aspect of their asceticism were generally ignored or circumvented by the use of special flesh-kitchens. Many of the monks dined separately and had their own private rooms. In fact, some monasteries had so completely abandoned community life that they resembled men's clubs. Due to a lack of vocations, many of them were almost completely manned by hired lay servants. In many monastic institutions the practice of corrody, whereby the monks received members of the laity, promising them an annuity for life (consisting of food and lodging) was common. However, the "lodgers" often lived on for many years after the lump sum they had paid was exhausted.

The office was seldom recited in choir, or it was regulated by a rotation process with a few old monks doing the chanting. In most monasteries learning was at a standstill and the monastic ideal forgotten. As an English bishop aptly remarked in the early fifteenth century, "religion was perishing" in the monasteries.

Life in convents had also lost much of its pristine religious fervor. Many of them had become comfortable boarding houses for the unmarried daughters of the wealthy. We read of nuns being beguiled into apostasy by wandering minstrels and of the prioress of a convent in Leicestershire who was wont to go haymaking with the local chaplain *sola cum solo*. The nuns of certain monasteries in France were known to don secular clothing on certain feast days and dance with the people of the neighborhood. Nicholas of Cusa, in attempting to reform his diocese of Brixen, fought a long and futile battle with the abbess of the Benedictine convent in Sonnenburg. The nuns, recruited almost exclusively from among the Tyrolean nobility, were completely ignorant of the rules of the order. They seldom recited the office, and frequently left the convent to attend the public baths and wedding festivals. They distributed the income from the convent properties among themselves. In spite of excommunication the nuns continued to resist reform and hired a group of mercenaries to defend them. They were finally expelled from the convent at sword point, still refusing to amend their laxities.

More actively involved in the social and economic affairs and, hence, more open to the scrutiny of the laity, were the ubiquitous mendicants, especially the more numerous Franciscans and Dominicans. Although both orders were formed in response to the urgent need of an age engaged in a struggle for privilege and exemption, an era when the Church had been victimized by a dried-up theology, they soon succumbed to these very evils their founders had aimed at eradicating.

The history of the Franciscans as we have seen was one of continued internal division and struggle between two groups: one advocating a purely spiritualistic concept of the friars as a brotherhood following Christ in perfect poverty, the other envisioning the followers of Francis as a legal corporate body controlled by the papacy. Constant changes in Franciscan vocation and a relaxation of the rule led to frequent attempts at secession and lapses into revolt and heresy. In addition there was constant bickering between the Franciscans and the Dominicans regarding the comparative excellence of their theory and practice of poverty. The Franciscan claim to utter poverty was an attractive force for support and recruits. Their claim to holding property only through "spiritual friends" as a third party often amounted to a little less than having their own private bankers. The Dominicans claimed the legal fiction of the Franciscans was an open violation of the vow of poverty and that it was impossible to find two followers of the Poverello who agreed on what apostolic poverty actually was. The syllogistic arguments between the two groups, often revolving about the question of whether the sword Peter drew in the garden was his own personal property, continued for centuries. Meanwhile both litigants accumulated vast wealth.

During the fifteenth century their animosity toward one another shifted to the question of the Immaculate Conception of the Virgin Mary. The Franciscans followed the lead of Duns Scotus who is generally acknowledged as the herald and champion of the doctrine which claims that the Mother of Christ was free from original sin from the moment of her conception. They soon became the violent advocates of a doctrine that in the minds of many was tantamount to denying the universality of Christ's redemption. The Dominicans, following the lead of Aquinas, whose canonization in 1323 was looked upon as an official sanctioning of his doctrine, soon attacked the immaculists. By the fifteenth century the issue had involved not only the members of the mendicant orders but the papacy and the leading universities as well. The thirty-sixth session of the Council of Basel had declared the doctrine a matter of faith, and it had been accepted as such in many parts of Northern Europe. A provincial synod at Avignon, in 1457, had imposed the penalty of excommunication upon anyone who dared to attack the doctrine either in the pulpit or in public discussions. The controversy continued unabated however. Numerous tracts were published by the partisans of both views. In 1475 a Dominican, Vincent Bandelli, published a work on *The Truth of the Conception of the Blessed Virgin Mary,* in which he described the immaculist system as erroneous, impious, temerarious, and more dangerous than the heresies of Pelagius, Celestius, and Julianus. In bitter polemic he speaks of this belief as a diabolical dogma that undermines the foundations of Christian belief. The advocates of the doctrine are guilty, he protests, of seducing the people under the pretext of piety and the hope of lucre. They corrupt Holy Scripture, condemn the Fathers, and by exalting the Blessed Virgin with false honors, nefariously slander the blood of Christ. The excess of both parties resulted only in hatred which was enflamed by heated and disgraceful discussions.

The quarrel reached an almost tragi-comic climax in Bern, Switzerland, in 1509. A mentally retarded psychopathic tailor by the name of Jetzer, from that city, had been persuaded to enter the Dominican novitiate. He was soon prevailed upon by four of the brethren to announce to the public a miraculous apparition from the Blessed Virgin. The visionary gave a detailed account of the event and pointed out that the Virgin had expressed her distress at the attempts of the immaculists to have the Pope declare the dogma of the Immaculate Conception. Jetzer's vision was supported by all of the conventional proofs of the supernatural. He had seen a bleeding Host, and the picture of the Virgin in the chapel was also reported to have undergone an effusion of warm blood. Excitement reached a high pitch in Bern when it was announced that Jetzer had the stigmata.

Investigations later proved that the entire plot had been planned by the Dominican Chapter in Wimpfen. After Jetzer left the novitiate, he reported to a jury that his reluctance to continue with the hoax had brought about attempts on his life—the brethren had attempted to kill him with a poisoned Host. Four of the friars were defrocked and executed by the civil authorities and Jetzer was banned from the city.

But the problem of Mary's Immaculate Conception continued until long after the outbreak of the Reformation. During the fifth session of the Council of Trent the question was brought before the assembled fathers. Cardinal Pacheco, the head of the Spanish bishops, suggested that the conception of Mary be dealt with in connection with the definition of original sin. He urged that since the greater part of Christendom piously believed in the Immaculate Conception a definition would be especially pleasing to France and Spain. Pacheco's suggestion met with a volley of objections from the Dominican bishops since the Cardinal had acted upon the advice of his counselor, the Franciscan theologian Andreas de la Vega. Peter Bertano, the Bishop of Fano, recommended that the question be dropped since the matter was a difficult one which the Church herself had been unable to unravel. If the Council were to define this doctrine, he argued, the discussions would continue for months and this would be playing into the hands of the Protestants and bring dishonor on the assembly. Bertano suggested that the most sensible way of dealing with the problem would be to impose perpetual silence on all who would henceforth wish to speak on the question. Finally the Jesuit Lainez arranged a deletion of the doctrine from the decrees of the Council, observing that its adversaries based their position on the fact that the Fathers of the Church, and many of the great scholastics, while commentating on the text of St. Paul concerning the universality of original sin, made no mention of Our Lady.

The Jansenists carried the controversy into the seventeenth century. Adam Widenfelt, a convert from Protestantism, summed up what was the opinion of many sober-minded Christians before and since on the turbulent problem. In a work he wrote on the Blessed Virgin dedicated to "her more indiscreet venerators" he put these words in the mouth of the Virgin: "Love that is contentious is not beautiful. Stop devouring one another in your wrangling over my privileges; it serves no purpose except to upset the listeners. And why do you presume to decide what was neither revealed by God nor defined by the Church? Deal with the work of truth, and avoid profane and empty talk."

The envy and hatred that reached such a disgraceful pitch among the friars was equalled only by the bitter animosity that prevailed between themselves and the secular clergy. The struggle between the friars and the secular clergy at the universities of Paris and Oxford had not ceased since the thirteenth century. We have seen how Gerson was involved in this struggle as Chancellor of the University of Paris. Both Popes Eugene IV and Nicholas V were forced to intervene and protect the right of the friars to lecture at the university. Here as elsewhere the granting of immunities to the friars helped to increase the antagonism toward the source of those immunities, Rome. If the prophetic and evangelical vocation of the mendicants had become subordinate to the demands of ecclesiastical politics, it had also succumbed to a spirit of acquisitiveness and greed that provoked the undying hatred of the diocesan clergy. The conflict between the mendicants and the diocesan clergy had of course begun soon after the approval of the mendicants by Honorius III, in spite of the decree of the Fourth Lateran Council that no new orders be created. Although St. Francis had warned his followers against forcing themselves into a diocese or a parish against the wishes of the bishop, the friars soon began to encroach upon the preserves of the secular clergy. By the middle of the thirteenth century they were threatening a serious loss of clientele and income for the parochial clergy.

Since many of them were more widely travelled than the seculars, they were able to fascinate their audience with tales of the Holy Land and the marvels of Rome. Generally better trained in the art of preaching, they drew greater crowds with their dramatic accounts of miracles and fanciful presentation of dogma. Well established in most of the larger cities they acquired a clientele among the well-to-do. Many of their penitents, fascinated by the amazing treasury of spiritual gifts one accrued through burial in the friars' cemeteries—a share in the daily Masses of the brethren—turned over their wills to the mendicants. In this way they often deprived the parish clergy of the customary burial fees and legacies upon which they depended for financial support.

Another grievance voiced by the secular clergy against them was that they encouraged sin and moral laxity by doling out light penances in confession. The Archbishop of Armagh, speaking before the Pope in 1375, said, "For I have in my diocese of Armagh, as I suppose, two thousand subjects, who every year are involved in sentences of excommunication on account of sentences passed against willful homicides, public robberies, incendiaries, and the like; and all such men received the sacrament like other men, and are absolved or said to be absolved; nor are they believed to be absolved by any other except by the friars, without doubt, for no others absolve them."

The Provincial Council of Canterbury in the early fourteenth century, after denouncing the friars because of their abuses respecting the privilege of preaching, confession, and burial, complains of the effect they have on the laymen who come to them for confession. "By these circumventions the ears of the laymen are hardened and turned against their parish churches and their rectors, and these laymen presume to work contemptuously against the liberties of the Church. The parish priests suffer from the neglect and interference of these laymen and are reduced to beggary, whereas the friars grow rich and erect grand buildings. The parish priests end up by begging the help of the bishop of the province against their enemies."

Toward the middle of the century the same Chapter of Canterbury lashed out again against the friars as slanderers of the clergy, flatterers of magnates, and overindulgent confessors. "These religious, to whom the quest of beggary ought to provide a living, go about on noble palfreys of their own, with saddles and reins most exquisitely ornamented. They surpass the ostentation of the greater prelates and become their most biting detractors. They handle secular and spiritual affairs relating to the King and other nobles and magnates of the land, and so prejudice the clergy and the English church. They are clearly more hostile to the Church than the laity. They are astute and one-sided middlemen, corrupt and disguised under the veil of religion. They frequently become mediators of contracts of marriage, illicitly and of their own free will, and they are deceitful agents of business. By their blandishments they acquire the good will of the lords and ladies of the realm of England to such an extent that very many churches of this realm to which they are opposed are outrageously oppressed in their legal rights. What is more lamentable, being the confessors of such noble lords and ladies, nay rather the betrayers and notorious deceivers of their souls, they convert to their own gain the compensation for wrongdoing which by earthly and heavenly law ought to be restored to the injured parties. Thus a pillow of flattery is put under the sinner's head as he sleeps in his sin. Loaded with goods, they stuff their ruddy cheeks and blow out their bellies; and when they are deservedly rebuked for fomenting sin in this manner, they daily prepare intolerable plots against the English church, and secretly commit things concerning which it is not expedient to speak at present, since they hold such sway. Wherefore your clergy pray that for the salvation of the English church you would cause to be applied some timely remedy against these insolencies of the said mendicants, in this present council or by provision of the Apostolic See."

Mathias Janov, well-known canon of Prague, described the mendicant orders as a third hand on the body of Christ that had taken from the right hand of Christ, the secular clergy, all of its power and glory. He proposed that the religious orders with the exception of those stricter observances, the Carthusians and Cistercians, be consolidated within the secular clergy. Only in this way, he said, could the respect and honor of the faithful for the priesthood be reestablished. There has never been a period in the history of the Church when the suppression of the mendicant orders has not been suggested by those who feel their contributions to religion are overshadowed by the false asceticism they foster.

Like the monks before them they had lost faith in their own traditions and had failed to adapt themselves to a changing world. The monasteries were no longer the marvel they had been in a less complicated society that was more direct in its religious outlook. Both the monks and the friars had become the unconscious victims of the changing social and economic fabric of the times. The disintegration of monasticism was not entirely unlike the breakup of knighthood. In both cases the ideals had been pitched too high and the asceticism practiced became an obstacle rather than a means to genuine piety.

Perhaps the real cause of the bitterness felt toward the religious orders in the late Middle Ages was their having outlived their purposefulness. The ideal of poverty, originally intended to demonstrate to the poor that their plight could be voluntarily shared by others, had lost its cogency in a society where money rather than land tenure had become the criterion of wealth. The friars themselves were faced with the dilemma of claiming absolute renunciation of property and yet finding it necessary to act as wage earners. The great majority of them had entered the orders at an age when idealism was at its highest pitch; seldom were novices out of their early teens. In establishing the quintessence of Christianity in the evangelical counsels they set a goal whose non-achievement, in many cases, resulted in a depreciation of the entire message of Christ. Of no period does the observation that the spread of piety does not mean a growth of charity seem more appropriate than of the pre-Reformation era.

It is not without significance that it was the monasteries that nurtured the great leaders of the sixteenth century reform—Luther, Bucer, Capito, Bullinger, and others. Nor can it be denied that those areas of Northern Europe where the Christian message was first carried by the monks, Augustine in England, Boniface in Germany, Anglo-Saxon Benedictines in Scandinavia, were those very lands that broke away from Roman Catholicism in the sixteenth century.

6

Martin Luther: from church reform to doctrinal change

"In truth had this man been prudent, had he restricted himself to his first propositions, and not entangled himself in manifest error about the faith, he would have been not only favored but adored by the whole of Germany."

CARDINAL CONTARINI

Although it may be somewhat of an exaggeration to identify the Reformation with the personality of Luther and to equate Protestantism with his doctrines, nevertheless, from an ecumenical point of view we must accept the widespread conviction that "the principle of Protestantism is basically reflected in the person of Martin Luther." There is scarcely a single instance in history in which one individual has such significance in a tremendous historical upheaval as Martin Luther assumes in the Reformation. To consider him merely as the enunciator of ideas traceable to a number of early theologians or to maintain, as Haller does, that his contribution to the Reformation was small (that it was, as it were, the spark that ignited the powder and that he was an occasion, not a cause, of the Reformation) is a view that no serious student of the period now accepts.

However complicated politically and doctrinally Protestantism may have become, its basic and primary design must be attributed to Luther. What occurred within his soul and mind and the manner in which he expressed this in his writings gave the impulse and direction that dominated the entire Protestant movement. As Döllinger sagely remarked of Luther a century ago in appraising the tremendous contribution of Protestantism to Christianity, one simply cannot condemn the most powerful conductor of religion that Christianity has produced in eighteen centuries for a few pages in a hundred volumes, for his matrimonial advice to Philip of Hesse, or for his exhortation to exterminate the revolted peasants. In Luther were clearly reflected the two central themes of the Reformation, the renovation of the fundamental message of the Gospel and the establishment of a more practical and personal means of presenting it.

Luther was born on November 10 in 1483 in the Thuringian village of Eisleben. His parents, Hans Luder and Margaret Ziegler, had recently emigrated from the farming community of Möhra where the Luder family had lived for many generations. As was the practice of the time, the child was baptized the following day by the local pastor, Bartholomew Rennebecher, and as it was the feast of St. Martin of Tours, was named after the sainted Roman soldier.

Within a year after his birth the family moved to Mansfeld where the father was employed as a laborer in the copper mines. Although Luther's early childhood was beset with poverty, there is no indication that this fact or his father's sternness as a disciplinarian created an abnormal atmosphere. By the turn of the century his father's financial situation had improved and in 1511 he became owner in a number of mines and foundries of the area. He was elected to the city council in 1491. Young Martin was enrolled in the local Latin day school in 1488 where he began the traditional study of Latin grammar, the requisite *sine qua non* for any higher education. In 1496 he was sent to Magdeburg where he remained until Easter of the following year at a school conducted by the Brethren of the Common Life. The next semester he transferred to Eisenach because he had relatives there. Here he found lodging in the household of a well-to-do merchant, Henry Schalbe. The Schalbe family, especially the wife, was extremely pious and was greatly influenced by the Franciscans from neighboring Wartburg. The friars were frequent visitors to the Schalbe household.

In April of 1501 Luther matriculated at the University of Erfurt and enrolled in the bursa of St. George, a sort of hospice or college for young students, well-regulated in the manner of present-day seminaries and, like the latter, quite lacking in academic freedom.

The University of Erfurt was in a sense one of the oldest schools of its kind in Germany. Already by the middle of the thirteenth century there were over a thousand students pursuing a *studium generale* here. It was not until 1379, however, that a bull of foundation was granted by Clement VI. It was later renewed in 1389 when the institution transferred its obedience to Urban VI. By the time Luther had enrolled the school had become a stronghold of nominalism. Two of his professors, Jodocus Trutvetter and Bartholomew Arnold von Usingen, were followers of the *Via Moderna*. Whether Luther was deeply influenced by nominalism is still a moot question. The picture drawn by Denifle that portrays Luther as an ossified Occamite is no longer tenable. Although Luther, in his later life, remarked that he belonged to the school of Occam, he did not, on other occasions, hesitate to refer to the nominalists as "hoggish theologians."

Nor was Luther, as his Catholic biographers contend, a "crass ignoramus." He received his baccalaureate in 1502 and immediately began the required studies for a master's degree. In January of 1502 he passed the master's exam after the shortest period of study possible, standing second in his class. His courses followed the traditional trivium and quadrivium of the medieval university. He studied the *Summales Logicales* of Peter of Spain, and the *Physics, Politics, Nicomachean Ethics* and *Metaphysics* of Aristotle. Although the young Luther had but a slight knowledge of Greek, he was well acquainted with classical Latin authors. Ovid, Virgil, Plautus and Horace were well known to him. He was also fairly well acquainted with humanism. The humanist Jerome Emser had lectured at Erfurt during the summer of 1504, and Luther was familiar with the *Ecologues* of the Latin humanist Baptista Mantuanus. Grotius Rubeanus was a close friend of the young Luther and was painfully shocked at his decision to enter the monastery.

In the summer of 1505, Luther, influenced no doubt by his father, began the study of law. Sometime in July of the same year, while returning to Erfurt from a visit to Mansfeld, he encountered a severe thunderstorm near the village of Stotternheim and, as a lightning bolt threw him to the ground, he vowed to St. Anne in a sudden panic that he would become a monk. To assume that the decision to enter the monastery was as impromptu as it is often depicted does Luther an injustice. His strict religious upbringing, his natural bent toward piety, and above all the experiences of the last few years at the university were unquestionably factors in his move. In 1503 he had severely wounded himself by accidentally cutting the artery in his thigh and had spent many weeks in meditative recuperation. In the same year one of his closest friends, a fellow student, had died suddenly. The plague that struck the city of Erfurt in 1505 had made him keenly aware of the pre-eminence of death. When he was about twenty years old he had seen for the first time in his life a complete Bible, and, as he relates, soon purchased a Postel, or a book of sermons. All of this indicates that a call to religion was something that had probably been in his mind for a long period of time.

Nor is it without significance that he chose to enter the monastery of the Hermits of St. Augustine. The city of Erfurt boasted a Dominican, a Franciscan, and a Servite monastery in addition to the Black Cloister, a member of the Observant, or stricter, congregation of Saxony, which was by far the most severe of the religious houses in the city. On July 16, 1505, much to the chagrin of his parents, who were already selecting a future bride for the student of law, Luther entered the novitiate of the Hermits of St. Augustine. Luther's novitiate lasted longer than the prescribed year. Soon after his profession, the exact date of which is not known, he was told to prepare himself for the reception of Holy Orders. He was ordained a deacon by the suffragan bishop of Erfurt, John von Laasphe, on February 27, 1507; he received the priesthood in the Erfurt cathedral on the following April 4. His father, along with some twenty relatives and friends, attended his first Mass on May 2, 1507. The tale of Luther's fear to continue with the Mass when he came to the words of the Canon—*Aeterno Deo, vivo et vero*—until urged on by his Prior is of course unfounded. Its origin can be traced to a normal hesitancy on his part during the process of learning the Mass ceremonies and the subsequent urging of his Prior at that time.

Needless to say, the Augustinian community had plans for the young *magister artium* who had entered their ranks. Soon after ordination, Luther was sent to Wittenberg where the order held two professorships at the Elector Frederick's newly founded university. The university itself was hardly impressive as an institute of higher learning. When Luther arrived there in 1508, there were probably no more than 300 students. John von Staupitz, vicar-general of the Saxon congregation of the Augustinians, held the chair of scriptural theology and Luther was given the chair of moral philosophy in the arts faculty. In addition to lecturing on the Nicomachean Ethics, Luther was also obliged to continue his theological studies. He received his baccalaureate in theology in the spring of 1509. The following autumn he returned again to Erfurt where he continued with his study of the *Sentences* of Peter of Lombard, and lectured on philosophy to the students in the Augustinian monastery there.

Luther's studies were interrupted in 1510 when he was selected to accompany Staupitz to Rome. The vicar-general had for years been identified with the reform group in the order who sought to unite the observant, or stricter, group in the order with the more numerous "conventuals." Because of a failure to bring about the conjunction and thus introduce a stricter discipline, Staupitz had been summoned to Rome.

Luther probably spent a month in Rome, visiting its many shrines and churches. He was not particularly edified with the horde of unlettered clergy whom he encountered there, many of whom were unable to hear confessions. He later observed that the priests said Mass in such a cocksure and slipshod fashion that it reminded him of a juggling act. Yet there is little evidence that the scandals of Rome had any bearing on the gradual religious transformation that was taking place in his mind.

After returning to Erfurt he was again sent to Wittenberg in the late summer of 1511. In October of 1512, he received the doctorate in theology and was assigned to the theological faculty, succeeding Staupitz as professor of Scripture. The next five years were of vital importance in the development of Luther's theological ideas. During this period he lectured on the Psalms (1513-15), on the Epistle to the Romans (1515-16), the Epistle to the Galatians, and the Epistle to the Hebrews (1517-18). One gains some idea of the competence of the man in considering that in addition to following a monastic and academic schedule, he also preached at the castle church, and held the office of Augustinian vicar of the district of Meissen and Thuringia.

We gather some ideas of Luther's care and solicitude for his fellow religious in a letter he addressed to the Augustinian Prior at Mainz, John Breche, in 1510: "I have been recently grieved to learn that there is with your reverence one of my brothers, a certain George Baumgartner, of our friary in Dresden, and that, alas, he sought refuge with you in a shameful manner, and for a shameful cause. I thank your faith and duty for receiving him and thereby bringing his shame to an end. That lost sheep is mine, he belongs to me; it is mine to seek him, and if it please the Lord Jesus, to bring him back. Wherefore I beseech your reverence, by our common faith in Christ and our common Augustinian vow, to send him to me in dutiful charity either at Dresden or at Wittenberg, or rather to persuade him lovingly and gently to come of his own accord. I shall receive him with open arms, only let him come; he has no cause to fear my displeasure.

"I know that scandals must arise. It is no miracle that a man should fall, but it is a miracle that he should rise and stand. Peter fell, that he might know that he was a man;

today the cedars of Lebanon, touching the sky with their tops, fall down. Miracle of miracles, even an angel fell from heaven, and man from paradise. What wonder is it, then, that a reed shaken by the wind and a smoking flax be quenched? May the Lord Jesus teach you and use you and *perfect you in every good work*."

If peace of mind had been one of the motives for Luther's entering religion, he found it to be illusory. He gradually grew aware of the vast abyss between what he felt himself to be in his innermost self and the demands of God. He was increasingly conscious of the power of sin, even repeated confession brought him no peace. Further, the complacency that he felt at doing good seemed, as he said, "to poison his soul as the frost nips flowers in the bud." There were times when he felt as if on the brink of hell and the verge of despair. He tells us that while contemplating the righteousness of God in the monastery tower, probably in 1512, a new concept, a new illumination came to him—"the gates of paradise were opened!"

Original sin was no longer seen in the scholastic tradition as the *carentia gratiae,* but rather identified itself with its effects. The real nature of concupiscence and of all sin was selfishness. It was selfishness that dominated the entire instinctive and volitional life of natural man. Not that it destroyed freedom of choice, which is essential to human will, but it destroyed the capacity to will freely and cheerfully what is good. This selfishness is, in a final analysis, idolatry, as it rejects God and relies upon oneself for righteousness.

The study of Paul's Epistle to the Romans had convinced him that the justice of God before which he trembled is not exacting, does not condemn, but is wholly beneficent. It is a justice that reinstates the sinner qua sinner in the eyes of God, in virtue of Christ's redemption.

Though he still answered the question "How can I get rid of sin?" in the same way as did the traditional scholastic teaching—through grace that is infused—he gives it a different interpretation. Justification was no longer an instantaneous transformation whereby sin is suddenly destroyed by the supernatural quality of grace infused into man's soul but was a spiritual and psychological miracle which produces a new disposition, namely a faith, or an unreserved confidence in the forgiving favor of God. As a result, a personal communion is established between the soul and God with a subsequent moral renewal. Even if man considers the sorry results of his moral endeavors, he will not despair because he knows that Christ has made satisfaction for him and that God reckons Christ's righteousness to his account. The whole process is a humble and obedient surrender to God effected by Him through the Holy Spirit which enables the sinner to trust the promise "Thy sins are forgiven." This surrender simultaneously awakens in man a certain confidence that all other promises of God will be realized. Hence faith is not only trust, but also hope and expectancy, a childlike confidence that God who has put such trust in man's heart is disposed to love and favor him. It is, in brief, a doctrine of God's acceptance of the sinner without any objective sanctification through sanctifying grace. Christ's justice fills the chasm that yawns before God and the sinner, provided the sinner appropriates that justice by faith. Faith then, as Luther sees it, is born out of humility, a realization of man's complete and total dependence upon God.

In explaining how this phenomenon is produced, Luther logically rejects the traditional teaching of the Church. For justification, no longer an objective transformation but rather an ethical process, is produced by the word of God, the Gospel. It is in, with, and through the Gospel that God works upon the soul through His Spirit. The soul remains passive and receptive like a woman in the act of conception. One is forcibly reminded of the works of the Catholic liturgy read after the Gospel of the Mass—"May our sins be blotted out by the reading of the Gospel." The word of God thus becomes more important than the sacraments; it is, in fact, the great sacrament.

The word is also the means by which Christ founded the Church and continues to preserve and govern it. In the preaching of the word He Himself is always instrumental and is constantly creating new members. Thus Luther makes an extremely personal experience the center of a new theory of salvation that is no longer in harmony with the one traditionally taught by the Church.

These ideas were only gradually formulated, but a study of the glosses and the notes kept by Luther's students during the years 1513 to 1518 leaves no doubt that by then they had formed the basis of his religious thought. They would have probably remained within the depths of his own spiritual struggle and never spread beyond the confines of the classroom where he lectured, were it not for a series of events which brought the focus of all Christendom on the Wittenberg monk and changed the course of history.

Albrecht of Brandenburg, brother of the elector Joachim,

at the age of twenty-three, was elected Archbishop of Magdeburg and was, at the same time, given the administration
of the diocese of Halberstadt. Both his age and the accumulation of two bishoprics were in direct violation of canon
law; nor were his personal characteristics becoming for a
successor of the apostles. The Holy See condoned the appointment and a year later the same pluralist was elected
Archbishop of Mainz, a position that automatically made
him prince elector, Reich-chancellor and primate of all Germany. The move was undeniably inspired by political aspirations since it gave the Hohenzollerns two votes in the
electoral college. Yet it was paid for at an incredibly high
price. For the dispensation to hold benefices in three dioceses
Albrecht had to pay the Curia a sum of 10,000 golden
ducats. Another 14,000 was demanded to pay up the arrears
in pallium taxes for the see in Mainz. (It had been vacated
three times in the previous ten years.) A deal was made with
the Curia whereby, for allowing the Peter's Indulgence to
be preached in his episcopal territories, one half of the income was to go toward the construction of St. Peter's, the
other half to the Archbishop. The House of Fugger was
called upon to finance the undertaking with a loan of 24,000
Rhenish gulden. The sums involved came to well over a
million dollars in present monetary terms.

As principal agent for this sordid simoniacal act, the Fuggers chose the well-known indulgence preacher, John Tetzel.
Tetzel, a member of the Dominican house in Leipzig, had
been engaged in the work of dispensing indulgences throughout Germany since 1504 and had been eminently successful.
It was often his wont, after opening an indulgence drive with
a sermon and procession, to walk to the indulgence chest
with a certificate for his father or some close friend, and
then loudly announce that it was no longer necessary to
pray for their souls—their salvation was now assured. Nor
were his services cheaply acquired. For his cooperation in
the Mainz indulgence enterprise he demanded eighty gold
gulden monthly in cash, and ten gulden extra for his servant. Free maintenance and transportation were also provided. Charges against his morals, for example that he sired
two illegitimate children, have never been proved, but there
is little doubt of his overbearing intellectual pride, a characteristic not uncommon among those whose mission is preaching to illiterates. He once boasted that several universities
in Germany had offered him degrees in theology. He was
not a university graduate.

Luther knew nothing of the indulgence agreement between the Fuggers, the Curia, and the Archbishop of Mainz. Nor was he particularly interested in Tetzel. Frederick of Saxony had obstinately refused to allow the indulgences to be preached in his territories. Neither Albrecht's appointment to the see of Magdeburg, formerly held by Frederick's brother Ernst, nor the take-over of Mainz, had pleased the Saxon elector. There was even speculation that Frederick himself had aspired to the Mainz position. He was still single, although he had at least two illegitimate children. It was only when Tetzel began to preach the indulgence in the towns of Jüteborg and Zerbst on the northern boundary of Saxon territory that Luther felt it was his duty to admonish his Electoral Highness, the Archbishop of Mainz and Magdeburg, of the difficulties Tetzel was causing. He wrote him on October 31, 1517: "Papal indulgences for the building of St. Peter's are hawked about under your illustrious sanction. I am not denouncing the sermons of the preachers who advertise them, for I have not seen them, but I regret that the faithful have conceived some erroneous notions about them. These unhappy souls believe that if they buy a letter of pardon they are sure of their salvation; also that souls fly out of purgatory as soon as money is cast into the chest, in short, that the grace conferred is so great that there is no sin whatever which cannot be absolved thereby, even if, as they say, taking an impossible example, a man should violate the Mother of God. They also believe that indulgences free them from all guilt of sin."

On this same day the young monk nailed his famous ninety-five theses on the door of the castle church in Wittenberg and announced his intention to hold a debate on the value of indulgences "out of love for and the elucidation of truth." What had been for years a question in the mind of Luther, a matter of theology, now became a matter of reform. Most of these theses were not opposed to traditional Catholic doctrine. In the first four Luther sets the tone of the entire draft and protests that the Lord's statement "do penance" meant that the entire life of the Christian should be one of repentance. Hence, penance was not to be construed as an occasional transaction performed speedily with the help of an ordained priest, but rather an inner process that continues throughout the whole life of the Christian.

Poenitentia is derived from the latin *poena*—punishment. Therefore penance and impunity, penance and evasion of punishment, are antithetical, if not mutually exclusive. He who performs penance in a proper manner will never cease to punish the old Adam, that is, to mortify himself with all kinds of ascetic disciplines. In treating the question of indulgences Luther points out that the Pope can remit only punishment attached to purely ecclesiastical laws. In the matter of guilt, God alone has the power of forgiveness. Regarding indulgences for the dead, he denies that the Pope possesses jurisdiction over the souls in purgatory. Once a penitent is dead all canonical penalities are effaced. It is true that the souls can be helped by intercession, but no one knows whether this is favorably received by God. Buying indulgences is actually sinful if in so doing the purchaser neglects the poor to whom the money could better be given. Anyone who actually believes that the purchase of an indulgence is a guarantee for salvation is as guilty of damnation as the person who teaches this doctrine. In the eighty-second thesis he asked: "Why does not the Pope, if he has the power, out of Christian charity empty purgatory of the suffering souls all at once?"

In the main, these theses voice Luther's protest against egotistic religiosity which regards exemption from punishment as the supreme good. This he contrasts to his own concept of religion, an ethical piety which views the greatest evil as being not so much punishment but guilt, and looks not so much to exemption from punishment as to forgiveness of guilt and spiritual improvement. Rather than a quest for personal happiness the Gospel teaches a desire to do the will of God and perform works of mercy for our brethren in Christ.

It is doubtful that Luther could possibly have foreseen the storm that his theses let loose. Within a few months they were being read and acclaimed throughout the entire Empire. The Bishop of Merseburg regretted that they could not be posted in public places so that the poor might be warned of the fraudulent activities of Tetzel. An old Franciscan in Muldenstein exclaimed: "There is a man who will do something!" A priest in Hamburg summed up the sentiments of many when he said after reading them: "You speak the truth, dear brother, but you will accomplish nothing. Go back to your cell and say, 'God have mercy on me.'"

Tetzel, who was in Berlin at the time the theses were published, showed them to the Bishop of Brandenburg and boasted, "Within three weeks I shall have the heretic thrown into fire." Tetzel of course was supported by the members of his order, and to confirm their confidence in his theological competence he was later given an honorary degree in theology from Rome. Luther's own attitude toward his antagonist was anything but hostile. Later on, when he heard that the poor man had been stricken with a fatal illness he wrote him a consoling letter saying that the unfortunate affair was in no way the Dominican's responsibility; its roots lay much deeper. As indeed they did.

In early February, Luther presented the Bishop of Brandenburg a series of *Resolutiones* on the theses requesting that the Bishop strike out whatever in them he found displeasing. He wrote: "I know that Christ does not need me. He will show His Church what is good for her without me. Nothing is so difficult to state as the true teaching of the Church, especially when one is a serious sinner as I am." He ended his letter of explanation by urging reform of the Church and pointing out that, as recent events had proved, namely the Lateran Council, the reform is the concern not of the Pope alone or of the Cardinals but of the entire Christian world. The Bishop answered Luther, informing him that he found no error in the *Resolutiones* and that in fact he thoroughly objected to the manner in which the indulgences were being sold.

Meanwhile the Dominicans, with their curial connections and their even closer association with the powerful House of Hapsburg, had taken the case to Rome. They were still recovering from the execution of four of their brethren in Bern less than a decade before, and were determined that no Augustinian hermit would embarrass them once again in German-speaking lands.

Rome had already been alerted to the dangers contained in Luther's novel doctrine by the Archbishop of Mainz. In view of the recent negotiations between Albrecht and the Curia it is understandable that his protest was interpreted in terms of declining revenues rather than threatened dogma. However, with the powerful Dominican order now denouncing the Wittenberg professor, Rome had no alternative but to act. Following an established pattern, the Roman authorities, having failed to silence Luther through his own order, instigated a formal canonical process against him.

The provincial of the Saxon province of the Dominicans, Herman Rab, induced the fiscal procurator, Marius de Perusco, to have the Pope instigate charges against Luther. At the procurator's request, an auditor of the Curia, Jerome Ghinucci, was entrusted with the preliminary investigation.

At the same time a Dominican, Sylvester Prierias, Master of the Sacred Palace, was commissioned to draw up a theological opinion of Luther's doctrine.

A thoroughgoing Thomist, Prierias handled Luther's writings as if he were conducting a scholastic disputation. His *Dialogus* was nothing more than a polemic aimed at tagging the various theses "erroneous," "false," "presumptuous," or "heretical." A citation was drawn up demanding that Luther appear personally in Rome within sixty days to defend himself; the citation and the dialogue were dispatched to the General of the Dominican order, Thomas de Vio, commonly known as Cajetan, probably the outstanding theologian of the century. They arrived in Wittenberg in August of 1518.

During the same month, the Pope, now informed of Emperor Maximilian's willingness to prosecute Luther, instructed Cajetan, whom he had appointed as his legate to the Diet of Augsburg, to cite the accused to appear before him. An order of extradition was also sent to Frederick the Wise, Luther's territorial sovereign, as well as to his provincial, Hecker, who was commanded to arrest him.

Upon receipt of the citation, Luther took immediate measures to forestall his appearance before what he considered anything but an impartial tribunal. Supported by Frederick the Wise, he demanded that his case be tried in Germany and by a group of competent scholars. Frederick managed to obtain a promise from Cajetan of a fair hearing and pledged safe-conduct to the young monk.

On October 12, Luther appeared before the Dominican Cardinal and his entourage of Italian jurists. It is interesting to note that Cajetan was in agreement with Luther on many points. Like him, he defined an indulgence as a remission of the penances imposed by the priest in confession and he was similarly opposed to the view that an indulgence may be procured for the dead without their having confessed and received absolution in the regular manner. Like Luther he was also opposed to the extreme legalistic mentality of many curial officials. Cajetan was never a popular figure in Rome. It was his hope to obtain recantation by paternal exhortations. Luther obstinately refused to make an act of revocation maintaining that he would not do so as long as he was not convinced of his errors on the basis of scriptural proof. He flatly denied the validity of Pope Clement VI's decretal on indulgences, *Unigenitus*. When Luther suggested that the decretal be submitted to the

opinion of a council, Cajetan accused him of being a Gersonist.

It was finally agreed that Luther put his opinions once
again in writing and await Rome's decision. Luther made a
formal statement before a notary and two witnesses refusing
to acknowledge the competence of the judges who had thus
far conducted the inquiry on the grounds that they were
biased. He asserted once again that he was not bound by
the Roman citation and terminated his statement by ap-
pealing to a better-informed Pope. On the 16th of October
he informed the Cardinal of his willingness to stop com-
menting on indulgences and his readiness to listen to the
Church. He apologized for his violent outbursts against the
Pope. Yet there was not a word of recantation. He wrote
to the court chaplain, Spalatin, "I will not recant a syllable
and I shall have in my defense what I presented today,
printed so that he may be refuted throughout the entire
Christian world if he continues to deal with me as outrageously as he has begun." To his brethren at Wittenberg
he wrote: "The Cardinal may be an able Thomist, but he
is no clear Christian thinker, and so he is about as fit to
deal with this matter as an ass is to play the harp."

Cajetan, thwarted in his attempt to reconcile Luther, demanded that the Elector Frederick extradite Luther and
send him to Rome for trial. On November 28 Luther appealed to a General Council. The appeal was actually a
legal device intended to stay the civil effects of the excommunication that was now imminent.

Yet the delay of the excommunication of Luther was not
due so much to this legal maneuver as it was to a developing
political situation that was to involve the papacy once
again in the affairs of Germany. The Emperor Maximilian
had since 1513 been planning the election of his grandson,
Charles, Duke of Burgundy and King of Castile and Aragon,
as Holy Roman Emperor. The election of Charles would
have constituted a threat to the territorial independence of
the Pope because of his sovereignty over Naples. Hence, the
Curia, favoring an election of either Francis I of France or,
preferably, Frederick, Luther's sovereign, made every effort
to delay any move that would antagonize the Elector. To
win the support of Frederick, one Karl von Miltitz, a swag-
gering, alcoholic Saxon holding the office of papal notary
in the Rome Court, was sent to the Elector with a plan to
have Luther tried in a German ecclesiastical court, preferably in Trier. In addition he was to present the Elector

with the Golden Rose, a sort of papal award, as well as a letter of legitimization for Frederick's two children. None of the supporters of Luther was, however, deceived by the boastful Saxon. In fact his presence in Germany supported their conviction that politics, not theology, was behind Rome's denunciation of Luther.

Charles V was elected Holy Roman Emperor on June 28 in spite of Rome's opposition. His election had cost over a million gold gulden, and as in the election of Albrecht it was the firm of Fugger that supplied the greater part of the outlay of bribes, indemnities and pensions. After over a year's delay the Curia once again took up the case of Luther. In February of 1520 a committee of theologians presided over by Cardinals Cajetan and Accoli once again examined the theses of Luther. John Eck, a nominalist and university professor from Ingolstadt who had been the first of Luther's opponents in 1518, joined the group in May and at his recommendation the propositions were condemned *in globo* as "erroneous, scandalous, and heretical." A blanket condemnation was hardly what the commission desired but the vociferous Eck prevailed upon them to make all of the theses appear at least erroneous.

It was generally believed that Eck, who had debated with Luther at Leipzig in the previous year, was the man most familiar with his views. A bull of excommunication, *Exsurge Domine,* was issued in Rome on June 15 and Eck was commissioned to promulgate it throughout the Empire. In September he published the bull in the diocese of Brandenburg and in the diocese of Saxony. Before the sixty-day time limit, within which he had to submit, Luther again appealed to a General Council. The appeal did not, however, delay the final bull of excommunication, *Decet Romanum Pontificem,* which pronounced sentence on Luther on January 3, 1521.

It is one of the strange turns of history that Luther was never officially prosecuted in his own country, although excommunication, by labeling him a heretic, made him liable to the death penalty in the Empire. A number of circumstances combined to render the ecclesiastical and civil penalties ineffective. In the first place there was a strong public reaction which rebelled at the prospect of condemning a man who for all practical purposes was the outright spokesman of their own grievances against corruption in the Church. The conviction that until a council had actually pronounced against him, he and his followers were not definitely cut off from the Catholic Church, was widespread. Finally, the majority of the German bishops, still influenced by conciliarism, were hardly inclined to stand in the way of a man whose attacks on papal claims to ecclesiastical supremacy were but an expression of their own opposition to Romanism.

Almost everywhere the publication of the bull met with strong opposition. In Luther's home diocese of Brandenburg the local ordinary, Schulz, did not dare to publish it. The University of Wittenberg brushed it aside as a further example of Eck's skullduggery. In Erfurt the document was cast into the river, and in Leipzig a riot of the students at the University forced the executor to flee the city.

The University of Vienna was finally forced to acknowledge it only after direct intervention on the part of the Emperor. In many places it was impossible to find printers willing to print the bull. Nor was the commanded burning of Luther's writings carried out with any amount of enthusiasm. Perhaps one of the reasons behind the reluctance of the German hierarchy to promulgate the excommunication was the fact that an insignificant professor of an unknown school in Ingolstadt, John Eck, had been commissioned to execute it. Many bishops felt that a public burning of Luther's works would only worsen the situation. Even Albrecht of Mainz, who more than any other bishop had suffered the immediate effects of Luther's attack on the sale of indulgences, refused to cooperate with the Roman authorities.

During the summer and fall of 1520, Luther wrote what many consider the most important of his works after his translation of the Bible. In a series of pamphlets entitled, *An Appeal to the Nobility of the German Nation, On the Babylonian Captivity of the Church,* and *On Christian Liberty,* he outlined what he felt would be a program for reforming and revitalizing the Church. The first edition (some 4,000 copies) of the *Appeal to the Nobility* was sold out in five days between August 18 and 23. In the preface to this edition, which he addressed to Nicholas von Amsdorf, a fellow professor at the University, he remarks: "The time to keep silence is past and the time to speak, as Ecclesiastes says, has come. I have, according to our plan, brought together some propositions on the improvement of the Christian estate and have addressed them to the Christian nobility of the German nation, to see whether God will help His Church through the *laity,* since the clergy, to whom such

matters pertain, have become completely oblivious of them."
He then proceeds to point out the three walls that the
Romanists have built about themselves which constitute the
main obstacles to true reform and are responsibile for the
decline of Christianity: the claim that civil government has
no rights over them, the superiority of papal decrees over
Scripture, and, finally, the superiority of the Pope over a
council.

Regarding the authority of the Pope, the most sensitive
area of all previous reform programs, Luther recommends
that the papacy extricate itself from temporal affairs. The
Pope should relinquish his territorial claims to the north of
the Appenines in order to avoid a repetition of Julius II's
bellicose policies. He should also renounce the temporal
powers indicated in the Donation of Constantine. This document he claims is a clumsy forgery. The Pope's right to
crown the Emperor is in no wise an indication that he is
the Emperor's superior.

In treating the Curia, Luther recommends that it could
be radically reduced without any loss to the Church. A
small staff of officials with a fixed salary would be sufficient
to deal with all ecclesiastical affairs within the Pope's competence. The number of cardinals should be reduced to
twelve and supported out of the Pope's own purse. The payment of papal taxes, especially annates, must be abolished
as well as the reservations of benefices and the accumulation
of them. The right of nomination to benefices must be
restored to bishops so that they could cease acting as mere
figureheads. In the future bishops should be invested by
metropolitans and not obliged to swear allegiance to the
Pope. Disputes involving the laity or temporal affairs should
no longer be called to Roman courts. Only litigations between archbishops should be reserved to Rome. There must
be a reduction of the number of religious orders, and those
monasteries that are allowed to remain must return to the
spirit of their founders. All religious must refrain from
begging. Papal dispensations, especially those effecting the
third and fourth degrees of blood relationship and spiritual
relationship, must be abolished. Excommunication is only
operative in the spiritual sphere and interdicts and other
spiritual censures must be done away with. Saints' days
should be transferred to Sundays since they are spent in
drunkenness, gambling and idleness. There should be a curtailment of pilgrimages, especially to the city of Rome. A
reduction of the number of foundation Masses must be

ordered and each community should choose its own parish priest. In order to put an end to certain moral abuses the council should do away with clerical celibacy. It is a shameful thing that Christians permit brothels. The principal sinners in these places are the clergy. Begging should be prohibited throughout Christendom and each city should take care of its own poor rather than providing for pilgrims and mendicants. The Bohemian schism should be healed and the Church should openly confess its guilt in the burning of John Huss and Jerome of Prague.

The universities should be reformed by removing the *Physics, Metaphysics, De Anima* and *Ethics* of Aristotle from the curriculum. No one has really ever understood Aristotle and studying his works is a waste of time as well as a burden to the soul. A poor potter has more knowledge of natural science than is contained in all his works. It is a painful tragedy that this cursed, arrogant, heathen has made fools of so many of the best Christians. The *De Anima* denies the immortality of the soul and the *Ethics* runs directly counter to God's grace and Christian virtue.

In early October Luther penned his second famous work, *On the Babylonian Captivity of the Church*. While his *Appeal to the Nobility* was an attack on the century-old abuses of the Church and contained little that was novel, this next work openly struck a blow at the sacramental system and the sacrifice of the Mass. Written in Latin, it was intended for theologians and scholars and opened the eyes of many, for the first time, to the radical elements in his new doctrine. Erasmus declared that it precluded all possibility of peace with the papacy. The third great work of this period, *On Christian Liberty*, continued to strike out at the roots of papal Christianity by emphasizing the primacy of Scripture, the priesthood of the laity and the doctrine of justification by faith alone. In emphasizing Christian liberty he stresses the freedom expressed in doing obedience to God and service to one's neighbor. He traces the religious implications of justification by faith and impugns the idea that good works are the mechanical performance of ecclesiastical laws. Rather they are the fruit of faith from which they flow. Although these three writings in a certain sense epitomize the salient features of the early Lutheran movement, it would be unjust to say that they are the very heart and soul of Luther's doctrine. Neither would it be correct to assert that Luther or his followers felt that they had in any way separated themselves from the Catholic Church by condemning the abuses within it.

In March of 1521 the Emperor Charles V, at the incessant prompting of the papal nuncio Aleander, cited the Augustinian monk to appear before the Estates of the Holy Roman Empire. It was a decision that was made with great deliberation, for by this time Luther's popularity had spread beyond the borders of Germany and the Electors, particularly Frederick the Wise, were in no way inclined to condemn him. On April 16, with a letter of safe-conduct, Luther entered the city of Worms and two days later made his now famous statement in answer to the accusation of heresy: "So long as I cannot be disproved by Holy Writ or clear reason, so long I neither will withdraw anything, for it is both criminal and dangerous to act against conscience. So help me God." The fearlessness shown by Luther in appearing before the assembled rulers of Germany can only be appreciated by realizing that his chances of returning alive were probably even less than those of Huss and Jerome of Prague a century before.

He wrote to George Spalatin, the Elector's chaplain, some months before the summons: "If I am summoned I will go if I possibly can. Even sickness will not deter me. For it is not right to doubt that if the Emperor summons me it is the same as a summons from the Lord. He lives and reigns who saved the three Hebrew children in the furnace of the king of Babylon. If He does not wish to save me, my life is a little thing compared to that of Christ who was slain in the most shameful manner, to the scandal of all, the ruin of many. Here is no place to weigh risk and safety; rather we should take care not to abandon the gospel which we have begun to preach to be mocked by the wicked, lest we give our enemies to boasting that we dare not confess what we teach and shed our blood for it . . . I should prefer, as I have quite often said, to perish only at the hands of the Romans, so that the Emperor may not be involved in my cause. You know that nemesis dogged Sigismund after the execution of Huss; he had no success after that and he died without heirs, for his daughter's son, Ladislaus, perished, so that his name was wiped out in one generation and his queen Barbara became infamous, together with other misfortunes which befell him. Yet if it be the Lord's will that I must perish at the hands not of the priests but of the civil authorities, may His will be done."

Unlike Sigismund, Charles remained true to his promise

of safe-conduct and Luther was allowed to leave Worms unmolested. However, the Emperor was determined to uphold the Roman and Apostolic faith. He informed the Electors, "You have heard Luther's speech and now I say that I regret that I have delayed so long to proceed against him. I will not hear him again. He has a safe-conduct. But from now on, I regard him as a notorious heretic and hope that all of you, as good Christians, will not be wanting in your duty." From the summer of 1522 until the autumn of 1529 the Emperor Charles was absent from Germany futilely attempting to consolidate his vast territorial holdings. It was an effort compromised by an alliance of Catholic France with the Turks and later further confused by alliances between the same power and the Protestant princes within the Empire. The papacy itself, at variance with his territorial aspirations, was almost as great an obstacle to his plan for religious pacification as were the Lutherans. It is one of the ironies of history that out of interests purely political, the King of France, the last of the Holy Roman Emperors to be consecrated by the Pope, and the Pope himself, frustrated the only possible means of solving the religious crisis in Germany, a general council of the Church. Charles' decision to turn over the affairs of the hereditary Hapsburg lands in Austria to his brother Ferdinand also jeopardized his position vis-à-vis the reformers. The dependence of Ferdinand upon the support of the Lutheran princes in his war against the Turks undermined any strong policy he may have hoped for in executing the Edict of Worms. While returning from Worms Luther was kidnapped by the agents of Frederick the Wise and placed in hiding at Wartburg where he continued to pour forth his scriptural and reformatory writings. The years between 1521 and 1525 were the most decisive periods in the reform movement. Since neither the bull of excommunication nor the Edict of Worms were actually put into effect in the Empire, the Lutheran movement continued to flourish. A number of events, however, caused the movement to lose much of its original momentum. As a popular uprising it was thwarted by the very forces that Luther had originally hoped to liberate. For several generations the peasants in the south and west of Germany had threatened local governments with grievances arising out of the economic and sociological changes of this transitional period. The doctrines of Luther, particularly his teaching on Christian liberty, were quickly transformed into demands for social reform. Eventually, peasant uprisings broke out in the Black Forest region in June of 1524 and spread throughout Swabia, Franconia, Thuringia, and part of the Rhineland. Luther firmly opposed the revolt asserting that rebellion would stir up more ills than it would cure. In defending the harsh treatment of the peasants he wrote: "I have two fears: if the peasants become lords, the devil would become abbot; but if these tyrannical princes become lords, the devil's mother would become abbess." Luther's refusal to help the peasants cost him the support of many of the lower classes and turned him against any form of religious innovation that did not conform to his own doctrines, thus preparing the ground for dissention within the reform movement.

The failure of the revolt and the urging of Luther that the civil authorities step in to stop the political anarchy that was threatening large areas of the Empire gave a definite impetus to the formation of territorial or state churches. These had undergone a gradual development and were for practical purpose in existence long before Luther. Hence it is incorrect to trace the so called state-controlled church to the Wittenberg Reformer. The dukedom of Cleves had for several decades enjoyed almost complete independence in the direction of its religious affairs, and the same trend was in evidence in smaller territories throughout the Empire. The Lutheran movement's contribution to the territorial Church was in giving it a new theological direction.

In the fall of 1526 Philip of Hesse summoned a synod in Homberg. There, under the direction of a former Franciscan, Franz Lambert of Avignon, a new church ordinance was imposed on the territory of Hesse, monasteries and other ecclesiastical properties were confiscated, Catholic pastors were removed and the Lutheran adaption of the Mass was introduced. The following year in Saxony a commission of lawyers and theologians, after a series of visitations to the parishes in the area, published regulations governing divine service and the establishment of schools to instruct the faithful in the new Gospel teaching.

To implement the regulations Luther wrote his Large Catechism, a manual of instructions for pastors, and his Small Catechism, which was both a devotional work and an instruction for the faithful in the fundamentals of the Christian religion. This use of catechism for religious instruction was later adopted by the Council of Trent and, for better or worse, has to this day remained the normal means of instruction in the principles of belief for Catholics as well as Protestants. These instructions or formulas for the guidance of churches were soon adopted with certain modifications by many of the principalities of northern Germany. The imperial cities of Strasbourg, Magdeburg, Nuremberg and Hamburg also introduced similar reforms.

The Church ordinances afford a good example of the ambivalence that characterized the reform at this time and for generations to come in German lands. Most of them indicate that the Lutheran Mass liturgy retained the Introit, Kyrie, Gloria, Epistle, Gradual and Sequence. The liturgical directives continued the use of vestments. The great number of major feasts were still celebrated, especially those of our Lady. The feast of the Immaculate Conception endured in certain areas for generations. In the administration of the sacraments very little of the ancient Catholic practice was altered. In baptism, for instance, the exsufflation, the use of salt and spittle, the anointings, and the *abrenuntio,* all remained. An ordinance in Lower Saxony emphasized the need for confession: "No one shall approach the sacrament of the altar until he has seen a priest, confessed and received absolution." In the matter of fast and abstinence practically all of the ordinances retain the traditional fast days and urge that in individual cases the practice should not be limited to periods stipulated, but should be a general practice aimed at sanctifying the soul. The Elector Maurice of Saxony not only ordered that fasting be observed on certain days, but also forbade the very sale of meat during the Lenten period.

The loss of humanist support inflicted on the cause of Lutheranism a blow even more severe than that incurred with the disaffection of the peasants. In October of 1520, while the bull against Luther was being promulgated, the Elector Frederick had asked Erasmus, the acknowledged leader of the humanists, "How has Luther sinned, and why has he been condemned?" Erasmus answered, "In many things has he sinned, he has struck at the bellies of the monks and the crown of the Pope." Then Frederick was commanded by the papal nuncios to imprison his troublesome subject. Once again he approached Erasmus and asked whether the great scholar stood by his earlier expressed support of Luther. When Erasmus replied in the affirmative the Elector returned to Saxony and shielded Luther for the rest of his days.

In speaking of the greed of monks and the tyranny of Popes Erasmus was not using the words of Luther. Neither was his eye on the egg that he was supposed to have laid for Luther to hatch. He desired the reformation of the

Church to follow along the lines that he and his emulators had been pursuing long before 1517. Thus until the full significance of the interview between Erasmus and Luther's secular protector is studied, one of the great problems of the Reformation must remain unsolved—the interplay between reform and humanism. A fundamental ambiguity of the Reformation is that we find the same educational and religious program nurturing contrary religious tendencies that have not even as yet completely articulated themselves.

Both the humanists and the early Lutherans envisioned a religious reform that would be basically educational. The whole Lutheran movement is set within a pastoral and instructional framework. The ninety-five theses crackle with the phrase "Christians should be taught." The *Babylonian Captivity* bears down heavily on the instructional value of the sacraments. In fact, Protestantism after Melanchthon subsumed all churchly activities under the notion of *doctrina*.

For the humanists the task of theology was to teach piety. Like Luther they attacked scholastic theology chiefly because it was utterly unfit to do so. Instead of teaching Christ, scholastics befuddled the people with intricate subtleties. Their argumentative method generated a spirit of arrogance and fierce competition which positively obstructed the gentle stirrings of piety. Like Luther also, the humanists turned aside from the Aristotelian notion of theology as *scientia*, knowledge of God and of divine things, and embraced instead a patristic view, holding theology to be an eloquent persuasion to piety and virtue. Men were moved to piety by a "certain sweetness of speaking," above all by that eloquent exposition of Scripture in which the Fathers excelled. Scripture was in itself even more efficacious. Erasmus would have men at the plow and wives at their spindles singing scriptural songs with the text itself laid before them in their own tongues. True theology was thus the means to genuine piety among the faithful. Christian liberty and *bonae litterae* were joined inseparably.

Monks' bellies and papal tyranny were the enemies of both. Friars were zealous promoters of dubious ceremonies as well as archchampions of scholasticism. Instead of nourishing itself on Scripture and finding expression in daily life, ran the Erasmian critique, the piety of the layman was dissipated along with his money among mounds of sacred bones presided over by smiling friars. Popes and monks collaborated to promote indulgences, a practice more profitable to themselves than to the people. The extreme papal centralization of the Church obstructed Christian liberty by needlessly imposing external obligations on the people. Binding man to fast under pain of mortal sin was unlikely to rouse in him a free and spontaneous love of Christ. Friars reciprocated their patron in Rome by an exaggerated defense of papal authority. If *bonae litterae* were to work a renewal in the Church, the friars and their allies were not to be allowed to gain the upper hand.

A few years before the Lutheran affair the great Hebraist Johann Reuchlin had aroused the suspicion of the Dominicans in Cologne by dabbling in the Kabbala. He had angered them further by persuading the Emperor to abandon their project of burning all Jewish books in the realm. The controversy was finally brought to the attention of the Pope, who found Reuchlin innocent. His indictment, however, had two important results as far as the humanists were concerned. It convinced them that their rivals would use charges of heresy in order to submerge the new learning, and it implanted in them a fear that the real interior power of the Church lay with their enemies. Luther had raised the banner of liberty and *bonae litterae* and had been set upon by the Dominicans. The humanists had no alternative but to recognize him as one of their own. Tetzel was a Dominican, so was the man known to have written his defense against Luther, the Frankfurt Thomist Wimpina.

At Louvain Erasmus was attacked as the archpriest of the new heresies preached by Luther. In the fall of 1520 a Carmelite theologian at Antwerp, seeing Erasmus in the congregation, interrupted his sermon on Christian charity to point out the man who had, he alleged, started Luther on the road to perdition. If Erasmus had disassociated himself from Luther, he would have aided his enemies. He could not remain silent for, long before the official Church recognized the danger, he foresaw the threat of a schism. Taking the only course, he defended Luther.

Yet Erasmus never completely subscribed to Luther's revolutionary tendencies. His early letters to Wittenberg called for moderation. As early as November of 1519 he admonished the young monk by saying: "A just wrath has carried him too far." He rightly feared Luther's intemperance would provoke schism. Yet, while not identifying Luther's teaching with his own, he did nonetheless identify himself with the movement to secure Luther a fair hearing because he feared that if their common enemies managed to burn Luther the humanist reform would be doomed. In May of 1521 he wrote in despair to Archbishop Warham of Canterbury. If these men who love their bellies succeed in crushing Luther, he warned, "nothing will remain except for me to write the epitaph of Christ who will not come to life again."

The papal party had been after Erasmus to take up the cudgels against Luther for some time before the gentle humanist finally agreed to do so. When the nuncio Aleander first plied him with the promise of a bishopric he is said to have answered: "Luther is too great for me to write against. I learn more from reading one page of his books than I would from the whole of Aquinas." In January of 1522 Erasmus' old friend Adrian of Utrecht was elected Pope and he almost immediately wrote to Erasmus to come to Rome and write against Luther. Once again Erasmus discreetly refused. Finally in the fall of 1524 Erasmus published his famous *Diatribe on Free Will*, in which, with all the wit and moderation he could muster, he condemned Luther's doctrine on the freedom of the will. Undogmatically, as in all his writings, Erasmus sums up his position on this controversial subject by saying: "The opinion of those who attribute much to grace but something to free will pleases me best. God helps the man as a father supports the first steps of a young child; only God does not do it all."

In denying the freedom of the will it must not be assumed that Luther intended to deny individual responsibility. Throughout his life, beginning with the theses, his appeals to the Church had been one of repentance. A denial of responsibility would have completely nullified this call. In his writings against Erasmus Luther actually asserts that man is lord over the things that are under him and that in so far as they are concerned he has the right and free will (*jus et liberum arbitrium*). The real problem for Luther was not whether man is able to do what he wants to do; it is whether man is able to do as he should do. Moral judgment goes astray when it endeavors to appraise man according to the measure set up by the moral sense itself. Repentance must lead directly out of the sphere of reflections that are merely human. The call to God deals a destructive blow to what is purely one's inner nature, one's self-determination. Before God autonomy cannot achieve comprehensive fulfillment. It remains merely an egotistical demand.

It is particularly on the question of God's forgiveness that reason must be accused of overstepping its natural boundary. For when it attempts to explain the miracle of God's justifying the sinner it not only flounders in waters too deep to comprehend, it also devises an escape that is at variance with God's redemptive plan. Luther says: "The human heart does not understand nor does it really believe that so great a treasure as the Holy Spirit is given simply because the individual is asked to believe. Therefore it argues that there must be a *quid pro quo* situation. Something so great as forgiveness of sin, righteousness, and eternal life must be paid for. Free forgiveness is something beyond the human reason to grasp. Christian righteousness is an unspeakable gift that goes beyond any rational explanation. The mercy of God is beyond words, our minds are too small to understand it, let alone put it into verbal concepts."

It is at this point that traditional Catholic thought balks at the doctrine of Luther. Medieval Catholicism had been conditioned to accept man's justification as the result of a long process of moral achievement. The scholastics had taken the strictly religious viewpoint of St. Paul and sacrificed it upon the altar of Aristotelian metaphysical categories. In his work *Against Latomus* Luther asserts that grace must be properly understood as the favor of God, not as the Thomists say as a quality of the soul. Grace has become the medicine of immortality and justification is simply a matter of being virtuous. Luther is particularly vitriolic in placing the blame for this at the feet of Aquinas. It was Aquinas's great synthesis that formed the pagan Greek as an unwanted intruder into the realm of the supernatural. Thomas, he says, first takes some opinions out of St. Paul, or the other great apostolic writers, and then proceeds to interpret them in the light of what Aristotle has said. It is the fault of Aquinas that Aristotle has been elevated into the place of Christ, obscuring Him and replacing Him with moral virtues and endless opinions.

It is commonplace among contemporary critics of Luther to equate his attack upon scholasticism as an attack upon both Catholicism and reason. Yet it would be an oversimplification to say that his attitude toward scholasticism made him "a destroyer of Catholicism" or that his "heresy was a deviation of the intelligence," simply because of his attitude toward reason. In his *Commentary on the Galatians* written in 1535, we catch a glimpse of his more mature thought on reason and faith and particularly on his motives for rejecting the traditional medieval notion of grace and merit which in a certain sense forms the basis of his theology. Like Gerson and Cusa before him, Luther is deeply concerned with the limitation of human reason in the realm of the divine. In order to perceive the things of the spirit, the Kingdom of Christ, one needs an eye other than that of reason. Reason is fettered to its own sphere of activity, possessing no perception for things unseen. Hence, the very concept of sin cannot be reasoned to.

Essentially then, for Luther, the supernatural world is completely beyond the powers of discursive reason. This however does not imply that reason is unable to carry out the offices for which it was intended in the fulfillment of political, domestic, and natural affairs. He admits that "a man immersed in impiety and enslaved to the devil nevertheless has will, reason, freedom of choice, and the power to build a house, serve as a magistrate, navigate a ship, and perform other duties over which man was given dominion." These things, procreation, government, the management of household affairs, have not been taken away from man. Yet, in the face of God, *coram Deo,* reason can do nothing. Man may achieve a sort of civil righteousness, but this righteousness is of no avail before God. In the realm of theology there is no right reason and good will except in faith. The guiding principle of conduct for the believer is no longer natural reason but reason enlightened by faith. Faith takes the place of reason—right reason in spiritual matters *is* faith. It becomes a new reason, a *nova ratio.* For reason must first be illuminated by faith before it issues in works. Yet there is a definite limit, a definite boundary which man's reason must observe.

The basic disagreement between Luther and the humanists as represented by Erasmus and his followers originally lay in the area of method rather than that of objective. It was Erasmus's conviction that a barbed pen could remove abuses without splitting the Church. This was a policy that as far as Luther was concerned bordered on the blasphemous. On one occasion he likened Erasmus to Democratus, the laughing philosopher of antiquity, and according to Luther the times demanded tears rather than laughter. Yet, Erasmus could say that everything Luther demanded, he too had taught, less stridently. In the judgment of Luther, Erasmus tended to treat the Christian religion as a mere prop for the institutions of Christendom. Erasmus, claimed Luther, had nothing to say of the fundamental doctrine of faith in Christ. His was that moralistic attitude of mind that turns Christ into a lawgiver. Against any who would so reduce religion to a mere observation of laws, Luther was constantly opposed.

The break with humanism and the growing interference

of German political leaders turned the attention of the Reformer to the more practical implementation of his design. The controversy on the Eucharist which arose at the same time that Luther wrote his *De Servo Arbitro* made it obvious that some strong clarification of doctrinal position was necessary if the movement was not to dissolve into warring parties. Luther's clearest position on the Eucharist was not enunciated until 1528 when he published a Confession concerning the Lord's Supper. His belief in the real presence was vested not only in the biblical proofs of traditional Catholic belief but also upon his firm conviction that all communion with God must, because of man's sinfulness, have a visible medium that can be apprehended by faith. Christ as God-man is the mediator of salvation, and because of the indissoluble unity of His person He is present in the Eucharist in His divine as well as His human nature. Although he had attacked the doctrine of transubstantiation in his *Babylonian Captivity,* he did so because he felt the terminology used in presenting this doctrine created a barrier to faith. It was his intention that among the faithful there be a belief that Christ's body and blood are contained in the bread and wine, with no emphasis upon the how and where. No theory was to interpose itself between the act of Holy Communion and the faith.

Regarding the Mass it would be wrong to say that he repudiated it as many of his critics contend. For him the Mass was, according to the will of Him who instituted the sacrament, a renewal of the remembrance of the death of Christ and of all His benefactions. Hence, he recommended that the words of institution be distinctly and clearly spoken or sung publicly before the assembly. Here the proclamation of the word should not be a mere demonstration but rather something whereby the faith of the hearers is awakened, strengthened, and confirmed by Christ's word. For Luther the sacrament of the altar, like the other sacraments, was a street, a bridge, a door, a ship, and a stretcher on which and by means of which we journey from this world into eternal life. In his *Formula of the Mass (Formula missae)* Luther declares that he never thought of doing away with this form of divine worship altogether, and he gives his reason for this when he says: "For this we cannot deny that Masses and Communion of the bread and wine are a rite instituted by Christ." Regardless of how much he deviates from the externals of the medieval Mass he always considers that ceremonial elements are indispensable. This is especially

in evidence in his stand on Communion under both species
and his insistence that all the congregation participate.

In 1534 Luther wrote: "Herewith therefore I now confess
again before God and the whole world . . . that where
Mass is celebrated according to Christ's directive, whether it
be among us Lutherans or in the papacy or in Greece or in
India, although there is only one form . . . that there under
the forms of bread and wine there is the true body of Christ
given for us on the cross, under the wine the true blood of
Christ shed for us." "It was," he says further, "a sacrament
which was to be a constant memorial of His bitter suffering
and death, and of all His benefactions, a seal of a new covenant, a comfort for all troubled hearts, and a constant bond
and union of Christians with Christ their Head, and among
one another." Earlier he had said of the Mass, "The closer
any Mass approaches the first of all Masses, which Christ
celebrated at the Supper, the more Christian it is."

Nor was Luther opposed to ceremonials as such. In answer
to a criticism of the Ansbach Counsel of 1524 he wrote:
"There are in use certain ceremonies that are partly an orna-
ment of Christian churches, in order not to treat the sacraments of the Church in a manner so empty and plain, and in
order that there may be a difference between sacred and profane things. Some are signs of spiritual and divine things."
It was in fact his position on the eucharistic ceremony that
caused the first break in the Protestant movement.

Doctrinal divisions within the reform movement accentuated by the eucharistic controversy at Marburg in 1529
had their counterpart in the political sphere. Between 1524
and 1529 the political leadership of the Lutheran movement
gradually passed from the Saxon electors to the Landgrave
Philip of Hesse. At the Diet of Speyer in 1526 it was already apparent that a division between the Catholic and the
Lutheran princes within the Empire was taking shape. There
was as yet no final split into two religious parties. The Lutheran group was comprised of the Elector of Saxony, John
Frederick, Casimir and George of Brandenburg, and the imperial cities of Augsburg, Nuremberg, Ulm, Frankfurt and
Strasbourg. Many of the other principalities of the realm
maintained a neutral position, and of course the Spiritual
Estates remained strongly Catholic. Nevertheless the gathering at Speyer made it plain that the Emperor's failure to
summon a council was provoking a situation that would leave
no alternative to an introduction of reform by individual
states. The group that favored Lutheranism introduced a

memorial that advocated freedom to preach the Lutheran doctrine, the abolition of private Mass, confiscation of monastic property, and clerical marriage. They further urged a national council that would implement these reforms and suspend prosecution of the Edict of Worms.

Confronted with a Turkish invasion of Hapsburg territories, the Emperor's representative Archduke Ferdinand made a compromise with the estates which guaranteed a postponement of the settlement until a council could be assembled. Three years later in 1529 at the Second Diet of Speyer this policy of postponement was rejected by the Lutherans and they protested against the imperial demand that Catholic forms of worship be tolerated in their territories. The protest, subscribed to by the Elector of Saxony, the Margrave George of Brandenburg, Landgrave Philip of Hesse, Dukes Ernest and Francis of Brunswick-Lüneburg, Wolfgang of Anhalt and fourteen cities of the Empire represented by Jacob Strum gave birth to the expression "Protestantism." Their famous protest concludes with the words: "In matters which concern God's honor and salvation and the eternal life of our soul everyone must stand and give account before God Himself."

The following year at Augsburg, Melanchthon, Luther's closest associate at Wittenberg (he had already attempted to systematize Luther's teachings in his *Loci communes* in 1521), drew up the *Confessio Augustana,* a final embodiment of the basic Lutheran or reformed doctrine. An examination of the document gives some insight into the perplexities of the religious situation as it stood after almost twelve years of religious controversy. It also demonstrates the ambivalence that invested the expression "reform" long after the Edict of Worms. Melanchthon maintained the conviction that he had not departed from the teachings of the Catholic Church in a single dogma, and Elector John of Saxony strongly rejected the accusation that the signers of the confession had separated themselves from the Church. The Confession addressed to the Emperor laid down the fundamental points of the new doctrine and repudiated all rival doctrine.

The first article on the Godhead demonstrates the strong traditional elements of the Confession. "Our churches, in mutual agreement, teach that the decree of the Council of Nicaea in regard to the unity of the divine essence and the three Persons, is correct and should be believed without doubt; or, in other words, that there is one divine essence which is called and is God, eternal without body, indivisible,

infinite in power, wisdom and goodness, the creator and pre-
server of everything, whether it be visible or invisible, while,
at the same time, there are three Persons—the Father, the
Son and the Holy Spirit—each eternal, and each with the
same essence and power. Moreover, the term 'person' is used
as the Fathers used it, that is, to signify not a part or quality
of something else, but rather that which exists of itself.

"We condemn every heresy which has sprung up contrary
to this article, such as the Manicheans, who adopted two
gods, one for good and one for evil; also the Valentinians,
Arians, Eunomians, Mohammedans and the like. We also
condemn the Samosatenes, both old and new, who, arguing
that there is only one Person, fallaciously and irreligiously
contend that the Word and the Holy Spirit are not different
Persons, but that 'Word' means the spoken word, 'Spirit,'
the created motion in things."

The long article on faith and works indicates perhaps more
than any other the conciliatory mind of Melanchthon on the
preeminence of faith as the central doctrine of the Church:
"Our teachers are wrongly accused of forbidding good
works. Indeed their published writings on the Ten Commandments, and other writings of the same importance, show
that they have instructed beneficially about all conditions and
duties of life, as regards to what states of life and what
works in every calling are pleasing to God. Until now, preachers had taught little about these things, and encouraged only
childish and unnecessary actions, such as holy days, particular feasts, brotherhoods, pilgrimages, ceremonies in honor
of saints, the use of rosaries, monasticism, and the like. Since
our adversaries have been warned about these useless practices, they are now forgetting about them, and do not preach
on them, as they did before. Moreover, they are beginning
to speak on faith, about which there was once only striking
silence. They teach that we are not justified by works alone,
but joining faith and works, say that we are justified by both
faith and works. This doctrine is more tolerable than the
former one, and affords more consolation than their old belief.

"Since, therefore, the doctrine on faith, which should be
the main one in the Church, has so long lain unknown (for
everyone must grant that there existed a very deep silence
in sermons on the righteousness of faith, while only the doctrine of works was dealt with in the churches), our teachers
have instructed the churches on faith as follows:

"First, our works cannot appease God or earn forgiveness
of sins, grace and justification, but we can obtain these by

faith alone, when we believe that we are received into favor for Christ's sake, who alone has been placed as Mediator and propitiation (1 Tim 2,5), so that the Father may be appeased through Him. Anyone, therefore, who trusts that by his works he merits grace, despises the merit and grace of Christ, and looks for a way to God without Christ, through human strength, even though Christ has said of Himself: 'I am the Way, the Truth and the Life' (Jn 14,6).

"This teaching about faith is everywhere dealt with by Paul (Eph 2,8): 'You are saved by grace through faith, and not by yourselves; it is the gift of God, not of works,' etc.

"And for fear that anyone should craftily say that we have invented a new interpretation of Paul, this whole matter is given support by the testimonies of the Fathers. Indeed in many volumes Augustine defends grace and the righteousness of faith against the merits of works. Furthermore, Ambrose, in his *De Vocatione Gentium,* and elsewhere, teaches the same thing. For in his *De Vocatione Gentium,* he says the following: 'Redemption by the blood of Christ would have little value, and the mercy of God would not have preeminence over man's works, if justification, which is brought about through grace, was due to previous merits, so that it was not the free gift of the giver, but the reward due to the worker.'

"Yet, although this teaching is hated by the ignorant, still Godfearing and anxious consciences discover by experience that it brings the most consolation, since consciences cannot find peace through any works, but only by faith, when they know that, for Christ's sake, they have a benevolent God. As Paul teaches (Rom 5,1): 'Being justified by faith, we find peace with God.' This entire doctrine must be related to the conflict of the terrified conscience; nor can it be understood apart from this conflict. Thus, ignorant and profane men judge wrongly on this matter, who imagine that Christian righteousness is nothing but the civil righteousness of reason.

"Up to this time, consciences were afflicted with the doctrine of works, nor did they hear any consolation from the Gospel. Some people were driven by their consciences into the desert, or into monasteries, hoping there by the monastic life to merit grace. Some devised other actions by which to merit grace and make satisfaction for sins. There was a very great necessity to renew and deal with this teaching of faith in Christ, so that fearful consciences should not be without consolation, but instead, that they might know that grace, the forgiveness of sins and justification are understood by faith in Christ.

"Men are also warned that here the term 'faith' does not mean merely the knowledge of the history, such as is held by the ungodly and the devil, but rather a faith which believes, not just in history, but also in the effect of history—namely, this article on the forgiveness of sins, that is, that we have grace, righteousness and forgiveness of sins through Christ.

"Now a man knows that he has a Father reconciled to him through Christ, since truly he knows God, that God cares for him, and that he calls upon Him; simply, unlike the heathen, he is not without God. Indeed devils and the irreligious cannot believe this article on the forgiveness of sins. Thus, they despise God as an enemy, do not call upon Him and do not expect any good from Him. Augustine likewise admonishes his readers about the word 'faith' and teaches that the term 'faith' is used in the Scriptures not to mean knowledge such as in the ungodly, but confidence, which consoles and encourages the terrified mind.

"Moreover, it is taught by us that it is necessary to do good works, not because we should desire to merit grace by them, but because it is the will of God. Only by faith are grace and the forgiveness of sins understood. And since the Holy Spirit is received through faith, our hearts are renewed and endowed with new affections, so that they can produce good works. In fact, Ambrose says: 'Faith is the mother of a good will and righteous actions.' For man's strength without the Holy Spirit is full of ungodly desires, and is too weak to do works which are proper in God's sight. Furthermore, it is in the power of the devil, who urges men to diverse sins, to unholy opinions and to outright crimes. We may see this in the philosophers, who, although they sought to lead an honest life, could not succeed, but were strained with many open crimes. Such is the feebleness of man when he is without faith and the Holy Spirit, and rules himself through human strength alone.

"Hence it can be readily seen that this doctrine must not be interpreted as prohibiting good works, but should be commended, for it shows how we are enabled to do good works. Truly, without faith, human nature can in no way do the works of either the first or second commandments. Without faith, our nature does not call upon God, accept anything from Him, or bear His cross, but endeavors and hopes in man's help. And thus, when faith and trust in God are absent, every sort of lust and human device rules in the heart. For this reason, Christ said: "Without Me you can do nothing.' "

The article concludes significantly with a verse from the liturgical sequence of Pentecost, *Veni Sancte Spiritus,* written by the thirteenth-century Archbishop of Canterbury, Stephen Langton: *"Sine tuo numine, nihil est in homine, nihil est innoxium"* (Without Your divine power there is nothing in man, nothing but what is harmful).

The treatment of the Mass, which after the question of faith and works was the most controversial, also indicates an attempt to clear a middle path. Significantly, no mention is made of its sacrificial nature. "Our churches are incorrectly accused of abolishing the Mass, since the Mass is retained by us, and celebrated with the greatest reverence. All the usual ceremonies are likewise retained, except that the parts sung in Latin are interspersed occasionally with German hymns, which were added to instruct the people. Indeed ceremonies are needed for this alone so that the unlearned may be taught. And not only has Paul ordered a language understood by the people to be used in the Church, but it has also been instituted this way by man's law.

"The people are accustomed to receive the Sacrament together, if there are any worthy of it, and this practice increases the reverence and devotion of public worship. In fact, none are admitted unless they are first approved. The people are also advised about the dignity and purpose of the Sacrament, that is, how it brings great consolation to fearful consciences, so that they might learn to believe God, and ask and expect of Him all that is good. This worship is pleasing to God, since use of the Sacrament promotes true devotion to Him. It does not seem, therefore, that the Mass is celebrated more devoutly among our adversaries than among us.

"However, it is clear that, for a long while, it has been the open and most grave complaint of all good men that Masses have been basely profaned and used for the purposes of gain. Indeed, it is not known how far this abuse has progressed in all the churches, by what kind of men Masses are said just for fees and payment, and how many celebrate them contrary to the canons. Paul harshly threatens those who use the Eucharist unworthily, when he says: 'Whoever shall eat this bread and drink this cup of the Lord unworthily, shall be guilty of the body and blood of the Lord.' Thus, when our priests were warned about this sin, private

Masses were discontinued among us, since hardly any private Masses were celebrated except for the sake of gain.

"Nor were the bishops ignorant of these abuses, and if they had corrected them in time, there would be less disagreement now. Up till this time, by their own neglect, they have permitted many corruptions to creep into the Church. Now, when it is too late, they start to complain of the troubles of the Church, seeing that this disturbance has been brought about simply by those abuses, which were so obvious that they could be no longer supported. Great dissensions have arisen about the Mass, and the Sacrament. Perhaps the world is being punished for such continuous profanities of the Mass which for so many centuries have been tolerated in the churches by the same men who could have and should have corrected them. Indeed, in the Ten Commandments, it is written (Ex 20): 'The Lord will not hold him guiltless who takes His name in vain.' Since the world began, nothing that God ever instituted seems to have been so abused for filthy gain as the Mass.

"There was also added the opinion which greatly increased private Mass, namely, that Christ, by His passion, had made satisfaction for original sin, and had instituted the Mass in which an offering should be made for daily sins, venial and mortal. From this view has arisen the common opinion that the Mass takes away the sins of the living and the dead, by the outward act. Then they began to argue whether one Mass said for many was worth as much as special Masses said for individuals, and this brought forth an infinite number of Masses. Our teachers have given special warning about these opinions, namely, that they depart from the Holy Scriptures and decrease the glory of the passion of Christ, because Christ's passion was an oblation and satisfaction, not just for original sin, but also for all sins, as it is written to the Hebrews: 'We are sanctified through the offering of Jesus Christ, once and for all.' Likewise: 'By one offering He has perfected forever those that are sanctified.' Scripture also teaches that we are justified before God through faith in Christ, when we believe that our sins are forgiven for Christ's sake. If the Mass takes away the sins of the living and the dead by the outward act, then justification comes through the action of the Masses, and not through faith, and this Scripture does not permit.

"However, Christ commands us (Lk 22,19): 'Do this in remembrance of Me'; therefore, the Mass was instituted that the faith of those who use the sacraments should recall what benefits it receives through Christ which cheer and comfort the anxious consciences. Because, to remember Christ is to remember His benefits, and realize that they are truly offered to us. Nor is it sufficient to only remember the history, for this the Jews and irreligious can also remember. Thus, the Mass is to be used for this purpose, that in it the Sacrament (Communion) may be administered to those that are in need of consolation; as Ambrose says: 'Because I always sin, I must always take the medicine.'

"Now since the Mass is such a giving of the Sacrament, we believe in one Communion every holy day, and also on other days, for the Sacrament is given to anyone who asks for it. Moreover, this custom is not new in the Church; indeed the Fathers before Gregory do not mention any private Mass, but they speak very much of the common Mass (the Communion). Chrysostom says that the priest stands daily at the altar, inviting some to the Communion, and turning others back. And it appears from the ancient canons, that someone, from whom all the other presbyters and deacons received the body of the Lord, celebrated the Mass; indeed, this is what the Nicene Creed says: 'Let the deacons, according to their order, receive the Holy Communion after the presbyters, from the bishop or from a presbyter.' Furthermore, Paul (1 Cor 11,33), on the Communion, commands: 'Wait for one another,' so that there may be a common participation.

"Therefore, inasmuch as the Mass with us has the example of the Church, taken from the Scriptures and the Fathers, we are confident that it cannot be disapproved, especially since the public ceremonies have, for the most part, retained the same as those previously in use; only the number of Masses is different, which, because of the obvious great abuses, without doubt might be profitably reduced. In olden times, even in the churches most often attended, the Mass was not celebrated every day, as is witnessed by the Triparte History (Book 9, Chap. 33); 'Again in Alexandria, every Wednesday and Friday, the Scriptures are read, the doctors expound them, and everything is done except the celebration of the Eucharist.' "

The Confession does not mention the question of papal supremacy, but its author on several occasions expressed his willingness to accept papal primacy "according to human law." An examination of this most famous sixteenth-century reform document might dispel some of the prejudices of those who share the opinion of Grisar and his disciples that it was the "abasement of practical Christianity and fostered a religion without dogma."

Nowhere is there greater evidence that Luther was not relying solely upon Scripture as the source of all revelation than in the Confession of Augsburg. In the first article it is plainly stated that the decrees of the Nicene Synod concerning the unity of the divine essence and concerning the three Persons is true and must be believed without any doubting. Thus Church doctrine is primary and it is the word of God which gives it a stabilization. The Scripture is the rule and guide of doctrine as elucidated by the councils. The various Protestant confessions that followed continued the theme of the Augsburg Confession in accepting the dogmas of the ancient Church. Augsburg gave a direction to Protestantism in that by accepting the dogmas of the ancient Church it submitted voluntarily to a control that cannot be otherwise construed than tradition.

The claim of the Augsburg Confession that it contained nothing that deviated from the Catholic Church merely emphasized the claim of Luther that he had never given up the idea of the universality of the Church. To Luther the Church designated a Christian communion or assembly, or better yet, a holy Christendom. He often stresses the fact that his followers have the same baptism as the old Christian Church has. In 1524 he had defined the Christian Church as the multitude or assembly of all those who believe in Christ, who live and will continue to live in unity of spirit, faith, hope and love. It is because of this unity that the believers are called a communion of saints. The Confession also emphasizes the supraterritorial unity of the Church. The Church is catholic not because it unites definite people into an external body politically, but rather because it unites people who are scattered over the entire world and yet are in agreement in the message of the Gospel, have the same Christ, the same Holy Spirit, and the same sacraments regardless of human traditions. Thus Luther writes in 1539: "Now where you hear or see this word preached, confessed and practiced, have no doubt that in that place there certainly must be a true, holy, catholic church."

The crux of the problem of unity, at least in the eyes of the Lutherans, was that unity of ecclesiastical policy rather than unity of doctrine was the object of the papal party. It is therefore incorrect to assume that the notion of the Church as understood by Luther and his immediate followers was a new church in opposition to the ancient Catholic Church. In a work entitled *Wider Hans Worst* which he published in 1541, he states that what the reform has done has been to restore the ancient Church by repudiating the strange novelties that had become identified with it. The Church has been returned to the pure word and sacraments and is ready to be guided by the word of God which is the only Way, Truth and Life. The life and substance of the Church is in the word of God, *"Tota vita et substantia Ecclesiae est in verbo Dei."* The word of God which is creative in the Church is Jesus Christ Himself, the Word that became incarnate in His historical body.

Yet the Church, though spiritualized as the Mystical Body of Christ, nevertheless has, like other forms of human life —the family, the state, etc.—a constitutional aspect. The Church like the individual is at once justified and a sinner. Externally it is involved in the unredeemed world of the old man, but according to its inner aspect it is holy and justified. Luther's experience with the papacy had made him feel that the Church as the creature of the Word and as the community of the faithful was constantly threatened and obstructed by an historical and visible structure. This was especially true since that visible structure had laid claim to institutional independence which amounted to nothing else than a secularization of the Church. Against this tendency of the Church of Rome Luther insisted that freedom must be created within the visible and physical world for a Church whose essential nature was determined by union with Christ—not by union with a human individual who claimed to be his vicar. The Church had to have freedom to live within the external world in a way appropriate to its inherent spiritual nature. It had to possess freedom to live within the framework of history but at the same time to transcend it.

In this respect he frequently uses a sacramental analogy. The communion of the saints in Christ forms an invisible and spiritual body, but it is marked with an external sign. Christians, are, he says, signed with the word, with baptism and the sacrament of the altar whereby they are distinguished from all other peoples not only before the world but also before God.

In making the Gospel the chief architect of the Church, Luther is speaking of the spoken not the written word. It is the spoken word that forms as it were the bridge between the spiritual and the visible Church. The word must be proclaimed before a public assembly. It is by the oral and public voice of the Gospel that one can know "where the Church is and the mystery of the Kingdom of Heaven." Accused by one of his contemporaries, Thomas Müntzer, of building a church as Plato wanted to build a state, one that would be nowhere, he defends himself by pointing out that invisibility as predicated of the Church does not mean a pure communion in spirit. The Church for Luther is invisible in exactly the same sense as all the other constituents of faith are invisible. It must be believed contrary to all appearances. It is not invisible in a Platonic sense but in the scriptural sense of being hidden (*abscondita*).

After the Diet of Augsburg in 1530, which he was not permitted to attend (being refused safe-conduct by the Emperor), Luther tended to remain more and more aloof from the political developments which continued to detract from the religious aspect of the reform movement. The Augustinian monastery in Wittenberg had become secularized and was finally deeded to Luther in 1532. With few interruptions Luther continued to teach at the university until his death. Part of his salary was provided from the appropriation of the income from founded Masses at the castle church where he had posted his theses. In 1532 and again in 1536 his salary was increased until he was receiving 400 gulden a year.

One of the reasons for Luther's concern over money matters was the fact that in 1525 he had married one Catherine von Bora. Some sixteen years his junior, she came from the town of Lippendorf near Leipzig. At the age of five she had been sent to the Benedictine nuns near Brehna; four years later she transferred to a Cistercian cloister near Grimma where her aunt was abbess and an older sister a nun. She took her vows there in 1515, but during the troubled times in 1523 joined in the exodus from her convent. Wittenberg had become a refuge place for the hundreds of monks and nuns who left their monasteries during these years, and it was here that she met Luther. Luther at this time had no intention of marrying. He wrote Spalatin in November of 1524, "Not that I lack the feelings of a man, for I am neither wood nor stone, but my mind is averse to matrimony because daily I expect the death decree for heresy." The death penalty was actually never lifted in Luther's case and this fact certainly had some bearing on his constant concern over the growing division within the ranks of his followers.

The marriage caused a great stir in Europe. Erasmus, in

correspondence with Luther at the time on the *Diatribe,* attributed the failure of Luther to answer his letters to his marriage. He wittily remarked that in comedies troubles are wont to end in marriage with peace to all. He added that he felt the marriage was timely as he heard that a child was born ten days afterwards. It was his hope that Luther would be milder in his attacks on the Church since even the fiercest beasts can be tamed by their female mates. Later on he apologized for his inference about the child, remarking that he had always been skeptical about the old legend that the anti-Christ would be born of a monk and a nun. Were this true there would have been too many anti-Christs in the world already. Henry VIII of England was especially loud in his denunciation of Luther's marriage. Yet from all accounts the marriage was hardly the dire and unhappy union that his enemies predicted. The Luther household became a gathering place for needy priests, poor relatives and indigent students. In addition to his own six children, four of whom survived their parents, Luther also brought up eleven orphaned children. Luther's almost reckless hospitality and generosity to friends necessitated income greater than his professor's salary provided. He constantly refused the honorarium demanded of students in the German universities and turned down frequent offers for the sale of his manuscripts. The practicality of his wife (whose business acumen was far greater than his) kept the household from falling into debt.

During these years Luther continued his commentaries on the New Testament and revised many of his earlier writings. During his lifetime he published over 400 works which more than fill a hundred volumes. With the possible exception of Goethe, no single writer influenced the development of German literature as did Luther.

Luther's later years can hardly be described as happy. He was in fact an embittered and often disappointed man. Plagued with frequent illness (like Erasmus he suffered from "the stone"), and keenly aware of the growing schisms within the reform movement, he often complained of the contempt with which many of the Reformers regarded him. Writing to Nicholas von Amsdorf in 1545 he remarked of the Swiss Reformers, "These men are fanatic, proud, and yet they shrink back from genuine efforts toward reform. In the beginning of the Reformation when I alone sweated to bear the fury of the Pope they kept silence and watched my dangers and my success. Yet as soon as the power of the

Pope was somewhat broken they burst forth in triumphant boasting, saying that they owed nothing to others, but all to themselves. Thus does one labor and another enjoy the fruit of his labor. Now at last they turn and attack me by whom they are freed. They are a cowardly swarm of drones, skilled only in filching the honey others have made. Their judgment will come upon them. If I see best to answer them I shall do it briefly, merely reiterating my condemnatory opinion. But I am determined to finish the book against the papacy as long as I have the strength."

Luther's support of Philip of Hesse in the celebrated case of bigamy did little to enhance the Reformer's cause. As he had done earlier with Henry VIII Luther recommended that bigamy was preferable to divorce since it had been condoned in the Old Testament, even practiced by the patriarchs. In so arguing he was not entirely at variance with many contemporary Catholic theologians including Cajetan. The convocation of the Council of Trent gave him little hope that any reconciliation between Protestants and Catholics would result. In one of his final works against the papacy he refers to the Council as a juggling contest. Luther died of a stroke on the morning of February 16, 1546, at Eisleben, where he had been attempting to arbitrate a dispute between the counts of Mansfield. It is typical of the man that in one of his last letters to Melanchthon he informs him of the progress of the arbitration and denounces the litigants because of their misinterpretation of law. He writes: "I have offended the defendant because I am angry at the severity and sharpness of the law; but he has offended me by his enormous and ill-considered vice of proclaiming victory before the battle. A little learning makes lawyers bad. Almost all of these men seem to be ignorant of the real use of the law, caring not at all for peace, and the state of religion about which we care now as always." It is significant that Luther's last days were spent as was his entire life in an endeavor to free the Church and religion from the evils of legalism.

News of Luther's death did not reach the fathers assembled at Trent until a month later. The Cardinal of Augsburg, Truchsess von Waldburg, regretted that he had not been taken captive, brought to Trent and burned at the stake. The conciliar secretary, Angelo Masserelli, noted in his diary: "Would to God all men of his stamp either listened to reason or were promptly removed hence."

7 The reform divides Christendom

"And since familiarity breeds contempt, in growing old this heresy will not make further progress, but the important thing is, that neither will it diminish, and will remain, like an incurable paralysis, in these very noble parts of Europe."

ST. FRANCIS DE SALES

The Reformation outside of Germany, although not lacking in leadership and enthusiasm, never quite attained the momentum that marked it within the Empire. A number of factors were responsible for its failure to take root in Latin lands. In Spain a long tradition of forcefully suppressing heresy, recently accentuated by the expulsion of the Jews and the revival of the Inquisition, hampered the movement. Spanish monks were in the vanguard of those who had attacked Erasmus and the moderate reform he advocated. Toward the end of the century a number of monastic reforms were undertaken in Spain and the bishops of Toledo and Seville had introduced revisionist measures that strengthened the position of the episcopate against both the king and the papacy. As a result of the Hundred Years War both France and England, in contrast to Germany, enjoyed strongly centralized governments. Thanks to the Pragmatic Sanction of Bourges, a century-old policy of royal control over ecclesiastical affairs enabled the king to appoint bishops, and abbots as well, in France. A concordat drawn up between Francis I and Leo X the year before the Lutheran affair guaranteed the continuation of this control. A number of bishops had attempted to reform the monasteries in their dioceses, men like François d'Estraing of Rodez and Pocher of Paris. Their efforts, however, were compromised by the coercive tactics of the papal legate Cardinal d'Amboise. For a decade before the appearance of Luther humanists like Jacques Lefèvre, Jean Standonck, Clichtove and Guillaume Briçonnet, later Bishop of Meaux, had attempted to reform the Church by urging a

267

return to patristic theology and Gospel studies. There is evidence of the same trend in England with Thomas More, Colet, and Wolsey.

The Reformers in Italy, humanists like Juan de Valdés, Paolo Ricci, Pietro Vermigli, and the Capuchin preacher Bernardino Ochino, were either too isolated to bring any influence to bear or fell victim to the Inquisition. It must be remembered that large areas in Italy were under Spanish control, and flowers do not bloom in the shadow of ecclesiastical dictatorship. In general the indifference of the bourgeoisie to religious issues and the illiteracy of the peasantry blocked any enthusiasm for rejecting the ancient faith. The papacy, in spite of its constant interference in political affairs, was too great a prize to be sacrificed for the sake of reform in Italy.

The turmoil and political unrest that were associated with the reform in the Empire, especially the Peasants' Revolt, had the effect of creating the suspicion that the movement fostered sedition and anarchy. Hence, it was against the background of governmental opposition that the Reformation was to force its entry into most of those parts of Europe lying outside of Germany. Its chief prophets were frequently men who had at one time or another been banned or forced to flee arrest. Whereas Luther spent his entire lifetime unmolested in the cloister where he had first sounded the call to reform, the partisans of evangelism elsewhere were men harassed by civil authorities and the victims of a growing spirit of intolerance. It was this confrontation with governmental opposition that gave Protestantism in other parts of Europe one of its chief characteristics, a strong organizational pattern directed toward a self-adjustment to the existing modes of municipal and royal government.

The second wave of Protestant Reformers, Zwingli, Bucer, Calvin, were far more sophisticated than the men from provincial Wittenberg. Keen observers of the political scene, they had watched the shifting alliances for and against the movement in Imperial Germany. They planted the movement in the larger centers of population and identified it with civic and social responsibilities. In many cases they succeeded in actually interpenetrating the government itself. These men placed a greater emphasis than had Luther on the introduction of reform into society as well as the Church. They gave to Protestantism its strong ethical coloring, linked with the transference of responsibility for the maintenance of Christian morality in the state. They adapted the movement to the social virtues demanded by the emerging commercial classes: frugality, thrift, sobriety. Holiness of life, not membership in a world-wide organization, was their criterion of the true Christian. Although for these reasons Calvin is often called *le fondateur d'une civilisation,* he was anticipated in his grand organizational design by both Zwingli and Bucer.

The Reformation in Switzerland shared a great many similarities with the movement in Germany. In both areas it was identified with a political agitation aimed at establishing a more confederate form of government. In both areas it was responsible for a permanent division of the country along confessional lines. Perhaps the greatest importance of the Swiss reform, however, lies in the fact that it gave the movement an international character and an organizational framework that enabled it to take root in the great urban centers throughout southern Germany, especially in the imperial cities. In the hands of Zwingli, the reform was molded to fit into the republican municipalities that had formed within the decaying Empire through adaption to their concern for civil liberty and responsibility.

Ulrich Zwingli was born in 1484 in the small mountain village of Wildhaus about 40 miles from Zurich. He received his early education in Latin and rhetoric from a clerical uncle who was the dean at Wessen. In 1498, he matriculated at the University of Vienna which had, under the patronage of Maximilian, become during this period one of the leading centers of humanistic studies in Europe. During his years in Vienna he came under the influence of the Erasmian Glareanus, but here there is also evidence that the *via antiqua* played a role in his intellectual formation. For unknown reasons, Zwingli left Vienna in 1502 and transferred to the University of Basel where he received his master's degree in 1506. After receiving orders he was given a parish in the village of Glarus. He spent the next ten years continuing his studies and acting from time to time as military chaplain to the Swiss mercenaries engaged in the Italian campaigns. His visits to Italy were no doubt responsible for his later attacks on the superstitious elements in Catholicism and his disdain for the political papacy.

In 1518, he was selected by the chapter of the cathedral church in Zurich to act as municipal preacher. The appointment marked the beginning of his reformatory efforts. These were aimed at an amelioration of preaching methods along Erasmian lines and a purging of the liturgy. In 1521, he became a member of the cathedral chapter in the city and was thereby automatically made a member of the city council. He soon introduced evangelical forms into the divine service, revised the canon of the Mass, and altered the baptismal ritual. It was during this time that he began his literary defense of the Swiss Reformation. In 1522, he published a work entitled *Architeles,* addressed to the Bishop of Constance, wherein he outlined the drastic changes that had been introduced into the Zurich community, the rejection of papal authority, clerical celibacy, transubstantiation and the veneration of images. The Mass was abolished the following year and replaced by a more simple communion service.

Under Zwingli's leadership, Zurich gradually assumed all of the theocratic characteristics that Calvin later introduced in Geneva. Unlike Luther, Zwingli's aim was the establishment of a totally Christian community. In his eyes, being a good Christian was tantamount to being a pious, honest citizen. In order to consolidate the gains of the reform in Switzerland he formed a Christian Civic League in 1528 which included the cities of Berne, Basel, Constance, Mulhouse, Schaffhausen, St. Gall and later Strasbourg. The alliance was formed to protect the reformed cities from attacks by Austria and the Catholic cantons.

Envisioning Zurich as the head of a great evangelical confederation, Zwingli also undertook to establish a political alliance with the German Protestants. In 1529, he was invited by Philip of Hesse to join forces with the imperial cities of Ulm and Nuremberg in a united front against the Emperor. However, because he refused to accept the Lutheran doctrine on the Eucharist at the colloquy of Marburg, he was forced to look elsewhere for political support. He approached the Republic of Venice and the French court, but neither responded to his overtures. Taking advantage of the isolated position of Zurich, the Catholic cantons attacked the area in 1531 and Zwingli was slain in a fray at Cappel. Had he lived, the course of continental Protestantism might have been less ridden with internal divisions.

Two important issues separated Zwingli from the German Lutheran party: the question of the real presence in the Eucharist, and the importance of the absolute sovereignty of God, an element which permeates his entire ecclesiology. He was one of the few early Reformers who saw that the Eucharist was the key to the success of a unified reform. For Zwingli, Rome's claim to juridical control over the Mystical Body was wrapped up in its claim to the control of orders. In a work he composed in 1526, *On the Lord's Supper,* he clearly expresses what he feels is the error in both the Catholic and Lutheran positions on the real presence. His rejection of the notion of the real presence is systematically presented within the content of the twelfth-century condemnation of Berengar. Certainly no other Reformer used the methods of scholasticism with greater lucidity in arguing against the doctrine.

"The papists might complain that we do not take the words literally in the scriptural phrase: 'Thou are Peter, and upon this rock I will build My church.' Does it mean that we automatically fall into error if we do not maintain this interpretation? Not at all. For we find that Christ alone is the rock, Christ alone is the Head, Christ alone is the vine in which we are all secure. Therefore the natural sense of the scriptural phrase is that Christ Himself is the rock upon which the Church is built. The papacy's application of the words is not natural. They are quite contrary to faith and reason and unacceptable to true believers. So too with Christ's words: 'This is My body.' To refer them to His physical flesh is not the natural interpretation. To the believing heart it is the most unintelligible of all, and it can find no basis in the word of God, as we shall see later. According to their proper signification these words cannot have this sense, as we already have seen. The third error, which is that we eat the body of Christ arisen from the dead, we shall oppose in a second article.

"We shall now turn to the papal canons in order to show that there is no justification in Christ's words for the view that in this sacrament we partake physically of the body and blood of Christ. When I appeal to papal laws, it is not my intention to prove anything to the true believers, but simply to show those who accept the papacy that it is possible to reach the truth even by way of the papal canons. For God has ordained that even in those writings which the anti-Christ has exhalted there shall be found that which subverts the erroneous doctrine of the anti-Christ. The text of *De Consecratione,* dist.2, ca. Ego, is as follows: 'I, Berengarius, an unworthy servant of the church of St. Maurice of Angers, confessing the true, catholic and apostolic faith, anathemize all heresy, including that of which I have been so long suspected, which maintains that the bread and wine which we place on the altar is, after the consecration, only a sacrament, that is, a sign'—notice how even the papacy uses the word sacrament—'and that it is not the very body

and blood of our Lord Jesus Christ, and that it is handled
and broken by the priests and pressed by the teeth of the
faithful only symbolically and not literally. But now I agree
with the Holy Roman Church and the Apostolic See, and
both with my lips and in my heart I confess that I, in respect of the sacrament of the Lord's table, hold the same
faith as that which my noble Lord Pope Nicholas and the
holy synod prescribed and confirmed on evangelical and
apostolic authority, namely, that after the consecration the
bread and wine are not merely a sacrament but the very
body and blood of our Lord Jesus Christ.'

"Now first let the thoughtful believer consider how the
devil may transform himself into an angel of light. This
Berengarius lived about 1,080 years after Christ. He felt
that there had been serious error in relation to the sacrament, for there have always been those who perceived the
error. But the Pope intervened and prevented this window
from being opened, and he forced him to make a ridiculous
public recantation, in which it is quite obvious that what is
said concerning the physical flesh of Christ is utterly false.
And there are some historians who testify that Berengarius
was so pious that after his death many princes said that
they would rather follow Berengarius than the Pope, notwithstanding the fact that he was under suspicion right up
to the time of his death; as though in his heart he had
never abandoned the view that is stated in the first of his
recantation. He made what is obviously a false recantation
in the face both of his conscience and of that of all men.
Second, let us consider what is involved in the recantation.
It involves a confession that on his lips and in his heart he
believes that the body of Christ is perceptibly taken and
pressed by the teeth of the faithful. But these three statements are all essentially false, like the devil's words to Eve:
'You shall surely not die, but shall be as the gods.' For
where is the priest that ever took the body of Christ perceptibly? For if the body were really there, how would they
elevate it? And is it not an outrage upon Christ to enclose
Him in a dark and stinking tabernacle? If the priest can perceive Christ, then surely He can perceive Himself? If so,
then surely, too, He suffers the discomfort and cold. But
here they argue that we are not to take the word perceptibly
so badly or literally, but to read the gloss. Answer: Tell
us then how we are to understand the word. You reply:
As it says in the gloss. And the gloss says the same as
you do, that we must understand the word properly, and

then it goes on to say that these things are to be understood of the two forms bread and wine. But what else was it that Berengarius maintained when he said that the body is broken sacramentally? Is it not that to refer to the two forms, bread and wine?

"Berengarius was forced to confess that the very body of Christ is taken and broken and pressed with the teeth. Do not these words make it quite plain what is meant by the word 'perceptibly'? For it is clear that if they insist upon a literal interpretation of the word 'is' in the saying of Christ: 'This is My body,' they must inevitably maintain that Christ is really there, therefore, they must also maintain that He is broken and pressed with the teeth. Even if all the senses dispute it, this is what they must maintain if the word 'is' is to be taken literally. If the sky is red at dawn, we can say: It will be stormy at evening; and if it is red at sunset, we can say: It will be fair tomorrow; and yet we are quite blind to the fact that if in the bread Christ is miraculously present, or if the bread is actually flesh, we must be able to perceive it. If we say that, although the bread is flesh and that the flesh is literally eaten, this takes place miraculously so that the flesh and blood are not perceptible, is it not evident that we are lying and deceiving ourselves?"

Zwingli's mature position on the nature of the Church and the sacraments is outlined in a work that he addressed to the King of France in 1531. Nowhere in the literature of the reform is the central belief that justification is the sovereign declaration of God by which those who are chosen by Christ are redeemed by His merits alone presented as in the *Ratio Fidei*. An examination of the work reveals how deeply he shared in the nominalistic belief in the omnipotent freedom and sovereignty of God. With the possible exception of Calvin, no other Reformer rejected more forcibly the notion that God can in any way be man's debtor. Few writers struck more devastatingly at the Catholic sacramental system. He begins his assault by stressing God's primacy and the uniqueness of His power.

"All being is either created or uncreated. God alone is uncreated for only one thing can be uncreated. For if there were many uncreated things there would be many eternal, for uncreated and eternal are closely related, so that one is also the other. Were there to be many eternal things there would also be many infinite, for these too are very similar and interrelated, so that if a thing is eternal it is also infinite, and if it is infinite, it is also eternal. But only one thing can be infinite, for once we allow that there are two infinite substances, the one is immediately limited by the other. Hence, it is certain that God alone is uncreated. This is the origin and source, the basis of the first article of the Creed. When we say: 'I believe in God the Father Almighty, maker of heaven and earth,' we state emphatically that ours is an infallible faith because it rests upon the one and only God. Pagans and unbelievers and those who trust in what is created have to admit that they may be deceived in their belief or opinion because they trust in what is created. But those who build upon the Creator and the beginning of all things, who never began to be but caused all other things to exist, can never fall into error. Certainly no creature can be the object and the basis of the unchangeable and never wavering power which is faith. For that which had a beginning, at one time did not exist. When it did not exist, how could anyone trust in what is was not? That which has a beginning cannot be the natural object or basis of faith. Only the eternal and the infinite and uncreated God is the basis of faith."

Zwingli proceeds from these premises to a condemnation of the excessive trust placed in saints, sacraments and other intermediaries. He believes that reliance upon such means has produced a superstitious dissipation of the honor and worship due to God alone:

"Hence the collapse of all that foolish confidence with which some rely upon most sacred things or the most holy sacraments. For it is in God that we must put our firm and sure trust. If we were to trust in the creature, the creature would have to be the Creator. If we were to trust in the sacraments, the sacraments would have to be God. Not only the Eucharist, but in the sacrament of baptism the laying on of the hands would have to be God. The absurdity of this proposition may be judged not merely by scholars but by all intelligent men. To help divines to the truth, we gladly hold out to them light. When they maintain that we are to employ creation, but to enjoy only God, they say exactly the same thing as do we, with the exception that they un-wittingly disregard their own words. For if we are to enjoy only God, we must trust only in God; we must trust in what we are to enjoy and not in what we are to employ.

"As the true reverence for the saints and the sacraments we transmit and teach that which Christ himself transformed and taught. 'If you are the children of Abraham, do the works of Abraham.' This is the example we should follow in respect to all the saints and all holy men. For instance, if as the mouthpiece of God some prophet or saint has communicated to us some divine warnings, we must receive that which is set before us by the Holy Spirit with the same honor as they themselves received and imparted it. If they have adorned their religion with holiness of life, we must follow in their steps and attain the same piety and holiness and purity that they have.

"Concerning baptism, He says: 'Baptize them in the name of the Father and of the Son, and of the Holy Ghost.' Concerning the Supper, He says: 'Do this in remembrance of Me.' And by the mouth of Paul: 'We are one bread and one body, the whole multitude of believers.' Neither in regard to the reverence of the saints nor the institution of the sacraments is it maintained that they have the power and grace which belong to God alone. If God Himself did not give to created things the power which we ascribe to them, it is frivolous to teach that the saints or the sacraments can remit sins or confer blessings. For who can forgive the sins save God Himself? Or from whom comes every perfect gift, as St. James confesses, except from the Father of lights and every good thing?

"We teach therefore that the sacraments should be reverenced as holy things because they signify most holy things, both those which have already happened and those which we ourselves are to produce and do. Thus baptism signifies that Christ has washed us with His blood and also that we are to put on Christ, that is, to follow His example, as St. Paul teaches. Similarly the Supper signifies all the divine favor bestowed upon us in Christ, and also that in thankfulness we are to embrace our brethren with the same love with which Christ has received and redeemed and saved. The question whether we eat Christ's natural body in the Supper is one which I will discuss more fully later.

"To sum up: the source of our religion is to admit that God is the uncreated source of all things, and that He alone has the power over all things and freely bestows all things. This chief principle of faith is destroyed by those who ascribe to the creature that which belongs only to the Creator. For in the Creed we confess that we believe in the Creator. Therefore it cannot be the creature in whom we are to believe."

After Zwingli's death the leadership of the reform in Zurich was assumed by Heinrich Bullinger, son of a parish priest in Bremgarten. He had been educated at the University of Cologne and since 1523 had been associated with the Cistercian monks in Cappel. He was instrumental in drawing up the First Helvetic Confession of 1536. Gradually, however, the center of the Swiss reform movement shifted from the German-speaking cantons to the French-speaking area around Geneva where Calvinism was to flourish.

In contrast to the militant Zwingli, who died sword in hand fighting the Catholic cantons, Martin Bucer's role in the reform movement is that of an irenicist and reconciler. His life-long efforts to bring about an understanding between the growing factions among the Protestants and to establish a rapprochement with the Catholic party mark him as a real political leader of Protestantism.

Bucer, like Luther, was the product of a monastic upbringing. Born in the Alsatian town of Sélestat in 1491, son of an improverished shoemaker, he entered the Dominican order at the age of fifteen. He completed his education at the University of Heidelberg, where in 1518 he made his first contact with the Wittenberg professor. Unlike Luther his exit from monasticism had ecclesiastical approval. He received a dispensation from his vows in 1521 and joined the ranks of the secular clergy. Supported by Franz von Sickingen he obtained a chaplaincy at the court of the Palatinate and was later given a parish in Landstuhl. Denounced by the local clergy for preaching Lutheran doctrines, he was excommunicated by the Bishop of Speyer and in 1523 made his way to the great center of Protestant refugees, Strasbourg. Here he joined forces with Matthew Zell and Wolfgang Capito in reforming the Imperial City.

The reforms introduced during these years before the Augsburg Confession were the prototype of the ordinances that soon appeared wherever non-Lutheran Protestantism was established. The congregation was given the right to call, invest, and dismiss its pastors. There was a strong emphasis on educational and charitative changes. A program of relief for the poor and a municipally controlled education system was introduced. Bucer exerted a profound influence, especially in the realm of the liturgy. Two years before Luther he formulated a German Mass and radically modified the ceremony by doing away with the traditional Catholic vestments and ritual. Baptism and the other sacraments were given an instructional as well as a symbolic role. Congregational singing was fostered and the Matins and Lauds of the monastic office were sung by the entire congregation in the vernacular. Between 1527 and 1530 he published the

first of a series of exegetical works. His commentary on the
Gospel of St. Matthew developed those politico-religious
ideas that were later to be transmitted by Calvin into all of
Western Europe. Bucer insisted that Christians must transform their faith into an active love for all mankind. They
were to live out in the political and economic sphere those
same practices of mutual charity which bound them as
baptized persons to the Mystical Body of Christ. The Kingdom of God upon earth was the *Res publica* of those who
were moderated by the spirit of Christ at every level of
private and public life.

For Bucer, Christ is not only the Redeemer of the Christian, He is the great Reconciler of men. The Church which
is His body cannot and must not exercise force and coercion.
Christ rules solely by His word and His spirit, never by
external power. Faith for Bucer seems at times to play a
secondary role in the economy of salvation. Without deeds
of charity and mercy, he wrote, there can be no "communion of saints." Without mutual forbearance there would
be no Christians, for faith without deeds is dead. Thus the
Kingdom of Christ is identified with His priesthood and its
principal operation is the sanctification of sinners and intercession on behalf of the sanctified. It is the terrestrial expression of divine love and its ultimate purpose is to lead
all of mankind back to the love of God.

Not unlike Aquinas, Bucer sees the Church as the extension of Christ in space and time. Comparing the Church
analogically with the Incarnation, he qualifies individual
subordination to the common good with the notion of an
ordered rather than an organic unity. The Church is to be
governed through the dispensors of the mysteries of Christ:
pastors, doctors, bishops, presbyters and deacons. Through
them the entire flock is compacted and built into Christ
as in a communion of love. As in the body of Christ all
the various members are mutually ordered to one another
in a constant service of mutual love and concern.

Following the Marburg Colloquy Bucer assumed leadership in the group seeking to reunite the Protestant front
now divided on the question of the real presence. In his
conciliatory eucharistic theory one can see the Thomistic
background, especially in his insistence upon the substantial
rather than the quantitative presence of Christ. During the
period from 1533 to 1535 Bucer was also the driving spirit
behind the attempts that were made to bring about closer
collaboration between Catholics and Protestants in France.

A series of discussions undertaken with the consent of Clement VII were carried out under the direction of Jean du Bellay, Bishop of Paris and his brother Guillaume, Viceroy of the Piedmont.

Concessions, including the retention of papal and episcopal authority, were conjoined with a demand for the lay chalice and a relaxation of clerical celibacy. Melanchthon and John Sturm participated in the exchange as did the humanists Gaspar Hedion and Ulrich Geiger. In 1535 Philip of Hesse, for whom Bucer had prepared a new church ordinance, also joined in the dialogue. However the political overtones, the hope of inducing Francis to ally himself with Philip's anti-imperialistic designs, were so much in evidence as to prevent serious consideration of doctrinal questions. Bucer was present at each of the Colloquies that took place in the Empire during the forties, those attended by Witzel, Gropper and Contarini of the Catholic reform party. Had his attempt to introduce a reform into the Archdiocese of Cologne under Bishop von Wied met with success, it may well have changed the entire course of the Reformation in Germany. Upon its imposition, Bucer opposed the Interim because he saw it as direct governmental interference in a matter of conscience. After the defeat of the Schmalkaldic League he left Strasbourg. He had been invited to the Universities of Copenhagen and Basel, but he chose England. This was probably motivated in large part by his long continental association with such English reformers as John Hales and Christopher Mont. He had dedicated his Commentary on Romans to Cranmer and was acquainted with Foxe.

Cranmer was instrumental in according Bucer a professorship at the University of Cambridge. However, the old leader of Protestant reunition was by this time a disappointed and ailing man. The plague had carried off his wife and five children in 1541 and the failure of Regensburg weighed heavily upon him. Still in England he hoped to find a base from which the reform movement might once again be reorganized and projected onto the continent. To this purpose he composed for Edward VI the *De Regno Christi,* a utopian program aimed at the complete Christianization of society under state auspices.

The *De Regno Christi* is one of the most comprehensive pieces of reform literature to appear during the sixteenth century. Blending elements from Plato's *Republic* and *Laws* with Old and New Testament norms, it outlines an ideal Christian state in which a religious ethic transforms every aspect of public life. Since the family is considered as the basis of society, the state is empowered to regulate it according to scriptural directives. The catechizing of children is treated with the same reformatory zeal as recommended in changes in the penal code and laws affecting agriculture and the cloth industry. Relief to the poor and the regulation of Sunday observance are combined with such divergent measures as the Christianizing of the theater and public entertainment. Elemental to the proper establishment of these comprehensive reforms is the institution of a Council of Religious which would be entrusted with supervision of the entire program. A genuine reform would not be promulgated by government edict alone; it would be proclaimed throughout the countryside by well-instructed preachers. The clergy were to be trained in theological studies instead of law or rhetoric, the offices of bishop, presbyter, and deacon restored to their original roles as in the primitive Church. The liturgy was to be purged and private Masses abolished, and lastly, pluralism and absenteeism were to be eliminated.

The *De Regno Christi*, however, was Bucer's swan song. He passed away in March of 1551. One can gain some notion of his popularity in England from the fact that over 3,000 persons attended his funeral. He exerted considerable influence on men like Parker, Grindal, and Latimer. The Book of Common Prayer was modeled to a great extent after the program he had prepared earlier for the Archbishop of Cologne, Hermann von Wied.

Far more successful in adapting the spirit of the Gospel to the social and economic needs of the time was the Frenchman John Calvin. He succeeded in establishing at Geneva a base for this vast enterprise. It became a model for Reformers of every country in Europe to study, a community based upon Scripture that incorporated many of the ideas contained in the *De Regno Christi*.

John Calvin was born on July 10, 1509, at Noyon, an old cathedral city in Picardie, a fact which has led many of his biographers, without any real justification, to envision his as a Latin rather than a Teutonic reform. He was the second of four sons of Gérard Calvin (or Cauvin), an ambitious artisan who had risen to the petty bourgeoisie and become a secretary to the ruling bishop and a procurator of the Chapter of Noyon Cathedral. Little is known of Calvin's mother, Jeanne, daughter of Jean Le Franc, an innkeeper at Cambrai, except that she had a great reputation for piety. Because of his standing with the Bishop

and the Chapter his father secured for John at the age of
twelve an appointment to a chaplaincy in the Noyon Cathedral. Supported by this benefice he enrolled in the College de
La Marche at the University of Paris. There Calvin studied
under the distinguished Latinist, Mathurin Cordier, to whom
many years later he entrusted the organization of education
at Geneva and Lausanne. Calvin soon moved for some unknown reason to the College de Montagu, the much maligned
butt of Erasmus' *Colloquies,* where the atmosphere was more
ecclesiastical. Noël Béda (or Bédier), the former head of
the school, was still on the faculty and one of the most open
critics of Luther. In addition to Béda there were other
distinguished masters: Antonio Coronel, John Mair, Fourcy
de Cambrai, and Guillaume Cop. While they undoubtedly
acquainted young Calvin with the writings of Lefèvre,
d'Etaples, Luther and Melanchthon, there is no evidence
that Calvin went, at this point, beyond a humanistic criticism
of Rome.

In 1528, Calvin received the degree of Master of Arts,
but instead of continuing his philosophical and theological
studies, he returned to the study of law at Orleans, where
Pierre de l'Etoile, regarded as the best French jurist of the
time, was teaching. Calvin's father had always intended
him to enter the priesthood, but he persuaded his son to
abandon theology for law because he had become involved
in a dispute with the Church dignitaries of Noyon, upon
whom he had relied to provide his son with a first-class
appointment. Calvin obediently took up the study of law
and pursued it with great success. Among his teachers was
the professor of Greek, Melchior Wolmar, a convinced
Lutheran who doubtless made some efforts to convert Calvin
to his views. From Orleans, Calvin went to Bourges, where
the famous Italian interpreter of law, Alciati, had just become a member of the faculty of Roman Law. Alciati's
pompous discourses and unjust attacks upon de l'Etoile dis-
pleased Calvin deeply, prompting a defense of his Orleans
master in a preface he wrote for a book by his friend
Nicholas Duchemin.

In 1531, Calvin was forced to leave Bourges rather suddenly upon receipt of news that his father was seriously
ill. Once home, he and his brother Charles tried fruitlessly
to gain a remission of the excommunication that the Chapter
had weighed upon their father, the only result being that
Charles himself incurred the ban. How much this incident
influenced Calvin's later decision to abandon his faith is

not known. The death of his father did leave him free to choose his own career. From Noyon he went to Paris where he devoted himself to literary study at the royally founded independent college with its trilingual courses. Here he continued his Greek studies and began studying Hebrew under Vatable.

On April 4, 1532, Calvin published his first book, a commentary on Seneca's *De Clementia*. This work, which showed a remarkably mature knowledge of classical authors, both Latin and Greek, resembled his later commentaries on the books of Scripture, but it made exceedingly little use of the Bible. There seems to be the possibility that this work was intended to bring Francis I to consider a policy of clemency toward the Protestants. But it may have been simply a challenging attempt to develop a more thorough treatise of Seneca than Erasmus had done a few years earlier. The commentary gives evidence of Calvin's continued preference for humanism. He greatly admired Stoicism, insisting upon its "natural" law, and attempted to accommodate the notion of natural law to Christian principles. The book was met with cold disapproval by its intended readers, who considered it the presumptuous work of a young man thinking himself capable of imitating the venerable Erasmus.

Calvin soon returned to Orleans. He visited Noyon's General Chapter on August 23, 1533, and by October of the same year was settled back in Paris. Here Calvin's life soon began to take a new direction through an experience which, in an introduction to his *Commentary on the Psalms* written in 1557, he describes as a "sudden conversion." During these years scholastic philosophy and theology were becoming discredited, while the humanists and other advocates of a moderate Reformation with the support of Margaret of Navarre and Francis I openly enjoyed royal favor. Calvin's old friend, Nicholas Cop, had just been elected rector of the University and was called upon to deliver an address according to tradition in the church of the Mathurins on the Feast of All Saints. The oration, which was certainly approved but hardly composed by Calvin, attacked the censors of the Sorbonne and defended reformed views, in particular the function of the Gospel and justification by faith. The day after the oration, Cop and many of his associates, including Calvin, were summoned to appear before the parliament of Paris. Failing to gain support of either the King or the University, they fled, Cop going to Basel while Calvin escaped to Angoulême.

Here he had access to his friend Louis du Tillet's excellent library and began the studies which resulted in his great work, the *Institutes.* From Angoulême Calvin paid a visit to the venerable Lefèvre, who was under the care of Marguerite at Nérac. After this meeting of which we know no particulars, Calvin made a brief visit to Noyon in order to surrender his benefice to the Canons there. His mind was made up. He had finally decided to break with Rome. The affair of the placards in October, 1534, by provoking the authorities to violent reaction against everyone suspected of being associated in the "plot" imputed to the Lutherans, put an end to Calvin's days of quiet study. Realizing the imminent danger of remaining in the country, he chose flight to Basel, one of the chief centers of reform evangelism in Europe. At this city, in March, 1536, appeared the first edition of his great work, *The Institutes of the Christian Religion.* As soon as he had finished proofreading he left Basel for Italy to visit Renée, the Duchess of Ferrara, who favored the Reformation and was giving shelter to a number of refugees. Calvin tried to strengthen her in her faith and, in fact, later became her spiritual director. Then a problem concerning the family heritage once again called Calvin to Paris.

From the French capital he started out for Strasbourg, but the war between Francis I and Charles V forced a detour through Geneva, a circumstance which changed the entire course of Calvin's life. For it was here that Guillaume Farel, who had succeeded in securing the city's churches for evangelical preaching but who was in desperate need of help, entreated Calvin to devote himself to the work of reform in Geneva. He consented, feeling spiritually obligated, and began his career as a reformer in Geneva with the status of Reader of Holy Scripture to the Church there. He was soon elected a minister by the Magistracy, but the austerity of the discipline exacted in his attempt to completely free the Church from state control met with much animosity. A crisis broke in April 1538, when he and Farel refused to administer the sacrament according to Bernese rites on Easter Sunday, and the two were banished from the city.

A few months later Martin Bucer convinced Calvin to accept the position of minister to the refugees offered in Strasbourg. He spent a fruitful three-year period, not only carrying out his pastoral duties of preaching and organizing the French congregation, but also teaching theology at the college of Strum and publishing numerous writings including his *Commentaries,* the first of a series of brilliant exegetical works, and also revising and editing a more complete edition of his *Institutes.* They no longer resembled an elaborate catechism, but a copious manual of dogmatic theology. During this period, largely at the urging of Bucer, he attended the religious conference in Frankfurt and the later colloquies at Hagenau, Worms and Regensburg. At Regensburg he was accredited as a delegate from the city of Strasbourg. In August, 1540, it was again Bucer who encouraged and convinced Calvin to espouse Idelette de Bure, the widow of an Anabaptist and one of his own converts.

Meanwhile the situation in Geneva had grown unstable and disorganized. It was to Calvin that the Genevese turned, requesting that he resume his work. Undecided for almost a year, he finally determined to carry out his whole original scheme of reform, including recodification of the Genevan laws and constitution. So he accepted the invitation and returned to Geneva on September 13, 1541. He was to remain there until his death on May 27, 1564. During the remainder of the sixteenth century Geneva became the nerve center from which the Calvinistic ideas of reform pulsated throughout all of Northern Europe. In 1559 a college and an academy were established there from whence well-trained preachers departed to England, Scotland, France, Poland, and Hungary. The Netherlands in particular became one of its strongest bastions. By the end of the century Calvinism, or the Reformed Church, was the most completely organized and strongest opponent of the ancient Church. International in character, possessed of a cogently logical ecclesiology, and led by a group of well-disciplined clergy, it was the most formidable foe of the Catholic Church during the Counter-Reformation. Little wonder that the papacy regarded Geneva as the center of a diabolic international conspiracy that was subversive to all government and religion.

Some historians have compared the *Institutes* of Calvin with the *Summa* of Aquinas for its role in the religious struggle that continued for the next century and a half to win men to the Kingdom of God. It is an almost complete synthesis of Calvin's doctrine since he spent his entire life improving and revising it. In its first form the work, written in Latin and published during March, 1536, consisted of only six chapters, and purported to be a brief catechism of Christian doctrine. The first four chapters followed the classic order of religious teaching dealing with the law, the

Creed, the Lord's Prayer, and the sacraments of baptism and the Lord's Supper. To these were added a fifth and sixth chapter, considerably more polemical than the others, treating false sacraments and Christian liberty. The successive editions of the *Institutes* were many, and with each there was a continual growth in its volume and excellence until the completion of the Latin edition in 1559 and the French in 1560, which represent the culminating point in this work of an entire lifetime. Instead of the six chapters of 1536, the reader is confronted by four sections comprising eighty chapters in all.

It is his assiduous reading not only of the Bible itself but also of the Fathers of the Church that must be taken into consideration in determining the influences which molded Calvin's thought and religious mentality in his ever progressive and lifelong development of the *Institutes*. Among the Greek Fathers he seemed to favor St. John Chrysostom, although upon other points of doctrine Calvin also borrowed heavily from St. Augustine both for inspiration and argumentation. There is also evidence of Erasmus and Bude, but it seems Calvin depended very little upon Lefèvre d'Etaples and even less upon Zwingli, whom he considered a second-rate theologian. From 1536 Melanchthon, who later became his friend, must be considered one of the sources of Calvin's thought through his *Loci Communes*. The expositions in Calvin's *Institutes* upon law, upon faith, hope, and charity, upon repentance and upon Christian liberty, and upon the sacraments and baptism, all include characteristic reminiscences of Melanchthon's famous dogmatic work. Deep disagreement on free will and predestination eventually moved Calvin away from Melanchthon.

Luther's influence is easily recognizable in Calvin's dogmatic exposition. Calvin was entirely in agreement with Luther in regard to all the fundamental doctrines concerned with justification, sinning and original sin, Christ the Savior and Mediator, the appropriation of salvation through the Holy Spirit, the word and the sacraments. It can be said that the central teaching of Luther on the justification of faith and regeneration by faith was preserved more faithfully by Calvin than by any other dogmatician of the Reform. After 1536 Calvin disagreed with Luther over the question of the Lord's Supper; and later on the differences became more acute, whether it was a question of the canon of Scripture, of predestination, of the doctrine of the Church, of Christology or of the sacraments. Although the thought to both of these men was entirely dominated by the person of Jesus Christ, the reason for their divergence lies in their different conceptions of the relation between Christ and the believer.

Bucer also played an important role in the development of Calvinistic theology. As early as the *Institutes* of 1536 there is evidence of Calvin's careful reading of Bucer's commentaries. In fact, in his chapter on prayer Calvin reproduces the whole sequence of ideas expressed by Bucer on the Gospel of St. Matthew. Subsequent editions of the *Institutes* reveal even more extensively the degree to which Calvin adopts Bucerian ideas. Special developments concerning predestination, the permanent validity of the law, and the equality of the two Testaments, found in Bucer's *Commentary upon the Epistle to the Romans,* are incorporated in Calvin's *Institutes* of 1539-41. In the areas of repentance and Christian life, he also had a distinguishable influence upon Calvin, but it is above all in regard to Calvin's idea of the Church, its organization and discipline, that Bucer is most evident as the source, in particular, his *Commentary* of 1530, his *Catechism* of 1534, and his *Treaties on the Cure of Souls* of 1538. The influence of Bucer on Calvin was considerable, yet Calvin's utilization of his ideas never involved any servile imitation, but always carried the predominant character of Calvin's personality.

Calvin undertook the writing of the *Institutes of the Christian Religion* with the intention of producing an exposition, as complete as possible, which would serve as an introduction to the reading of the Bible. It was an endeavor to systematize scriptural data into a coherent whole. He was concerned primarily with pointing out to his readers what they should search for in the Scriptures, and to what end they should relate what the Scriptures gave them. Probably the most dominant preoccupation of Calvin was to present the divinity of Jesus Christ in the strongest light and guard it against the slightest depreciation.

Calvin believed the principal article of the Christian religion to be justification by faith, describing it as "the principle of the religion." As with Luther he denies that regeneration is any sort of a *qualitas* that man could present as a value to God. He, however, distinguishes justification from sanctification, claiming they both proceed from the same source, Christ, but remain independent and logically distinct. The bond that unites these two benefits proceeds from union or other communion with Christ. Sanctification can only be begun in this life, since regardless of what progress the faithful may make here, they remain sinners to their death. Justification, on the other hand, is perfect from its first reception, as perfect as the righteousness of Christ with which it clothes us. Unlike Luther, Calvin does not accentuate justification, but holds that justification and sanctification are two graces of equal value. For Calvin, justification includes the idea of an extrinsic righteousness which is however imputed without any prejudice to one's being in a state of sin. Thus the very basis of justification is to be found in the remission of sin. Although man certainly cannot satisfy the judgment of God through personal work, through faith the believer receives justification. Being grafted onto Christ, his sins are forgiven, he is accepted by God, and is thus considered by Him as righteous, the righteousness of Christ being imputed to him. Although man's works are still contaminated by sin after his reception of faith, God does not impute them to him as sins but holds them acceptable.

This reasoning led Calvin to formulate his doctrine of double justification: the justification of the sinner, and then the justification of the justified, or more accurately of their works. The righteousness of the works of the justified depend, just as the justification of the sinner, upon the grace of Christ, for "God cannot be gracious either to His children or to their works unless He is receiving them in Christ rather than in themselves." Thus not only the man but also his works are justified by faith alone. However it must be emphasized that faith is nothing in itself. It acquires its value only in its context; that is, through Jesus Christ. "We say that faith justifies not because it is accounted as righteousness to us for its own worth, but because it is an instrument by which we freely obtain the righteousness of Christ." It is evident in this sentence from the *Institutes* that Calvin sees the real value not in the instrument but in Christ and His work. Calvin thus emphasizes the point that faith justifies, provided it is considered as no more than a means by which we are brought into relation with Christ. For indeed, "it is solely by means of the righteousness of Christ that we are justified before God." Calvin was careful not to exaggerate the part faith played in justification, for too heavy a reliance upon it incurs the risk of detracting from the work of Christ and the glory of God.

The external means, by which God unites men into the fellowship of Christ and advances those who believe, are the Church and its ordinances, particularly the sacraments.

The purpose of the Church is to be an instrument to our vocation and an auxiliary to our sanctification. The preaching of the Gospel and the institution of the teaching ministry purport to awaken the faith and to aid in the collective sanctification of the members of the ecclesiastical community by establishing between them what Calvin calls "the consensus of faith." The universal Church is the multitude gathered from diverse nations which, though separated by time and place, agree in one common faith. All who are thus animated by the love of God constitute one religious and social community, an organism representing the body of Christ, with Christ as its master. Wherever the word of God is sincerely preached, and the sacraments are duly administered, according to Christ's institution, there is beyond doubt a Church of the living God. Just as God had made use of the Incarnation of His Son to reestablish the severed bond with fallen humanity, so too He must employ earthly means in order to advance the sanctification of those to whom He has given the gift of faith.

These earthly and human means are constituted by the various functions and offices that have been given to the authority of the Church. God has chosen these as the most appropriate for the accomplishment of the work of Christ glorified upon earth. Thus the Church can be called a divine instrument, not only insofar as it is the body of the faithful, but also in its ministries and the functions apportioned to them. Although God remains free to communicate His grace according to the pastor's preaching and the use of the sacraments, since the will of God cannot be constrained, we however are bound to the Church and to its means of sanctification by the very fact that it has been instituted. We are members of the Church in the most literal sense, being parts of it, from the fact that we enter into communion with Christ, whom the faithful constitute as a living organism. The supreme Church of Calvin is the invisible one composed of all the elect, living or dead, while the Church with which we are concerned during our earthly life is the visible Church formed by the gathering of Christians in unified parishes. It includes all the elect and therefore coincides precisely with the Body of Christ. Calvin knows of only one Church, but distinguishes between two distinct aspects of it: one presents the Church as an object of faith and the other as an object of experience. The former represents the Church as God sees it, while the latter refers to the Church that men see. Because of the unity of the

Church, one can use the invisible Church as the criterion in judging the visible Church.

Besides preaching the Gospel and administering the sacraments, thereby uniting its members in the communion of Christ, the Church must guide and aid its members in their sanctification. Constant self-examination is essential for the Church in order to avoid all error. Regarding its members, it must employ ecclesiastical discipline in order to preserve its character as the Church of Christ. For it is necessary, by means of discipline, to maintain respect for God and Christ in the Church, and to protect members guarded from evil. It must also induce sinners to repent and thus come to amendment. The function of discipline therefore is educational, acting as a measure of defense and a means of sanctification, and for this reason discipline is merely an aspect of the organization and not essential to the notion of the Church. In classifying ministries and their ecclesiastical functions, Calvin makes a fourfold distinction: pastors, doctors, elders, and deacons. The first two are the most important, since they teach doctrine and expound the Scriptures. The elders' chief function is to superintend morals and discipline in the name of the Church, while to the deacons is entrusted the care of the poor.

It is through these four specialized ministries that the Church carries out its special functions: preaching and administering the sacraments, teaching doctrine, maintaining good order by discipline and promoting charity. The Church finds the right to impose its prescriptions upon its members by claiming that it possesses a spiritual power. This power, Calvin writes, "consists of three parts, which are doctrine, jurisdiction and the faculty of ordaining laws and statutes." Calvin points out that the first right of the Church's spiritual power, that of defining doctrine, belongs not to the members of the Church in themselves, but to the word of God as infallibly written in the Scripture. Calvin bases his argument for the other rights of the Church, ecclesiastical jurisdiction and legislature, upon the obvious sociological fact that in any organization there must be order, and no order can be maintained without certain laws and a body of police to enforce the laws and make them operative in achieving their end.

After pointing out the numerous differences between the spiritual jurisdiction of the Church and the temporal jurisdiction of the Magistracy, Calvin recommends a system of close collaboration between the two powers, believing that they ought to be complementary and assistant to one another.

Just as the purpose of the Church in teaching doctrine and explaining Scripture is to awaken the faith and act as an instrument in the collective sanctification of its members, so too the chief function of the sacraments is to maintain the faith of believers and thereby assist in their individual sanctification. Thus the sacraments supplement the Gospel. They are considered by Calvin as instruments that the Holy Spirit makes use of in order to reach us and bring us to Christ. The sacraments for Calvin are only two in number, baptism and the Eucharist, for these alone are confirmed by the Scripture and "clearly present Jesus Christ to us." These two sacraments, representing as they do the remission of sins and the redemption respectively, sum up for Calvin the work of the Christ on earth.

Baptism, however, is more than just an outward sign of the remission of sins, and Calvin instructs his reader that he has "to take it with this promise, that all those who believe and are baptized will be saved." The power of the sacrament to purify does not reside in the water of baptism itself, but in the very blood of Christ. The primary significance of baptism is its ablution assuring the remission of our sins, but a further consequence is that it "shows us our death in Jesus Christ, and also our new life in Him." In addition, baptism bestows upon our faith a third benefit, namely that "we are so united with Christ that He makes us sharers in all His goods."

In explaining the religious content of baptism, Calvin attacks the Catholic doctrine of the sacrament, claiming that baptism does not restore us to the state of purity, in which Adam had been created, but rather it assures us that our sins and the resultant punishment which we would have to suffer have been remitted by God, who looks upon us as righteous by imputing the righteousness of Christ to us. From this it is evident that the doctrine of baptism is logically conjoined with that of justification.

In addition to conferring our faith, baptism also serves as a confession toward men. "It is a mark and sign," writes Calvin, "by which we profess that we wish to be numbered with the people of God, by which we testify that we consent and agree to the service of one God alone, and of one religion with all Christians, by which, lastly, we publicly declare and avow what our faith is." This public confession functions as an instrument in promoting the glory of God.

The second sacrament, the Supper of the Eucharist, Calvin considers a spiritual feast where Christ attests that He is the lifegiving bread by which our souls are fed. Christ in the Supper attests and seals that sacred communication of His flesh and blood whereby He transfuses His life into us. He uses this bread to put forth the efficacy of His spirit whereby He fulfills what He promises. Through the action of the Holy Spirit, God overcomes the infinite distance between Christ who is in heaven and men who are on earth. In this way, Christ descends into us at the Supper and lifts us up, even to Himself, uniting us with Him, body and soul. In the mystery of the Supper, Christ is truly shown through the symbols of bread and wine which represent His body and blood, in which He fulfilled all obedience for the obtaining of righteousness for us. Calvin emphasizes the point that Christ is not affixed to the bread or in any way circumscribed.

Despite the difficulty of seeing how Calvin could maintain that the faithful "really" receive the body and blood of Christ in Communion, the means by which this contact is established, namely, the intervention of the Holy Spirit as the agent of the union, does, in effect, establish a symmetry between the doctrines of baptism and of the Eucharist. Furthermore, this parallel enables Calvin to make both sacraments dependent upon the preaching of the word, which is the focal point about which Calvin constructs his theology.

It is thus apparent that the central idea of Calvin's theology is neither the notion of predestination nor of the glory of God, nor the preservation of Christ's divinity from depreciation, but rather the idea already expressed by Luther: *"Omnia quidem habemus a Deo, sed non nisi per Christum"* (We indeed receive everything from God, but only through Christ.) Like most of the sixteenth-century Reformers Calvin often uses the Scriptures to support a doctrine already accepted in advance. Yet as the formulator of an amazingly well-organized doctrine he was able to attract an intellectual elite from all over Europe. For his aim, as Acton remarks, was not to create a new Church but a new world, to remodel not only doctrine but society as well.

Strong as was Calvin's determination to obliterate the monstrous perversion that was the Church of Rome, he exhibited throughout his entire life a vivid hope of achieving unity among the reformed Churches. He once wrote Cranmer that his concern for Church reunion was so great that to effect it he was willing to traverse the ten seas. Writing to Cardinal

Sadoleto, the humanist Bishop of Carpentras, he said, "May the Lord grant, Sadoleto, that you and all your party at length perceive that the only true bond of ecclesiastical unity consists in this: that the Lord Christ, who has reconciled us to God the Father, gather us out of our present dispersion into the fellowship of His body, that we may, through His one word and spirit, join together with one heart and one soul."

The Reformation in England, whatever else it may have been, was, as the English historian Powicke remarks, an act of state. The King took to himself the power that for centuries had been the uncontested claim of the papacy in governing the English Church. While Henry VIII's matrimonial difficulties, his desire to obtain an annulment from Catherine of Aragon, and his subsequent bedroom affairs have tended to obscure the deeper issues involved, what happened in England in the sixteenth century was to a certain extent the culmination of a trend toward an independent national Church that had been at work for many years. Although there was a long tradition of resistance to the claims of the medieval papacy, the main impulse in the revolt in England was hardly in the realm of theology. Not unlike the Empire England had more than its share of pluralists and illiterate clergy and these did provide the Reformers with cogent arguments. Yet in a sense the thinking that justified the separation of England from the Church of Rome was to be found in the conciliarism of the post-schismatic Church.

While England produced no great conciliar theorist in the preceding century, it would be wrong to assert that the country as a whole was not interested in the movement. Even Gerson remarked that there were in England many subtle and imaginative minds insofar as conciliarism was concerned, though they had not the solid foundation of the Parisian theologians. It was the support given the conciliarists at Constance by the divines at Oxford that gave the movement its greatest hope in determining the future course of the Church as a more democratic and representative body. The Bishop of Winchester had been a moving force in the Council's futile efforts to introduce reform.

Henry's efforts to have his marriage difficulty settled by a general council rather than the Pope were but one aspect of the role of conciliarism in the English reform. Since the beginning of the Reformation in England in 1529 and until 1547 the King played a definitely obstructive role in the conciliar proceedings of the Pope. Whenever there were conflicts between himself and the Emperor, or whenever the Emperor was successful against the Turks or in promoting the cause of the Council, Henry turned to Francis I. Whenever there were conflicts with France over Calais or Boulogne, or whenever Francis was conspiring with the Pope in conciliar proceedings, Henry turned to the Emperor. Whenever signs of a papal threat grew ominous he would turn to the Schmalkaldic League.

It was in the context of the ecclesiological discussions concerning the visibility and unity of the Church that conciliarism played its most important role in determining the direction taken by the Anglican Church. Both William Tyndal and Robert Barnes held to a spiritualistic view of the Church and defined it as the congregation of true believers, pure and clean without spot and wrinkle, and thus excluded the Roman Catholic Church with her well-known abuses. Barnes was of the opinion that a papal council empowered with the right of excommunicating others was an unlawful council, and that a council that was not the assembly of all Christians from all parts of the world would not be unerring in matters of faith. During the years between 1533 and 1535 episcopalism and conciliarism were the weapons of Henry's *bellum nervorum* against Rome.

In 1534 two conciliar works were widely circulated in England, one entitled *A Glasse of Trueth*, the other *A Litel Treatise Ageynste the Mutterynge of Some Papists in Corners*. The former was principally concerned with Henry's divorce, and with the help of the canons of the ancient councils endeavored to prove that the marriage of Arthur with Catherine of Aragon was indispensable. It stressed that the Roman Church was but a daughter of the Universal Church, and that the Bishop of Rome was to govern the Church by the means of the council in accordance with the law of God. It supported this contention with the canons of the Councils of Constance and Basel reinforced by pronouncements attributed to Augustine, Hilarius, and Popes Celestine, Damasus and Zozimus.

The *Litel Treatise* was much more legalistic. It pointed out that the Pope had been chosen by men without aid of miracle or revelation. He was merely a Bishop in the diocese of Rome, subject to Scripture and general council. He was a member of the mother Church, if he were a truly Christian man, but he could in no case be the head of the Church. The King's cause was determined by the Church of England in which the Holy Ghost was as resident as in the one of Rome. Meantime, Henry needed a more comprehensive political theory justifying a position that would put the Church of England somewhere between the "new fashion" of Lutheranism and the papalistic Church. It was the civil lawyer Thomas Starkey who provided, under the auspices of Cromwell and Cranmer, just such a theory.

In his book entitled *An Exhortation to the People Instructynge Theym to Unity and Obedience* published in 1536, Starkey succeeded in adapting to English Church policy the doctrine of Marsilius of Padua with a few additions from Melanchthon's adiaphorism. Starkey made a strong distinction between "things of their own nature good," "things by nature idle" and "things of themselves neither good nor idle." Things of their own nature good had been defined by God's own words as were things ill of themselves; but all things indifferent to salvation and neither demanded nor forbidden by God should be left to "worldly pollycie." In this latter sphere, unlike matters concerning the articles of faith, there could not possibly be any kind of unanimity, nor should there be. In view of maintaining unity and concord among people, therefore, one should obey the order of the princes. The general council was not necessary for the conservation of faith and doctrine, since these had been conserved for almost five centuries without councils.

Originally, the ordering of "things indifferent" belonged to the business of every Christian prince. However, the Pope came to meddle with these affairs in the council, with the end result that princes began to decree against the canons of the councils. The canons of general councils had originally remained without authority until princes accepted them in their own countries with the consent of the people. Hence, what is decreed in this land by the common authority of parliament as regards the abuses of "things indifferent" must be accepted with obedience. The definition of the articles of faith may demand the intervention of a council, but in the case of "things indifferent" the voice of the council is merely exhortative. It was the Emperor Justinian who gave power of law to the canons derived from the See of Rome and its general councils. Hence, their acceptance or nonacceptance was the prerogative of each individual nation.

It was Starkey's hope that within the framework of a *via media* policy some positive use of the general council could still be acceptable. He wished that the Henrican Supremacy could obtain the sanction of the Church through the decisions of a general council. In 1536 he wrote to the

King expressing the hope that the King's "plukking downe
of the prymacy of Rome" might be brought before a general
council for its approval. Christian hearts were much desirous
now to have a general council for restoring peace to the
world; yet there was little prospect for a council because of
the enmity between the "mighty pryncys of the world." The
King should induce the warring parties to peace and unity
so that there might follow a general council. With the holding
of a Council, the old quietness would return, and then Henry
would be judged to be worthy of immortal glory and "the
veray hede of all churchys eternally."

The middle path which Starkey advocated, impractical as
it was, became the core of the Anglican Church policy. Before 1536 the Reformation in England had been characterized
by the traditional conflict between the *sacerdotium* and *reg-
num* and the publicist literature had been concerned with
explaining the new position of the Church of England within
the Universal Church. If the authority of the council had
been cited, it had been to exalt the regal power and authority
over the ecclesiastics or to stress the independent position
of the English episcopacy. Once the marriage question was no
longer pivotal, after Catherine died in 1536, the task of the
theologians was to consolidate the nature of ecclesiastical
authority in the light of constitutional inquiries. Here again
conciliarism played a very important role.

An anonymous tract, *Concerning General Councilles, The
Byshoppes of Rome and the Clergy,* appearing in the later
years of Henry's reign, indicated the connection between the
rejection of papal supremacy in England and the anti-curalist
theories of the fifteenth century. The author points out that
at the First Council of Jerusalem there was no primate
over others; it was only with the decrease of love toward
God that it became necessary for someone to sit in judgment over others in order to avoid schism and division.
Even if Christ had made Peter head over the other apostles,
this did not imply that the Bishop of Rome held the same
distinction. Peter was made the prince of the apostles, not
because of his stay in Rome, which is historically open to
doubt anyhow, but because of his faith. Even were the Roman
residence a fact, this primacy did not perdure since some of
the bishops of Rome were heretical and most of them were
corrupt. Petrus was therefore but an image of the entire
Church, as Augustine and others have said. There are in
fact certain canons of general councils which decree that no
bishop may be called the head or universal priest. In the

event that the Bishop of Rome had been given the primacy over others, the primacy lacked immutability as does any other law. It is the law of nature that people should be ruled by whom and in whatever manner is coincident with the demands of each individual community.

The relationship between the Bishop of Rome and a general council is therefore in no way like the relationship between a bishop and his cathedral chapter; for a council can make canons binding on the Pope, while the cathedral chapter cannot legislate to bind its bishop. It follows then that the Bishop of Rome is not principally the vicar of the Church and secondly the vicar of Christ. The earlier Councils of Nicaea and Constantinople determined many things concerning the princes and laity, but only insofar as they affected the unity of the Church. The principal function of a council was, then, to act as a judge in a case of heresy and to define matters of faith in accordance with "the word of God and the apostles" and not according to any manmade traditions.

In order to maintain unity and concord all should be left at liberty to act as they will in things "indifferent." Attempting to bring about uniformity of opinion in every light matter was the cause of division in the Church. The "cause why the Church of Christ is brought to so smale a number" was "that we cutt of to hastely the branches that Christ hath sett in his vineyard." Love rather than fear of judgment must be used to bring about obedience. Among the matters that are beyond the competence of the Pope since mundane in origin are: matrimony, confirmation, confession and "satisfactyon," benedictions and hollowings, the ceremonies at Mass, and ecclesiastical orders, i.e., such names as Pope, Patriarch and Cardinal. Though the simple people may believe these are of divine origin, they are not.

In the primitive Church, the apostles did not force but only advised the people to come to a council; no coercive measures such as excommunication or interdict were taken against those who refused to come, as is illustrated by the example of the Council of Jerusalem. All such measures of the Bishop of Rome derive from the spirit of pride. Therefore it is most pleasing to God and the easiest way to encourage the conversion of infidels for every king and prince to reform this pride in their own realms. A council called by kingly authority, in which only those who were neutral had voice, would accomplish more in a single session than many of the popish councils of the past had ever done. The treatise finally denies the right of the Pope to preside at a General Council not only because of his partiality but because the belief that his primacy is based on the Scripture is obviously false and unfounded. The reason that had once given the Bishop of Rome this right no longer exists. At the time of the institution of that office, Rome was the greatest city in Christendom and most neutrally situated. Then the Roman Emperor ruled the world, but this glory of Rome is no more. Because of the corruption not only of the Pope and the cardinals but of the entire city, this supremacy of Rome was now bringing to the whole estate of Christendom more harm than good. The final solution is, therefore, that "it were easyer to make a newe hedd than to reform the olde."

The conciliar theory, so much a part of the reform literature in England, must also be evaluated in terms of its bearing on the parliamentary supremacy theory which set up the Anglican Church. In 1533, Thomas More publically warned the English people that laws made and ratified by the general councils were in peril of being repudiated by one individual. He was referring to the eminent lawyer Christopher St. Germain, who had written that in temporal matters both laity and clergy should obey the law established by parliament and that a statute made by the authority of the Parliament of England could not err. He went so far as to say that it was the Parliament representing the clergy and the laity and therefore was the *ecclesia tota* in England, and not merely a convocation representing only the clergy that ought to interpret Scripture. This principle of the supremacy of an unerring parliament was practiced by men like Cranmer and Cromwell and by Henry himself. Nor can the canonist ideas that formed the background of conciliarism be ignored in explaining the practical identification of the parliament with a general council. The equation of *ecclesia* with *civitas* and the principle of *quod tangit omnes* were also powerful weapons in establishing the state church in England. It is little wonder that Bishop Giberti of Verona called the Parliament of England a *conciliabulum*, a diminutive council. Thus while the estates of the Empire were attempting in vain to achieve through a national assembly and the reform of abuses and errors a unity of faith and peace on the continent, this end was quietly and efficiently accomplished in England by the assertion of parliamentary supremacy within a loosely defined framework of Catholicism.

Of equal importance in the establishment of the Anglican Church was the ancient notion of the *translatio imperii* which had been significant in medieval political theories from the time of Charlemagne. The convocation at Canterbury in 1536 pointedly referred to this in establishing England as an independent empire. As early as 1531 the Duke of Norfolk had informed Charles' ambassador, Chapuys, that the King of England had a right of empire in his own kingdom and recognized no superior. This claim was considered as a revival of the imperial tradition of the Anglo-Saxon kings as well as that of the Byzantine emperors. Henry did not claim the Empire of England as an empire of universal authority, but maintained as a matter of simple fact that no such universal empire any longer existed. His was one of many empires existing severally in many kingdoms. The imperial idea gave the Anglican Church the same position in the universal Church as the one enjoyed by the ancient Byzantine. Here was the jurisdictional independence from the Church of Rome that had been enjoyed by the ancient churches of the Orient and Africa. If Constantinople had been a *nova Roma,* why not Canterbury? Henry was *hiereus kai Basileius.*

The idea that England was an empire also helped to give the government of Henry that other important feature, peace and tranquillity. Peace, unity, concord, and obedience were the slogans of Henry's reign, and they were closely associated with the dignity of an empire (especially in the traditions of imperial Rome and Byzantium). They endowed his peaceful overtures to Wales, Scotland and Ireland with a certain majesty.

Unlike the continental Reformers who were so violently opposed to all that the papacy represented, Henry followed a mean between the two extremes of Rome and Wittenberg. The *via media* was thus a reformed Catholicism characterized by its positive attitude toward ecclesiastical traditions and "indifferent things." Although it was a compromise with many obscurities and concessions on both sides it can nevertheless be described as a fairly coherent theoretical entity. It still acknowledged the universally valid judicial authority of the general council, and in politics made appeal to law, reason, the early Fathers, and the councils as well as to Scripture. It recognized the use of ceremonies and the divine historical origin of the episcopal office. The Church was not merely an institution divinely established from above, but also a corporation consisting of many societies with the right to regulate their own lives. The marks of the Church were the true teaching of the word of God and the proper administration of the sacraments. The Church of England had nothing to do with the Church of Rome, but held it possible that the Roman Church could, if faithful to the teachings of Christ, also be of His family.

All of this is not to say the English people abandoned the Faith with alacrity; many of them felt the evil of the changes that were being made. For the most part, though, they were bewildered and confused as to the right or wrong of the question. We must remember that in England at that time "the King's word was law." By the influence and prestige of Henry VIII, together with a marginal amount of overt force, internal resistance to the reforms was quelled. There were those who made courageous and vehement protests such as Bishop Fisher of Rochester and Sir Thomas More, but these were as small voices protesting an irrevocable trend.

The dissolution of the monasteries, though coming somewhat later than Henry's schism with the Pope, further reflects the changes in thought and outlook among the English people, because it too was an act of state. This great turning point in the history of the Church in England involved the extinction of some 550 houses and the dispersion of some 7,000 religious. This was not, as we are sometimes led to believe, a cold-blooded, savage pillage of Church property and slaughter of defenseless monks and nuns. Though some monks were executed, their executions were connected not so much with the actual confiscation of the monasteries as with their staunch denial of the King's right to do so. In fact, the systematic eradication of the monasteries establishment was a typically English operation; it was a disinterested, business-like execution of state policy.

Another common fallacy that has been foisted on the modern generation by various histories is that the dissolution of the monasteries in England brought about a catastrophic social upheaval.

It is not so much the lack of ensuing turmoil after Henry took over the monasteries that is surprising, but the ease with which the English people, including the displaced monks and nuns, accommodated themselves to the change. The land and buildings were taken over by the country gentry. This was no radical change in administration, since they had more often than not acted as auditors, bailiffs, receivers and other hired administrators before the control of the property was wrested from the hands of the Church. Thus, a large portion of the Church holdings in England had been leased to laymen, and they managed to buy lands that they had leased.

During the period in which the Pope and the Roman Church were eliminated from English life, there was a continuity maintained to a degree unknown to any other country except Sweden. The system of episcopal government, the assembly of the clergy in convocations and synods, the general diocesan system, the method of exercising discipline, and for twenty years the rites and ceremonies developed in the past to give expression to the doctrine of the Church, were retained. Until the latter part of the reign of Edward VI, ecclesiastical life in England presented a picture of unity despite acute differences of opinion. This is mainly attributable to the strong personality of Henry VIII and the powerful support of the public opinion. There were neither Catholic recusants nor Protestant dissenters. As Powicke reports "a few people were executed because they denied the royal supremacy, and a few more were burnt as heretics for rejecting some of the dogmas of the Catholic Church. Aside from these few incidents, the Reformation was taken in stride by most Englishmen."

Although the doctrine and the ritual remained basically the same as that of the Catholic Church during the reign of Henry VIII, there is little doubt that a separate Church existed in England after the Supremacy Act of 1534. The Church was a secular one and the nation was united in both religious and temporal powers under a single ruler, the King, the embodiment of the English people. Much was done during the reigns of Edward VI, Mary, and Elizabeth to introduce Protestant teachings into the English Church and to destroy any link that still remained with Catholic doctrine and ritual. These things, however, seemed anticlimactic to the central fact of the English Reformation, the initial break with Rome.

After the death of Henry and the reign of Edward VI, the efforts of the radical Protestants continued. The first thing to be attacked was the *Act of the Six Articles* imposed to bring uniformity to the Church. An examination of this document shows how basically Catholic England had remained: "Where the King's most excellent majesty is by God's law supreme head immediately under Him of the whole Church and congregation in a true, sincere, and uniform doctrine of Christ's religion, whereupon, after a great and long and deliberate disputation and consultation had been made concerning said articles, as well by the consent of the King's highness as by the assent of the lords spiritual and temporal and other learned men of his clergy in their convocation, and by the consent of the commons in this present parliament assembled, it was and is finally resolved, according, and agreed in manner and form following—that is to say, first, that in the most blessed sacrament of the altar, by the strength and efficacy of Christ's mighty word, it being spoken by the priest, is present really, under the form of bread and wine, nor any other substance but the substance of Christ, God and man; secondly, that Communion in both kinds is not necessary *ad salutem* by the law of God to all persons, and that it is to be believed and not doubted of but that in the flesh under the form of bread is the very blood, and with the blood under the form of wine is the very flesh, as well apart as if they were both together; thirdly, that priests, after the order of priesthood received afore, may not marry by the law of God; fourthly, that vows of chastity or widowhood by man or woman made to God advisedly ought to be observed by the law of God, and that it exempteth them from other liberties of Christian people which without that they might enjoy; fifthly, that is meet and necessary that private Masses be continued and admitted in this the King's English Church and the congregation, as whereby good Christians ordering themselves accordingly receive godly and goodly consolations and benefits, and it is agreeable also to God's law; sixthly, that auricular confession is expedient and necessary to be retained and continued, used, and frequently in the Church of God."

The chief opposition to the acts centered on the Holy Eucharist; other issues might crop up from time to time, but the Mass was the center of the storm. The main point of the dispute was whether or not the Eucharist should be received in both species. Of course, the conservative elements vehemently demanded that it should be received only in the form of bread, as it had been for centuries, while the reforming elements urged that it be received in both kinds, bread and wine. The period 1547-53 witnessed the appearance of the Prayer Book, the Ordinal, and the Articles, all intended to bring some measure of unity to the English Church. A definition of doctrines and rituals was sought in order to find a compromise between the liberals and the conservatives. Also during this period, the right of the clergy to marry was acknowledged by convocation and a crusade was undertaken against images, crucifixes, and so-called idolatry of all kinds. As usual, such innovations brought forth both champions and critics. The critics, who were the real conservatives, eventually sustained defeat.

The conservative stand on the Eucharist increasingly weakened and with this process came the de-emphasis of the Mass and the replacement of the altar with a table. That Communion was received under two species was not strictly a heresy since papal permission had been given for this in Germany, but illustrative of the propensity for change then existing in England.

Protestant ideas, however, increased with the passage of time. The publication of the second Prayer Book under Edward VI saw the eucharistic sacrament as founded for the sake of reverence and uniformity, as a signification of grateful acknowledgment but repudiated any suggestion of adoration. Any concession to the belief that the bread and wine do not "remain still in their very natural substance" was firmly rejected. This is an effective illustration of the extent to which the government of Edward VI had moved in the direction of Protestantism. The Church of Henry VIII which was still Catholic, though separate from Rome, was transformed into a vehicle which introduced Lutheranism, Calvinism, and Zwinglianism into England.

The people of England accepted with indifference the breach with Rome, the dissolution of the monasteries, the supremacy of the King, and the assumption of authority in religious affairs by the secular power. But they resented the visitations, the destruction of altars, the attempts at inquisitorial discipline because these measures affected their private lives. Having no knowledge of theological controversy, they took little interest in it, but they would be quick to resent the destruction of their neighbors by the agents of what they had come to regard as an alien power. During the reign of Edward VI, there was widespread hostility between opposing religious factions which at times approached outright rebellion. The government at this time was directed toward a national unity in religious practices and belief by means of a clear statement of doctrine and ritual ratified by parliament. Internal strife persisted because no compromise could satisfy all opposing parties.

The brief restoration of Roman Catholicism under Mary Tudor, 1553-58, indicated how difficult it would be to reestablish the ancient faith. The persecution of evangelists and alliance with Spain did a great deal to encourage a popular trend toward Protestantism. Yet the efforts of Cardinal Reginald Pole, former protégé of Henry VIII and papal legate at the opening session of Trent, did give the country a

brief glimpse of a Catholic reform that was neither revisionist nor radical.

Few of the Catholic reformers of the humanist party
shared more deeply the conviction that the main responsibility for the Church's degradation lay with the hierarchy
than did Pole. His activity in England indicated his conviction that the reform of the ancient Church was the only
way to restore Christian unity. In 1546 he had told the
fathers at Trent that they as shepherds should make themselves responsible for the ambition, avarice, cupidity, and
other evils that burdened the flock of Christ. Returning to
England in May of 1554, Pole inaugurated an effort intended
to be more than a mere restoration of the religious status
quo before the reign of Henry. It was a renewal that sprang
from the same fonts that had inspired men like Seripando,
Contarini, and Sadoleto. It was based, like their efforts, upon
neo-Platonic Christianity and evangelism. He informed parliament that he had come not to destroy but to build, not to
condemn but to reconcile. Pole regarded it as his first and
most important duty to fill the vacant episcopal sees with
men of humanistic rather than scholastic leanings. Men
like Christopherson of Chichester, founder of Greek studies
at Cambridge, Baynes, the chief promoter of Hebrew studies
in England, and Glynn were installed.

In December of 1554 Pole made a series of concessions
which confirmed ecclesiastical foundations, court judgments,
and preferments made during the schism. The clergy were
restored to whatever ecclesiastical authority they had previously possessed. A national synod was called for November of 1555 and its reform decrees were published in February of the following year. The document reprimanded the
clergy for their ignorance and covetousness. First on the reform agenda was the insistence that all pastors reside in
their parishes. All priests including bishops were obliged to
fulfill their preaching duties and to use the Scriptures in instructing the faithful in the principles of the faith. Clerical
celibacy was to be enforced and married priests deprived
of their benefices. Greater care in the selection of priests
was urged and colleges were to be founded for the education
of the clergy. Simony in any form or shape was made pun-
ishable by deprivation of office and excommunication. The
decrees of the synod were to be implemented by frequent
visitations and inspections. Pole set the example in this regard by visiting his metropolitan see in 1556. The synod ad-
ditionally undertook preparations for a new standardized

book of homilies, a catechism, and an English translation of the New Testament.

Yet moderate reform was as doomed in England as elsewhere in Europe. The same forces strangled it: papal politics and reactionary Catholicism. The Caraffa Pope's hatred of Spain read into Mary's Spanish marriage a possible crowning of Philip's territorial ambitions. Pole was remembered as a moderate who had once expressed his view on the role of faith by advising that one believe as though saved by faith, and act as though saved by works. Deprived of his legative power and excommunicated, Reginald Pole died in 1558, just twelve hours after his Queen.

By the time of the death of Mary Tudor, all the issues concerning the English Church had either been raised or could be foreseen. The main fabric of the Church stood unshaken and its titles, deeds, statutes, and ordinances were all in order. The task of eradicating the uncertainties and strife fell to Queen Elizabeth. She was eminently qualified for this task, for she had at her disposal both the Privy Council and the Ecclesiastical Commissioners. Through Elizabeth's guidance the English Church began to move away from the controversies of the reformers and the restorers.

The Elizabethan Church had a medieval constitution and a comprehensive liturgy in which ancient, medieval, Lutheran, and Zwinglian elements were welded together and put into a language understood by the laity. Many English clerics tended toward a Calvinism mingled with some elements of Erasmian Catholicism, and produced a unique English doctrine from this theological diversity. The episcopacy was respected and had authority, but it was subordinate to the Crown to which it owed its dignity and privileges.

It was not necessary for Elizabeth to regain the royal supremacy after the reactionary reign of Mary, for the Crown had withstood all attempts to weaken it during this period. When Parliament conferred upon Henry VIII the title of supreme head of the Church, it did not bestow this title upon him, but merely asserted that the primacy in religion had always existed and was inherent in the sovereignty of the Crown. Therefore the Supremacy Act in 1559 did not formally invest Elizabeth with the title of supreme head of the Church, but merely reenacted the legislation repealed in Mary's reign. It comprised an oath in which the Queen was described as the "only supreme governor in this realm as well as in all spiritual and ecclesiastical things or causes as temporal."

The Elizabethan settlement of the Church was political rather than theological. Although she worked through parliament to the same degree as did Henry VIII or Edward VI, Elizabeth did not seek so much to impose doctrine upon the realm as to create unity and harmony within it. While concerned with ecclesiastical discipline, she strove to avoid the conflict caused by over-strictness. Occasionally it was to her advantage to hold statutes and injunctions in reserve, and to enforce them rigidly. Fortunately, the Queen and her ministers tempered the ecclesiastical discipline with good political sense. Her principal motivation was not the desire to make the Church conform to her own ideas. She was guided by the political expedient of enforcing some kind of religious conformity upon her realm in order to weld it into a strong state firmly under control.

Heresy and schism meant more or less the same thing in Elizabethan England. Within certain limits, the only real heresy was to deny or qualify the monarch's claim to supreme ecclesiastical power. Hence, Elizabeth's reign was not so great a period of religious persecution as is often believed. The Catholic and Protestant martyrs of those years were the willing or unwilling victims of the law which protected the Queen against treason and the Church against schism. In reality, treason and schism were interchangeable crimes. The martyrs were not executed as heretics, for their crime was first one of treason. Heresy in the legal sense of the word was unusual, and even the rare cases of legal heresy were tried not by ecclesiastical courts, but by the Queen's High Commissioners.

For these reasons the so-called Elizabethan settlement was characterized by moderation. It was an attempt to satisfy as many of her subjects as possible in terms of religious belief. The advent of the Jesuits, spearheading the Counter-Reformation, was as resented by many loyal Catholics as it was by the Protestants. It is noteworthy that Elizabeth was not excommunicated by the Pope until 1570, twelve years after her accession. Toward the end of the century, Catholic intrigue, political rivalry with France and Spain, and especially the Armada of 1588, did a great deal to encourage the acceptance of a more radical reform in England. A new generation of Calvinist and Bucerian enthusiasts from the continent began to appeal to the intellectuals of the kingdom. By the reign of James I the anti-Catholicism of Calvin and the early Puritans was well established.

Seven years after the historic event of 1517 at Wittenberg, the Protestant doctrines of Martin Luther were introduced into the Scandinavian kingdoms. His teachings had already found fertile ground in the duchies of Schleswig and Holstein. They rapidly advanced through a variety of channels not the least of which was the "active and ceaseless" intercourse between Scandinavian *entrepreneurs* and Germanic merchant seamen. The new doctrine was also spread by scholars recently returned from the University of Wittenberg, where the lectures of Melanchthon and Luther himself fired youthful minds. Of equal importance among the events which brought the Reformation to Scandinavia were the overtures of political disharmony and the decadence of the Roman Catholic Church—especially moribund in Denmark.

Perhaps nowhere in Europe, excepting Rome itself, had the spiritual structure of the Church sunk to such a low level of decay as in the Nordic lands. The bishops were closely associated with the nobility and they were generally more than willing to prostitute the powers of their ecclesiastical offices to earthly pleasure. This condition caused the breach between the bishops and the parochial clergy to grow wider than anywhere else in Europe. The Scandinavian people were in the hands of a largely uninstructed priesthood appointed by ignorant prelates. The regular orders were equally corrupt, earning from the masses a singular contempt.

The geographical situation contributed greatly to the rapid spread of Lutheranism in the North. It would be a mistake, however, to underestimate the effect which political events had upon the establishment of national Lutheran Churches. In Denmark, where the Protestant group was strongly supported by King Frederick's eldest son, the future Christian III, and the leading nobility, it gained quick recognition.

After achieving formal institution at Schleswig, the reform movement stretched into Denmark proper. The death of Frederick I in 1533 occasioned political unrest and civil war. But by 1536 Christian, with the aid of a mercenary army, had succeeded in the reconquest of the kingdom. He immediately dismissed the former bishops and completely secularized all Church properties. Henceforth, Christian decreed, Denmark was to be governed by the temporal authorities. The Crown assumed responsibility for paying the evangelical bishops and undertook the support of schools and hospitals.

By 1539 an ecclesiastical constitution, approved by Luther, had been adopted and the Danish Reformation was consummated.

The movement in Schleswig was foreshadowed as early as 1520 by the work of two "biblical humanists" whose services to the cause of the Danish Protestants were invaluable. The Carmelite friar Paulus Helie vehemently disavowed the worldliness of his contemporaries and denounced the "fables and superstitions" taught by the religious. Helie's sympathies, like those of Erasmus, whom he greatly admired, remained with the Church. Like Erasmus, too, he came to reject the tenets of Luther, although at one time he had "looked upon the Reformer as an ally." Scarcely less important were the activities of Christian Pederson, a canon at Lund. Unlike his counterpart, Pederson was quick to accept the reform movement and did not hesitate to give his entire support to the Reformation. He undertook a Danish translation of the New Testament and contributed vernacular editions of the Psalms and numerous Lutheran tracts.

The successful introduction of Protestantism into Denmark prepared Norway for the reception of Luther's teachings. Although the Norwegians initially succeeded in opposing the religious persuasions of Frederick I, the elevation of his successor to the throne in 1536 assured the success of the movement. Christian's accession precipitated the end of an independent Norway as well as the dissolution of the supreme authority of the Roman Catholic Church.

The work of the Reformation in the Norwegian dependency proved to be a difficult task. It was never a popular movement, such as that experienced in Denmark. The natives clung tenaciously to the old Roman Catholic beliefs and traditions that could be observed in their lives for many decades to come. No less antagonistic to the efforts of the Reformers were the problems of a language barrier and the extremely low moral standards maintained by clergy and laity alike.

The Lutheran Reformers began their task in the year 1528 with the activities of the German monk, Antonius. Despite the efforts of the competent and zealous Peder Palladius, the Danish King's ecclesiastical advisor, and such earnest men as Bishop Pederson and Jorgen Eridsson, Bishop of Stavanger, it was not until 1607 that a Norwegian Church Ordinance was officially proclaimed.

The introduction of Protestantism into Iceland was another strenuous challenge to Denmark's evangelism. The personal intervention of Bishop Palladius combined with the

literary achievements of Oddur Gottskalksson and the young
Gissur Einarsson effected some progress. But the true triumph
of Icelandic Protestantism belongs not to the contemporaries
of the Palladian period, but rather to those who came after
the era of the Reformation. Especially fruitful were the reform efforts of Gudbrandun Thorlakkson, the Bishop of
Hólar from 1571 to 1627. Under his prudent guidance
the Lutheran cause on the island was greatly strengthened
through clerical training, Christian education, and the first
complete translation of the Bible into the vernacular.

Contemporaneous with the introduction of the Lutheran
Reformation into Denmark a similar movement arose in the
Swedish state. Provoked by the ambitions of Gustavus Vasa,
recently proclaimed King of Sweden, it was to develop in a
more violent manner than its Danish counterpart. The labors
of the Swedish reform movement were principally directed
by Olavus Petri, his younger brother Laurentius, and Laurentius Andreae. Ironically enough, all three at one time or
another incurred the wrath of Gustavus and had legal proceedings instituted against them. These incidents however
were of a temporary nature in every case.

Despite the endeavors of Gustavus and his various ministers, notably George Norman, superintendent of the Swedish
Church, the progress of the Reformation was slow. Not
until the convocation at Uppsala, in 1536, were any considerable advancements made. Even then, Gustavus' suspi-
cious nature nearly cancelled the work of the synod, and his
subsequent ruthless policies precipitated a serious revolution
in the southern provinces. Gustavus was forced to rescind
his recently pronounced Protestant edicts and proclaim the
older Swedish system.

In consequence of this, the Swedish monarch determined
to make a complete break with Roman Catholicism. From
his resolution sprang the important Diet of Västerås. Here,
in 1544, it was officially announced that Sweden was to be
an evangelical kingdom. This pronouncement was given a
concrete basis when in 1572 a synod at Uppsala formally
endorsed a set of Church Ordinances.

The violent tenor which characterized the Swedish Reformation was absent from that movement's introduction into Fin-
land. The Protestant teachings of Luther were first advocated in this Swedish dependency by Peder Sarkilas. Teaching at the cathedral school of Åbo, he greatly influenced
the local youth. Sarkilas was an important influence in the
development of the Finnish Church, but the great figure in

its Reformation was Mikael Agricola. A large part of its quick success resulted from Agricola's extremely tolerant attitudes and "stress on practical Christian life."

Viewed as a whole, the Protestant reform movement won a "more complete victory" in Scandinavia than in any other area of Western Europe.

The Reformation in Poland was an unusual phenomenon because it continued for almost fifty years without great hindrance from either the Polish government or Church prelates. Poland was fractured into many irreconcilable factions in the early sixeenth century: country versus town, noble versus burgher, and peasant versus noble, to list a few. As a result of this disunity a Reform Church, *per se,* was an impossibility and heresy far more likely.

The Polish hierarchy was both wealthy and corrupt despite the worthwhile measures taken by the king in 1505 and 1523 when he forbade noblemen to acquire bishoprics. Abuses continued until in 1549 the first notable attack on the Polish bishops was delivered by the Erasmian John Ostrorog speaking before the Diet. He accused the Pope of overextending his authority with regard to the Polish Church and rebuked the Pontiff for the shameful prices of indulgences, Church offices, and suits brought before the Roman Curia.

The Jagellonian kings were indifferent to Ostrorog's attacks on the papacy and, in fact, appeared quite disinterested in the whole reform movement. This attitude was largely due to the real danger of a definitive, pro-Catholic stand spelling the ruin of the Polish nation. The Slavonic population of the south and east was Greek Orthodox and the Hussite heresy had spread over the western lands. Lutheranism had first come to Poland by way of Polish Russia, that western part of the territory of the Teutonic Order ceded to King Casimir III in 1466. The Lutherans chose Danzig as their base, and in 1525 threw out the civil authorities and placed themselves in charge. The Church hierarchy was helpless and Sigismund I's efforts to keep the Reformation in check were ineffectual. In Königsberg the Polish printer Jan Seklucjan published Luther's Small Catechism in 1530, and in 1550 the New Testament appeared.

Because of the weakness of the central government and the feudal authority of the aristocracy the spread of dissidence was sporadic and diverse, taking such forms as the anti-Trinitarian heresy taught in Cracow by Francisco Lismani, the Italian Franciscan. Attempts to try heretics in the ecclesiastical courts, for example, were frustrated by the various privileges which the nobles enjoyed, making them immune to such tribunals. The King had little real power to contest the will of the nobility and his successor, Sigismund Augustus (1548-72), was equally distracted and helpless. The Polish Reformation attained its high-water mark during his reign.

A Polish counter-reform of sorts was led by the moderate Frycz Modrzewski whose plans were both conciliatory and reasonable. However he was unable to procure the authority he needed to carry out his reform measures. With Augustus' consent in 1552 a diet did ask the Pope for a number of concessions: the vernacular Mass, Communion of both kinds, marriage of priests, and a national council for reform. Pope Paul IV answered by denouncing the King and the reform movement in general.

In the late 1550's it seemed as though the Reformation had triumphed. In reality, the lack of unity between the various protesting sects was to prove ruinous to the movement. By 1570, when the Synod of Sandomierz was convened, there was still little unity and the best the Synod could effect was mutual toleration between the Reformers. At the time of Sigismund Augustus' death (1572), the Polish Reformation had neither permeated the peasant class nor succeeded in attaining the necessary unity. In 1564 Bishop Hosius placed both his colleges and his abortive Catholic reform movement into the hands of the Jesuits. From the time of this action onward, the Counter-Reformation was to enjoy repeated successes.

Protestantism spread rapidly into both Transylvania and Hungary. Lutheranism was strong enough to ecclesiastically organize in Transylvania by 1545. It reached the same level in Hungary five years later and Calvinism was recognized by the two countries in 1563 and 1565 respectively. Both sects spread unchecked until the mid-1560's when the Counter-Reformation began.

While Ferdinand worried about defending Hungary and Austria from the Turks, the diets were advancing Lutheranism in Bohemia. Protestantism had permeated the Utraquists and the Bohemian Brethren. In 1535 the Brethren accepted a new confession that incorporated much from the Confession of Augsburg. After 1540 Calvinist and Bucerian doctrines spread throughout the kingdom. The Bohemian Archbishop of Prague, Anton Brus, was an ardent reformer who at the Council of Trent had sought to obtain the concession of the chalice for Ferdinand's Bohemian subjects. Brus's ambition was to bring about a reconciliation between the Catholic and Utraquist elements in Bohemia. Pope Pius IV granted his request in 1546 and the chalice was made accessible to both factions. At the same time the Jesuits, headed by Canisius and steadily supported by Ferdinand, were hard at work in the Catholic reaction throughout the Hapsburg dominions. In 1555 they had entered Prague and quickly established a college in direct opposition to the Utraquist university.

Although the Reformation was largely the work of the men whom we associate with the larger denominations within present-day Protestantism: Lutheranism, Calvinism, and Anglicanism, modern historians are wont to speak of a fourth dimension in the reform movement. Historically referred to as Anabaptists, a term popularized by Zwingli, this group, like the Erasmians among the Catholics, suffered from a poor press. Often the attacks of reformers against them actually surpassed similar efforts against the papists. In terms of persecution and bloodshed this Protestant left wing supplied the real martyrs of the Reformation. Perhaps the chief reason for the high feeling against them was their unfortunate identification with Thomas Müntzer and the New Jerusalem at Münster.

While still studying for the priesthood the Thuringian-born Thomas Müntzer became acquainted with Luther and witnessed his 1519 debate with Eck in Leipzig. Luther's daring made a favorable impression on the young cleric. Luther was pleased with Müntzer's zeal and it seemed an alliance had been formed. Then in 1521 the two Reformers split over the biblical prophecies of one Nicholas Storch. According to this former weaver the day was at hand when all ecclesiastical and civil authority would be swept from the earth. Luther generally placed little confidence in "biblical prophets" and considered Storch's position far too radical. Müntzer, on the other hand, tended to support this extremist. Storch had an ever-increasing influence on the impressionable Müntzer and the rift between the latter and Luther was never closed.

Müntzer appeared at Allstedt, a mining town easily swayed by his eloquence. His marriage to a nun seemed to have a temporary sobering effect, and he wrote many hymns during this period. However, his dissatisfaction with the Lutheran practices of the wealthy princes remained acute. It was here at Allstedt that Müntzer suddenly discovered his "New Mission." Central in this calling was the formation of a covenant with God as the Jews had done in the Old Testament. This covenant described a biblical kingdom on earth in which a regenerated Church and godly state would be joined. The elect, said Müntzer, would rise up and destroy the godless so that the second coming could take place and the millennium begin.

Through his great ability as a speaker and his inborn vitality he quickly drew support for his crusade. By early 1524 his teaching bore fruit in rebellion. On May 15, 1525, the combined armies of Prince George of Saxony and Prince Philip of Hesse slaughtered between four and five thousand peasants at Frankenhausen. Müntzer was captured and beheaded two weeks later. He is important as the first Protestant religious leader to identify himself with social reform.

Swiss Anabaptism owes its origin to Conrad Grebel and Balthasar Hubmaier. "The Brethren," as the "praying circles" came to be known, published their *Directory for Christian Living* as a basic formula of belief and discipline in 1524. They resolved to separate from the Church of Rome, live according to the precepts of the New Testament, protest against the sacerdotal system, and adopt the idea that baptism must be received in faith. From the beginning the Swiss Anabaptists recognized civil government. In 1528 Hans Marquardt declared that the Anabaptists would accept all wishes of the government that did not obstruct God's will. Four years later at Bern the Brethren quietly paid government taxes and tithes. Finally in 1538 Swiss Anabaptists disavowed the belief that God wished to abolish civil government. In understanding this period it is necessary to remember that in the ten years 1524-34 over five thousand Swiss Brethren were martyred.

In southern Germany Anabaptism centered around the town of Augsburg. For practical purposes historical Anabaptism was brought to Augsburg in the spring of 1526 by the Swiss leader Balthasar Hubmaier, who, like most of the early Anabaptist leaders, was tortured and killed. John Denck, who had once belonged to the Erasmus circle and was a highly esteemed humanist, then led the movement until August, 1527. At that time the evangelist repudiated his Anabaptism, and returned to his early mysticism. Leadership then passed to George Nespitzer (Jorg von Passau). In less than a year he was forced to leave by the Augsburg mass executions. Over eight hundred Anabaptists were executed and the movement never fully recovered.

In the Netherlands, too, persecutions constantly harassed the Anabaptists. Melchior Hoffman had preached radical doctrines in the Low Countries until his arrest. An energetic baker by the name of Jan Matthys assumed leadership of the movement in Amsterdam, Zwolle and Deventer. Unlike the Anabaptists in the South he did not hold to the creed of non-resistance. Under his able leadership the Netherlands branch of Anabaptism grew rapidly. One hundred baptisms are recorded to his credit in a single day. Matthys soon realized that taking a city by force if necessary would best serve the interest of Anabaptist unity. Münster in Westphalia was chosen as the site of the new Zion. In 1529 a young Erasmian canon turned Anabaptist, Bernard Rothmann, had attracted the attention of the townspeople through his preaching. He was especially popular with the artisan guilds of Münster and their leader Knipperdolling. In 1532 he was elected preacher by the town council. The new bishop, Franz von Waldeck, sought to expel Rothmann, but the guilds acted to block this move. Civil war raged in the bishopric until in 1533 Philip of Hesse intervened. Münster was admitted to the League of Schmalkald, winning toleration for Rothmann. When Philip realized that the man was an Anabaptist he withdrew his support and the strife was renewed.

Early in 1534 Jan of Leyden, a disciple of Jan Matthys, entered the town and was well received by the Anabaptists. In February they seized control of the city council. The bishop was sufficiently alarmed to reissue the imperial edict against the Anabaptists, but this only served to further incite them to action. The Münsterites wanted to build a true kingdom on earth and they were prepared to fight for it. Jan Matthys arrived sometime in February and took over the work of Rothmann, Leyden, and Knipperdolling. One of his first acts was to insist that nonbelievers either leave the city or be rebaptized. A type of communism was introduced during the siege, food, clothing and other items being rationed. Greatly depressed with the events of the past few months Matthys surrendered himself to the bishop's troops in April, 1534, and was promptly executed.

Jan of Leyden then assumed leadership and had himself elected king. He dismissed the town council and in July, 1534, declared that polygamy was to be followed by all believers. There were two principal reasons for this peculiar edict. First, there were about five thousand women and seventeen hundred men in the city when the siege began. To them living in an Anabaptist city closed to the outside world, polygamy seemed neither immoral nor impractical. Secondly, the Anabaptist doctrine of separation could be used to support divorce: marriage between a nonbeliever and a regenerated mate was invalid by the standards of many Dutch Anabaptists. The city was organized after the model of the Old Testament. All opposition was extinguished in blood and the saints enjoyed a momentary triumph. Dissension soon arose and one disaffected Münsterite gave information to the bishop's soldiers, leading to the recapture of the city in June, 1535. Leyden, Knipperdolling, and Rothmann were either killed in battle or executed.

Although the events at Münster had stigmatized the movement as one of fanaticism and immorality, the majority of the Anabaptists were sincere individuals devoted to carrying out what they considered Christian principles. The nineteenth-century Catholic student of Ranke, Cornelius, first brought to light the true nature of the Anabaptist movement. He conducted an intensive study of the documentation in the Münster archives. Ludwig Keller later established a link between the Anabaptist movement and the free spirits of the late medieval period. Ernst Troeltsch relied heavily on these findings in developing his thesis that the Reformation was not a complete break with the medieval concept of the corporate Church.

The Anabaptist movement was basically a new concept of Christianity as a discipleship, a new concept of the Church as a brotherhood distinguished by love and nonresistance. Firmly opposed to the notion of a state Church, a characteristic distinguishing them from Lutherans, Zwinglians, Calvinists and Catholics alike, the Anabaptists regarded the true Church as an association of believing people. They saw any institution which baptized infants before they could either possess or exercise faith as a subversion of true Christianity. The entire movement, especially its Mennonite wing, was an attempt to reproduce as literally as possible the primitive Church in all of its original purity and simplicity. It sought a restoration of individual and collective responsibility toward the brethren of Christ. The Anabaptists were subject to constant attack from both Catholics and Protestants because they rejected the idea of the Church as a *Corpus Christianum*. External and juridic elements, whether ruthlessly imposed in the Catholic camp or slightly modified among the Protestants, ran counter to a true idea of responsibility. Both the *sola fide* of the latter and the *ex opere operato* of the former were rejected in favor of the direct action of the Holy Spirit. The fundamental impulse of the movement was restoration of Christianity as a brotherhood of the saints, a collective life according to the teaching of the Sermon on the Mount.

Franklin Littell, a contemporary authority on the Anabaptist movement, finds the core of its belief lying not in its theology or its ritual, but rather in its dominant view of the Church as the absolute center of Christian life. It was a rediscovery of peoplehood and the rejection of the institutionalized mass establishment. It was the reassertion of the biblical role of the laity and the local congregation.

Perhaps the Anabaptist movement's greatest contribution to the reform was its rejection of politico-religious union. This attitude paved the way for religious toleration and freedom of conscience, ideas that were not to bear fruit until the age of the Enlightenment and the American Revolution.

8 Catholic reform or papal recovery

"If our own father were a heretic, we would carry the faggots to burn him."

POPE PAUL IV

The election of Cardinal Alessandro Farnese as Pope Paul III in October, 1534, gave rise to the hope that now, after almost two decades of postponement, a general council would put an end to the growing break in the Church by inaugurating a policy of genuine reform. Pope Adrian VI, the last of the non-Latin Popes and the tutor of Charles V, had attempted an abortive reform of the Curia after his election in January of 1522. Yet his efforts had come to naught because they aimed at eradicating the very abuses upon which the financial bases of the papacy rested and further, as a foreigner, a barbarian from the North, he wielded little influence over the Italian members of the Curia. He was, however, personally aware of the papal responsibility for the crisis in which the Church found itself and sincerely determined to remedy that evil. In a letter which he asked his legate Chieregati to read before the Diet of Nuremberg he publicly acknowledged the sins of the clergy and the Holy See. "We know very well that even in the Holy See there have over the past years occurred many scandals, abuses in spiritual matters, and violations of the commandments that have become an open scandal to all. Hence it is not surprising that this sickness has been transplanted from the head to the members." Never again in history would the papacy come forward with such an unprecedented admittance of guilt. Unfortunately Adrian passed away in September of 1523 without having been able to take a single step toward convening a council.

His successor, Giulio de Medici, who took the name of Clement VII, made no progress in this direction either. His failure to call a reform council was due not only to the political maneuvering of the King of France and the Emperor, it was based upon a genuine fear of conciliarism. This fear of the Pope was compounded by anxiety over his illegitimate birth. Even the great martyr of the papal cause, Thomas More, had once suggested to Henry that the marrige affair with Catherine of Aragon might be brought to a happy conclusion if postponed until a council could depose Clement.

One of the first to congratulate Paul III on his elevation was Erasmus of Rotterdam. In January of 1534 he wrote the Pope from Freiburg expressing his joy at the choice of a man whose forty years of association with the court of Rome and the cardinalate had won for him world renown as a man of integrity and learning. He was especially pleased that Farnese had taken the name Paul which of itself was an omen of good things to come since it signified in Greek peace and tranquillity and in Latin meant gracious humility. He then briefly outlined what was in a certain sense the heart of his program for reunion and reform. He felt that it was not necessary for a council to pronounce on matters that should be regarded as mere opinions but rather to pass judgment on what constituted the substance of Christian belief. There were in the Christian message certain matters which the Apostle Paul had left open to individual interpretation. Questions on the matter of ceremonies should not be an occasion for perpetuating the schism. Differences could be tolerated without injury to the unity of the Church.

We have already encountered Erasmus in the early stages of the Reformation. Although historians no longer give credence to the saying coined by the Franciscans of Cologne that Erasmus had laid the egg that Luther hatched, he nevertheless did lay an egg that nurtured a reform movement which continued until the Council of Trent. It was especially during the critical decades of the thirties and forties that his reform program gained momentum throughout Europe. No single Reformer of the period, Luther and Calvin included, was unaffected by his influence. All of them shared to some degree his constant call for a return to the spirit of the Gospel and the traditions of the patristic Church. All were in agreement with his condemnation of the ignorance of the clergy and their hardly disinterested devotion to ceremonies. All shared in his fear that the invisible Church was in grave danger of being absorbed by the visible.

Long before the Lutheran movement had spread beyond the confines of Electoral Saxony he had been the acknowledged leader of a group who felt that the Church could be cleansed by a return to evangelism; this to be characterized by a new concept of tolerance and Christian forbearance. It is a group that must be studied if we are to understand how, in a certain sense, the reform of the sixteenth century was no more successful than the reform of the previous one. It is, in fact, one of the great tragedies of history that it failed, and one of its most perplexing problems is the frustration of the Erasmus program. Not unlike the disciples of the Enlightenment of two centuries later, its partisans were represented at almost every court in Europe. Included in their numbers were the English Bishop Tunstall, the Polish Archbishop Dantiscus, the Danish reformer Helie, the archbishops of Basel and Augsburg, the Italian humanist Sodaleto, Margaret of Navarre and Granvelle, the right hand man of the Emperor. It would be difficult to imagine a group wielding greater political or religious influence.

It can hardly be alleged that their failure was due to a lack of orthodoxy on the part of Erasmus himself. Down through the years he constantly professed his allegiance to the Church of Rome. Early in the conflict he wrote: "Though the theologians of Louvain try to drive me into the camp of Luther, neither death nor life shall be able to separate me from the communion of the Catholic Church." Writing to Conrad Pelikan he stated: "When I shall see a Church better than this one, which I follow, I will cease to call it Catholic. But as yet I see none." In his *De Libero Arbitrio* Erasmus uses the same argument that must have occurred to every other Catholic of his time: "Granting that the Spirit of Christ could have let His people fall into error on some secondary point, with no immediate repercussion for the salvation of men, how can you admit that He left His Church in error for 1,300 years, and that from among this multitude of holy men, He could not find one to whom He could show that what we late-comers pretend constitutes the very depth of the whole evangelical doctrine?" Nowhere does Erasmus advocate a wholesale relaxation of the doctrines already defined by the Church. His loyalty to the consensus of the Catholic Church was too great for that. "If the Church had adopted Arianism or Pelagianism, I would have adopted it with her."

In a letter he wrote to the Bohemian John Schlecta in 1519 Erasmus outlined a plan for reform and renewal of the Church. "In my opinion," he said, "many would be reconciled with the Roman Church, in which all are now gathered as if in one head, if we did not wish to define every little thing as if it were a matter of faith. It is sufficient that we rely upon those things that are expressly stated in the Scripture or which of themselves constitute what is essential for salvation. These are small in number. The smaller the number of things to be believed, the greater will be the number of the believers. At this time, however, we make out of one article six hundred. Many of these are of such a nature that they could readily be passed over or doubted without any serious loss to piety. The more we pile up definitions the more we lay the foundations of dissension. The nature of mortals is such that when a thing has once been established they cling to it stubbornly. The sum of the philosophy of Christ lies in this, that we know that all our hope is placed in God who freely gives us all things through His Son Jesus Christ; that by His death we are redeemed; that we are united to His Son Jesus Christ; that we are united to His body by baptism, in order that dead to the desire of the world, we may so follow His teaching and example as not only not to admit any evil, but also to deserve well of all; and that if adversity comes upon us we should bear it in the hope of the future reward which is in store for all good men at the advent of Christ."

The previous year he had written to his friend John Lang of his fears of coercion in matters that were nonessential to true piety. "Without a doubt, the uncontrolled authority of the Pope, sustained by the impudent adulation of the Dominicans, is the plague of the Christian religion." The same line of thought is evident in a work that he fathered in 1552 entitled *Consilium Cujusdam*. "The present controversy evidently arose from evil beginnings, doubtless from hatred of *bonae litterae,* by which theologians thought their own authority to be obscured. Further they have preached and written things about indulgences and the power of the Roman Pontiff which pious and learned ears cannot tolerate. They would undermine liberty altogether by their policy of threats and bookburnings. It is enough for tyrants to coerce and for asses to be coerced. Certainly it especially befits theologians to teach with all mildness. The bull excommunicating Luther, so incongruous with Leo's gentle nature, reads like something these men have fabricated. It is important for the peace of Christendom that the issues Luther raises be *impartially* settled."

During the two decades that separated the condemnation of Luther and the opening of the Council of Trent, the Protestant movement had undergone a profound metamorphosis. It had passed from what had originally been considered by many as just another squabble between monks to a movement that had changed the entire religious complexion of Northern Europe. Whereas historians until recently have tended to describe the events of these years in terms of a politico-religious struggle between those who identified Christianity in terms of papal supremacy and those who found its clearest expression in the Gospel alone, it is now evident that the majority of those who sought a cleansing of the Church followed a path of reconciliation rather than a forced imposition of religious convictions. Opinions shifted this way and that with the current of events. For example, a man who hoped for Christian reunion might stretch his beliefs in an irenic sense if hope seemed feasible.

The feasibility of such hopes ranged from the sometime alliance of the papacy and the Valois against Charles V to such insignificant circumstances as the Protestant placards nailed on the King's door in Paris or the incontestable feeble-mindedness of the only surviving son of Duke George of Saxony. During this period two sustained efforts, both independent of the papacy, that aimed at Protestant-Catholic reunion were carried out. One was initiated by Francis I in 1533 and lasted until 1535; the other was inaugurated by Duke George in 1539 and adopted by Charles V who supported a policy of reconciliation until 1548. In both instances it was the spirit of Erasmus and his general program of reunion that dominated the tone of the discussions. Bucer, Melanchthon and Sturm were, as we have seen, active on the French scene, while in the Empire men like George Witzel, John Gropper and Contarini may be called representatives of the part of moderation on the Catholic side. Erasmus did not himself participate in the discussions, having died in 1535. Nevertheless his last great work on ecclesiastical concord, *De Sarcienda Ecclessiae Concordia,* served as a platform for the party of the middle, the most prominent group in this final effort to forestall a permanent division in Christendom.

The work itself is a commentary on the eighty-third Psalm in which Erasmus weaves a beautiful allegory of the Church as the *Domus Domini,* the House of the Lord. It is a unique expression of the messianic hope that just as God kept His promise of mercy to the chosen people, so He will restore and mend the Church if it will but expunge its sins. Erasmus puts the entire question of reform and reunion within the framework of the central themes of Erasmian theology, spiritualism and interiorization. He voices his conviction that spiritualism is the expression of an inner intellectual renewal based on the hope that it will bear fruit in a personalization of religion. The work is thus directed more to the universal assembly of faith and charity than to the hierarchical, visible organization.

Rather than restricting our treatment of so central a work to commentary, we give here a few of Erasmus's own views on the perplexing problems that were separating Christian from Christian in the sixteenth century and continue to do so today: "Meanwhile put aside ambition and the obstinate endeavor to overcome opposition; give over your private hates and tone down the filthy bawling of your insane quarrels. In this way peaceful truth will finally come to light. Thus a spirit of accommodation will prevail so that each party will be willing to make concessions to the other, concessions without which no accord will be achieved. But care must be taken that the fundamentals be not removed and that human weakness be considered. In this way we will gradually arrive at the things that are more perfect. However this should be borne in mind, that it is neither safe nor conducive to concord rashly to do away with those things which have been handed down with the authority of the past and which long usage and general agreement have confirmed. Nor should anything be changed except under pressure of necessity or for evident benefit.

"Concerning the *freedom of the wills:* this is a thorny question rather than something that can be profitably debated. If, however, it must be ironed out, let us leave it to competent theologians. Meanwhile we can at least agree that man of his own power can do nothing and is wholly dependent on the grace of God, in virtue of which we are what we are, so that in all things we recognize our weakness and glorify the mercy of God. We must all agree in acknowledging the importance of faith provided we admit that it is a special gift of the Holy Spirit and that it is open to more meanings than the ordinary individual can comprehend. It cannot be adequately explained by merely saying, 'I believe Christ has suffered for me.' Let us agree that we are justified by faith, i.e., the hearts of the faithful are thereby purified, provided we admit that the works of charity are necessary for salvation. Nor is true faith inoperative, since it is the font and garden of all good works. Rather let us distinguish that justice which cleanses the dwelling place of our mind, which is rightly termed innocence, and that embellishes faith which is enriched with good works. God is properly speaking no man's debtor, unless perhaps because of a gratuitous promise. And even there we must fulfill certain conditions; it is from His own munificence. The expressions reward or merit ought not to be rejected because God accepts and weighs that grace which is in us or operates through us. Let us not have any argument then concerning words, provided they agree on the essentials. If not, the false doctrines will fall within hearing distance of the ignorant crowds. The expressions that the quality of our works, provided we have faith, have no special meaning, or that all our actions are really sinful, although true in a sense, will be misunderstood by the ordinary person.

"Take the expression, 'Christ died for our sins.' Does it mean that He died so that we might live in sin, or rather that washed by His blood we might abstain from all contamination? He died and rose again that in imitation of Him we might die to sin and rise in a newness of life. He tasted of the cross for us but at the same time He tells us: 'Whoever does not take up his cross and follow Me is not worthy of Me.' Whoever by their daily crimes crucify Christ who dwells within them will profit nothing more from His death other than a postponement of the impending approach of punishment. It is characteristic of certain pious individuals to believe that the prayers and good works of the living may profit the dead, particularly if they take care that this be done during their lifetime. To this practice I would give this warning: whoever provides for pompous funerals and Masses for his own glory loses his reward. It would be much more profitable if their legacies be used for pious purposes in aiding those who are still alive and healthy. But if we are not of this persuasion we should not disturb the simplicity of those who are: rather we should be more generous to the needs of the poor. It is better to apply oneself to good works than to believe that the devil can be helped by the good deeds of the living.

"It is also a religious practice to believe that certain saints who, while living, were able to expel demons and recall the dead to life, are still able to do this. Those who do not share this opinion should pray with sincere belief to the Father, Son, and Holy Spirit, and should not disturb those who out of superstition implore the intercession of the saints. Superstition, which I must admit is quite widespread in the invocation of the saints, should be corrected. Yet we must tolerate the pious simplicity of some, even when there is a certain amount of error involved. If our prayers are not heard by the saints, Christ, who loves simple souls, will give us what we request through the saints.

"Certain individuals cannot bring themselves to be persuaded that what in these times is termed sacramental confession was instituted by Christ. They ought to at least agree to retain it as something that is salutary and useful to many and has the approval of many centuries of practice. It is safer in this matter to recognize that its usefulness depends upon ourselves. We should choose an upright, educated priest who can hold his tongue, to whom we should confess as to Almighty God our certain and serious sins. This we should do without forcing him to extract our sins because of our vague and ambiguous manner of stating them. The serious sins I would list are: adultery, murder, theft, voluntary drunkenness, detraction, which is a type of murder, perjury, deception, rape, and sins of that nature. They are serious whether they have actually been perpetrated or whether they have been merely intended, lacking the occasion to perform them.

"There should be no superstition, repetition of confession, no minute enumeration of circumstances, no flying to another priest if we have forgotten something in a previous confession. Our chief concern ought to be to detest the sin we have committed and to return to our original innocence. Most important of all we should determine to lead such a life as to avoid serious sin entirely. If we do this there is no need for confession.

"It is hardly possible in this life to avoid little failings, yet with God's help we can avoid serious sin provided we have a deep love of God and our neighbor. This should be the basis around which we should center our actions. If, by accident, we should fall into sin, we should immediately make our peace with God, and await a favorable opportunity to confess the sin to a priest, rather than rushing off to a confessor. Certainly a priest can be consulted in dubious matters relating to the legality of actions. There are many cases of this type, for example questions concerning usury, marriage restitution, and vows. In general, let those who believe that Christ founded confession in its present form observe it with the utmost care; but on the other hand they should allow others to retain their own ideas on the matter until a council of the church has given a definite judgment. In this way Christian concord will be preserved and the weak will not fall into open licentiousness.

"As far as the Mass is concerned, wherever there is superstition or corruption it should be reasonably corrected. I see no reason why the Mass itself should be suppressed. It consists of psalmody, the doxology, prayer and canticles, lessons from the prophets and from the apostles and from the Gospels, the Creed, thanksgiving, or as it is called, the Eucharist, the commemoration of Christ's death, then prayer again including the Lord's Prayer, after this the symbol of Christian peace, then the Communion, the sacred canticle and prayer. Finally the priest blesses the people and as a group commended to his protection bids them depart in piety and mutual charity. What is there in this that is not pious or does not arouse reverence? Those who dislike the dirty crowd of hired priests should dismiss the unworthy and retain the good. Those who do not approve of the sequences, especially the unlettered, should permit this feature to be by-passed. The Church of Rome does not have this practice. The same holds for the various songs that are sung in some churches after the consecration—for peace, against pestilence, or for a good crop. They can be omitted without any bad effect on religion. The same holds for other novelties.

"In ancient times the people did not run about to see what the priest did, but rather in a prostrate position gave thanks to Christ the Redeemer who had cleansed us with His blood and redeemed us by His death. This practice is not known in Rome. In the chapel of the Pope there is but one altar and one divine service. There are many churches today where, in imitation of the practice in Rome, it is not permitted to celebrate private Masses, especially when Mass is being offered at the main altar.

"We must reprove the insolence of those who walk about the church when Mass is being celebrated, talking of their own private affairs, and when it is finished go find a priest of their own to say a special Mass for them. The same holds for those who at Vespers seize upon any priest they meet and compel him, even with violent threats, to say separate Vespers for them, though he may have already finished his own. This practice, whether done publicly or privately, ought to be condemned. Some may not approve of modern harmonized music and the use of organs. These can be omitted without any loss of piety. If they are retained, then care should be taken that the music is suitable for divine service. However, whatever is in the service by prescription should not be omitted or curtailed because of preference for music, as happens in some churches. Sometimes the readings take up almost an hour, whereas the Creed is abbreviated and the Lord's Prayer is omitted. There are large concentrated passages, a single verse often taking up a considerable time span, lengthening the usual form of the service and making it tedious.

"There is a great deal of superstition also in the increased numbers of special Masses; the Mass of the foreskin of Christ, Masses for those who travel by land and sea, the Mass of the crown of thorns, the Mass of the three nails, Masses for barren women, for persons sick of quartan and tertian fever. In this matter a great deal could be either tolerated or corrected. There is no need that the Mass, accepted for so many centuries, should be stamped out like some impiety or pestilence. Those problems relating to the quality of the Mass, the *ex opere operato,* and the *ex opere operantis* elements ought to be laid aside until a general council has made a pronouncement concerning them, or left them to the judgment of some arbiter. The expressions 'sacrifice' and 'immolation' were accepted by the ancient Fathers.

"I must admit, the Christ having once died, will die no more, but this one sacrifice is renewed daily in symbolic rites, whereby we receive new grace as from an inexhaustible font. We offer up the victim for the living and the dead, in the sense that we implore God the Father through His Son. Finally, since every prayerful action that consists of praise and thanksgiving is a sacrifice, this would seem an appropriate term for the Mass as it contains all these holy actions.

"There are those who demand that all participate in Holy Communion at Mass. And surely this is the way Christ instituted it and the manner in which it was so long observed. The fact that this is no longer so is not due to the priests but rather the laxity of the laity in whom charity has grown cold. The celestial food should not be forced upon those who do not wish it, or the sick, but those rather who request it. How can there be general communion when in many cases the churches are almost empty at the time for receiving it? Some people leave after the Asperges, even before the Introit. Others leave the moment the Gospel has been read, which, of course, they don't understand. At the time of the Preface, after the priest has said, 'Lift up your hearts' and 'Let us give thanks,' then especially there should be a participation with the priest in silent communion with God. Instead they stand gossiping in the marketplace or drink in wineshops, which practice, bad as it is, is not so disgraceful a thing as the irreverence of those who stay in Church chatting during the entire service.

"And finally, even today, there is not, just as there was not in antiquity, a complete sharing of the symbols of the sacrament on the part of those assisting at Mass. Nevertheless there is a participation in the same divine doctrine, the pious prayers and exhortations as well as the acts of praise and thanksgiving. This is the communion which vivifies and it does so without this sharing of the elements. Some may have objections to adoration given to the Eucharist. If Christ is totally present in the sacrament, why should it not be adored? Although He is only there in the form of bread and wine to be received in a pure devotion, not to be made a display of at public games or processions nor to be carried about on horseback through the fields. This may be an ancient practice but it is at the same time a concession to ignorant fancy that never should have been made.

"Some think themselves quite pious if whenever they see a priest exposing the Host, they rush up and gaze fixedly upon it. It would be much more religious if, like the Publican, they stayed at a distance or prostrated themselves in adoration of the Crucified.

"There is nothing so stupid as to adore what is human as divine in the person of Christ or to worship the bread and wine instead of Him. Since, however, no one is really certain, except the priest himself, as to whether he actually consecrates the elements, all adore with this tacit condition. Furthermore, what we adore in Christ is always present with us. Besides, if there is no sacrament so slowly that we do not uncover our heads when it is administered, as for example with baptism and confirmation, who would want to call this idolatrous that we bare our head to this sacrament even if Christ be there only symbolically?

"The plethora of feast days, which either bishops in deference to popular wish have introduced, or Popes have instituted for no real reason, they themselves ought to discreetly reduce in number. I would list among these the feast of the Immaculate Conception, the Nativity of the Blessed Virgin and the Presentation. I really feel that no feasts should be celebrated that have no basis in Scripture, with the exception, of course, of Sunday. There would be no objection to fewer feasts provided we keep those we have with greater devotion. We need not consider that a day is profaned when a man, by honest labor, earns enough to support his wife and children or helps his neighbor in need.

Those feasts which sodalities have set up on their own authority ought to be suppressed by the civil magistrates. They are nothing more than the ancient revelries of Coma and Bacchus.

"Fasting and special regulations about food are only enjoined by the Church for health of body and mind, and are not binding on those who cannot stomach fish or who find their strength diminished by fasting. But when people are all the better for these abstinences, it is mere contumacy to reject useful practices just because they are ordained by the Church. Let no one sit in judgment then. If you eat meat, don't condemn those who do not and vice versa. Let God be our judge. I feel the same way with regard to the other constitutions of bishops. If they are good and useful let them be observed as always. If the idea of enforcement is repulsive then consider them as merely counsels. If a servant whom you have employed for little or nothing offers you advice that is useful, then listen to him, not because he is your servant but because what he says is for your best interests. Should we reject the advice of those who are in public office and those who take the place of the Fathers and the Doctors of the Church?

"I take this stand, not because what I say should be taken as absolutely certain or because I wish to dictate what the Church should do. It is rather that while awaiting a council we must cut off, so far as in us lies, the causes of dissension. Let us not do anything by force, and certainly do unto others what we would wish them to do unto us. Let us beseech heaven and earth but in no way force anyone into a religion that repels him. It is equally important that those, who do not want to be forced in the matter of religion, refrain from attacking the religion of others, especially when that religion is sheltered behind ancient practices. Let this warning be listened to by both factions: If moderate accommodation lessens the intensity of the disagreements, the medicine of the council will more easily work toward concord."

Erasmus's final work on ecclesiastical concord was written at the insistence of and dedicated to the Catholic Bishop Julius Pflug. Yet it increased suspicion among the more conservative and reactionary Catholics that he had in his old age defected to Lutheranism. The reaction in Rome was that the book was no defense of orthodoxy, *Non isto defensore*. It was condemned by the stronghold of protectionism, the University of Louvain. Perhaps the real reason for its censure was its statement of the central theme of reform humanism as dogma controlled by the interests of piety. Erasmus and his disciples considered the task of greatest urgency in the restoration of piety to be a return to sources. This meant not only a restoration of scriptural and patristic texts, but a focusing of the Christian's attention on the teaching of Christ Himself. Since dogma exists only for the sake of piety, only as an aid to men's salvation, and since a complexification of dogma disrupts the precious peace of Christ in the Church, dogma must be confined to those immediately practical truths that each man must know for his salvation. It seemed to the Erasmians a ridiculous thing to destroy the unity and peace of Christendom through controversy over the Pope's jurisdiction in purgatory or disputes on man's intrinsic or extrinsic justification.

In spite of growing opposition to the Erasmian message, his ideals as summed up in the work *On Mending the Peace of the Church* continued to exert influence until the time of the Counter-Reformation. Nicholas Perronet, Charles V's minister, kept them alive in imperial circles until the time of his death. Cornelius Shepper and Johann von Weeze were Erasmian partisans at the court of Ferdinand I, as were Simon Pistoris at Dresden and Conrad Heresbach at the court of Cleves. Perhaps the most dedicated of the expectants, as these men were called, was the convert priest George Witzel.

He was one of the earliest supporters of the Lutheran movement, but later turned with a vengeance against the "Pope on the Elbe" because he found little similarity between the Church of Wittenberg and the Church of Jerusalem. Filled with an enthusiasm for reform that was matched only by his ofttimes misguided zeal, he was one of the few polemicists whose efforts toward ecumenism and ecclesiastical reform spanned the periods both before and after the Council of Trent. Born in 1501 in the little village of Vacha, near Fulda in modern Hesse, he received his early education in Schmalkalden and Halle and entered the University of Erfurt in 1516. There his remarkable ability as a classicist distinguished him as a member of the recently founded Erasmian Sodality. Attracted to the teaching of Luther, he transferred to Wittenberg at the age of twenty and soon plunged into a study of the Scripture and the early Fathers. Ordained a priest the following year, he availed himself of the new *Libertas Christiana* and married one Elizabeth Kraus. Deprived of his vicarage in Vacha because of his marriage, he made his way to Eisenach, hometown of his wife, and received a new vicarage there. This was the first in a long series of flights and harassments that his outspoken criticism of both Catholics and Protestants was to incur.

In 1538 Witzel was appointed as consultant in religious matters to the court of Duke George of Saxony. One of his first duties in the Saxon court was to assist in drawing up a reform program that would follow a *via media* between papal and Lutheran extremes. In 1539 he attended the religious colloquy at Leipzig along with Christopher Carlowitz. Here in close collaboration with Bucer, he worked out a reform program that was modelled after the ancient Church. Much of the proposal was based upon the *Apology* of Justin written in Rome in the year 150 and it followed this first account of the liturgy of the ancient Church in advocating the simplicity and communal nature of the early divine service. Private Mass was to be abolished, the Latin and German languages were to have equal standing, the canon of the Mass was to be revised, and the number of feast days was to be reduced. The colloquy, like others that followed, was based upon the hope that if the secular rulers were able to work out a religious compromise they could force the Emperor to convene a national council for its adoption. It was felt that agreement could be achieved if they used as their authorities the teaching of the apostles, the early councils, and the Fathers up to the pontificate of Gregory the Great.

Many of the ideas contained in this program were later expanded by Witzel and published in 1540 under the title of *Typus Ecclesiae Catholicae*. This work, which underwent at least a half-dozen printings, is a collection of quotations from the Fathers ranging from Clement to Bernard of Clairvaux, and demonstrating the historicity of current Catholic practices as opposed to papistical innovations. It depicts the *formae* or exemplars of the Church in both the East and West and follows a ceremonial rather than a juridical description of what the Church is in practice rather than in theory. The work follows the theme of Vincent of Lerin's *Commonitories,* a defense of the antiquity and universality of the Catholic Church against profane innovations of all heretics. Like the fifth-century monk, Witzel stresses that faith is based upon the authority of divine law which must be understood and interpreted according to the tradition of the Church, this tradition consisting of what has been believed everywhere, always, and by all. For Witzel as for Vincent, this principle does not exclude progress or doctrinal development. Progress is for both a growing of doctrine from within its own orbit, whereas change implies a belief that a thing is transformed into something else. For Witzel there have been changes out of accord with true development in both the Catholic Church and the more recent Protestant movements. Thus the Church of antiquity is the ideal type or form for a renewed Church.

The Church is not a spiritual edifice but rather that visible assembly of the faithful one encounters in his baptized neighbors and of which he himself is a member. It is holy, universal, catholic and apostolic. It is the community of those who break bread together, the community of saints. It is a community charged with making its visible presence known in this world. If belief in Christ is certain then so is a belief in His Church.

Yet this Church, regardless of how corrupt it may have become, lives on in the Roman Church (*Ecclesia Romanensis*). Witzel sees the attack of Luther on Rome as God's punishment for the vices and greed of the present-day papacy, and its continued refusal to reform itself. Nonetheless the Church of Luther is lacking in tradition. It is a modernity completely out of touch with the ancient edifice. *"Tanto recentior, quanto nocentior."*

Witzel criticized the degenerate customs of the Curia as few others have, but found that Rome retained the basic elements of the faith. This faith, he repeatedly affirmed, did not differ radically from that taught so long ago in Jerusalem and Antioch. It is to the merit of the Roman Church that she first preached the Gospel to the German peoples. "She has educated us and yet we act as if we did not know her." In controversy with Justus Jones, Witzel points out that it has always been the authority of the Church of Rome that has settled disputes in the East and in the West as well. It is a mistake, he says, to judge the Church solely on the basis of her present state, oblivious of what she once was. There is a proneness on the part of too many to see only what is evil in her. He undertakes a lyrical defense, saying: "This mother I love as much in age as I loved when young. Whoever feels the springtime pleasant and beautiful, should also like the fall. A mother's scars and blemishes pain me more than death and I long to remove them even with the loss of my life." In answer to Luther's remark that things would be otherwise were the Popes of four centuries ago with us today, Witzel retorts: "Yes, if those Popes reigned today, your sect would be nothing more than buttermilk."

Witzel held that there was no justifiable reason for separation from the Church. Her defects, however, impose upon all Christians the need to recognize and remedy them within the established framework of her traditional and time-honored teachings. It is not so important that some members of the Church are lacking in the fervor of the early Christians. The Church is a large edifice and it is not possible that all its furnishings be of gold or silver; wooden and earthen vessels will always be found. This has nothing to do with the content of faith; the essential thing is that unity be maintained. We see in Witzel that element of reform that sets the Erasmian group apart from the conflicting parties of the movement, a sense of history that evaluates not on a basis of dogmatic and *a priori* judgments, but on a critical assessment of documentary evidence.

The death of his patron George of Saxony, in 1539, once again forced Witzel and his family to flee to Meissen. It was not until two years later that he found any kind of a home for his family. He was then able to settle down in Fulda and become advisor to Abbot Johann von Henneberg. As temporal ruler of the territory, the Abbot was preparing a new Church ordinance. Witzel was largely responsible for the contents of the ordinance as he had been for a similar one prepared in Berlin two years before. The Berlin ordinance, prepared for the Elector Joachim II, had been presented to Luther for inspection. After reading it Luther claimed that it "smelled Witzelish" because of its stress on ceremonies.

In the Fulda program the whole theme of the reform was to inculcate fraternal charity, unity, and peace. The reform urged that the Gospel be preached clearly and distinctly and that sermons avoid points of dispute. The common man is to be taught what is said and sung in the churches. On Sundays all are to participate in Communion and the chalice is to be given to the layman if so desired. The use of both the German and Latin languages is recommended. Also suggested in the program is the establishment of schools for the education of future clergy where Latin, Greek, and Hebrew are taught. The reforms show Witzel's concern for the erection of orphanages and other charitable institutions. In all his reforms he was particularly aware of the vicissitudes of the poor, and the need for social reform accentuated by the troubled times. He urged that defunct monasteries be used for this purpose and that rundown convents be turned into training centers for indigent girls. Mainz, Meissen and Strasbourg also witnessed Witzel's reform efforts, and there is evidence that he exerted an influence in the moderate reforms introduced into the Dukedom of Cleves.

However, it was as a publicist that he exerted his greatest influence in the conciliatory movement of the period. Author of more than 130 books, he stands in the forefront of those who found the pen mightier than the sword in promoting ecclesiastical concord. Like Luther he had a fine command of colloquial German, and although many of his works were written in the heady classical Latin of the period, his appeal to the common people was enhanced by his rural origins and his ability to reduce issues to commonly understood vulgate expressions. Nowhere in his writings does he go into the deeper aspects of the theological problems of the time. He generally avoids such issues as the primacy of the papacy, the cogency of ecclesiastical laws, and the nature of justification. He uses, for example, the parable of the rich man who promises a poor guest a heritage to be shared with his son provided he fulfill certain duties, or that of the king who displays a purse containing ten thousand gold gulden in a field and asks that all interested race for the reward. All who run will be rewarded regardless of their previous merit; the running is what really matters. To avoid any taint of semi-Pelagianism he compares man's role in salvation to the plow, the fertilizer, and the reaping of the harvest, all of which have no significance when considered independently of the field, the rain, and the sun which Christ supplies. Man's activity has nothing to do with the latter, it cannot be merited.

The most popular of his writings on ecclesiastical concord was a little work entitled *Methodus Concordiae Ecclesiasticae* which was first published in 1539. Since it contains in general outline the aims of all his later reforms and strikes out at what he feels are the basic reasons for discord, it warrants examining in detail.

He begins his appeal by pointing out that the present storm which threatens to destroy the Church is due chiefly to the blindness and indifference of those entrusted to direct it. The most prudent realize that the storm must be quieted but it must be quelled without giving rise to greater evils; the cure must not kill. It must be realized that the Church with Christ as its Head spares the broken reed, tracks down and rescues lost sheep, and bears injury rather than inflicts it.

The book outlines the main areas of contention between the factions and the Catholic Church following the articles of the Confession of Augsburg. In the matter of doctrine, he urges that the Church should be prepared to make certain concessions by dropping some of its scholastic definitions. Scholastic jargon, he feels, has been responsible for much of the tragedy that afflicts the present century. "If modern theologians would be content with ancient theology rather than continuing to concoct novelties, the Church would not be afflicted with so many heresies." He warns the scholastic theologians to recall that the mentality of the people today is much different from the days in which this system was developed. Many of the prophets, apostles, martyrs, and doctors of the Church were no less servants of God because they were ignorant of the theology of the Sorbonne. The Church, since it is composed of diversified elements, demands a certain flexibility in order to govern with unanimity. Certain traditions, as long as they are in basic agreement with the Scriptures, should be permitted. Whatever is good or pious in either scholastic or schismatic theology should be retained.

With regard to Scripture, he urges that the Bible be translated into the vernacular, not by one individual, but by a committee of experts who will insure a version that can be used intelligently from the pulpit. A desire for edification rather than dissension and hate must motivate all preaching. In the question of the Eucharist, he recommends a return to the ancient doctrine of the apostles. If Catholics would do away with the shameful superstitious practices associated with the saying of Mass, concord will be achieved. The impious practice of saying Mass for money or of celebrating in private must be abolished. Those who say private Masses do so for the most part merely for the pecuniary profit derived. It would be much better if a few Masses were celebrated piously than to have a multiplicity of sacrilegious rites take place.

In speaking of Holy Orders he writes with unrestrained wrath of the deplorable state of the clergy. "If ecclesiastics would not command us to believe as oracles of the third heaven the imaginings of scholastic theology, the sects would then return to peace. This theology has dramatized the nature of Holy Orders far beyond the testimony of Scripture and the orthodox Fathers. On the other hand, it is of utmost necessity that the Church ordain bishops, and that they in turn ordain and consecrate priests and deacons. It is an incontrovertible fact that Sacred Orders are not the four-year-old figment of some Pope's imagination. Nor did the Church begin to ordain her stewards yesterday. If the sects themselves do not put the ordained in charge of the non-ordained of the Church, people who have little knowledge of the faith will not be drawn after those not in orders. Certainly the Church has ample documentation in this matter."

Although not entirely opposed to the monastic life, Witzel nevertheless urges a reduction of the number of monasteries, many of which are home for the lazy and the superstitious. The monks are more interested in their man-made devotions and the pious practices they peddle to the laity for profit, Witzel asserts, than they are in following the commandments of God. The incessant quarrels which they carry on among themselves constitute an open wound which feeds the present schism. Certain monasteries should be devoted to educational purposes, especially the ones that are equipped with good libraries. The gospel of Aristotle that is preached with such devotion among the monks, and the fables relating to their origins must be toned down if they are to survive the scorn that the people feel toward them.

Throughout all of his writings Witzel stresses the point that the real causes of the schism rending the Church are the abuses associated with the celebration of the Mass. "Let the ecclesiastics correct the shameful abuses of the Mass and its stolid superstitions and there will be happy accord. Masses for money, Masses read for the dead on various anniversaries, and Masses read by those living in concubinage must be abolished. Let priests celebrate the Mass at all times mindful of the Victim, religiously, seriously, and with such a disposition of mind that God may be thereby glorified and our neighbor edified." Addressing the Lutherans in particular he states: "It is necessary for us to admit, with a groan and great anguish of heart, that a great number of Masses are celebrated not according to the law, but murmured swiftly and unwillingly by the impure and the gluttonous. We unanimously defend the adoration of the Eucharist as worthy of Christ, but meanwhile let us do something about those of our brethren who by their miserable sacrificing plunge their souls into hell, since they eat and drink judgment perpetually to themselves."

For Witzel the Mass is first and foremost a public affair to be participated in by the entire community. The very expression "liturgy" could be understood only as a public Mass. To emphasize his reform programs as based upon a liturgical foundation, he speaks always of a *publica liturgia*. "Just as in the Pater Noster we recognize God as the Father of all, so in the liturgy there must be the essential note of communal petitioning and thanking of God. Yet because of the present multiplicity of Masses the Church has been afflicted and punished with blindness, discord and other evils. It is the cause of the increased number of ignorant clergy. All must agree that its continued practice will be harmful to both the Church and the state, as the people can no longer bear the financial burden of so many Masses."

Instead of daily Masses he urges a daily gathering of the community for liturgical services. Once this practice of public worship has been introduced, communal prayer will lead to a unity of all Christians in Christ *("unitas omnium hominum christianorum in Christo")*.

External cult he sees as a doctrinal as well as a devotional effort. The purpose of worship is to insure that one walks in a manner worthy of his vocation, worthy of God, and worthy of the Gospel. Where true understanding is, he often reiterated, there is true devotion. The real remedy for the religious discord that beset the Church of his day was a reeducation of the people by explaining the various rituals and ceremonies used in the administration of the sacraments and the Eucharist. Witzel voices what might be considered the central point of Catholic reform humanism, the de-emphasizing of the *opus operatum* element in the character of the Mass and the sacraments. It is an impious abuse, he writes, to put one's faith more in the work of the priest than in the benefits of Christ, as if once the Mass has been read, we can continue to sin seriously. It is repugnant to him that the Mass be applied indiscriminately to one or to many, or for the living or the dead, equally or unequally, as if God doled out the fruits of the Mass according to the determination of the person offering the sacrifice.

For Witzel the sacramental sign must become once again a symbol that is operative in the inner piety and imagination of the participants. In the sacrifice of the Mass he urges the people to recall to mind the whole tragedy of the sacrifice of Calvary. In the administration of the sacrament of baptism he urges the entire community to participate and to renew their own baptismal vows so that they will know what happened to them when they were incorporated into the Mystical Body.

First on the agenda of all the Church ordinances he composed is, significantly, the abolition of the private Mass. All his liturgical works are an attempt to bring into focus the communal nature of the sacrifice and to demonstrate it as something to be participated in and understood by the laity. He aimed always to restore to Christian people, and especially the common man, a loving understanding of the *cultus divinus,* and thereby a more religious appreciation of it. His studies of the Fathers of the Church had brought to light the true nature of the liturgy as essentially a social work. It is a prayer of the Mystical Body and therefore must restore a contact between the minds of the faithful and the sacred texts and norms used in the celebration. It must recall communities to nourish their minds as well as their souls. The reception of the Eucharist was for Witzel the most concrete and profound manner of participating in the sacrifice which was the center of the liturgy. His ideal was to create around the altar a family of the children of God, adding their voices, responding to the dialogue, ratifying the prayers, singing God's glory and imploring His mercy.

In directing his reform efforts toward a renewal of the liturgy, there is evidence in Witzel of a strong conviction that in it, whatever else may have been corrupted by monasticism and scholasticism, there was still to be found an inner principle of unity. As it once had united the East and the West, the Byzantine and the Barbarian, so now it could unite the sectarians of the sixteenth century. The liturgy was the very center of that Christian culture that had run aground in the centuries that separated his time from the golden age of the early Fathers. Yet his enthusiasm for the liturgy of the ancient Church was in part motivated by a deep sense of the aesthetic. The close proximity of the early liturgical practices to the cultural elements of Graeco-Roman antiquity with their "noble simplicity" gave them a value that transcended their sacramental worth. In this we see the deep influence of Renaissance humanism.

In the living testimony of the primitive Church he perceived a cogent moral force. It had fostered the heroism of the early martyrs and confessors, the first witnesses to Christ. Now it could once again inspire and unite the *plebs sancta* in the face of disrupting forces. Humanism had produced an awareness of the ethical value of antiquity. The liturgy was the bridge that could once again restore that inner vitality and life, lost during the centuries in which the Church had become the domain of a juridic and caste-minded clergy.

The outbreak of the Schmalkaldic war, which Witzel had repeatedly forecast, forced him and his family from Fulda. The Protestant troops plundered his home and ironically unfurled the flag of the Protestant league from his rooftop. No one had striven more tirelessly for its motto: "The Word of God remains forever." For a time he found asylum in Würzburg and in 1547 the Emperor summoned him to the Diet of Augsburg. Here many of the ideas in his *Methodus,* since they followed the general outline of the *Confessio Augustana,* found their way into the Interim. During the next two years he composed a number of *Gutachten* or reform programs for the Emperor. His work *Pro Concordia Ecclesiae Repurgandae et Restituendae* was used in the discussions at the Reichstag of 1555.

Witzel's final refuge was in Mainz where he was to spend the rest of his career resisting the evils that he felt were being perpetuated by the Council of Trent. Belatedly both the Emperor and the Pope recognized his efforts for reunion. In 1561 he was given one degree in theology at the insistence of Ferdinand and another by the papacy at the request of Commendone. The Bishop of Mainz entrusted him with several inspections of the diocese and listened to many of his reform plans. However, the forces of the Counter-Reformation were soon to victimize him more completely than any of his Protestant adversaries ever had. St. Charles Borromeo invited him to attend the final period of Trent because he considered him to be the theologian most conversant with the doctrinal views of the Protestants, but Bishop Hosius thwarted the attempt. The Bishop attacked Witzel as married, though his wife had long since died, and condemned him as an advocate of the lay chalice. Shortly before his death in May of 1564, Ferdinand again requested that Witzel draw up an outline of his irenicist doctrines. These were later incorporated into his final work, *Via Regia,* a book widely read during the next century and republished by Conring in 1650.

The Jesuits arrived in Mainz in 1561 and brought with them the beginnings of the Baroque piety that Witzel so detested. Their devotional practices and their educational system, both at variance with what Witzel had advocated for over two generations, soon stifled any hope of a reunion based upon a more intelligible liturgy and an education of the laity. The biased misjudgments of Peter Canisius on Witzel soon reduced both his reputation and his liturgical reforms to the oblivion of history. There was little to be recommended in a person who found so much good in evangelism and who believed that the essence of Christianity consisted in fraternal charity and a willingness to make concessions. Witzel passed away in February of 1573 continuing to protest Trent's militant defense of nonessentials. There was a note of pathos and prognosticism in his oft-repeated lament: "Would that this Council had been able to see what was really necessary!"

While Witzel, and others like him in the lesser clergy, strove to stem the tide of dissolution on a more local level by framing Church ordinances and penning popular works, the spirit of irenicism also reached the highest plateau of government in the imperial diets.

Unlike the better known encounters between the conservative Catholic party and the early Lutherans at Heidelberg and Leipzig, the discussions at Hagenau, Worms, and Regensburg were summoned with the realization that Protestantism in Europe was now a *fait accompli* both as a religious and a political factor, and could no longer be dealt with in terms of imperial edicts or papal denunciations. For a clear understanding of the reunion policy of these years, however, one must realize that neither the Catholic reform group nor the moderate Protestants had yet elaborated any well-defined policies or universally recognized standards of identity. Two basic ideas lay behind the ecclesiastical motives that brought these endeavors into being: Erasmianism and evangelism. Both aimed at achieving understanding through clear delineation of Christianity's substantial beliefs.

Although Charles continued to hope for a reconciliation after his defeat of the Schmalkaldic League and his publication of the Interim (drafted by the friend of Erasmus and Witzel, Bishop Julius Pflug), the Diet of Regensburg in 1541 can be said to be the high-water mark of Protestant-Catholic dialogue. It distinguished itself from all previous attempts at settlement by focusing its attention on the most fundamental question of the Reformation, justification by faith.

Two important figures, John Gropper, Chancellor of the Archdiocese of Cologne, and Gaspar Contarini, former ambassador of Venice to the Imperial Court, dominate the colloquy and in a sense epitomize the hopes and aims of the Catholic reform group before the Council of Trent. Both men were schooled in the humanistic tradition of the Renaissance and were advocates of a reform based upon a return to the norms of the pre-scholastic Church. Both possessed a deep appreciation and sympathy for the aims of the Protestant Reformers.

John Gropper, born in Soest in 1501, had attended the University of Cologne during the time of the Reuchlin struggle and was associated in his youth with the humanistic group, Sobius, Neuenahr and Caesarius. These figures had witnessed the first open conflict between those who looked for a reform of the Church in terms of doctrinal readjustment and those who represented the intransigence of Roman conservatism. In 1525 he was appointed Bearer of the Seal, or Chancellor of the all-powerful curia of the metropolitan of Cologne. As the most influential of the spiritual estates in the Empire and the largest ecclesiastical province in Europe, Cologne was the key to the success or failure of the reform movement in Germany. It was also pivotal in the Emperor's plan to renovate the Empire. Its Bishop-Elector, Hermann von Weid, was one of the earlier supporters of Erasmus and had once invited the great humanist to teach at Cologne's famous university. Largely at Gropper's insistence, Weid convoked a great synod in the city in 1536, with the purpose of instigating a reform in his vast territory. Hope had long vanished that the papacy, in spite of Paul's intentions, would ever relinquish its vacillating conciliar policies. The assembly was attended by representatives of the bishoprics of Liège, Utrecht, Osnabrück and Minden, and was by far the most impressive ecclesiastical gathering to take place in Europe during this period. An examination of the decrees that were published under the direction of Gropper leaves no doubt as to the sincerity of those who attempted to reform the Church in the face of papal obstructionism.

The central theme of the Cologne synodal decrees is a restoration of the Church as the community of believers in Christ. Filled with references to the New Testament, the document compares the present situation in the Church to the episode where Christ is awakened by His frightened disciples on the Lake of Genezareth. It admonishes its readers to follow the example of the disciples and turn to Christ, the true leader of the Church, and thus seek direction in the great storm that threatens destruction. The first section puts before the Church leaders the ancient ideal of the bishop as the shepherd of his flock and urges greater discrimination in the selection of candidates for the priesthood. "It is better," it says, "to have a few worthy priests who can properly preach the word of God than a multitude who are nothing but a hindrance to religion." A strong evangelical influence is seen in the recommendation that "No priest should ever be found without the Scriptures in his possession."

A number of articles are concerned with the monastic life in the diocese, with a particular effort to place the monks under episcopal control in the matter of preaching and administering the sacraments. The monks, and there were more than a fair share of them in Cologne, are especially admonished to avoid the practice of interspersing their sermons with unfounded fables concerning the saints and to orient them more toward a biblical interpretation of Christianity. Although the Mass is to be defined as a sacrifice for both the living and the dead, it must be emphasized that it is a living representation of the one death of Christ. In connection with the reception of the Eucharist it is recommended that the ancient practice of public confession be reintroduced. Changes in the liturgy are also recommended, especially the use of the vernacular.

A final section of the synodal decree speaks of the sociocharitative elements of the reform. Hospitals and orphanages should be of primary concern for the clergy and there should be a special solicitude for the poor. In order to implement these regulations it is recommended that visitations take place to insure the Church authorities of their complete reception. In addition, local synods are to take place each year and a full provincial council embracing the entire archdiocese is to assemble every three to four years.

Excommunication is to be abolished except in matters that pertain to purely spiritual crimes; the granting of benefices or stipends to those who have not as yet reached their majority is to be done away with; itinerant preachers who collect money for indulgences or for the construction of churches and thus exploit the uneducated laity are to be suppressed; processions with the Blessed Sacrament are to be limited to once a year; and finally, no one is to be professed in a religious order until he has reached the age of twenty-five.

As a supplement to the decrees of the reform council of 1536, Gropper published, in 1538, a work which many historians consider the most comprehensive theological tract emanating from the Catholic camp in the years before the Council of Trent. The popularity of this work, entitled *Enchiridion Christianae Institutionis,* may be judged by the amazing number of printings it underwent, over fifteen between 1541 and 1555 in Verona, Venice, Paris, Antwerp, and Cologne. It was received with enthusiasm wherever men seriously strove for Christian reform. The "handbook" is an exposition of basic Christian belief including an explanation of the Creed, the sacraments, the Lord's Prayer, and the decalogue. The entire tone of the five-hundred-page work is conciliatory and the reader will find in almost every line an attempt to evaluate Luther's position in a more modified presentation of traditional Catholic dogma. More pugnacious partisans of the Catholic reaction, such as Eck, Cochlaeus and Emser, dissipated their efforts in personal attacks on Luther's character and scattered their shots at the periphery rather than the center of Luther's doctrine. Gropper sympathetically analyzes the Reformer's teaching and sets it within a more intelligible framework. The *Enchiridion's* aim is primarily doctrinal and educational, a concrete rather than an abstract presentation of Christian dogma.

In treating the notion of the Church he distinguished between the expressions: "I believe in God," and "I believe in the Church," which is to say: I believe that the Church has been assembled by God. In this way the Creator is distinguished from the created, and the divine from what is merely human, a note that explains the weakness and imperfection of the Church. A sharp distinction is made between the Church Militant and the Church Triumphant. The Church here on earth is composed of those who reside in the house of God and are temples of the Holy Ghost. They are the beautified city of Jerusalem that descends from the heavens and is constructed upon those living stones of which the Apostle says: "Though many we are one body in Christ." We see here a reliance on the doctrine of Augustine, especially his *Enchiridion de fide spe et caritate*, wherein the Bishop of Hippo speaks of the Church as the house, the temple of God.

Gropper, however, does not identify the Church with the Civitas Dei as Augustine did. This concept, to which Luther had devoted some energy, is thoughtfully avoided by Gropper. The Church is catholic since she is bound to no particular place and because before the end of time she will announce the word to the ends of the earth. She is one, not in terms of or according to a corporate body in a given country or province, but according to a spiritual community united in one sacrament of faith, in one confession, one flock, one stable, under one shepherd and one chair (*cathedra*).

In speaking of the authority of the Church, Gropper emphasizes that its present authority is that ancient power of the keys which was essentially the commission to preach the word of God (*"potestas ecclesiastica in docendo verbo Dei"*). The power of the Pope does not consist in the fact that he stands over all others in the order of the priesthood, but rather in his primacy in terms of administration, government, and authority. The authority is centered in one office more for the purpose of demonstrating and preserving unity than for direct rule (*"ut ecclesiae unitas monstretur ac conservetur"*).

It is in the formulation of his ideas on justification that Gropper exhibits his strongest efforts to bridge the gap between Luther's *Sola Fide* and the traditional Catholic position. Although certain historians (Ranke) have traced the notion of *justitia duplex* to the Italian conciliarists or to the writings of Pighius (Döllinger), Jedin has definitely proven that it was Gropper who first formulated this famous doctrine in his *Enchiridion*. The basic problem that Gropper attempts to solve is whether justification is merely a forensic or an external act. He emphasizes with great decisiveness that justification is not only the remission of sin but also an inner renewal of the sinner through the Holy Spirit and His gifts, especially the infusion of charity. This latter aspect is not, as the scholastics held, a result of the justification, but is actually conjoined with it and is the operation of the *justitia Dei*. The means or instrument whereby we participate in this operation is faith. For Gropper there are two types of faith. The first, historical, moves us to believe God exists and that whatever has been revealed concerning Him can in no way be an illusion. Essentially it does not differ from the belief of the demons in God and is therefore merely the beginning or foundation of the spiritual edifice.

Through the other faith, the Christian fullness of faith, we hold as true those things contained in the Scripture and which the Church identified as revelation. Through it also we hope in the divine promises and put our trust in them. By this belief in God we are united with Christ and become one spirit with Him, and as members of His body are reconciled with God. In describing the psychological evolution of the process of justification Gropper places the law at the very beginning. Contrition begins with historic faith and servile fear which derives from a recognition of the law and the penalties threatened by it to the sinner. The inner trepidation which follows this awareness is the penance demanded by John the Baptist and by Christ. It would lead to desperation if the sinner did not proceed immediately to the contemplation of divine mercy and thereby through hope to fiducial faith, which transforms this servile fear into one that is childlike and trusting. This process from historic to fiducial faith and from servile to childlike fear in exceptional cases begins with a spirit of penance. However, in both cases the totality of the process takes place under the influence of grace. God infuses the sinner with good thoughts and prepares his will so that he tends toward faith. This preparation is the work of *gratia praeveniens*. Following the preparation God heals the will through the grace of justification and in this stage of the process the will must itself consent. After justification the justified person demands still another grace for action, the *gratia cooperans*. There is consequently no place in the process of preparation for charity.

Gropper is aware of the Luther critique of the scholastic formula *fides caritate formata* (faith formed by love) and particularly aware of his insistence that the scholastic call a spade a spade and attribute justification to charity rather than to faith, which is obviously without scriptural foundation. For Gropper, as for Luther, there is an attempt to point to a faith that *works* through love rather than justifies through love. The Cologne theologian follows Luther in admitting an historic faith, assent to the Gospels, that is of itself too weak to warrant justification. For Gropper as for Luther, the process of justification is something more than actual moral attainment. Charity is a gift of God to the soul in the process of justification itself. It is granted as soon as the fiducial faith is present and unites the sinner with Christ. Man must become aware of this fact and must be absolutely certain of it in such a way that it in itself becomes an object of faith. Assurance of the possession of faith leads to the recognition of his possession of charity, a recognition that must be confirmed through experience. Merely looking to the works produced by charity would not be sufficient to convince one that justification had really taken place. It is the spirit of God that bears witness to the fact that we are the sons of God.

The final phase of the process of justification is the incumbent obligation on the part of the justified to fulfill the law with active charity. The good works performed are not to be separated from the justifying faith and the renewing grace, for in them are to be found the basis for growth in justification as well as the constant intercession of Christ for the justified. Yet according to Gropper we may not place our trust in our own strength or in good works but rather must rely exclusively upon Christ. Works performed even while in the state of grace are imperfect; they become pleasing to God only insofar as they are accomplished in Christ and as a member of His Body. We must appeal to His mercy, and that which our works lack must be supplied by the works of Christ. The justification entered upon by means of this mystical union with the person of Christ gives to works a higher dignity and compensates for the imperfection inhering in them. In this way the *justitia imperfecta* is supplemented through the *justitia Christi*. This compromise formula on justification, though independently arrived at in varying shades of difference by a number of other theologians, Catharinus, Vega and Seripando, was strikingly similar to the formula worked out by the papal legate at the Diet of Regensburg.

It was not without good reason that with the opening of the diet in April, 1541, the Emperor nominated Gropper as chief representative of the Catholic party. He was assisted by Pflug and Eck. Melanchthon, Bucer, and Pistorius represented the Protestant group. It was, however, the appointment of Gaspar Contarini, a papal legate to the diet, that gave rise to the false hope that after years of allowing politics to obstruct its reform efforts the papacy had now come to discuss reunion on equal terms with the dissidents. This was seen as an indication that now at last the Vatican had been convinced that the complete destruction of Christianity was hardly the price to pay for the victory of one party over another.

Son of a distinguished patrician family in Venice, Contarini was born in 1483, the same year as Luther. Like Gropper in Germany he had been identified with a reform-minded humanistic group in Italy. Reginald Pole and Jacob Sadoleto were close associates. His renown as a statesman had long been established in Europe. As ambassador to the Imperial Court during the critical years from the Diet of Worms in 1521 until the peace that followed the imperial victory at Pavia, he had been in constant contact with Charles V. Few men were more keenly aware of the religious crisis raised in every part of Europe by the question of how man is justified. Few men had observed at closer range the entanglement of the papacy in power politics or assigned it more clearly as the real cause of inefficient leadership in the matter of reform.

Representing the Venetian Republic he had appeared before Clement VII in 1529 and demanded that he drop his territorial claims. This, Contarini asserted, was a condition sine qua non for a universal peace in Christendom. "Let not your Holiness," he said on this occasion, "suppose that the welfare of the Church stands or falls on these insignificant reactions of worldly dominion. Before their acquisition the Church existed, and indeed she then existed at her best. She is the common possession of all Christians, the papal states are like any possession of an Italian prince. Therefore your Holiness must set in the forefront of your responsibilities the welfare of the true Church which consists in the peace of Christendom and allows the interests of the temporal state to fall for a time into the background."

He had authored, while still a layman, two important works: *On the Duties of the Episcopal Office* and *The Power of the Papacy,* neither of which voiced a belief in the extreme claims of the papacy in doctrinal matters. Yet more remarkable than his many accomplishments as diplomat and author was the amazing religious transformation that he had undergone some thirty years before as a young man in Venice. Much has been learned of this from a recently discovered letter written by Contarini on April 24, 1511, to two former companions who had become monks. He explained how, during preparation for his Easter confession, he suddenly came to the realization that salvation was a matter of complete and total trust in the merits of Christ. "No religious vows, no amount of external penances," he wrote, "but a trust in the saving grace of Christ who died for all sinners would alone bring peace to his soul."

In a work on the theology of Luther he was later to write: "There is no need for a council, or for disputations, syllogisms, or citations from scripture to do away with the Lutheran movement. What is required rather is good intention, a love of God and man, and a true spirit of humility. Let us put aside the spirit of greed, preoccupation with the things of this world, elegant furnishings, and household staffs, turning instead to what is plainly set before us in the Gospels."

In May, 1535, Paul III had unexpectedly, but to the great joy of all the conciliarist party, raised Contarini, layman and high official in the traditionally anti-curial Venetian government though he was, to the College of Cardinals. There were a number of reasons for the unprecedented choice of Contarini. His astute abilities as a statesman were known to Paul, as a layman he was above sacerdotal professionalism, while few nonclerics had a better knowledge of the inner workings of the Curia. His reputation as a scholar was equal to the esteem in which he was held as a diplomat, and above all, his piety and outspoken criticism of the abuses of the Roman Church made his nomination to the College a great proof of change in the vacillating policy of the papacy toward reform and reunion. Few men of the age were more thoroughly convinced that neither reform nor reconciliation with the Lutheran party would be achieved unless the head of the Church itself be purged. *Purga Romam, purgatur mundus* had a real meaning for Contarini.

The year after his appointment during the summer of 1536, Paul called together a special commission to outline a program of reform that would affect that core and center of ecclesiastical abuses, the Roman Curia. What startled many observers was the lack of curial canonists in the commission which included Contarini, Pole, Sadoleto, and Caraffa. The deliberations of this commission resulted in the celebrated *Consilium de Emendanda Ecclesia* which was presented to the Pope in the presence of twelve cardinals in March, 1537. The boldness of the proposal astounds the reader of today. It begins with the terrible accusation that the root of the evils affecting the Church must be placed at the feet of an exaggerated theory of papal authority. "Flatterers," it says, "have led some Popes to imagine that their will is law, that they are the owners of all benefices so that they are free to dispose of them as they please without taint of simony." It is from this sort of sophistry and false principles—as from a Trojan horse—"that the mass of corrupt practices that are carrying the Church to its destruction emanate." The document goes on to list the abuses that cripple the effectiveness of the Church at all levels, in the Curia, in parishes, monasteries, and schools.

The College of Cardinals is cited for avarice and neglect of responsibility, the Curia for its toleration of moral turpitude. Attacked are the misuse of episcopal authority and diocesan administration, the corruption in the administration of papal pensions, reservations, and provisions as well as the practice of appointing coadjutor bishops with the right of succession. These evils are to be ruthlessly uprooted. Only such men are to be ordained whose fitness has been carefully scrutinized. The granting of bishoprics and benefices for the care of souls must not be for the purpose of providing a living but rather to secure good shepherds. Since the reforms are aimed at improvement of the pastoral ministry, such practices as the selling of dispensations, absolutions and indulgences must be halted. To achieve higher standards in the pastoral ministry bishops and pastors must reside in their dioceses and parishes—"Almost all the shepherds have forsaken their flocks and entrusted them to hirelings." It would be for the welfare of the Church if many of the lax religious orders were either suppressed or allowed to die out. The entire document teems with the basic conviction that the ideal of pastoral care of souls and the realization of the apostolic ideal of the same cannot be achieved unless there be a radical change in the Curia's administrative system.

Nor is the Pope himself spared in the document. The final section of the *Consilium* states: "Now that we have summed up all matters pertaining to the Pontiff of the universal Church, as much as we have been able to recount, it remains for us to say a few words about matters relating to the Bishop of Rome. Rome is both the Mother Church and the mistress of other churches, and for this reason divine service and moral uprightness should flourish in her especially. And yet, Holy Father, every stranger who enters the Basilica of St. Peter is horrified to find dirty and uncouth priests celebrating Mass, clad in vestments and garments that would not be used without shame even in the filthiest homes. No man can tolerate this disgrace. Therefore the Archpriest or Penitentiary of Rome must be ordered to see to it that this scandal be removed from this church as from all other churches. In this city prostitutes walk about or ride mules through the city like matrons of the nobility, and are attended in broad daylight by nobles from the households of cardinals and by clerics. In no city do we find such corruption except in this the exemplar of all cities. They reside even in the greatest homes. This disgraceful condition must be removed. Enmity and hatred between private citizens run rampant in Rome, and it is the duty of her Bishop to terminate these feuds and conciliate her citizens. This task of removing hate and conciliating the citizens can be accomplished by the cardinals who are especially suited to this work . . .

"These, Holy Father, are the abuses which, according to the poverty of our nobility, we have brought to attention for correction, and it seems to us that they must be corrected. May you govern all things by your goodness and wisdom. We have at least satisfied our own consciences, although we have not the strength to remedy the matter. It is our hope that under your principate we may see the Church of God purged, as a beautiful dove, in harmony with itself and united in one body with the everlasting memory of your name. You have taken for yourself the name of Paul, who was chosen as a vessel to carry the name of Christ to the Gentiles. We hope that you have been chosen to restore the name of Christ, now forgotten by the Gentiles and by us clerics, in their hearts and ours. We hope that you will heal our sickness, bring back the flock of Christ into one fold, and take away from us the wrath of God and His punishment we so deserve and which now threatens our necks."

In the face of the storm of protest the *Consilium* aroused among the more conservative elements of the Curia, Contarini held fast to his principles. The aging Guidiccioni who felt that its proposals would lead to the dissolution of the Church indicated that it would bring a revolution rather than a reform.

In an endeavor to answer his critics and at the same time elaborate the basic proposal of the *Consilium*, Contarini wrote two brief treatises addressed to Paul III. Protesting his acceptance of the doctrine of the plenitude of papal authority, he insisted upon defining it in terms of its original and legitimate form. The Pope, he wrote, is a *dispensator* and *servus*, not a *dominus* in the sense that he can exercise his authority arbitrarily. The legalists who attempt to expand this authority debase it to the most corrupt kind of license for exploitation and abuse, and thereby expose the Holy See to the ridicule of the Lutherans. "Rest assured," wrote Contarini to the Pope, "that nothing will disarm the calumnies of the Lutherans, and intimidate the King of England more effectively than a reform of the Curia and the clergy. The attempts to justify all the actions of all the Popes would be an arduous and in fact an endless undertaking. We cast no stones at your predecessors, but from you the world expects better things."

The reform of curial officialdom came to naught in spite of the tireless efforts of the commission. Contarini's admonition to the Pope not to stray from the path of Christ for the sake of a few thousand ducats fell upon deaf ears. The bureaucratic makeup of the Dataria and the Penitenzieria, with their interest in ancient remumerative practices, were to continue in one form or another long after the Council of Trent. One may question whether they have changed basically to this day. Reform for the Curia was and remains merely a suppression of abuses that scandalize rather than a change in the structure of the Church.

Nowhere in the *Consilium* is there any reference to doctrine or to the laity. In fact among the more irenic Protestants it proved a disappointment. Johann Sturm was commissioned by Bucer to reply and although applauding the cardinals' projected restoration of discipline, he remarks significantly: "For if we would have the world amended, we must have the people well instructed and taught; they must be as a field well tilled. Man is well tilled when he has a good preacher, in whom is great knowledge, zeal, and a pure mind, without which preachers, neither the people can be well taught nor the Church flourish." Strum points out that Catholic people are nowhere "well instructed in points of doctrine," and concludes that: "Christ must needs be unknown there, where His benefits with all His acts are unspoken. Surely the cardinals suppress the truth of this fact deliberately for fear of offending the Pope. You cannot be ignorant in this matter, for the whole world knows that the Gospel of Christ is taken from your Churches."

If Contarini's attempt to reform the Curia had failed, he had at least launched an attack on the cause of abuse in the Church and exposed to the world the reluctance of the Church to begin a true reform from within. His selection as papal legate to Regensburg was perhaps the greatest step taken on the part of the papacy toward the cause of the restoration of religious unity in the West.

His entrance into the city in March of 1541 was greeted by unbounded enthusiasm from Protestant as well as Catholic representatives. The publication of the *Consilium de Emendanda Ecclesiae* in Germany had endeared him to the reform party in that country, and his persuasiveness over the vociferous Eck indicated the authority he enjoyed among the extreme right wing of the Catholic partisans. The Emperor himself gave every indication of his joy at finally arranging peaceful settlements of religious affairs in the Empire. The Protestant cities had received him with jubilation and he had responded by suspending the ban and postponing the trials against Protestants then pending in the Imperial Governing Council. Few men had negotiated for so long and with greater understanding with the German Emperor than Contarini, and for once the Estates would be dealing with a man singularly lacking in the acrimony of their fellow antagonists in the Catholic League.

The basis of the discussions which lasted from April until May was the so-called *Book of Ratisbon*. The document itself was the outgrowth of an earlier clandestine conference held in Worms between Bucer and Gropper. Contarini, as papal legate, held the most influential position in the proceedings, the Catholic collocutors were obliged to report to him before and after each of the discussions. Melanchthon, who had been the leading advocate for reunion at Augsburg eleven years before, stayed in the background. He had instructions from the Saxon prince to limit his position to the contents of the *Confessio Augustana*. With the majority of the participants strongly in favor of concessions based upon the essentials of Christian belief, the Diet was lacking in the disturbing hostility that had characterized previous attempts at reconciliation.

The first four articles of the *Book of Ratisbon,* those on creation and original sin, were considered with little or no dispute. The fifth article on justification, the question upon which the entire Reformation movement was based, proved to be a stumbling block. Yet by the early part of May a formula on justification by faith working through charity, was accepted by the Protestants as well as by the Catholic parties, including the reluctant Eck himself. It was the *justitia duplex* arrived at by Gropper. Contarini informed the Pope of this triumph and the Elector of Brandenburg was so enthused over the common accord that he ordered a serenade in honor of the legate of reconciliation. In the end such reaction was to prove premature since the formula was rejected with but one exception by the Roman cardinals as being equivocal. Cardinal Farnese informed Contarini that although the formula might agree with Catholic teaching, it would demand more clarification before the Holy See could approve of it. Yet Reginald Pole, whose absence from Rome at the time was no doubt a factor in its lack of support, later termed it a "precious jewel" always in the hidden treasure of the Church but only now disclosed to everyone.

Until notified of its rejection Contarini continued to entertain the belief that his formulation would now dispel the assumption of the past twenty years that Catholic doctrine was semi-Pelagian. In stating that man is justified in a twofold manner, Contarini felt, as did Gropper, that he had found the only means of confirming the merits of Christ as the sole source of salvation and thus emphasizing the significance of faith in the process of justification. The hope of salvation must be founded in the justice or righteousness of Christ alone, and not in the sanctity inherent in us. Inherent justice is both imperfect and inadequate unless fulfilled and perfected by the imputed justice of Christ; these are the two elements of salvation, but due to sin we cannot be justified unless an outside justice be imputed us. Thus the justice inherent in the Christian believer recedes before the justice of God which accomplishes salvation.

That this position on justification was Catholic and orthodox was later attested to by the approval of Contarini's works thirty years after Ratisbon by the theological faculty of the Sorbonne. The idea of *fides caritate formata,* shared by many other Catholic divines who were working for reunion at the time, was a genuine proof of the great merit they placed in the person of Christ. By placing His works and excellence with man's appropriation of them in the very core of the debate they strove to remove the dreadful misunderstanding that Catholic belief prejudiced the mediatorship of the Savior and universal efficaciousness of His grace.

The disappointment of Contarini over the failure of his formula of concord was a cross that more than ever proved his gentle humility and his Christian forebearance. Even while the Diet was still in session he was reprimanded by the Pope and his powers as procurator were curtailed. Caraffa virtually accused him of joining with Charles in capitulating to the Lutherans on important dogmatic issues. In Italy he was regarded in many circles as a heretic. He passed away the following year, a broken man.

In July of 1541 a sorrowing Contarini had admonished the entire assembly of Catholic bishops to instigate a truly Christian reform that would begin with themselves. The papal nuncio Marone, in face of the failure of the Diet and the repeated failure of the Pope to summon a general council, had even more explicitly pointed out to the bishops their obligation to initiate new reforms in the areas committed to their pastoral care.

Following this directive Weid now called Gropper and Bucer together to draw up a Church ordinance that would abate the growing religious discord in his own diocese. Once aware that the new reform envisioned an almost complete break with the basic structure of the old Church, Gropper broke with the Archbishop and led the Cathedral Chapter into open revolt against Weid and his Protestant collaborators. Weid was excommunicated and deposed.

The struggle for Cologne lasted for almost four years. It was in many ways a preview of the struggle known as the Counter-Reformation. The intervention of Spanish troops, the militant role of the newly-founded Jesuits (Peter Canisius), the gradual exclusion of Erasmian ideas, and the general defensive mentality that was to characterize Catholicism for centuries to come are all in evidence here. The publishing of a totally Lutheran Church ordinance in electoral Brandenburg in 1540, the reorganization of the Roman Inquisition, and the defection of the Capuchin General Ochino in the summer of 1542 were all indicative of a changing situation on the hitherto fluid fronts between Catholicism and Protestantism.

Yet even after the deposition of Weid and the appointment of Adolf von Shauenburg as Archbishop of Cologne, Gropper continued his efforts toward reunion. The Interim of 1548, although rejected officially by Catholics and Protestants alike, was nevertheless adhered to in many parts of the Empire. A study of the twenty-six articles of the Interim Declaration, with its irenic provision for a married clergy, administration of the Sacrament under both species and the use of the vernacular, shows the influence of Gropper. Julius Pflug, its author, corresponded frequently with the Cologne Chancellor during the period that the Interim was drawn up.

Although Gropper attended the Council of Trent during its second convocation (1551-52) and urged the assembled fathers to terminate the proceedings in order to more speedily clarify the Catholic position before all of Germany was lost, his pleadings were of little avail. Paul IV, the Caraffa Pope, summoned him to Rome in the fall of 1558 with the intention of promoting him to the College of Cardinals. Yet even this final chapter of his career was clouded with the ever-present suspicion of heresy. Through the intrigues of the Italian Inquisitor Zacharias Delphinus, his *Enchiridion* was found to contain heretical doctrines, particularly his position on justification and his teaching that James, not Peter, presided over the First Council of Jerusalem. The accusation delayed his reception of the cardinalate, and he died in Rome on March 13, 1599, in the midst of those forces of conservative, reactionary Catholicism he had fought so tirelessly to modify in order to renew, rather than forcefully restore, the Church.

The Council of Trent was finally convened in December of 1545 as the Schmalkaldic League prepared for war. Twenty-five years had elapsed since the appeal of Luther for a general, free, Christian council in German lands. There was very little that was impressive at the opening convocation. All together, there were some twenty-nine bishops present, most of them Italians. Nor was the specter of conciliarism absent. The fathers debated long and hotly on whether to designate the Council as being representative of the universal Church. The expression *"universalem ecclesiam repraesentans"* was finally deleted from the official record and not without a certain irony. There was also a repetition of the dilemma of Constance and Basel in a failure to agree whether the question of reform should have priority over that of dogmatic definition. If numbers meant anything, it was hardly ecumenical. The Council of Chalcedon numbered about six hundred thirty active participants and there were more than seven hundred bishops at the First Vatican Council. The Protestants of Northern Europe, although invited to the Council, repeatedly refused to recognize its ecumenicity. This they did on the grounds that it was dominated by the papacy, forbade lay participation, and rejected the principle of *sola scriptura.*

Yet in terms of its effect on the life of the Church, Trent far surpassed any council before or since. Its duration alone—some 18 years, from December, 1545, to December, 1563—marks it as the longest ecclesiastical assembly if one includes the two periods during which it was suspended, 1548-51 and 1552-63. Its decree on justification, which tended to place the sacramental system at the center of Catholic religious practice, emphasized the cooperation of human will with divine grace and the possibility of human merit, thus setting up a permanent obstacle to any rapprochement with Protestantism. The sacraments were declared to operate *ex opere operato,* rather than through faith in divine promises.

Scholasticism, which had borne the brunt of the attack of the early Reformers, was firmly entrenched. The *Summa* now replaced the *Sentences* of Peter Lombard as the basic text for theological studies. Aquinas was declared a Doctor of the Church in 1567. In the papal bull establishing the "perennial philosophy" of the Dominican theologian, not only did the Church herself, as Pastor remarks, "take the science of the Middle Ages under her protection against the hostility of Protestants and even some Catholics, but she also recognized the teaching of Aquinas as the richest fruit of an earlier scientific evolution and as an unperishable treasure. At the same time she proclaimed that she recognized her own doctrines as those of the great schoolman." His doctrine was, as Pius V said, in contrast to others, "more safe and secure." Whereas Christian scholarship had once gloried in the brilliant works of Northern Europeans: Anselm, Scotus, Occam, Eckhart, and Albert, it was now dominated by names like Cano, Soto, Vittoria, Medina, and Suarez. The Augustinian General, whose efforts to introduce the notion of double justice into the decrees of the council were frustrated by the Jesuit Laynez, remarked: "The storm which the heretics loosed upon the Church after Constantine's day has been renewed in Germany. But how lamentable is the difference! Then the heretics were laid low by the theologians, by their own weapon, the Scriptures, but we thought to oppose them with Aristotle and now we have become the subject of their scorn." When his compromise formula was rejected he sadly remarked that "nearly everyone at the Council aimed at excluding Christ's justice from the hearts of men." Nonconformists who attacked the Stagirite, like Giordano Bruno and Tomasso Campanella, were either burned alive or spent years in the dungeons of the Holy Office in Rome. Curiously the real Catholic revival took place in those very areas of Europe where resistance to the decrees of Trent was strongest. The "Devout Humanism" represented by men like Francis de Sales and Etienne Binet had little time for the quibbling of the scholastics or the dogmaticism of Rome. If history is in any way a matter of challenge and response, then Trent gave every indication of defending to the hilt whatever was attacked by the Protestants or ridiculed by the Catholic reformers. The cultus of the saints and devotion to the Virgin flourished as never before. Pilgrims flocked to Loretto to visit the house the Virgin had lived in after Christ's Ascension. It had winged its way there several centuries earlier. The practice of the reciting of the Rosary became widespread and the "Infant of Prague" made its way from Spain to Bohemia. Later in the century Antonio Bosio's archeological discoveries in the ancient catacombs of Rome provided an almost inexhaustible supply of relics. The remains of St. Cecilia and the skulls of SS. Valerian, Tiburtius and Maximus were exhumed and reinterred with pompous procession. When Mabillon visited Rome he was appalled at finding that Church officials were exporting to all parts of the Catholic world relics which were no more than the bones of simple Roman citizens who lived before the time of Christ.

In piety as in theology there was a dominance of the Latin. A glance at the catalogue of the canonized saints of this period gives the easy impression that the Mediterranean basin had become the sole refuge of the sanctified. The names were those like Antonio Zaccaria, Philip Neri, Francis Borgia, Alonso Rodríguez, Mary Magdalen dei Pazzi, Catherine dei Ricci. Novenas, pilgrimages, and confraternities increased as never before.

Since the bishops of the northern lands were often suspected of heresy or showed too great a tendency to bend to secular authority, there was a proliferation of papally controlled religious orders. The Visitandines, the Camillans, the Ursulines, the Daughters of Our Lady of Bordeaux, the Doctrinarians of Blessed Caesar de Bus, the Clerks of the Pious Schools, the Piarists, and the Society of Servants of Little Children were but a few of the new orders who indoctrinated a new generation of Catholics with the teachings of the Tridentine cathechism. The older orders were restored and played an important role in the introduction of Catholicism into the New World. Here among the natives they found a climate more congenial to their type of piety.

The efforts of the sixteenth-century liturgists to reform public worship by making it more intelligible to the laity came to a standstill. It was firmly believed that any real active or intelligent participation in public worship, any effort to understand what was taking place, was tantamount to Protestantism. Like so much else, the liturgy became a static element in the religious life of the people. No longer was it a spontaneous expression of the inner life of the Mystical Body. There was one Breviary, one Mass, one standard devotional norm. Little wonder that Calvin wrote: "The dignity and use of the Eucharist we explain with whatever praises we can; we show forth what great usefulness comes from it. Almost all these things are neglected among you. Forgotten is the divine benefit which comes to us, forgotten the proper use of so great a benefit, things that ought to be dwelled upon. You hold it sufficient if the people are astonished at the visible sign, without any knowledge of the spiritual mystery."

The great saint of the Catholic restoration, Francis de Sales, when about to receive episcopal consecration resolved always to say his beads when duty required him to attend public Mass. The antiquarian pageantry of the Mass service was increased and attendance at Mass became the test of one's loyalty to an organization as much as an act of devotion. New decrees on marriage placing constraints on unions between Catholics and non-Catholics gave rise to sociological problems that have never been resolved.

One of the most perduring of the instruments of the Counter-Reformation, and one that, like the Inquisition and the Index, was intended more to be a temporary measure to halt the spread of heresy than a permanent fixture in the Church, was the creation of seminaries. The origin of the seminary legislation at Trent can be traced to the *Reformatio Angliae* drawn up by Reginald Pole in 1556 during the brief restoration of Catholicism in England. In 1552, a German college had been founded in Rome with the hope that its presence in the Eternal City would lead to the formation of priests deeply inbued with a love for the papacy. It is to these two sources that what was to become the chief implementation of the decrees of Trent can be traced. The Reformation in Northern Europe had been, for the most part, the work of men associated with universities. Certainly they had been the breeding grounds of conciliarism, hence the thinking behind the decrees on the establishment of seminaries was to protect future candidates for the priesthood from contamination in these fonts of unorthodoxy.

As the system developed over the years it had the end effect of cutting off the Catholic clergy from the mainstream of intellectual development in Europe. It is one of the strange paradoxes of history that the institution that developed what is perhaps one of the greatest contributions of the Middle Ages to civilization, the university, severed itself almost completely from higher education after Trent. As the seminary system took shape it absorbed all the debilities of educational inbreeding. The curriculum was controlled from Rome. It consisted for the most part of expurgated selections from the classics, a smattering of Aristotelian logic and long tracts proving, through memorized arguments, the monarchical nature of the Church and the hylomorphic structure of the sacraments. Any form of critical study based on historical arguments was suspect. Dogmatic theology became for the most part a study of redemption and grace that was little more than a polemic against the doctrines of Luther and Calvin. What little Scripture was studied centered on the hackneyed proofs of Petrine supremacy, the septennial number of the sacraments and the sacrificial nature of the Mass. The dialectics so attacked by the humanists reached an almost incredible tempo in the struggle between the Molinists and Bannezians. Moral theology was dominated by Aristotelian ethics and canon law. The casuist tradition has continued for centuries. One of the most commonly used textbooks on moral theology devotes one entire volume to questioning penitents on sex aberrations, while it limits its treatment of charity to one paragraph.

Thus while the Council raised the general standard of clerical education, it tended to indoctrinate the clergy rather than to really educate them. Since illiteracy remained general among the vast majority of lay Catholics in Europe until after the Napoleonic wars, however, a training that enabled the clergy to administer the sacraments, make the proper distinctions in the nature of sin, and perform the ceremonies of the Mass continued to be adequate. Although efforts were made at Trent to reform the preaching methods of the clergy, the lack of literary training in the seminaries greatly hindered progress in this area. Preaching remained polemical rather than instructive and inspiring. Listening to stereotyped sermons became for many literate laymen an element of sacrifice which they somehow identified with the "offering up" aspect of the Mass.

Perhaps the greatest failure of Trent was its inability to arrive at an adequate definition of the essential nature of the Church. The ecclesiology of Bellarmine, distilled from the writings of the earlier antagonists of Luther and Calvin, came to dominate Catholic teaching on this subject. Completely saturated with juridic concepts and aimed at depicting an organization rather than an organism, it is rejected today even by conservative theologians. The Church was conceived as a sort of clerical corporation engaged in saving souls from Protestantism, Satan and the world. Universality became identified with conformism, sanctity with cumulative piety, and loyalty to the papacy the soundest criterion of the good Catholic. The Church continued to look to the institutions of the Middle Ages for inspiration rather than beyond them to the Gospel. There was a studied reluctance to admit that the Protestant reform had originated in the quietude of a monk's cell and that it had succeeded because of a widespread conviction on the part of many sincere Christians that the real *thesaurus* of the Church is the Gospel of the glory and grace of Christ.

The strongly centralized papacy after Trent felt that calling attention to shortcomings was to run the risk of causing more harm than good. All criticism was regarded as proceeding from a spirit of opposition bordering on dubious orthodoxy. It continued to spread ideas on sanctity and the perfection of the Church which were not always exact and which could not be realistically held without a refusal to see things in the light of reality. Sarpi's accusation that Trent was a highly successful maneuver on the part of the papacy to renew its power and frustrate reunion and genuine reform may have been an exaggeration, but even the most ardent of its defenders must admit that for centuries to come Rome was dominated by a siege mentality in which criticism of the Church was tantamount to heresy. Pope Leo XIII in his encyclical *Militantis Ecclesiae* could still speak unabashed of the *"rebellio Lutherana"* out of which came the *"ruina morum ultima."* Pius X in the encyclical *Editae*

Saepe labels the Reformers as *"corruptores"* and the destroyers of faith and morals. In a similar vein Chesterton, the recent spokesman for enlightened Catholicism, describes Protestantism as having substituted the mood for the mind.

The Dominican theologian of our day, Yves Congar, perhaps best epitomizes why the reform of the sixteenth century was in many ways a failure and indicates the relevancy of this fact to our own day when he writes: "In the greater number of reforms known to the Church, the problem was essentially one of reviving the observation of rules fixed in decrees or canons. Still, certain reforms were made or at least proposed in the name of a return to sources higher than the canons, the legitimacy of which were not questioned but which the proposed problem of renovation surpassed. Such was the case of the evangelical or apostolic movement that terminated in the twelfth century in the work of St. Francis and St. Dominic. Such was, at the beginning of the sixteenth century, the vision of reform of John Colet, Lefèvre d'Etaples, Cardinal Ximines, Erasmus, and men of lesser breadth. Such is, without doubt, the plan upon which the current reform is to be modelled. The problem is not to reform abuses. Very few exist. What must be done is to revise structures; that goes much further than a simple restating of the canons. It involves going back to the sources. For there is not only the question of tracing to its sources a form which has gone awry, but of finding new forms beyond the patterns actually operative, simply by setting out from the spirit and the essential type of the originals."

The same thought is evident in the exhortations of many present-day churchmen. Society today is going through what the late Cardinal Suhard termed a structural reform, a reform which is breaking the continuity of traditions and questioning consecrated values. The Church is experiencing what Newman calls a succession of seasons, autumns and springs. As the permanent Incarnation of the Savior, it is not merely a juridical organization but it is also the Mystical Body of Christ. An overstressing of the external, institutional elements led to the sixteenth-century rift in Christendom. The pressing demand for reform in our day cannot be met by a mere return to the Reformation of the sixteenth century, whether Protestant or Catholic. It must be a reformation of the Reformation, a transformation. This reshaping, this configuration of the old Reformation, can take place only by a return to the universal, ecumenical, catholic

Church. As Newman so aptly remarks, "It could never be that so large a portion of Christendom should have split off from the communion of Rome and kept up a protest for three hundred years for nothing."

Index

MENTOR Books of Protestant Thought

HERE I STAND: A Life of Martin Luther
by Roland H. Bainton

A vivid portrait of the man who spearheaded the Protestant Reformation. (#MQ544—95¢)

OUT OF MY LIFE AND THOUGHT by Albert Schweitzer

The remarkable autobiography of a great religious leader. With Post-Script 1932-1949 by Everett Skillings.
(#MP483—60¢)

THE PROTESTANT MYSTICS Anne Fremantle, editor

The spiritual experiences of sixty-seven mystics of various Protestant denominations, from Martin Luther and John Donne to E. E. Cummings and T. S. Eliot.
(#MQ628—95¢)

THE PURITAN HERITAGE: America's Roots in the Bible
by Joseph Gaer and Ben Siegel

A provocative survey of the impact of Judeo-Christian concepts on American history. (#MT592—75¢)

VARIETIES OF RELIGIOUS EXPERIENCE
by William James

A new edition of James' classic work on the psychology of religion and the religious impulse, with an Introduction by Jacques Barzun. (#MT320—75¢)

RELIGION AND THE RISE OF CAPITALISM
by R. H. Tawney

The influence of religious thought on the social and economic structures of the world. (#MT507—75¢)

ETHICS IN A BUSINESS SOCIETY
by Marquis W. Childs and Douglas Cater

A brilliant interpretation of a monumental inquiry into the nature of moral values in the modern world.
(#MT724—75¢)

THE MEANING OF THE DEAD SEA SCROLLS
by A. Powell Davies

The fascinating story of the Dead Sea Scrolls with a scholarly interpretation of their relationship to the Holy Scriptures and the origin of Christianity.
(#MP587—60¢)

SIGNET Books of Catholic Interest

JOURNAL OF A SOUL by Pope John XXIII

Spanning nearly seventy years of Pope John's life, here is a record of the spiritual journey of a man who captured the imagination and affection of the world.
(#Y2858—$1.25)

WIT AND WISDOM OF GOOD POPE JOHN
Henri Fesquet, editor

A collection of sayings and anecdotes which record Pope John's great wit, deep character, and humble spirit.
(#D2696—50¢)

WHAT MODERN CATHOLICS THINK ABOUT BIRTH CONTROL William Birmingham, editor

Catholic men and women discuss their Church's stand on birth control, and tell why they agree or disagree.
(#T2577—75¢)

OBJECTIONS TO ROMAN CATHOLICISM
Michael de la Bedoyere, editor

Seven informed and devout Catholics challenge some outdated practices of the Catholic Church.
(#T2965—75¢)

THE SEVEN STOREY MOUNTAIN by Thomas Merton

The spiritual autobiography of a young man who withdrew from a full, worldly life to the seclusion of a Trappist monastery.
(#Q2857—95¢)

I LEAP OVER THE WALL by Monica Baldwin

The story of a nun's return to the outside world after twenty-eight years of convent seclusion. (#P2067—60¢)

THE DELIVERANCE OF SISTER CECILIA
by William Brinkley

The suspenseful, true-life story of a courageous nun's flight from the Communists. (#P2068—60¢)